THE ULTIMATE
HOUSE
BOOK>

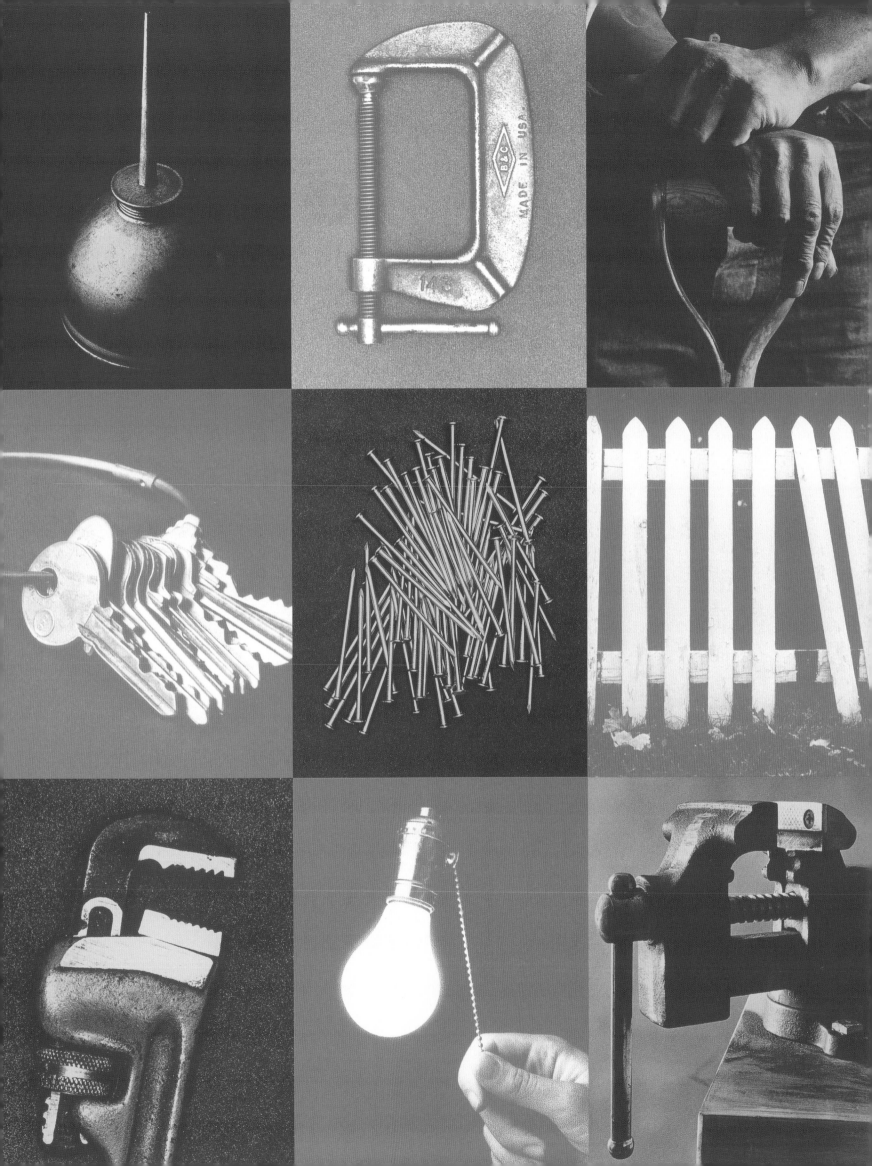

TERENCE >CONRAN

THE ULTIMATE HOUSE BOOK >

General Editor and Contributor Elizabeth Wilhide

TED SMART

To all my housewives, housekeepers, house children, house guests, house mice, house helpers, house builders, all who have taught me quite a lot about the house over the years.

First published in Great Britain in 2003 by Conran Octopus Limited a part of the Octopus Publishing Group 2–4 Heron Quays, London E14 4JP www.conran-octopus.co.uk

This edition produced for The Book People Ltd Hall Wood Avenue, Haydock, St Helens, WA11 9UL

British Library Cataloguing-in-Publication Data. A catalogue record for this book is available from the British Library.

ISBN 1 84091 356 8

Printed in China

General Editor and Contributor (Parts 1 and 2) Elizabeth Wilhide
Contributor (Part 3) Elizabeth Hilliard

Publishing Director Lorraine Dickey
Art Director Chi Lam
Consultant Design Alan McDougall
Design Broadbase
Project Editor Bridget Hopkinson
Picture Research Manager Liz Boyd
Picture and Location Research Clare Limpus
Production Manager Angela Couchman

CONTENTS

'If you have built castles in the air, your work need not be lost;
that is where they should be. Now put foundations under them.'
Henry David Thoreau

DREAMS OF LIVING

'Everybody, quite rightly, dreams of sheltering himself in a sure and permanent home of his own.' Le Corbusier, *Towards a New Architecture*, 1927

In the quarter century since the publication of the first *House Book* in 1974, there has been something of a major revolution in the field of home design. Those intervening years have seen the arrival of the urban loft conversion as the blueprint for contemporary living and spatial planning, the widespread acceptance of modernity, both in decoration and furnishings, and burgeoning consumer choice in terms of finishes, materials and fittings – a breadth of reference that was unthinkable even a decade ago.

Twenty-five years on and you see similar fashions on the street, self-consciously revived as 'retro' or 'vintage'. But whereas in those days interior design stood a little apart from the hectic fashion cycle, now it is fully enmeshed in it. To go with your vintage wardrobe, you can buy retro wallpaper and tongue-in-cheek Seventies furniture. 'Lifestyle' is defined not so much by what we do, but by what we buy.

While popular makeover programmes on the television have whetted the appetite for change on the domestic front, technological advances have also redefined the meaning of home, making possible new ways not only of living but of working. Like the telephone perched on its hall stand or the television console concealed in a cabinet, technology used to be the public intruder in the private domestic space. Nowadays, the fully wired home, with networked computers, interactive appliances, and programmable servicing, lighting and sound systems, has the potential to evolve into a smart skin, making it not so much a boundary as a communicator in its own right.

'The home has become a transparent and permeable medium for images, sound, text and data.' Terence Riley, Chief Curator of Architecture and Design, MOMA, author of *The Unprivate House*

Hand in hand with such developments have gone changes in expectations. What many people want from their homes these days is flexibility. Homes are no longer simply places of domestic retreat, but are in many cases places of work; they may also have to accommodate various permutations of the extended family some or all of the time. Such demands are leading to a departure from the traditional

'When I think of a dream house, it's more to do with a sense of light. It would be modern, with very large windows, in the country or by water. It would have to have stables. I'd love to have a wide, high corridor lined with books, rather than shelves in rooms. Lots of wood.' Mark, screenwriter, 34

⌐ The simple cube form of this contemporary house is an evocative distillation of the notion of shelter. The solid side and rear walls contrast with the open front, where the entire elevation is infilled with glass.

⌃ In the middle of a Finnish forest, a summerhouse bridges a pool stocked with salmon. The house is essentially one long glazed room flanked on either side by terraces. The timber used to construct the house is from trees felled and sawn on the site; the curved roof is corrugated metal. The pool was created by damming a stream farther up the site.

∧ Cabins, secret hideaways tucked in the woods, and the playhouses of childhood imagination shape our ideas of what home can be.

< Technological advances in both structural engineering and materials have made it possible to design houses with fluid boundaries between the interior and exterior. With space at a premium, particularly in urban areas, the emphasis is on open, flexible interiors with optimum conditions of natural light.

centuries-old house plan, where separate rooms are assigned specific functions, in favour of more open, transformable layouts that can be adapted and used in different ways as the occasion demands.

The blurred boundary between public and private space has had another impact: the increasing professionalism of the home. The trend started in the kitchen. The ubiquity of celebrity chefs and the rise of restaurant culture inspired a desire for catering-style fittings and equipment at home. The 'trophy' cooking range, a battery of utensils, vast refrigerators and acres of stainless steel made a statement of serious culinary intent, ironically at a time when less and less time was actually spent cooking at home. The emerging vogue for the home spa – combining the pampering luxury of the hotel bathroom with the exercise and relaxation facilities of a health club – is another instance of the same impulse. Home offices, atriums, panic rooms – all of which feature prominently on up-market consumer wish lists – are spaces that are not domestic in origin, but direct borrowings from the public realm.

Nevertheless, some things do not change. It was Robert Frost who defined 'home' as the place where, 'when you have to go there, they have to take you in'. What rings true about this rather wry definition is the way that it captures the sense of returning or belonging, which seems to be bound up with the whole concept of home. Home, for many of us, is somewhere you come back to. It is not so much a destination in itself, but the point of departure for other destinations or adventures. Homes house memories as much as people and possessions; home has a meaning for each one of us, which is unique and individual. It's the fixed point of our emotional compass.

'I never wanted a rock'n'roll house. I just wanted a normal house.' Liam Gallagher

Even those people who live much of their lives in hotel rooms find a way of imbuing their featureless, interchangeable surroundings with trappings of a more personal, settled nature, distilling the essence of home down to a few framed photographs, a favourite scent, a cushion or throw. It seems that without such familiar talismans, or symbols of what home life means, individuals run the risk of running adrift. In the 24/7 culture, the whole idea of home has become more rather than less important. Increased mobility has had a similar effect. Fewer and fewer people live their entire lives in the same town, let alone in the same house or apartment – Americans, for example, move on average every five years – but that does not lessen the ties of home or alter its central importance in our lives as a focus of security in times of rapid change.

If home is a fixed point, it is also a theatre for self-expression and change: it may well be one of the few places where we can enact our desires in the most fundamental sense. An important part of this process is the way in which we choose to design, decorate and furnish the spaces in which we live. Such decisions are not merely superficial or cosmetic, but have the power to affect our whole sense of wellbeing. There is nothing trivial about the quality of light, for example, or the way a space is planned and fitted, and it is with basic elements like these that we truly shape our homes.

'The house is the repository of our unmet needs, our unfulfilled dreams, or our nostalgic longings. It cannot really satisfy any of them, but perhaps that is why we have so much satisfaction in making the attempt.' Marjorie Garber, *Sex and Real Estate*

Homes may be made of bricks and mortar, plaster, paint and wood, but they also enshrine dreams of living. Everyone builds castles in the air. Even if few of these dream houses are subsequently realized, they still tell us a great deal about how we want to live. Not all dream houses, of course, are unattainable: one-third of those responding to a recent British survey said that the bungalow was their ideal home – a sort of apartment in the countryside, I suppose. The process of creative daydreaming is not merely wishful thinking, but can direct us to solutions that are affordable and practical as well as fulfilling.

It is a process that starts early in life. Children play house in tree houses, forts, Wendy houses and secret dens. I remember drawing my own dream house as a child: it was long and thin like a stable, with each room opening into the next without corridors to connect them. That first attempt at home design may have been one of the reasons why, in my early twenties, I was so smitten by the open and essentially linear nature of Nancy Cunard's converted barn in Lot, where I stayed with some friends during a memorable trip to France. That seemed like a dream home to me. The interior of the barn was arranged across a series of open levels, stepping down from a bedroom at one end, via a bathroom, to an open-plan living/kitchen/dining area on the ground floor, and then up again at the other end to a spare bedroom and bathroom. You could see right the way across the interior. A similar expansiveness and functionalism was evident in the houses featured in The Arts and Architecture Case Study programme (1945-66), the designs of which, with their easy informality, had an enormous impact on me as a young designer. Nowadays, I would have to add into the picture a location overlooking water with rolling countryside at the back.

> This series of small pod-like structures containing living and working quarters in rural Alabama were designed, built and are used by architectural students investigating forms of socially responsible and economic housing. The long arcade that links the individual structures serves as an outdoor room. Materials include salvaged or discarded items such as tyres, bottles, scrap timber and car windows.

⌄ Designed by Sir Nicholas Grimshaw, the architect of the Eden Project in Cornwall, Spine House near Cologne consists of a steel and glass box-like structure daringly bisected by an oval tunnel shaped like a fuselage. The tunnel progresses from the entrance at ground level to a 'cockpit' suspended in mid-air overlooking the countryside. Initially, the tunnel or 'spine' was going to be made by boat builders but was eventually crafted in sections by local joiners in Cologne.

∧ This family weekend retreat set in 22 hectares (55 acres) on the coast of New Brunswick, Canada, overlooking the Bay of Fundy, consists of a series of platforms projected out over the landscape. A simple shelter that interferes minimally with the site, the structure is anchored by a stone wall to the north which contains fireplace, heating, power and storage area, where everyday necessities can be kept between visits.

^ 'Fred' is a 3m (10ft) cube that expands telescopically to provide 18sqm (194sqft) of floor space, complete with bathroom, kitchen, sleeping area and windows. A prototype designed to address the need for mobile, temporary housing, Fred is made from wood and lined with thick insulation.

Your dream house, however, can take you by surprise. In her hugely entertaining and perceptive book, *Sex and Real Estate: Why We Love Houses*, Marjorie Garber quotes a popular saying in the real estate business, as divulged to her by a New York broker: 'Buyers are liars'. While most people would be forgiven for thinking that it is estate agents, with their coy euphemisms and misleading sales-speak, who are the ones that are economical with the truth, it seems that many house-hunters declare specific preferences with respect to location, price, type of house, number of bedrooms, and so on, and then proceed to fall for a property that fulfils none, or very few, of their original requirements. Put this together with a statistic recently published by a British estate agency, that the average house-buyer takes a mere 18 minutes to make up their mind to buy a property (less time than is usually spent deciding to buy an item of expensive clothing or pair of shoes), and it is evident that there is an x-factor affecting the way people respond to potential homes.

'Our sense of home develops out of our earliest experiences and the essence of it stays with us for the rest of our lives, affecting our sense of self and giving us the base from which we relate to the rest of the world.' Oliver James, psychotherapist

It is evident that a 'dream' house may be composed of significant elements of a 'remembered' house. There is no doubt that the first home we remember, the first room, the first kitchen, shape our notions of comfort and security. And not merely real remembered houses, but houses we may have encountered in fiction or in

film: the Manderleys, Bridesheads and Gosford Parks. Nostalgic tugs and memories that resist analysis may account not only for the 'buyers are liars' syndrome, but for the persistent affection for old houses and furnishings that, from a purely practical standpoint, do not serve contemporary needs or requirements very well.

Akiko Busch in *Geography of Home* quotes a survey carried out in the mid-1990s by *Metropolis* magazine that threw up interesting anomalies in the way people regarded their homes. The survey asked which room people would most like to add to their homes. The responses were fairly evenly split between up-to-the-minute home spas, home offices and exercise rooms and more traditional domestic spaces. The same survey asked readers to say which room they remembered most affectionately from their childhood. First was the bedroom, second the kitchen and third the basement or garage. As Akiko Busch notes, 'It occurs to me that the bedroom, the kitchen, and the basement reflect the three basic realms of home: the private and necessary sanctuary, the place of nourishment and community, the area where things get made. So long as the places we live can accommodate these three very different human activities, it might be called home.'

The homes that we make may be either forward facing or backward looking – or both. They might be places where we work, as well as the focus of our private lives. They may expand and contract with the comings and goings of a wider, looser household. But in the process of shaping our homes, in design, decoration and furnishing, we express who we are.

‹ A house within a house: an industrial-style warehouse shed encloses a typical suburban clapboard house for an intriguing tension of opposites. Huge garage doors on each side of the shed roll back to open the house to the garden, while the view from the veranda of the house within the house is not of a front lawn but a living room.

› Japan has one of the highest densities of population in the world, and the pressure on living space is correspondingly high. One solution to the problem of restricted garden areas is to take to the roof – sufferers from vertigo need not apply.

∧ Draped with mosquito netting and lit by lanterns, these "portaledges" suspended from the boughs of a cypress on the Northern Californian coast provide romantic shelters for local tree-climbing enthusiasts and unbeatable views of the Pacific.

"I'd like a slide from my room to a tree house and a secret doorway." Jack, 7

PART 1
HOME LIFE

Flexibility is increasingly what people demand from their homes. From the student setting up home for the first time, to the busy family or retired grandparent, each successive stage in life brings new requirements for space and servicing, new priorities, tastes and interests. And home life itself is changing – in Britain, for example, more than a quarter of all households are single person, and more people are choosing to work from home. This section looks at the basic elements of spatial planning, storage and fitted features, layout and activity zones (including outdoor spaces) in the context of specific life stages.

FLEXIBLE LIVING

The traditional house pattern has been incredibly persistent. Throughout the previous century, even as lifestyles were changing radically, most people's domestic lives were still defined by spatial arrangements that enshrined the social conventions of a previous age. In their layout and specification, our homes told us what to do and what they said was: eat in the dining room, sleep in the bedroom, live in the living room. In cities or parts of the world where the housing stock is still predominantly nineteenth- or early twentieth-century, the longevity and staying power of this traditional model is perhaps not astonishing. What is more surprising is that until recently many, if not most, new homes have also been planned and built in the same way.

But as our lives have become more fragmented and as the boundaries between public and private spaces, home life and working life, have eroded, things have begun to change. One of the significant turning points for this shift in domestic design has been the popular success of loft living; another is the trend for working at home. If loft living revealed the workability and freedom of the open plan, working at home has led to a total re-evaluation of domestic space.

Increasingly, we demand that our homes keep pace with the flexibility of our lives – shape-shifting to accommodate different family members at different stages, serving as workspaces all or part of the time, or simply providing day-to-day adaptability. The demand for flexible living by homebuyers is starting to have an effect on the way homes are planned and marketed. In line with consumer demand and expectation, some new developments now feature flowing ground-floor living spaces, "zones" rather than self-contained rooms; while others offer a choice of flexible interior layouts partitioned (or not) with transparent boundaries or sliding doors. The old hierarchy of bedroom size is also being challenged; in the sales literature for certain schemes, numbers of bedrooms are not specified and all interior spaces, except service areas, go unlabeled. "Bonus" rooms also feature – sunrooms, living spaces in attics or basements – spaces that could be used for any number of purposes, from in-law or au pair suites, studios or workrooms. Cynics might say that this amounts to no more than ordinary houses with the conventional labels left off, but, nevertheless, there is clear evidence of the need to rethink the way domestic space is planned.

Another contemporary manifestation of the flexible home are those designs where different areas or functions are articulated by panels, screens and modular, moveable pods. Pull out a couple of sliding doors, pull down a couple of beds and it's a two-bedroom apartment; unfold a working wall and it's a home office. No home is infinitely flexible or adaptable, but such ingenious build-outs provide a whole new way of looking at space.

Designing for life is difficult. When you set up house for the first time, you don't know what directions your life might take: how and where you will work, whether you will marry and have a family. And with each successive stage, things don't automatically become any clearer. What is clear is that the need for a home to be flexible and adaptable is only likely to increase with time.

> One apartment: 20 ways

Before conversion, this apartment, which is located on the 24th floor of a 1960s building on the outskirts of Brussels, Belgium, was conventionally partitioned into entrance hall, living area, kitchen and three small bedrooms. Now, with all internal walls stripped away and very few fixed points, it forms a flexible, quiet and calm environment in which its architect-owner both lives and works.

The main attraction of the apartment is the view it offers of the cityscape via windows on three sides, a panorama not only of bustling urban life but also of changing skies and light – an ideal backdrop for creative work. But perhaps the apartment's most surprising feature is that it can be reconfigured in as many as 20 different ways, according to need.

Aside from a kitchenette, bathroom and boiler (all housed in fixed blocks and concealed behind doors), everything else in the apartment is moveable. The basic elements, all designed by the owner, comprise three "sitting balls," three mobile tables, three mobile sofas and ten mobile cupboards. Each cupboard has a dedicated storage function, ranging from clothing to a home office.

The owner changes things around whenever he requires or wants a new interior. If guests come to dinner, the three tables are pushed together in the kitchen and the three sofas are put together to make a seating area. If someone stays overnight, a "mini-apartment' is configured from a table, sofa and cupboard. When there's a business meeting, the three mobile tables become a desk and the sofas are pushed out of the way. The owner admits he occasionally catches himself walking toward the wrong cupboard but this is a minor hitch compared to the feeling of spaciousness and the creative flexibility the design allows.

Key:

- ■ table
- ○ sitting ball
- ▬ cupboard
- ▬ sofa

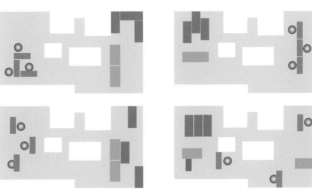

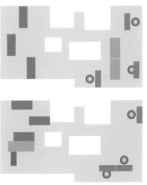

< Shift of gears

Shift of gears

When your lifestyle changes and your home no longer fits it isn't always necessary to move. In this case, a wholesale redesign has transformed a cramped Victorian studio flat into a light-filled open-plan apartment that perfectly supports the owner's shift from working as a chef to a new career as a food journalist. A key aim of the redesign was to maximize the living area and space for entertaining – the kitchen is the hub both of the owner's working and social life as it is where he likes to entertain friends.

To accommodate these roles and to create the sense of spaciousness the owner wanted, the original ground-floor flat was completely gutted to form a single fluid space from the entrance through the living area, on through the kitchen and, via French doors, out onto a garden terrace. To free up extra floor area, the bathroom was moved from the front to the back of the flat (shrinking to a shower room in the process). Taking advantage of the studio's high ceilings, a bedroom was slotted in on a mezzanine level with fitted clothes storage underneath. The bedroom is accessed by a built-in ladder flanked by two chrome poles.

Changes in level rather than walls delineate space. The kitchen is three steps down from the living area, and these steps turn the corner to form built-in bench seating, which doubles as storage, around the dining table. In a similarly neat move, an unbroken line of storage cupboards extends the entire length of the apartment from living area to kitchen. A concrete top, poured and sealed in situ, makes a beautifully robust unifying element.

Because so many elements are tailor-made and built-in, there is little need for much in the way of free-standing furniture and visual clutter can be kept to a minimum. This aspect of the design makes the most of the space and light while at the same time imposing a certain discipline of order and restraint.

FIRST HOME

First homes, whether bought or rented, are typically defined by a need for economy. Financial constraints generally mean some form of compromise: most first homes are on the small side, many are not in perfect repair or in an ideal location. Whether it be a student flat, bed-sit, or toe-hold on the property ladder, you still have to adapt the space to your needs as far as possible, which essentially means knowing where money is best spent. Since a first home is usually a stepping stone to somewhere else, it is as well to keep an eye out for improvements that will enhance your investment or, in the case of rented property, that will either move with you or be cost-effective for the length of time you expect to stay there.

If first homes are rarely dream homes, they do offer the first tantalizing opportunity for personal expression. Bringing your own spirit and personality into a place is the key to making it truly liveable. Where a first home is shared – particularly with a partner – taking someone else's opinions, tastes and possessions into the equation brings a whole new dimension into play.

PLANNING THE LAYOUT

Truthful self-assessment of needs and requirements, rather than wishful thinking, is the key to successful planning, particularly of small spaces. Take a good look at the way you presently live and work, and keep a relatively restricted time frame firmly in mind. One day, you may become an enthusiastic gardener; one day you may develop a passion for cooking elaborate meals for large dinner parties; if neither of these activities feature prominently in your life at the moment, you do not need to accommodate them.

At the same time, you need to take a long hard look at the assets and drawbacks of the space at your disposal. If you own your home and there are any trouble spots or elements requiring urgent repair, you must accept the fact that putting these right will have to take priority.

If you are in full-time employment, your home will essentially function as a place of retreat in the evenings and at weekends. Think about getting rid of conventional room arrangements to create an informal, open layout (and make sure you have given due consideration to security if the property will be empty for much of the day). On the other hand, if you need to work at home part of the time, a dedicated workspace is essential, which will mean that you may have to build in at least some degree of separation between living and working.

First homes generally coincide with a sociable stage of life. If you like entertaining, even if it is only having a few friends round to share a takeaway, an open arrangement again makes sense, as it will enhance the feeling of spaciousness and provide a more adaptable framework for different types of activity.

Affordable housing for first-time buyers is in short supply in many urban areas. A number of architects are currently responding to the problem by devising prefabricated micro-flats, living modules that can be manufactured off-site and delivered by truck, which dramatically cuts the cost and time of construction.

One such prototype, a 350-sq-ft micro-flat with walls and floors made of insulated panels, has been inspired by compact built-in spaces such as RVs, cabin cruisers and Japanese capsule hotels. Inside, a curved "utility module" houses kitchen, bathroom and bedroom storage. The bedroom at the rear is separated by a sliding screen, while the open living space leads directly to a balcony. Although such designs are only just beginning to make an appearance on the market, you can draw inspiration from their compact and functional planning when it comes to the layout of your own space.

Open layouts

First homes are often single spaces, but even when they comprise two or more distinct rooms, open layouts make a great deal of sense at this stage. Where space is confined, doing without conventional barriers and partition walls gives you the illusion of spaciousness as well as an important degree of flexibility in terms of emphasis and practicality. If you own your property and can afford to carry out simple structural alterations, you might consider knocking down walls between rooms or between the circulation areas of hallways and stairs to promote a freer, more adaptable internal arrangement.

Open layouts, however, are not successful where activities run together in a flurry and some forms of division are usually necessary. Flexible ways of defining different areas include free-standing partitions or storage units, half-height counters used to block views of a kitchen or cooking area, moveable screens and even furniture placement. Most people, even if they are living on their own, usually prefer some form of enclosure for a sleeping area. If there is enough ceiling height, a platform bed or mini mezzanine level can be a good way of separating a bedroom from the main space. Alternatively, a partition with openings on either side, serving essentially as an over-scaled headboard, can signal the shift between public and private areas within an otherwise open space.

Open layouts go hand in hand with built-in storage and to some extent built-in furniture. When there are no doors to close on clutter, built-in cupboards allow you to keep household paraphernalia out of sight when it is not required. The most elegant solutions, as well as those that maximize every inch of space, usually require some professional design input, but this is well worth the investment, especially if you expect to stay put for some time.

⌄ In an open-plan unit with high ceilings, a large free-standing box encloses the one area that requires privacy – the bathroom. Because the "box" does not extend all the way up to the ceiling, light is not blocked from one end to the other. The bathroom box is also positioned to segregate the living area from the more private sleeping area.

> Large panes of toughened sheet glass enclose a shower cubicle in an open-plan bedroom-bathroom. The glass provides a waterproof screen that allows in light from the window.

∨ The simple device of raising a bed – in this case, a simple mattress – up on a shallow platform helps to define different areas in an otherwise open layout. The base of the platform is used to store bedding.

˥ Small spaces are often awkwardly laid out. Here the odd angles under the plane of the roof have been fully exploited to create a built-in kitchen framing a dining alcove.

> Successful storage is the key to making a small space work. The galley kitchen, with built-in units on each wall is an efficient, practical layout where space is tight. A floor-to-ceiling wall of shelving organizes a range of different possessions in a coherent whole.

∧ Metal storage containers house kitchen paraphernalia on an open shelf under the sink workbench. Units or fitted elements that do not extend right down to the floor accentuate the sense of space.

∧ A new kitchen can take a sizeable chunk out of a home improvement budget. Unfitted kitchen elements, such as this storage unit slotted under a simple worktop on legs, allow you to take your investment with you when it is time to move.

≪ Junk shops and secondhand outlets are good sources of basic furniture, which can be revamped with a coat of paint. A sheet of Perspex upgrades an old wooden table; concertina loft lights provide practical directional lighting.

< Showers are more space-saving than baths, particularly when they are installed in a type of wet room arrangement draining directly to the floor. Fully tiled walls and water-proof floor means there is no need to enclose the shower with more than a simple shower curtain.

Kitchens and bathrooms

Those setting up home for the first time often find the service areas of kitchens and bathrooms particularly lacking, both in size and character. How much can be done to redress the situation depends largely on budget but also on lifestyle, particularly when it comes to kitchen planning.

The 'utility module' idea, as featured in the micro-flat design (see page 25) – and coincidentally in the service planning of many lofts and other free-form spaces – is a good one to adopt if you have the opportunity and the budget to plan your home from scratch. Grouping services makes practical and logistical sense, as well as maximizing space for more living-oriented activities.

If you are not a particularly enthusiastic cook, it makes sense to restrict kitchen facilities to the minimum. By the same token, if your entire social life takes place away from home – and if you tend to eat out a great deal – there is no real need to devote much space to a kitchen or to equip a cooking area with much beyond a kettle, mini-fridge or microwave. Compact kitchen areas that can be shut away behind a screen or sliding door when not in use are perfectly adequate if your idea of cooking is warming up a ready meal.

Small kitchens, however, can be highly efficient, provided they are properly planned. Where space is limited, fitted layouts are much the best solution – the simpler the better. A single-line kitchen, with appliances slotted under a worktop and wall-hung units is neat, efficient and unobtrusive. The same simplicity and discipline should be extended to equipping the kitchen. Avoid space-hungry appliances and gadgets; a restricted range of basic, plain ovenware and tableware is much less of a storage headache than different sets of glasses and plates for everyday and special occasions.

For those who are reluctant to spend much money on fittings and fixtures they will eventually leave behind, free-standing modular units and 'plug-in' kitchen 'workbenches' incorporating sink, hob, oven and fridge allow you to take your investment with you when it is time to move on. Similar designs include space-saving kitchens built into cabinets that simply connect to existing services. If there is very little in the budget at all, you can refresh tired or shabby kitchen units with a coat of paint and new handles or by replacing the doors and drawer fronts with new ones.

In a first home, the bathroom may not only be the 'smallest room', it may be positively minute. Short of moving walls around, there are a number of less costly and disruptive ways of easing the pressure on space. Replacing a door that opens inward with a sliding panel or screen can make a cramped bathroom seem a little roomier. Substituting a shower for a bath will also win you some additional floor area. Small sinks, particularly those that are wall-hung, are also space saving. Converting a bathroom into a fully waterproofed wet room is perhaps one of the more practical ways of making the most of a small area.

DECORATION AND FURNISHING

Even those on restricted budgets can put an individual stamp on their home. Basic decoration and a few well-chosen simple furnishings can transform the most unpromising surroundings. At this stage of life, necessity is most often the mother of invention: economic considerations can inspire lateral leaps that prove to be as aesthetically pleasing as they are cost-effective and functional. If you are

⌄ The use of mirror is a tried and tested way of doubling the sense of space. Here a large sheet of mirror over the sink helps to dispel a sense of enclosure in a small bathroom. Simple fixtures, such as the bowl sink, along with neat detailing, keep visual distractions to a minimum.

⌃ If you're short on space, you need not be short on style or personal expression. Quirky touches, such as this wall-hung loo-roll holder, add wit and humour.

⌃ For many people, their first home offers a welcome opportunity to express decorative instincts. When budgets are tight, improvisation can lead to surprisingly successful solutions. Here dishcloths have been stitched together to make a cheap and cheerful window shade.

⌃ Many retailers stock simple ready-made tab curtains, an instant and economical way of screening windows. A vivid ethnic-print fabric used as a bedspread injects bright color into an all-white room.

renting, make sure you study the fine print of your lease or consult your landlord before undertaking major decorating projects, particularly those that entail ripping out or painting over existing surfaces and finishes.

Cover-ups

A fresh coat of paint is instantly uplifting, not just on walls but on other surfaces and finishes that you may not be able to replace immediately, such as floorboards, cabinetry or tiling. Make sure you select the right type of paint for the job it has to do and follow manufacturer's recommendations with regard to preparation and undercoating. It's worth spending time filling cracks and dealing with other surface imperfections before you get out the paint roller. Time spent on preparation makes a vast difference in terms of the quality of the final finish.

White or light-reflecting shades are a good idea if the view is poor, the space is confined or the quality of natural light leaves something to be desired. At the same time, you have nothing to lose by being daring. First homes represent a learning curve in many ways and this is the chance to experiment.

Other economic and virtually instant cover-ups for walls include fabric stretched and tacked in position or blown-up photocopies of favorite images for a photomural effect. Good-quality wallpaper is not cheap, but a couple of rolls may be enough to paper one wall; a single plane picked out in this way can be a very effective means of introducing strong color or pattern.

Floors

The floor is a defining element in the interior; it also represents a substantial surface area which means that new flooring often can be costly, especially once fitting and underlay have been taken into account. If reasonably decent floorboards are lurking underneath layers of carpet or worn vinyl, one budget solution is to remove the old floor covering and paint, stain or sand and seal the boards. Wood laminate may not be as authentic as solid wood floors, but it is cheap and, in the snap-and-lock format, easy to lay. Sheets of plywood are another economic alternative. If you prefer the comfort, warmth and sound-insulating qualities of carpet or natural-fiber weaves underfoot, be on the lookout for suppliers selling remnants or discontinued ranges. Large plain rugs can hide a battered or stained floor covering if your budget is tight or your stay in your present accommodation is strictly limited.

Lighting

One of the cheapest ways of changing the atmosphere is by improving lighting – both artificial and natural. You cannot change the basic orientation of your home, but you can enhance the amount of daylight by keeping windows relatively uncovered. Shades, translucent Plexiglass panels or slatted screens allow more light through than heavy drapery – the more light, the greater the feeling of wellbeing and the greater the sense of space.

Where artificial light is concerned, the key is to increase the number of light sources in a room or area and to vary the direction of light. A single, central source, such as a pendant light, has a deadening effect on atmosphere, whereas individual points of light dotted around the room at different levels make a space seem bigger and more expansive. Reflecting light from ceilings or walls by using

∧ Paper lanterns, either in the form of pendant lights or mounted on metal stands, create a soft diffused background light and are so cheap they can be readily replaced as soon as they look battered or worn.

∨ Color is a highly economical way of adding instant uplift if you can't afford new surfaces or finishes. A warm red wall makes a vivid backdrop for retro junk-shop finds.

⌐ A plywood screen encloses a bed within an open-plan space. Bed frames can be improvised but a good mattress that properly supports your back is one purchase that should not be skimped on.

uplights or angled spots will also enhance spaciousness. Good-looking basic light fixtures, such as clip-on spots, desk lamps, aluminum pendants or variations on the theme of the paper lantern, are easy to come by and very economical. It is worth spending money, however, on having additional power outlets installed if there are only a limited number, as this will add greatly to the potential flexibility of lighting arrangements.

Flexible furnishing

Furnishing a home cheaply used to mean scrounging cast-offs from friends and family and improvising the rest. These days, however, there are plenty of retailers and other outlets where decent, basic furniture and furnishings are available, and where you can find pieces that offer both a veneer of contemporary design and an affordable price tag. In many cases, such furniture is flat-packed and self-assembled at home.

When you are short of space as well as money, look out for simple designs that can serve more than one function: a basic table can be used for both eating and working; futons and sofa beds fulfill a double purpose; anonymous chairs can work as occasional seating in a living area or as dining chairs; and stacking stools function as side-tables, additional seating or as places to perch a lamp. Modular designs, from sectional seating to storage units, which can be added to as living space and income allows, are another practical idea. Indoor-outdoor furniture in wicker, slatted wood or metal is lightweight, generally well designed and often very affordable; when you do make the move to a more established home, such pieces may well find a use in the yard or on the patio.

While improvisation still has a role to play, such as the stereotypical table that comprises a door balanced on trestles, or shelving made of scaffolding planks and bricks, it is worth spending as much money as you can afford on items such as sofas, sofa beds or mattresses that directly affect your comfort and wellbeing. A good-quality mattress may not be the most exciting purchase you will ever make but it will more than repay the investment.

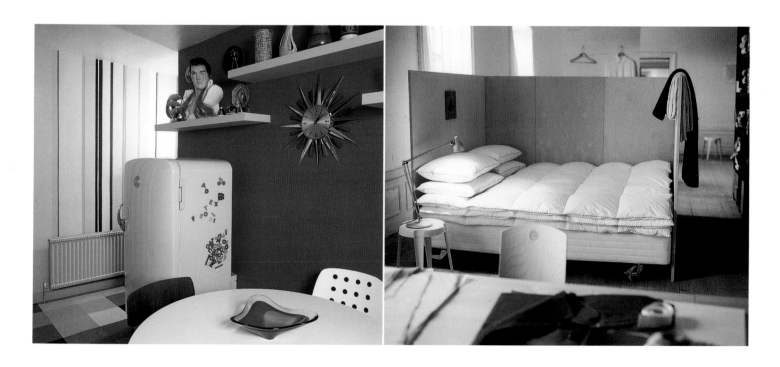

Where space is very tight, fitted furniture can be a good idea. Tables that pull out from the side of a kitchen counter or flap down from the wall, beds that fold down, and workspaces that are enclosed by sliding doors or screens when not in use keep the floor as clear as possible and provide the illusion of greater space. One proviso is that such features must be robust and truly workable, which often means custom design and construction.

Inherited or retro pieces can supply that sense of continuity or rootedness that a first home may otherwise lack. Retro furnishings discovered in junk shops are appealing not only because they are quirky and cheap but also because they provide a link with the past. Places generally begin to feel like home when they have a little history attached; here is a way to get it sooner rather than later.

STORAGE

One advantage of setting up home for the first time is that the number of possessions needing to be housed is generally fewer at this stage than in later life; the downside, however, is that storage space, indeed free space, may well be sorely lacking – few first homes come with convenient attics or basements where stuff can be stashed away. With this in mind, it can be a good idea to edit your belongings before you move. If you do not want to shed things permanently, consider renting storage facilities for those items you can do without on a daily basis but may find room for some time in the future.

Fitted storage makes particular sense in a small living space. Sacrificing a certain amount of floor area to build in cupboards along the length of one wall is a small price to pay for a more clutter-free life. Raised levels, such as platforms or mezzanines, provide the opportunity to fit out the space underneath; cupboards and shelving can also be neatly integrated into hallways if they are wide enough, or sited under the stairs.

Open storage, such as shelving and hanging rails, attracts attention and is best restricted to those inherently appealing possessions, such as books, which 'furnish' a room. If you opt for the shelving route, fitting an entire wall with shelves is a more satisfactory and wholehearted solution than dotting a few about here and there. Modular storage boxes in cardboard, metal or Perspex are an economical and unobtrusive way of organizing clutter.

SHARED HOME

If part of the pleasure of setting up home for the first time is enjoying your own territory and expressing your own tastes, when you set up home with a partner you may find yourself coming up against very different notions of decor and design. This may take the form of a typical gender divide, radically different approaches to domestic clutter or competing claims for personal space, or it may be as specific as blinds versus curtains, wood floors versus carpet. Compatibility in other spheres of life does not necessarily translate into shared preferences when it comes to wall colour or sofa design. The British DIY chain Homebase recently conducted a survey that reported that six out of ten couples had an argument during or after visiting their stores.

Living together entails compromise; in this context, compromise, where it is a true fusion rather than a watered-down solution, can result in a more distinctive result than one person getting their own way to the exclusion of the other's tastes

˅ Wooden vegetable crates given a coat of white paint stack up to provide a cheap and instant way of organizing shoes. There are plenty of such 'found' containers that can be used to keep clutter under control without spending a fortune.

˅ A more considered solution, which combines closed storage with accessible open display shelves, is this built-in bathroom cupboard with cut-out doors. MDF is a material that lends itself to this type of precision detailing and is easy to decorate.

∧ One of the simplest ways to create a built-in wardrobe is to fit an alcove with a rail for hanging clothes and a couple of shelves for shoes. Here the storage area is screened with a decorative Indian fabric; simple roller or bamboo blinds would work as well.

⌐ Fitted storage is the answer if you want clutter-free living. Sacrificing some floor area to build in cupboards and shelves is a functional and space-enhancing way of keeping all your belongings under control. Quality of design and construction is important if fitted storage is to work well in both practical and aesthetic terms.

and preferences. A shared home should express joint interests and that may mean redecorating in such a way that suits both people or making a few new purchases together. As difficult or as protracted a process as it may prove, making big decisions together, such as the purchase of a sofa or the choice of flooring, is important for long-term harmony; so, too, is making the effort to allow each person a degree of individual space.

Unavoidably, sharing a home means double the stuff. While hanging on to two copies of the same CD might express some pessimism about the longevity of a relationship, there is a his'n'hers (or mine'n'yours) element to most shared homes, a feature, moreover, that can persist well into middle-age. On a purely practical level, pooling your belongings may simply mean discarding duplicate items and hanging on to whichever is the better quality; equally it may involve accepting the fact that there isn't room for everything and either rented storage space or permanent disposal is the answer.

Another shared home scenario, and one that is becoming increasingly common as property prices in urban areas continue to escalate, is where a group of friends decide to pool their assets together to buy a home in the interests of gaining more space for their money in a better location than they could manage by going it alone. At a stage of life when friendships are often more enduring than relationships, this can be a sensible way of beginning the slow climb up the property ladder. But while this strategy might superficially seem no more than a

Even small outdoor areas can deliver many of the benefits of large gardens – a place to doze in the sun, somewhere to nurture a few plants and flowers, and a place to enjoy eating outside in fine weather.

Containerized plants and hard surfacing are practical for small gardens. Here, decking and stone chips create textural contrast underfoot; white painted walls make the most of available light.

Roof gardens, with their panoramic views of urban life, are places with special appeal. But conditions can be extreme, which presents significant gardening challenges. Plants need some protection from exposure to strong wind; you also need to check that the roof is strong enough to bear the weight of earth-filled containers, decking and any other surfaces.

This is gardening at its most minimal – a pair of pots hooked over a window railing provide a display of greenery to soften a city view. Planting scented or flowering species multiplies the pleasure.

logical extension of the shared student house or flat, clear rules and contractual arrangements are necessary from the outset in order to avoid disruptive and damaging disputes in the future. Obtaining a joint mortgage where the parties in question are friends rather than partners is no longer a problem with most financial institutions; it can be a problem, though, if one of the parties decides it is time to sell up and move on. It is therefore a good idea to get an additional legal document drawn up setting out some basic ground rules.

OUTSIDE SPACE

Gardening may not be high on the list of most people's priorities at this stage of life, but any outdoor space, however confined, is always an asset. Balconies, small paved terraces and even windowsills provide an opportunity to connect with the natural world and a place to display a few containerized plants, flowers or herbs. By framing views and drawing the eye onwards, well-tended outdoor spaces can have a great impact on the quality of indoor space, serving as a green buffer between your home and the surrounding environment. If there is space to sit out in fine weather, so much the better.

When you lead a busy life, perhaps much of it at work away from home, easy garden maintenance is essential. Hard surfacing such as decking, paving, stone chips or gravel is more practical than grass which will need to be mown on a regular basis. Where the garden immediately connects with a ground-floor area, using similar materials underfoot indoors and out enhances the sense of space. Drought-tolerant plants that will survive a little neglect and infrequent watering are a good idea if your gardening instincts are intermittent; suitable species include those that flourish in coastal conditions, as well as grasses, bamboos and other 'architectural' plants. For roof gardens, or other similarly exposed locations, plants need to be particularly robust in order to survive relatively extreme conditions and exposure to wind; some shelter in the form of trellising can help in this respect. You may need to consult a surveyor in order to establish whether the structure of an existing balcony or roof will support the extra load imposed by containerized plants and outdoor furniture. Timber decking can be a good way of covering up a poor surface, with the slats aiding drainage. You should also think carefully about safety. Secure screening with trellis, wire fencing or woven panels will not only provide better climactic conditions for plants and some privacy if necessary, but will also prevent accidents.

Simple planting is highly effective in small gardens. A balcony with a flowering climber threaded through the railings can be an intimate natural space; window boxes planted with the same species in the same colour have more impact – and are easier to look after – than lots of different containers planted with lots of different plants. Window boxes and other containers provide the opportunity to respond to the seasons, with a display of spring bulbs giving way to bright summer annuals. Scented species, such as lavender, or edible plants such as herbs, add to the sensory benefits.

In Japan, where population densities are very high and balconies are the closest many city-dwellers get to experiencing the great outdoors, every opportunity is taken to make the most of them. Furnishing an outdoor space with a simple table and a couple of chairs – and perhaps outdoor lighting – will mean that you are more likely to use it than ignore it.

⌄ An old blocked-up doorway lined with shelves makes a natural display area for a selection of plants in terracotta pots. Grouping containers in this way makes it easier to look after them as well as delivering greater visual impact.

STREAMLINED SPACE

Subtle 'tweaks' and the provision of extensive fitted storage have radically altered the perception of space in a two-bedroom maisonette in north London. The maisonette had been badly converted and felt very small; the owner's original brief to the architect was to make the most of the existing space and to add a rooftop extension in the form of a glazed box. Although the extension was eventually ruled out on grounds of cost, internal replanning has brought a new quality of light and air throughout the apartment that more than repays the investment.

An ungainly feature of the original conversion was that none of the walls lined up, thereby creating many awkward visual breaks. On the first floor, where the bedrooms are located, the hallway was small and the bathroom, which is set between the two bedrooms, was disproportionately large. Upstairs, the living room could only be accessed via the kitchen and the relatively low ceilings on this level accentuated the cramped feeling.

The first part of the design consisted of replanning the internal layout both to apportion space in a more effective way and to 'streamline' the walls so that they lined up

⌐ High-level cupboards were avoided in the working area of the kitchen because they would have broken up the wall area unnecessarily; instead a single timber shelf supports worktop lighting. Surfaces and finishes were kept simple and plain: basic units with MDF fronts, steel oven, hob and extractor, and a glass splashback.

‹ The dining area on the other side of the kitchen is framed by built-in cupboards housing food and kitchen equipment. The cupboards form an unbroken line from the living room right through the kitchen, accentuating the sense of space.

⌐ The worktop of thick iroko hardwood, with stainless steel sink inset, adds textural character and a sense of quality to the kitchen fit-out.

> In the living area immediately adjacent to the kitchen fitted cupboards provide a cohesive spatial element and turn the redundant fireplace into a place of display. Like all the cupboards in the apartment, these are custom-made from MDF and spray-lacquered for a silky smooth finish. The large orange L-shaped sofa provides a generous seating area and a welcome accent of colour.

∨ On both levels another unifying decorative feature is the treatment of the floors. Upstairs the original wooden floorboards have been painted dark brown, providing a foil for the crisp white walls.

⌐ Floor plans of the first level (left) and second level (right) show the location of the fitted storage cupboards and the effect of streamlining the spatial layout.

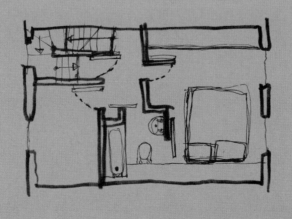

properly. On the first floor, the bathroom was reduced in size, which allowed the hallway to be widened to create a more generous entrance. The boiler, which had formerly been in the kitchen, was relocated to the bathroom. On the second floor, the kitchen and living room were opened out into one L-shaped space, which allowed light through into all areas.

The key unifying feature of the scheme, and the means by which the entire apartment was neatened and made more efficient, is the fitted cupboards which conceal clutter and possessions in every area. In the bedroom, a wall of cupboards houses the owner's wardrobe; in the bathroom, the boiler and lavatory cistern are similarly built-in. Fitted cupboards in the second bedroom are used to store files and other work-related items, which enables the room to double up as a study. Upstairs, a long line of cupboards runs from the living area right through the kitchen, breaking to form an alcove for the dining table.

The scheme perfectly illustrates two important points of successful small-space design. The first is to keep everything as simple as possible, with plain finishes and straight lines; and the second is to build in generous storage space to reduce visual clutter to an absolute minimum.

⌐ The bathroom is located between the two bedrooms and can be accessed from either the hallway or the main bedroom. A door connecting the hallway to the bathroom slides across a bookcase cleverly built into the space at the end of the bath. Cupboards conceal the boiler, lavatory cistern and pipework for a neat, integrated look.

≪ The bedroom has its own storage alcoves and cupboards which are seamlessly fitted so that they read as part of the architectural structure. Flush doors and the absence of handles or superfluous detailing make for a discreet, unobtrusive effect. The flooring throughout this level is dark rubber, which creates a sense of cohesion.

≺ A large sliding door provides access from the bedroom to the bathroom. The wall around the bathtub is tiled in mosaic. The lines of the bedroom wall continue through

to the bathroom and the opening between the two runs floor to ceiling, reinforcing the sense of spaciousness.

∧ The original intention was to add an extension onto the roof but the work required to flatten the existing 'butterfly' structure in order to gain the necessary floor area proved too expensive. Instead, a simple roof terrace, decked in hardwood, provides an outdoor living area. The decking wraps around a wall to create a low-level bench; cushions add comfort and a touch of colour. Wall lights allow the terrace to be used after nightfall.

≻ A rooflight positioned over the stairs to the roof terrace spills light down into the main living area on the second floor. Toplighting, particularly with natural light, enhances space enormously by accentuating volume.

SPATIAL CLARITY

Quite radical transformations can be achieved on relatively low budgets. In the case of this one-bedroom flat, located on the ground floor of a terraced house in south London, a new sense of clarity was achieved largely by rethinking the layout and redesignating room use, with new fitted elements and finishes providing a unifying theme.

The owner's brief to the designer was to make better use of the space overall and to make the flat more suitable for entertaining friends. The budget would not stretch to major structural changes, so these had to be kept to a minimum.

In the flat's original layout, the kitchen was sited where the bedroom is now, with the bathroom and lavatory leading off it. The key to the redesign was to swap these two areas over and relocate the kitchen in the former bedroom, where double doors leading to the garden provide better natural light and a more open, hospitable feeling. The lavatory was moved to separate it from the bathroom and positioned so that it could be accessed from the rest of the flat.

Where space is tight, fully open layouts can run activities together uncomfortably, but at the same time there is generally a need to improve internal views and make the most of natural light. The decision taken here was to open up the rooms so that they communicated with each other but were not entirely open plan, a strategy that also kept the level of structural alteration required within budget.

A new opening was made between the living room and kitchen-dining area. Two existing doorways were extended upwards so that all three openings were the same height, accentuating the high ceilings and enhancing the sense of space. These openings stop a little short of the ceiling, which is a cheaper option than running them floor to ceiling. To partially screen the working area of the kitchen, a low partition wall was built at the end of the worktop.

Whatever the budget, a sympathetic understanding between client and professional is the key to a successful scheme. The owner here has a strong sense of style, a good collection of furniture and preferences for materials and finishes, all of which complement the redesign and give the final scheme great vitality and character.

< The relocated kitchen is arranged in a single line of six units. Existing kitchen unit carcasses were reused and new doors fitted. A flush panel on the end wall conceals the boiler, which was moved from the bathroom. The worktop is white laminated birch ply; the splashback consists of layers of birch ply used side by side to reveal the grain. The same material crops up throughout the flat in the construction of fitted elements, providing a unifying effect.

L A low partition screens the counter and preparation area from the living room. To make the most of what might otherwise have been a dead corner, a flush door on the living room side of the partition wall gives access to a built-in washing machine.

> Over-scaled openings enhance the sense of space. The existing wooden floorboards were retained throughout the main living areas. The hallway is painted pink, giving a glimpse of warm colour.

∨ Moving the kitchen to where the bedroom used to be made a more sociable area and spread natural light into the living room. The bedroom, set on a lower level down three steps from the entrance hall, has a more private, enclosed feel.

⌐ A new fireplace was created by excavating the chimney breast and installing a poured-concrete hearth in place of existing floorboards.

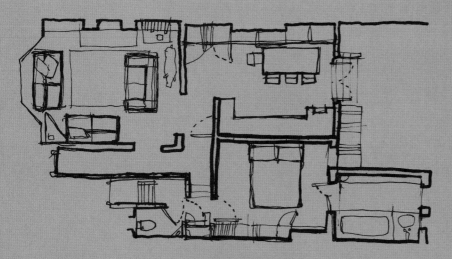

◁ Attention to detail reinforces the spatial clarity. The line of the bookshelf in the living room exactly matches that of the shelf in the dining area. Although the kitchen appears to be restricted to one wall, a tall built-in unit in the dining area on the opposite side of the room conceals the fridge-freezer. A low-level bench with pull-up flaps, also made in ply, extends along the wall, doubling as seating and storage for kitchen paraphernalia.

∟ In the bathroom the existing tub and basin were reused, the bath moved to line up with the basin, and the two under-mounted in white laminated birch ply. A long low ply bench provides storage space and conceals a radiator. The new en suite arrangement sets up a long sight line from the bedroom through to the bathroom window. White mosaic tiling provides a waterproof surface.

⌄ The exposed ply edge of the laminate used in all the fitted elements gives a sense of visual continuity. Side-mounted bath taps provide neat detailing.

▷ A key decorative feature of the more 'private' area of the flat is the striking Moroccan tiled floor that runs throughout the bedroom and bathroom areas. Sourced by the owner, the tiles were laid over a self-levelling sub-floor to take up the type of discrepancies in thicknesses that come with a handmade product. The 'panelled' wall in the bedroom, echoed on one wall of the bathroom, is actually a wood-effect laminate, and was also sourced by the owner.

LIVE-WORK

< A sense of light

As a photographer, the owner of this two-storey apartment has a keen appreciation of natural light. When she first began house hunting, she was looking for an old house and imagined spending years renovating it. Instead, she found herself purchasing a top-floor apartment in a new complex situated near one of the oldest and most vibrant areas of Amsterdam, Holland. The central location, with cosy restaurants, pubs and markets within walking distance, was a deciding factor, particularly for someone who works from home and travels a great deal.

The apartment is arranged on two levels, with a central void. On the upper level is the workspace, with doors leading to a roof terrace offering a spectacular view of the city and the barges passing by on the canal in front of the building. Year-round the interior is flooded with sunlight, an effect that is accentuated by a dominant use of white in the decor. Other more intense shades, defining different areas of the interior, were inspired by colours the owner saw in Argentina and northern India.

Simple changes allowed the owner to express her own personality in the new space. The kitchen units were repainted and fitted with new handles. Because she felt the living area was not large enough for a sofa, she commissioned a plasterer to make a built-in bench which is located next to the stairs. Rugged natural finishes are a favourite: wooden floorboards are left untreated and the steel-framed dining chairs are strung with leather.

A key consideration was room for display. To accommodate her large collection of photography books, she had a bookcase – essentially 12 open boxes – built to line one wall of her studio. Other treasured possessions are scattered throughout the interior: pots and bowls from around the world, African stools, cushions from Bali and her collection of found natural objects grouped in miniature still lifes.

One of the most notable ways in which lifestyles have altered over the past decade is the burgeoning trend for working at home. On current forecasts, it is estimated that nearly a third of the British workforce will be home-workers in less than five years' time, a statistic that is echoed by similar developments around the world. Advances in technology and communications, together with changes in the way modern companies are structured and staffed, mean that more and more people are choosing to work at home all or part of the time.

On the face of it, earning your living without having to face the draining horrors of the daily commute or put up with petty office politics may seem like a dream come true. Working at home supposedly means fewer distractions, flexible hours and setting your own pace and schedule, along with not having to ask anyone's permission to take time off to cope with a domestic crisis such as a sick child or broken washing machine.

That is the theory, at least. In practice, 'live-work' throws up a number of unique challenges that require serious consideration if home life is to remain enjoyable and work life productive. Many of these have to do with spatial arrangements; others are concerned with your working methods and preferences.

SELF-ASSESSMENT

Nearly everyone in full-time paid employment works at home some of the time. Scanning the pages of a report in preparation for a big meeting, making telephone appointments, finishing off a presentation over the weekend and similar overflows from office life can generally be accommodated without too much disruption to your household. But if you are planning to make the leap to live-work, it is important to spend some time assessing your needs and requirements and determining the implications of the changes to your working habits. While it can be difficult to predict which working methods and arrangements are really going to suit you when you have spent your entire career to date conforming to an office culture, unless you plan ahead and really know what you want, you may soon find yourself feeling nostalgic for all those aspects of office life you were initially so pleased to leave behind.

Aspects to consider:

> **The physical conditions required for your work** How much space do you need for a desk or workstation, for computers, printers, faxes, scanners or other equipment, for filing and storing supplies? Is your work dependant on good natural light? Are artificial lighting arrangements sufficient to support the work that you do? Is your work inherently noisy, which may distract others in the household, or do you require absolute silence to function effectively?

> **Technological support** Do you require additional lines of communication in the form of a separate telephone line, ISDN line or high-speed internet access? Will you need to buy special equipment? Are there essential support services, such as printers or photocopying shops within the vicinity?

⌐ Views aid concentration, particularly if you are engaged in creative work, and all working areas need good natural light. Here space has been partitioned in such a way that both living and working areas have the benefit of the garden view through floor-to-ceiling windows.

∧ Sliding opaque screens conceal the working area from the rest of the space when it is not in use. A neat array of shelves organizes files and work-related items; an ergonomic desk chair provides essential support for keyboard work.

> **Access** Does your work involve employees, clients, customers or suppliers visiting you on a regular basis? Do you need to maintain a professional image if they do? Can your work area be sited so that the rest of your home is not visible or accessible for working visitors?

> **Legalities and finance** Working from home, especially if you are employing others, may have legal and financial implications. If, for example, you charge the full cost of your home office out to your business, you may be liable for corporate capital gains when it comes to selling your house. Consult a financial adviser or accountant for current regulations. Are you liable for business rates? Are there tax advantages whereby a proportion of household expenses can be claimed against earnings? If you are working from home in order to have more time to spend with your family, can you get sufficient work done in the hours available to make ends meet and keep clients happy?

> **Future prospects** What flexibility is there for future growth? How do you envisage your career or business changing over the next five or ten years? Are your working arrangements able to cope with changes in circumstances, such as the arrival of children or a partner deciding to work from home as well?

> **Personal preferences** What sort of working environment makes you feel most comfortable and encourages your productivity? Do you find office-style fittings and fixtures reassuring and confidence-boosting or do you prefer a more relaxed set-up to stimulate creativity?

> **Social contact** Working from home can mean isolation, particularly if you are used to working in a team or lively office. Have you any strategies for combating loss of contact? Are there facilities nearby, such as health clubs, coffee shops or similar that you can depend on for social interaction?

SITING THE WORK AREA

Getting in the right frame of mind for work entails putting some psychological distance between you and the many distractions that home life provides. (Until you work from home, you may never have seen a pile of ironing or an un-mown lawn as potential distractions, but it is surprising how otherwise dreary chores can suddenly look appealing when a blank screen or deadline looms.) Perhaps the sole advantage of commuting is that it does at least offer a natural punctuation point that reinforces a shift of gears.

The siting of a working area is an obvious way of gaining the necessary psychological distance between home and work: if you have to climb a flight of stairs to reach an office in a converted attic, or if you can close the study door, such physical parameters can subtly signal the separation of different spheres of activity and push household matters out of mind. At the same time, sitting down to read the paper, tackle the crossword or deal with correspondence and admin at the beginning of the working day can prepare you mentally for the tasks ahead.

Views, which superficially may seem like potential distractions, are actually very beneficial for concentration, particularly for creative work. 'Staring into space' is not slacking, but part of the process of shaping ideas. If at all possible, try to locate a working area near a window; alternatively, an elevated workspace where you can gaze into the distance – on a mezzanine level, for instance – also offers the opportunity for creative daydreaming.

Psychological distance is equally important the other way round. Live-work implies a balance, which means that there must be the opportunity to relax and unwind away from the pressures of work. If you are the sort of person who cannot switch off if their work remains in view, your workspace should be located where you can walk away from it, or your workstation set up in such a way that it can be screened off or enclosed at the end of the day.

⌄ A horizontal internal window between a living room and a study set down on a lower level provides an unusual vantage point. Elevated workspaces, on a mezzanine level for instance, also provide the necessary psychological distance without the feeling of being entirely cut off from the rest of the household.

⌐ A dedicated working area tucked underneath a mezzanine level in a converted loft provides room for concentration. Where a working area is sited, just as much as how it is fitted and furnished, can have a great impact on productivity.

‹ Good natural light is a positive asset for most types of work. Here light floods into a high-ceilinged room through large windows. White fabric blinds provide a minimal degree of separation; glossy reflective finishes and flooring spreads the available light around further.

⌄ A spare room, or any room that is currently under-used, makes an ideal workspace, particularly if you are the sort of person who needs to shut a door on the rest of the household in order to concentrate, or if your work is not easily tidied away or screened at the end of the day.

‹‹ A compact workstation, with ample shelving for books, is slotted along one wall of a living area and screened by folding doors.

‹ You do not have to spend a great deal to create an efficient workspace. A bank of reclaimed metal filing cabinets with a counter on top is a neat way of integrating storage with an additional worksurface. An old kitchen table makes a practical desk for computer work.

INTEGRATED WORKSPACES

Paperless portable office technology – such as laptops, palm pilots and mobile phones – means that in theory you can work anywhere: in bed, on the kitchen table, in the garden or in a local café. In practice, however, a designated workspace is an essential anchoring point for any kind of serious endeavour upon which your livelihood depends.

Obvious candidates for workspaces within the home are any areas that are currently under-used, for example, if you have a dining room but tend to eat in the kitchen, if you have a spare room but overnight guests are infrequent, if a child has grown and flown the nest. All you have to do is stake a claim on the territory and fit it out accordingly.

Where space is in short supply, you may be forced to set up a workspace within a bedroom, living area or kitchen. That need not be as disruptive or as counter-productive as it sounds. In the case of otherwise communal areas such as kitchens and living rooms, if the rest of the household are out at work or school for most of the day, you will still get the peace and quiet you need during working hours. Similarly, bedrooms are chiefly occupied at night, and can readily accommodate a different daytime role.

Some rooms lend themselves to multipurpose use: an L-shaped layout, for example, allows you to set up a workspace in the shorter arm of the 'L' without the need for further visual distinction. Otherwise, you can maintain a proper separation of home life and work life by either opting for a built-in arrangement, whereby a working wall is screened from view with panels, folding doors, blinds or free-standing storage units; or by constructing some form of half-height or half-width partition.

Generous hallways, landings or understairs spaces may present highly practical options for siting a workspace, provided you are on your own during the day and thus not liable to the distractions of people passing to and fro, upstairs and down. But even if you do not choose to put your desk there, such spaces can usefully serve as storage areas for files, office supplies and working libraries, which means that the workspace per se can be more compact and self-effacing wherever it is located.

❯ A converted attic makes a good self-contained working area. Windows in the plane of the roof bring in natural light. If you will be using the space every day, a proper means of access, rather than a loft ladder, is important. Under-the-eaves space can be exploited for storage; these shelf units on castors make the most of every available square centimetre.

CONVERSIONS AND EXTENSIONS

Converting an attic or basement or adding on to your home can win you the extra space you need for a work area, either directly or indirectly. Think about your home as a whole and how it could best be reorganized rather than simply in terms of gaining an extra room. Extending a kitchen, for example, so that it is big enough for the entire family to eat in, can free up a dining room, which can be turned into a home office. In the same way, while converted attics often make good workspaces, you may prefer to shift your bedroom up there instead and set up your home office in your former bedroom, particularly if access is an important issue.

Carrying out conversions and extensions is disruptive and costly; while in most cases you will eventually recoup your investment in terms of an enhanced selling price, you should be certain that the expense and effort is warranted at the present time. If working from home may prove a temporary phase rather than a permanent lifestyle shift, it may be better to seek other solutions.

LOFTS AND LIVE-WORK UNITS

Lofts are where 'working where you live' meets 'living where you work'. Loft living, a phenomenon that has spread from major cities such as New York and London to urban (and suburban) areas around the world, has proved a crucial spur to the whole trend of working at home. The true loft – rather than the unremarkable apartment inflated by estate agent's hyperbole – makes an ideal live-work environment because it comes with no domestic baggage in terms of style or layout, thanks to its industrial or commercial heritage.

True lofts generally boast high ceilings and good natural light. Volume means that siting a separate work area on a mezzanine level is a natural arrangement, providing both a separation of activity and expansive views to aid concentration. The more rugged aesthetic of loft space also means that work-related equipment and furniture look less intrusive than they do in a conventional home.

One of the ways in which the loft movement has altered contemporary lifestyles has been the relaxation of formerly stringent planning regulations regarding change of use. Several decades ago, when loft pioneers occupied redundant warehouses, workshops, factories and commercial buildings, running battles with local authorities often ensued. Once the movement acquired momentum, however, and it became clear that loft living might have a beneficial effect on the preservation and regeneration of the urban fabric, planners began to relax their codes and look more favourably on more hybrid arrangements combining living and working in the same space. Significantly, this has led more recently to the loft offshoot, the 'live-work' unit.

Many live-work units come fully wired for the internet and hi-tech communication. In most areas, the amount of space that can be used for working purposes – generally between 30 and 50 per cent of the total area – is specified as part of the planning permission (conversely, this allocation should not, however, be used as an additional bedroom or living area). There are also restrictions on the type of business allowed in such units. Most of these concern the impact of your business on your neighbours, which rules out any activity liable to create adverse environmental factors such as excess noise, pollution or traffic. Any business operating from a live-work unit must not be the sort that relies on passing trade. Visitors must be by appointment only and you may not be allowed to advertise your presence with commercial signage.

Before taking on a live-work unit, look into the financial pros and cons. Generally, owners or tenants of live-work units pay a combination of business and local rates and are allowed to offset a certain proportion of household expenses against tax. If you are a self-employed home-worker, you are also allowed to claim back a percentage of household running costs, but do not have the added burden of business rates, so there may be no particular financial incentive to having a live-work unit.

∨ The rugged aesthetic and functional pedigree of lofts and other non-domestic buildings means that working areas are less of an obvious intrusion. Where space is particularly generous, there is also room for your business to expand.

❮ Original exposed wooden beams and rafters make an evocative contrast to sleek new finishes, including smooth plastered walls and hardwood flooring. With a gable end fitted with shelves to house a library and a simple trestle table serving as a desk, there is no obvious segregation of living and working.

∧ All the hallmarks of a true loft: exposed structural features, a high ceiling, good natural light and an open, free layout. The exposed framework of beams and rafters provides a natural way of defining areas of activity without the need for partitioning.

˥ Converted buildings that are double-height can be effectively divided in a vertical fashion with the addition of a mezzanine level. Here the mezzanine is used as a sleeping area, while the working part of the loft is screened by a fabric panel hung from the ceiling.

❯ Toplighting from generous rooflights creates an uplifting atmosphere for work.

∧ This Californian photographer's studio-cum-gallery is very simply constructed of plywood panels supported by a redwood frame. The redwood timbers were milled from fallen trees that had lain for years on the property and were thus already naturally weathered and seasoned. Inside the studio, oriented for northern light, there is one free-standing exhibition wall.

〉 The 'Yardbird', a home office designed by architect Neal Deputy, is supported by steel piloti and a concrete wall. The structure was assembled out of prefab elements: metal siding and louvred windows.

〉〉 If your garden is big enough, self-contained prefabricated units, including the humble garden shed, make good workspaces that are separate from the home. This version, designed as an office, has electrical connections and is insulated.

SHEDS AND ANCILLARY BUILDINGS

The humble shed, where traditionally men have sought refuge from the demands of family life among the deck chairs, old plant pots and gardening tools, is currently proving a surprisingly popular live-work option. The lure of the shed (and presumably why many men have been content to spend hours there) is its self-containment and separation from the rest of the household. That same isolation has long recommended the shed as a workspace for writers. Roald Dahl wrote in a shed; so do Phillip Pullman and Margaret Drabble. George Bernard Shaw's writing shed at his home in Ayot St Lawrence, in Hertfordshire, Britain, was on a turntable so that it could be pivoted to face the direction of the sun.

If you have a big enough garden, the shed as workspace has much to recommend it. That essential psychological distance is enhanced when you have to physically leave the house and set off down the garden path to go to work. For home businesses where clients, suppliers or customers need to visit on a regular basis, a shed or ancillary building that can be accessed without going through the house also makes a lot of sense.

At the simplest, an off-the-peg garden shed can be converted into a workspace with relatively little trouble; you will need an electrician to make the electrical connections and you may wish to install a telephone line (or not). If the garden-shed aesthetic does not appeal, one British company has recently responded to the trend for working from home by coming up with a compact home office with a more upmarket look. One advantage of such an arrangement is that planning permission is not required; sheds in kit form are also easy to install. However, if you need to keep expensive electronic equipment in the shed overnight, make sure it is fully secure and vandal-proof – the average shed is a great deal easier to break into than your home.

Converting an ancillary building on your property into the base for a home business will necessarily involve legal and bureaucratic hurdles. In some country areas, planners may take some persuading before they allow you to make over a redundant farm building or stable block. If you are just starting up a new business, it may seem like a great deal of expense and trouble, but the effort can pay off rapidly when the business begins to grow.

ERGONOMICS AND EFFICIENCY

Although some far-sighted companies make every effort to provide welcoming and human working environments, the average office, all bland neutral shades and regulation furniture, still leaves a lot to be desired. One of the most appealing aspects of working at home is leaving all of that behind and putting a more personal stamp on your surroundings.

What you should not leave behind when you shift to a home workspace, however, is ergonomic design. Office decor may not make your heart sing, but most contemporary office furniture is the product of detailed ergonomic research designed both to improve productivity and efficiency and to minimize work-related stress injury and illness. If you work from home you are no more immune from back pain, RSI (repetitive stress injury) or eye strain than you are in an office; in fact, you may be at increased risk if you are using furniture or equipment that are not properly designed for the job.

> **Lighting** For general working conditions, overall light levels should be between 500 and 1000 lux. Computer work demands a lower level of background light – between 300 and 500 lux – because the screen itself is a source of illumination. Glare-free background light can be supplied by uplighters, but you will need to provide extra task lighting for reading paper documents.

> **Worksurfaces** Placing worksurfaces at the correct height is essential. Since keyboards should, as a rule, be operated at a lower level than that required for general desk use, and monitors should be set a little higher, a worksurface that incorporates different levels or that has an inset keyboard tray, which can be slid back in when not in use, is most efficient. Rounded worktop edges protect the wrists and arms.

> **Keyboard** Working at a keyboard is most comfortable and least likely to cause stress injury when the keyboard is placed directly in front of the body, between 10 and 40cm (4 and 16in) away, and at a level where it can be operated without having to lift the shoulders and with arms and wrists straight. Choose an ergonomically designed keyboard if possible.

> **Chair** Sedentary work requires an ergonomic task chair, that is, one which accommodates a variety of movements and supports different postures. The chair seat should be padded, tiltable and with a rounded front edge; seat height should be adjustable so that you can sit with your feet planted squarely on the floor. The backrest should follow the curve of the spine and should also be tiltable to allow you to lean back, stretch or change position.

> **Storage** A work area at home may be relatively easy to accommodate within the space at your disposal. More problematic, however, is what goes with the work: files, accounts, reference material, supplies, invoices and tax returns. Few people have the discipline or sufficient faith in the infallibility of technology to run a truly paperless office. You may require two or three separate storage areas and systems to accommodate your working life at home: storage near or around your desk for work in hand or materials you use or refer to constantly; storage in an accessible location for bulk supplies, reference libraries or documentation relating to recent projects; and deep storage in an out-of-the-way and out-of-sight location for old tax returns, accounts and other files relating to your working history.

⌄ A home office on water: a concrete hull, built along the lines of barges used during the Second World War, supports a wooden frame covered in corrugated metal sheeting to make a floating architect's studio in San Francisco Bay, United States.

⌄ Farm buildings, barns and other ancillary spaces provide room for expansion when the one-person operation turns into a flourishing business. In many cases, you will need to obtain planning permission for change of use if you plan to convert a non-domestic building.

CONVERTED WATER TOWER

Loft living was born in redundant warehouses and factories in cities such as New York and Amsterdam; today a surprising variety of other utilitarian structures have been successfully converted into live-work homes. Few, however, have presented such a design challenge as this 365,000-gallon water tower made of solid concrete.

The tower, built in 1907 and decommissioned by the water company in 1977, stands on a ridge overlooking Yale University, with views across New Haven and Long Island Sound in Connecticut, United States. When the owners, two newly appointed Yale professors, spotted it, it was damp, windowless and derelict. But the sheer presence of the fortress-like structure, along with the views, had immediate appeal, as did the unusual cylindrical form.

The existing structural system of the tower dictated the new subdivision of the internal space. At ceiling level, two reinforced concrete beams run north to south and two others east to west, with four large concrete columns supporting the roof structure where these intersect. The owners wanted as little intervention as possible, but the home had to function for both living and working, as well as provide a degree of privacy. Accordingly, an upper level was inserted halfway up the four existing columns, supported by beams of Douglas fir. The upper level has tongue-and-groove

⌐⌐ The water tower in its original state – damp, window-less and with crumbling concrete walls. The external staircase-tower that gives access to the roof has been retained.

⌐ The main bedroom faces east, so the owners can wake up to the sunrise. A glass walkway connects the bedroom with the metal staircase, passing over the double-height library. A sliding door separates the bedroom from the walkway and a projecting boxed bay window increases the natural light.

L After restoration and conversion, the tower has the appearance of an elegant Mediterranean villa. In summer the large glazed doors are kept open to provide easy access to the terrace, planted with climbers and shaded by canvas awnings.

∨ The south-facing double-height living area, with its sweeping white walls, has a dark concrete floor that contributes to passive solar heating. The massive tiled fireplace was inspired by similar examples the owners saw in Switzerland.

« The central core or 'soul' of the house is the double-height library, framed by four structural columns. On one side is the staircase leading to the upper level; on the other side is the kitchen. Four skylights bring natural light into the library.

‹ The generous terrace, made from debris salvaged from the interior, provides a place for outdoor eating. The garden has been planted in as natural a fashion as possible.

› The second accommodation level is supported by great beams of Douglas fir, bolted onto the existing concrete columns. A glass walkway crosses the library at the upper level, connecting the main bedroom with the metal staircase.

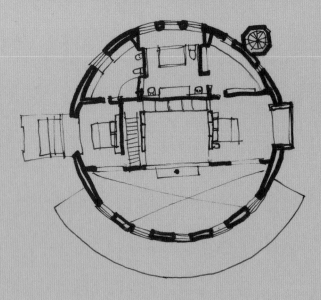

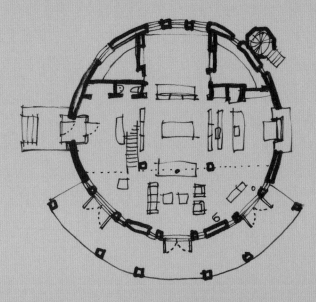

wooden flooring, stained black, with the underside, which forms the ceiling of the areas below, painted light blue.

Within the central square core defined by the four columns is the two-storey library that houses the couple's 150m (488ft) of books. At ground level, the library opens into a double-height living area. On the new second level, which is accessed by a metal stairway that leads from the entrance, the library is flanked by two bedrooms.

The 45cm- (1¹/2ft-) thick concrete walls provided a considerable structural challenge when it came to adding doorways and window openings. Windows were inserted around the circumference, four skylights in the roof and several large glazed doors on the south-facing elevation. The kitchen and main bedroom have boxed bay windows that stand out from the façade, bringing these areas closer to the outdoors. The interior is full of light which pours in from all sides and constantly changes as the sun moves round the building.

Instead of repairing the original concrete walls, which would have been an extremely expensive option, they were first insulated externally and then covered with stucco, tinted in an earthy ochre shade. Inside, the walls were sandblasted and washed in two coats of lime for a chalky, translucent finish. The massive concrete shell serves as an efficient thermal mass, cooling the interior in the summer and retaining warmth in the winter.

FAMILY HOME

As demographic studies show, the stereotypical family profile – mother, father and two-point-something children – no longer accurately represents the increasing diversity of the contemporary family. Modern families can be made up of lone parents bringing up single children to families where lodgers, au pairs, nannies or grannies also co-habit (or where grown-up children refuse to move out). But if families nowadays come in all shapes, sizes and permutations, they are all, by their very nature, multi-generational.

Where different generations live under the same roof, there are inevitably competing demands. Such demands may be as concrete as the rival claims for the same space – such as who has to share a bedroom – or less tangibly take the form of different attitudes to noise and clutter – an adult's 'loud' is typically a teenager's 'inaudible'. In such circumstances, planning the family home can demand the type of tense, delicate negotiations that would tax a professional arbitrator. In any event, compromise, in some form, is almost always needed to balance the requirements of different family members.

At the same time, if no single solution can be found to provide a workable blueprint for all families, no one solution can be expected to work all of the time. Where children are concerned, change is built into the equation. In a terrifyingly short space of time, the toddler getting under your feet in the kitchen will be transformed into the teenager blasting music from behind a bedroom door. This means that the type of planning and arrangement that would suit a family with young children will not necessarily work when those children reach school age, and will be positively outdated when the teenage years loom on the horizon.

Many families respond by moving at key stages: when more children come along, or when children become old enough to want a space of their own. But by building in flexibility to your living arrangements and making sure you get the basics right, it is possible to organize matters so that your home grows with your family and you stay one step ahead of the game.

PLANNING AND ARRANGEMENT

One of the big issues when it comes to planning the family home is getting the balance right between private areas and shared space. Although it may be tempting on days when sibling rivalry goes nuclear, no one would wish to return to the old hierarchical system, whereby children, relegated to night and day nurseries, were neither seen nor heard. At the same time, if every area of the home is a free-for-all, there can be little respite for either parents or children.

A shared space can be as small as a big bed or as all-embracing as an open-plan living-kitchen-dining area, but family homes do tend to work best where there is at least one generous area where everyone can gather together without worrying about spoiling pristine surfaces or finishes. However, this isn't merely a question of practicalities. A shared space means that other things are shared, too, and thus provides a framework for both communication and communal experience that family life at its best should be all about.

> Young at heart

The home of a husband-and-wife design team and their four children combines robust surfaces and finishes with a playful approach to furnishing and fitting. The house, which is set in the English countryside near the coast, was designed and built to a relatively low budget.

On the back elevation, huge windows make the most of garden views. Inside, materials for surfaces and finishes are no-frills: neutral-coloured plaster walls and concrete floors. The kitchen is clad in marine-blue swimming pool mosaic tiles, bought in sheets; the bathroom fittings are the type of stainless steel basins and lavatories generally used in hospitals. Hard-wearing, practical and easy to maintain, such elements are not only built to withstand the rigours of family life, but also provide a simple background that will go with any future decorative changes. Extensive built-in storage keeps clutter at bay.

While none of the furniture is precious, a lot of it is fun and children do not have to be told constantly not to touch. The two sofas in the living room were made from the family's old fishing boat, which was smashed up in a gale. The bow has been transformed into a play den in the garden. The dining table top was found in a skip and most of the rest of the furniture came from bargain sources such as car-boot sales, junk shops and markets – a reflection of the couple's keen interest in the eccentric as much as an attempt to create a relaxed and informal living environment. With a climbing wall at one end of the living room and a fish-tank-cum-lavatory cistern, the result is an easy-going, irreverent, practical home for small and big kids alike.

To what degree your children's lives and needs are woven into the fabric of your home depends to a great extent on your attitude to parenting. But where both parents work out of the house for much of the day and children are cared for by nannies, au pairs or childminders, it is also important to be aware that homes may have to accommodate different requirements on a daily basis, serving as a child-centred place during the day and providing more of an adult focus in the evening. Essentially this means that everyone in the family must have some space they can call their own.

FAMILY KITCHENS

These days, rather than more notional 'living' areas, the prime candidate for shared space tends to be the kitchen. Just as people tend to gravitate to the kitchen when you throw a party, the kitchen in most homes is increasingly where much of everyday living tends to take place. The inclusive kitchen, where food is prepared, cooked and eaten, and where many other incidental activities take place, from homework to music practice to routine household admin, provides a practical, hospitable and functional focus for the family home. It is all the better if the kitchen is located where there is an easy connection with outdoor areas, so that some of these activities can shift outdoors on fine days and children can rush in and out with an element of parental supervision.

Although there is an increased tendency in many busy families for food to be 'grazed' throughout the day, with snacks replacing settled mealtimes, a big robust table where everyone can sit down and eat together (once homework, colouring books and other paraphernalia have been swept down one end) provides an essential point of connection between family members. A generous family kitchen also means that children inevitably come in greater contact with routine domestic tasks and may even be persuaded to help out with the food preparation or washing up. A good way of gaining the space for a family-oriented kitchen is to absorb adjacent rooms or areas, such as separate dining rooms, or to extend a short way out into the garden, either to the side or the rear of the house, or both.

⌄ A big wooden table positioned in a sunny spot overlooking the garden makes a hospitable focus for family mealtimes. The open arrangement of kitchen and main living areas is underscored by extending the same flooring throughout.

⌐ Free-standing kitchen units raised on feet emphasize the spaciousness of this family kitchen by leaving the parquet floor in full view. Efficient mechanical ventilation to prevent stale odours from lingering is important in all kitchens, but particularly in those used for other activities aside from cooking.

⌐ A low-level counter, set at child height and incorporating its own sink, makes a practical space for creative play – ideal for messy activities such as painting, gluing or cooking.

> ⌃ Family kitchens are best positioned where there is easy access to the garden or other outdoor areas, so that when there is fine weather children can run in and out under the watchful eye of a parent. Here a sweep of worktop doubles as a counter for light meals and snacks.

LIVING AREAS

By accommodating many routine everyday roles, the inclusive kitchen can help to provide a more defined function for the living room as a place for relaxing and recharging one's batteries. In the old days, living rooms – sitting rooms, drawing rooms, parlours, front rooms, the terms themselves are class-ridden – had the clear purpose of communicating to visitors one's status, wealth and taste, with the result that many were hardly ever used at all in case anything got broken or messed up. More recently, living areas have functioned rather as the default space of the home, mopping up a range of different and often competing activities or, more passively, serving as the place where the entire family could flop on the sofa to watch the box. Nowadays, with more households owning two or more televisions and the kitchen increasingly serving as the hub of the home, there is an opportunity to re-evaluate what living areas are for and perhaps reclaim them as spaces for enjoying a book or newspaper, some music or good conversation.

‹ A sofa big enough for the whole family to snuggle up together and listen to music or watch television counts as a shared space, too. On the practical side, make sure sofa covers are removeable and washable.

⌄ Children are acutely aware of comfort and in the early years spend a lot of time in floor-based play. Hard flooring may be more practical and durable but at least some softer surfaces – rugs or carpeted areas – are also needed, to absorb sound as well as cushion falls.

∧ A semi-transparent glass panel separates a play zone from main living areas, thereby maintaining a sense of connection to the rest of the family but reducing noise levels and providing a dedicated area for toys.

› A pair of pedestal sinks can help to relieve congestion in a family bathroom, particularly at key moments of the day, such as early morning. Fully tiled walls make a practical wipe-down background.

While it is faintly ridiculous and, frankly, counter-productive to furnish and decorate a family living area in a 'hands-off' manner, it can be no bad thing to treat it as a space with a more adult emphasis where children have to be not necessarily on best behaviour, but at least on better behaviour. A recent television programme, half an exercise in Big Brother-style voyeurism and half social experiment, filmed what happened when a group of ten-year-old boys were left alone in a house for a week. No one was entirely surprised when the house was trashed in a remarkably short space of time. A living area that has been planned and arranged to please grown-ups, and which requires that children must take a little extra care, can help to usher them through the trashing phase, as well as spell out the message that adults have lives, too.

Although nowadays the television is the inevitable focus of any living room or space where relaxing is the prime activity, the old focus of the hearth still has an irresistible lure. Real fires – open fireplaces, stoves or even gas fires – have a powerful psychological appeal for both adults and children alike and create a warm centre at the heart of the family home.

BATHROOMS

The sitcom standby, the bottlenecked bathroom, indicates one area where a great many families feel particularly pressed for space. Two bathrooms, or at least an arrangement where the lavatory is separate from the main washing and bathing area, can go a long way towards making family life less fractious. An effective alternative is to site a bathtub or wet area within the main bedroom, so that an invigorating shower or relaxing soak can be taken without someone hammering on the door. Small washbasins in children's rooms are another practical idea – for washing out paint trays as much as for brushing teeth – or in years to come, for the teenager's interminable grooming sessions that can otherwise put the bathroom out of action for hours at a time.

PRIVATE SPACES

The greatest scope for shape-shifting flexibility within the family home is in the realm of private spaces or bedrooms. Family life is all about change, which at times can be both rapid and radical. While there's a limit to how often you can turn your home upside down, knock through walls or tack on extensions, moving bedrooms to suit different needs at different times need only take a weekend and a little muscle power. Babies don't need big rooms and may spend more time in yours in any case for the first few months at least, but by the time a child is walking, there is an increased need for space, particularly floor space. Young children up to the age of ten or thereabouts spend a lot of time playing and indulging in what psychologists term 'gross motor activity', which the rest of us know as romping or messing about. If you don't want them swinging from the chandeliers, and would rather the living room was not carpeted with Lego or bits of train track, it's a good idea to give children the space they need to be boisterous and expansive in their play. This may mean that the 'master' bedroom becomes the child's bedroom, an arrangement that is particularly advantageous when

⌄ Bathroom fittings and fixtures are not as a rule adjustable. Moveable steps or stools bring children up to sink – and mirror – height.

⌄ Plenty of floor area is not necessary in a bathroom but it undoubtedly contributes to a sense of relaxation. Here the bath itself is set into an alcove, which provides a comforting feeling of enclosure.

children are still young enough to share a room. As children grow into teenagers, on the other hand, smaller bedrooms can work surprisingly well. Many teenagers have a greater need for wall area to customize with posters and collaged ephemera than for floor area per se. Dividing a big bedroom into two small ones or shifting bedroom allocation around again makes sense at this stage.

CHILD-FREE ZONES

If you are pressed for space, your bedroom may be the only area within the home you can truly call your own. If it is, ensure that it serves as a true refuge or retreat. An understandable response to the hectic clamour of family life is to treat the bedroom as an exercise in cool restraint, where clutter is banished, colours are muted and pale, and furnishings kept simple. Decanting clothes storage to an adjacent dressing area or built-in closet can go a long way to making the bedroom a place where you enjoy spending time, instead of a mere dormitory. In some households, a closed bedroom door still has the power to stop children from making dawn raids on sleeping parents – make the most of it.

At the same time, it is possible to stake a territorial marker within an otherwise more communal area, such as a living room or kitchen, although such child-free zones may need more active defending. A desk placed in front of a window or in an alcove can provide valuable thinking or working space even if there is no door to signal the boundary.

⌃ Children are never entirely out of sight or out of mind (or out of earshot) but even the most devoted parents need a space to be by themselves, which in many cases is the bedroom. Simple furnishings promote a mood of relaxation.

⌃ All-white decor is peaceful and fresh. A large mirror propped against the wall spreads natural light from the bay window to the rest of the room. A squashy sofa provides somewhere to curl up with a good book in the odd quiet moment.

❯ Even if you are not an advocate of small children sharing your bed, it is worth investing in as large and as comfortable a bed as possible. Here, night tables have been improvised from a pair of chairs.

> One of the advantages of an open-plan layout is that it provides plenty of free space for children to let off steam – or practise their balancing skills. Sliding doors and internal partitions are a good way of retaining flexibility and providing a little privacy within an open space.

⌐ A mezzanine level fitted out with storage and worktops serves as a family study area and computer zone. Any activity that demands concentration or peace and quiet needs to be separated to some degree from more communal areas.

⌐ Even older houses, built and arranged in a traditional layout, offer the potential for opening up, both internally and from indoors to out. The free arrangement of the kitchen-dining and living areas on the ground floor is echoed in the glazed rear wall merging house with garden.

OPEN-PLAN

Fully open-plan layouts are rarely entirely successful ways of accommodating family life. It is particularly instructive that many couples who have happily enjoyed the wide open spaces of a loft, for example, find themselves putting up a few walls or partitions once children come along. The reasons are obvious: the need for privacy, intimacy, or simply some peace and quiet. Family life, however, does not necessarily entail a retreat into the conventional arrangement of separate box-like rooms. You can have the best of both worlds by dividing space into free-flowing public zones and more private areas, screening the two with flexible partitions, screens or moveable dividers.

Great spaces for children:

The run of the house

Window seats

Verandas

Hideyholes under the stairs

Dens

Wendy houses

Tree houses

Bunkbeds

Outdoors

Great spaces for adults:

Bed

Any room without a toy in it

Three floors away from music practice

Study

Workroom

Garage

Shed

Bathroom

A hotel room in another city/country

^ Beds placed at right angles to each other make the most of the corner window and leave maximum floor area clear. Underbed storage in pull-out drawers keeps clutter under control while toys and other belongings remain easily accessible. Giving each child an equal allocation of space and similar furnishings can help to prevent sibling squabbles.

CHILDREN'S ROOMS

A child's room is a psychological as well as a physical space; to a child, it is that all-important first place of their own, a bit of private territory, even if they are sharing with a sibling and the only exclusively private part about it is their bed. A children's room should provide space for the imagination, a springboard for creative activity, just as much as physical space for letting off energy or getting stuck into serious play. Above all, it should serve as a secure base, constant enough to provide a sense of continuity during years of rapid change, but also flexible enough to accommodate each new stage of development.

Unfortunately, children's rooms often say more about adults than they really ought to. A case in point is the relentlessly themed nursery, complete with co-ordinated wallpaper, curtains, borders and friezes. One of the problems with this approach to decoration is that all the imagining has been done on the child's behalf, leaving little scope for the child to put their own emotional or interpretative stamp on their surroundings. Other drawbacks are fundamentally practical. Most figurative nursery patterns have an incredibly short life span. Quite simply, by the time children are old enough to have views on the matter, they will probably prefer Thomas the Tank Engine or Barbie over rabbits and teddies, and in what may feel like only minutes later, it will be the members of the Manchester United football squad or the latest boy band. Few parents have the time, inclination or budget to redecorate children's rooms in line with a craze that may well be over by next Tuesday, so the best strategy is to keep the basics – walls, ceilings, floors and window coverings – relatively plain, and restrict expressions of allegiance or worship to items such as duvet covers or posters which can be easily and affordably replaced.

By the same token, nursery furniture, so heart-tugging in its miniaturization, rarely earns its keep. Children grow – fast. Furniture that is standard size and of decent quality is a better investment than pieces that will soon be outgrown. For young children, however, a low child-size play table and chairs can be very useful; some incorporate storage for art materials or reversible blackboard tops.

Babies

New parents are often daunted by lists of seemingly essential items that babies or children must have. A baby, however, will not care if it is changed on a mat on the floor rather than on a special rimmed changing table with integral storage for nappies and toiletries. Nor will it mind sleeping in a cot you bought on the high street rather than an antique heirloom trimmed with lace. For the first three months, all a baby really requires in the way of kit is somewhere to sleep – a portable basket, crib or cot which allows you to keep the baby by you is often a good idea – along with a changing mat and a minimal amount of storage for toys and clothes, which can be anything from drawer space to baskets and trunks.

All you will need (apart from sleep, which you won't get) is a comfortable chair for feeding and some means of dimming or lowering light levels for nighttime feeding and changing. After three months, as routines are beginning to establish themselves, a move to a proper cot is advisable. Choose a cot with adjustable sides that is robust and well made. If you acquire a hand-me-down cot from a relative or friend, it is important to invest in a new mattress.

Babies may have little to say on the subject of style, but they are far from oblivious to their surroundings. From birth, babies are stimulated by graphic shapes and bright colour; studies have shown that the first recognizable colour is orangey-red. They are also soothed and intrigued by sound. Musical, brightly coloured and mobile toys play an important role in early conceptual development.

Pre-school

Children's rooms really begin to come into their own from toddler-hood onwards. Between two and three, most children are ready to move into a proper bed. Buy the best bed and mattress you can afford: children get very attached to their beds and one that is of decent quality is more likely to see them through childhood. Guardrails are an option if your child tends to go bump in the night.

By this stage, gone are the days when your child's possessions will fit into a couple of baskets, and storage assumes greater importance. Make it accessible and easy to use, otherwise young children may be tempted to mountaineer in order to reach the toy or game they want when you're on the phone and not on hand to retrieve it for them. Visibility is all: make space for artwork and models and the display of favourite toys. A good deal of pre-school play is floor-level and a warm, resilient surface is kinder on young knees and quieter on adult ears.

⌄ Babies are highly stimulated by strong colour. Here, while the background is soothing and neutral, chairs and other elements deliver vivid eye-catching accents.

⌄ Pieces of small-scale nursery furniture, such as mini chests of drawers, are quickly outgrown and are often a waste of money. But child-size tables and chairs don't represent a huge investment and can help children focus on creative play or simply serve as props in games of make-believe.

┌┌ Built-in bed alcoves, with blue-painted interiors, give each child his or her own sense of territory, an important factor when children are sharing the same room. Cut-out 'windows' within the alcoves prevent any feeling of claustrophobia. A large low table means there's room for everyone to sit down and play.

┌ High-level beds maximize floor area when space is tight and provide room underneath for storage or work areas. Once children have reached a certain age you can safely dispense with guard rails.

≪ A bunkbed on a platform built around a doorway is accessed by sturdy metal rungs. A peg rail at low level provides accessible hanging space for clothes.

< Almost a miniature mezzanine, this metal-framed high-level bed provides a cosy sleeping space under the slope of the ceiling; there is plenty of shelving underneath for books, toys and games.

School-age

The next mutation of the child's room occurs during the school years, when it becomes both more of a private refuge and at the same time a social centre – sometimes a social centre by default as this is the most common stage for siblings to share a room. Homework may take place on the kitchen table, where parental assistance is conveniently at hand, but most children appreciate a desk of their own at this point. A good work chair and shelving for books and other school-related items can help promote a positive attitude to learning.

Flexible multipurpose furniture such as bunkbeds, floor cushions, platform-level beds with study areas underneath and modular storage can all help to rationalize space at this stage, particularly where two children are sharing a room. But the real challenge is keeping ahead of the game in terms of possessions. This is the age when children are not yet ready to discard beloved toys from infancy but at the same time are rapidly developing new interests and activities, which may include anything from constructing complex Lego models to roller-blading or basketball. Good organizational systems (along with diplomatic skills) are essential for keeping the additional clutter under control.

Teenagers

Less of a threshold and more of a frontier, the door to a teenager's room may not be emblazoned 'Do not enter' but the implication is there all the same. After puberty, child-parent relationships enter their most delicate phase. At a time when boundaries are constantly challenged and redefined, a new approach is also required when it comes to spatial arrangement.

What teenagers require is not so much space but privacy and autonomy. Many teenagers will put up with restricted space if that is the only way they can have a room of their own. If decibel levels look likely to become a serious bone of contention, you may wish to rethink room allocation so that the teen zone is as far away as possible from areas where you need peace and quiet. It's also a good idea to make some sort of provision for overnight stays, so you have the choice of offering a bed rather than a lift when a friend has missed the last bus.

Equally important is to allow teenagers freedom to customize their space to their own taste. Provided the basics are in place – a well-lit study area, enough shelving and storage space for clothing, sports equipment and the like – parents should be prepared to allow teenagers to exercise their fledgling sense of independence and individuality when it comes to decoration and furnishing. This may well take the form of 'anti-decor' statements such as lurid paint schemes or riotous collaging of every available surface – it doesn't matter. The visual assault on your aesthetic standards is only skin-deep and is generally reversible.

◣ Provided there is enough storage for the inevitable collection of CDs, books and sports gear, teenagers do not necessarily require big rooms, but do appreciate being able to customize decor to their own tastes. A wall-mounted bracket keeps a bicycle from occupying valuable floor space; an old couch covered in a bedspread makes a practical seating area.

⌄ A pair of painted wood trunks double up as storage caches and bedside tables. Teenagers, no less than younger children, like to surround themselves with their belongings, so building in display areas is a good idea.

FAMILY ROOMS AND DENS

If you have the available space – or an attic or basement ripe for conversion – family rooms or dens can alleviate many household bottlenecks as well as providing a useful generational buffer zone. The function and furnishing of such areas can evolve with the family, starting out as play areas and progressing to entertainment centres or chill-out zones. Here is a place for space-devouring or noisy and disruptive activities: train sets, indoor games, musical instruments, computers and music systems. Acoustic insulation can be added to floors, walls or ceiling if necessary. The one real drawback of such designated family rooms is that hiving off the livelier and more sociable activities into a separate area may well drain other living areas of much of their vitality and purpose.

STORAGE

Keeping things organized is one of the true challenges of family life. Many families consider moving not because there is not enough room for everyone, but because there isn't enough room for everyone's stuff. If children grow fast, so does the quantity of their belongings. As well as plenty of accessible and workable storage space, you will also need to instigate periodic clear-outs to weed out what is outgrown, outdated or unwanted.

Take every opportunity to shed excess baggage. Redundant items come in all shapes and sizes, from the impulse-buy gadget that you haven't worked out how to use to the pair of ice skates your child was desperate to have but has never put on. Many children's possessions have an in-built time frame of usefulness, some shorter than others. But the same is often true of adult possessions.

Most children, however, hate to part with things, even if the thing in question is too small, broken or not played with any more. One solution is to adopt a halfway approach and first move the items to an out-of-the-way location (attic,

⌐ A contemporary version of the old day nursery, the playroom, where everything is organized and furnished to suit the needs of children, can be a good idea if you have room to spare. A low storage unit houses books within easy reach, and provides room on top for toys and models.

⌃ It is important to make room for the display of artwork and other creative efforts. A pinboard or a wall lined in cork or felt means that underlying surfaces need not be damaged by drawing pins or Blu-tack.

⌃ A basement or recreation room, with additional soundproofing if necessary, is the ideal location for noisier family activities such as music practice or the rehearsals of a fledgling rock band.

garage, box room or basement, for example). After a certain amount of time has elapsed, and the items haven't been missed, children may be more willing to part with them permanently. However, it is important to respect the fact that at each stage there will be certain possessions that a child wants to hang on to, such as a few beloved picture books, treasured soft toy companions, prize models or artwork.

In many families an enormous amount of time is spent looking for things (games kit, homework, letter from school requiring reply) – particularly on a Monday morning. Establish dedicated places where such things are kept and stick to them. It may be a kitchen notice board for notices, bills or other items relating to school life, activities or household admin, or a dump bin under the stairs for sports equipment and kit, but it is important to limit the opportunities for possessions to float around and disappear without trace. In the same way, items used infrequently but which may be needed acutely, such as a first aid box, spare fuses, light bulbs, and the like, should always be kept in the same place so you know how to get your hands on them fast.

Make full use of deep storage areas in attics, basements, garages and sheds for items used seasonally or very infrequently, such as Christmas decorations, sports kit and suitcases. It can also be worth rotating clothing in and out of deep storage on the same basis. Anything you are hanging on to just for the sake of it should also be in deep storage – such as old files and records, old school work and artwork.

Small boxes and modular containers provide an invaluable way of storing like with like: photographs, CDs and videos, multi-piece games and toys, art supplies. Accessible and floor-level storage arrangements help to encourage smaller children to participate in the tidying up. Avoid large catch-all containers, which only encourage a child to tip the whole thing out on the floor in search of what is at the bottom. For young children, clothes should be stored in drawers, baskets or hung on low-level hanging rails that children can actually reach. Provide storage space for toys and games where children actually play to prevent unnecessary to-ing and fro-ing. In the early years, this may mean you will need a toy basket or container in the kitchen and living area.

Exploit between-spaces, such as halls, corridors and landings, as storage areas. Lining walls with shelving or cupboards concealed behind flush panels can accommodate a great deal of clutter that would otherwise silt up in living areas.

∨ Family life equals burgeoning possessions. Seamless fitted cupboards can house a surprising degree of clutter, especially items such as tapes and videos which lack the visual appeal of books.

⌐ A storage unit fitted with individual baskets provides a way of organizing diverse everyday things, including items such as multi-piece toys or sports accessories which need to be stored by type – or owner.

⌐ A wall of fitted storage in a children's room lifts clutter off the floor but still keeps belongings accessible and on view. Young children tend to forget what is stored out of sight and generally feel more secure when they can see their possessions around them.

⌄ In the family home, surfaces and finishes need to be practical and durable, capable of taking a degree of punishment without the need for intensive maintenance. But that does not have to rule out the expression of decorative taste.

DECORATION AND FURNISHING

Family life does not mean that you have to put your decorative preferences on hold. But it does mean that you have to be aware of what you are letting yourself in for in terms of maintenance and basic practicality. No scheme of decoration is fully child-proof, but some are easier to live with than others. The most successful family homes are often those where everyone feels relaxed and comfortable, where children are not intimidated and constrained by 'don't touch' surfaces and furnishings and where adults are not constantly fretting about scratches, finger marks and other unavoidable signs of wear and tear. This does not entail putting up with the lowest common denominator in terms of decoration or furnishing, but rather seeking out robust, simple designs, and surfaces and finishes that will not be irretrievably spoiled by sticky little fingers, muddy paw prints or an upset beaker of juice.

One strategy is to choose materials that will wear well and look the better for it. Wood, stone, terracotta tile, linoleum and other natural surfaces and finishes take a fair degree of punishment and acquire a certain depth of character in the process. A related approach is to ensure that basic finishes and furnishings can be easily maintained: washable loose covers for sofas and armchairs, for example, or wipable tile or paint finishes for bathrooms and kitchens will go a long way towards reducing parental anxiety levels. Smooth, glossy surfaces, such as glass and stainless steel, may well be chic and wear-resistant but show every smudge and mark and will require extra vigilance to help keep them in pristine condition. Paint is a much more practical finish than wallpaper as it is easier and cheaper to renew; a portion of wall painted in blackboard paint can provide a vehicle for creative expression in a children's bedroom or play area and a useful place for chalking up messages and reminders in a kitchen or family area.

Sound, comfort and resilience are other factors you should bear in mind when you are deciding on finishes and furnishings for a family home. Expanses of hard, ungiving materials, such as stone and concrete, for example, especially when they are combined with a relatively minimal approach to furnishing, will result in unacceptably high noise levels. Softer floor surfaces, such as carpeting, natural-fibre matting or rugs can be a good idea at upper levels of a house or on stairs, and particularly in younger children's play areas and bedrooms where they provide the necessary comfort for floor-based play.

While there is every good reason why children should be taught to respect their surroundings and learn more appropriate outlets for self-expression than scribbling on the walls and furniture, it is important not to expect the impossible. Accept the fact that when children are small, delicate and breakable items are best kept out of reach. The same goes for delicate fabrics, smart sofas or fine rugs, which might be snagged or ruined by stains.

FAMILY GARDEN

Some outdoor space, however limited, is a real asset when it comes to family life; for many people, the whole concept of a family home is bound up with the garden that serves as an extension of it. As with the planning and arrangement of indoor spaces, the design, planting and equipping of an outdoor area means balancing different generational requirements and desires. Whereas adults turn to gardens for relaxation and the sensual pleasures that contact with nature offers, children view outdoor space both as free-form play areas and the opportunity to create private domains of their own away from adult eyes and ears.

If you have a very large garden, such conflicting requirements can be met simply by setting aside different areas for different functions. In a small space, you may have to work harder to ensure that everyone is happy. Gardens, however, naturally evolve, and with a little flexibility in terms of overall layout and design, it is possible to shift the emphasis subtly as your family grows.

> **Lawns** Soothing on the eye, a lawn is a great all-purpose garden surface for kickabouts or lying on a blanket in the sun. For most children, however, a lawn is a sports pitch, which can mean that your patch of green quickly erodes into a patch of bare dirt or mud. Fine-leafed rye grass, or hard-wearing utility grass seed mixtures will stand up to greater punishment.

> **Planting** Delicate plants should be restricted to borders or beds away from children's play areas, or containerized in a location where trampling feet and flying footballs will cause no damage. Some common garden plants – including

L One way to curb children's natural tendency to add their own creative signature to walls is to provide them with a surface where they can doodle away to their heart's content. Blackboard panels or a wall painted with blackboard paint provide a practical focus for budding artists.

⌄ With careful planning, the differing needs of children and adults can be accommodated within the same garden. Shrubbery half conceals a wooden play platform, the timbers of which are stained dark brown to make them less obtrusive.

⌐ It is a good idea to set aside an area where children can get stuck into serious play, otherwise they may run riot in your carefully tended flowerbeds. This miniature adventure playground has a safe surface underneath made of bark chippings.

foxgloves (*Digitalis*), yew (*Taxus baccata*), bleeding heart (*Dicentra spectabilis*) and laburnum (*Laburnum anagyroides*) – are poisonous and should be avoided where children might be tempted by flowers or berries; other prickly or sharp-edged species should be planted away from play areas to prevent accidents. Encourage children to grow their own flowers or vegetables by giving them a small plot of their own or a few pots for spring bulbs. Vegetables such as radishes, lettuces and runner beans are easy to grow, as are flowers such as cornflowers, marigolds and poppies.

> **Water features** Water is one of the most evocative elements in garden design, but even shallow ponds pose a risk for toddlers and small children. When children are very small, it is best to do without a permanent water feature altogether and restrict water play to refillable paddling pools (closely supervised). In later years, a pond planted with water plants and stocked with fish and frogs can be a source of endless fascination.

> **Play equipment** There is a huge range of outdoor play equipment on the market, from slides and climbing frames to sandpits and trampolines. Aesthetically, play equipment can leave a lot to be desired, making a rather bolder statement than one might wish to in the garden. Provided children are at the stage where constant supervision is not required, such pieces can be sited out of full view and screened by planting. Make sure equipment is robust and conforms to safety standards; anchor it securely into the ground and provide safe surfacing, such as bark chippings, underneath. Sandpits (either temporary or built-in) should be covered when not in use to keep them dry and unfouled by animals. Try to position them where there is at least partial shade.

> **Special places** For children, gardens are often places of mystery and exploration. Secret dens, hideouts and forts can be little more elaborate than an overgrown pathway or a shady nook in amongst the shrubbery; other special places include tree houses, tents and teepees and Wendy houses. Neither are adults immune from the romantic lure of the summerhouse, gazebo, tree seat or hammock. Garden layouts that do not reveal all from one vantage point, but unfold as you move from place to place, keep alive this sense of mystery and surprise. Changes in level, as much as changes in direction, have the same appeal. The shady veranda, that traditional feature of vernacular buildings in hot climates, has a particular tug on the emotions.

> **Outdoor living** The transitional areas that connect house and garden make good locations for the more 'living' garden functions of outdoor eating, relaxing and entertaining, as well as for the messier and more creative forms of children's play. A hard surface such as terracing or decking provides a practical base for garden tables and chairs, and a non-muddy environment for outside games when the weather is less fair. With the ease of

‹ A decked terrace extends a living area outdoors and provides a safe surface for children to play on. Glazed doors that can be slid right back out of harm's way minimize accidents.

ʌ Play and sports equipment encourages healthy exercise and develops physical skills. Choose equipment that has been designed and constructed to proper safety standards and ensure that it is properly anchored to the ground.

access to indoors, this is also a suitable site for barbecues and grills, and for growing your own herbs to provide fresh flavours for the table. Providing some shelter from the sun or light rain in the form of awnings, pergolas or other types of cover means that you will be able to use the outdoor space more often.

> **Garden lighting** Lighting adds a magical dimension to the nighttime garden. Uplit trees and foliage, paths edged in lights sunk into the ground, lanterns, flares and shaded candles grouped around seating and eating areas multiply the pleasure of outdoor living.

SAFETY

Parenting is most often characterized as a nurturing role; equally important, however, is the need to foster independence and a sense of open-minded inquiry in growing children. Somewhere in the continuum between irresponsibly negligent and neurotically over-protective is the right approach to safety. All children have accidents and most learn from them rather than come to great or lasting harm. But at the same time, the average home presents hundreds of hazards to the health and safety of children, hazards that can be difficult to anticipate or guard against simply because they are so familiar and everyday. Until, for example, you have seen your toddler try to insert a key into an electrical socket it can be difficult to spot the similarity between a power point and a lock. Potential risks also vary according to age: once children have passed the auto-destruct, try-anything years, you can afford to relax (a little).

> **Fire** Fit a smoke alarm and keep spare batteries to hand. Make sure open fires have a protective fireguard or screen. Never leave children alone in a room with a living fire (which includes gas fires and lit candles). Keep matches well out of reach. Make sure gas appliances and fires are fitted with child-proof switches and controls. Have gas fires and flues serviced regularly to prevent toxic fumes from escaping.

> **Toxic substances** Keep all toxic substances under lock and key: household chemicals, cleansers and bleach; paints, seals and varnishes; insecticides, pesticides and other garden products; all medicines. Do not, however, lock a first-aid box (when you really need it, you may not be able to find the key), but keep it stored on a high shelf or somewhere else that is safe.

> **Preventing falls and accidents** Avoid trailing flexes that can cause a child to trip; keep light fittings and flexes out of the reach of very young children, who might be tempted to pull them over. Make sure stair carpets are secured and not worn or frayed; scatter rugs should be taped in place or laid over non-slip mats. Non-slip bathmats are advisable in baths and showers. Tall and heavy items of furniture, such as bookcases, should be securely bracketed to the wall to prevent them from toppling over. Fit window locks, particularly at upper storeys. Restrict bunkbeds to children over six years of age; make sure their ladders are robust and secure.

> **Child-safety devices** Not all children are daredevils, but some do require an extra degree of vigilance. Among the devices and products you may need to make your home safe are: socket covers; corner protectors for sharp table edges; safety film for glass doors or cupboard fronts; child-proof locks for appliances and cupboards; and stair gates.

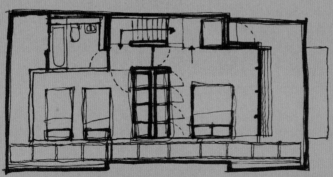

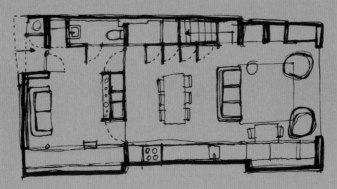

∧ The main living area leads directly onto the courtyard garden, with a floor-to-ceiling opening filled with metal-framed glass doors. The limestone flooring throughout the lower level extends outside; internally, it is laid over underfloor heating. The base of the double hearth is also limestone and the lintel is an old beam made of greenheart, a very hard wood, which was salvaged by the builder.

< The lower floor plan shows how the sloping roof stops short of the side wall, with rooflights infilling the gap, bringing natural light through the entire length of the house. The upper level is stepped back from street level; at the rear is a balcony overlooking the courtyard.

FROM SHED TO HOUSE

One way to ensure that your house fits your life is to design it yourself. For the architect-owner of this two-storey family home in west London, the opportunity to build his own house was something of a dream come true, even though the site was an awkward urban plot.

Like many urban plots in densely populated areas, the site already had a building on it – a garage workshop that had been disused and unoccupied for three or four years. Finding sites is always the hardest part of any new-build project. In this case, the owner was lucky and discovered the site was for sale before it went on the market and was able to buy it from a developer who had already negotiated permission for residential use.

The scheme that had previously been awarded planning permission was for a fairly traditional two-storey bay-fronted coach house. The architect, who wanted a much more modern design, took the trouble to meet all of the neighbours and talk through his plans with them to prevent possible objections. To preserve 'angles of light' in the gardens that adjoin the side of the property, the roof was designed as a sloping mono-pitch. The new scheme also preserved the existing garage walls, which not only meant less construction but also minimal alteration to the front elevation, a factor that won favour with the planners.

∧ The low-e (low-emissivity) glass rooflights above the kitchen units allow in light but not heat. They are opened by electrically controlled hydraulic motors which set up patterns of through ventilation.

< A divider separates off the kitchen-dining-living area from the study-spare bedroom at the front of the house. The divider contains a refrigerator and oven.

> Panel doors to either side of the divider can be folded back to open out the entire space from front to back. Cupboards housing the boiler, washing machine and a separate lavatory are tucked away under the stairs. The stair wall is painted an orangey-yellow, which picks up the terracotta colour of the external garden wall and increases the apparent width of the space.

Although the existing walls were retained, they were not in particularly good condition, so a new steel framework on piled foundations was designed to support the roof and upper floor. If seeing the framework go up in only two days was a highlight of the building programme, discovering that carpenters had knocked them out of plumb installing the timber joists of the first floor was a low point.

Unable to afford to rent a home during the building works, the architect and his young family set up a rudimentary one-bedroom flat at the far end of the garage, known affectionately as 'the shed'. The arrival of a new baby while they were braving the cold and covering holes in the 'shed' roof with tarpaulin meant they were more than delighted to move into their new home when it was finally completed some five months over schedule.

It was well worth the effort and the wait. Downstairs, the kitchen-living-dining area is bathed in warm sun from the huge south-facing opening at the rear and from the rooflights that run the full length of the house. A divider screens off a spare bedroom-study at the front. Storage is neatly integrated everywhere, from the long line of kitchen units to the cupboards under the stairs. On the second level are two bedrooms, a bathroom and shower room. The main bedroom has its own balcony overlooking the courtyard garden where 'the shed', now demolished, once stood.

⌐ The rear, south-facing elevation of the house with the glass doors folded back. A particular concern was that the doors should not prove a safety hazard. One door hinges flat and the other two slide out and dock in front of it so that nothing is protruding. The decked area is a parking space (off-street parking was a condition of the planning permission).

‹ The children's bedroom on the second floor has a horizontal ribbon of windows overlooking the side of the house. The sloping roof forms the ceiling of the entire second level. It is painted blue in reference to 'the shed' as the family had become accustomed to the cheerful sight of light shining through the blue tarpaulin with which they had patched its roof.

> The fitted kitchen units run down the length of the side wall, where they are lit by the rooflights. The units consist of basic carcases with MDF fronts, roller-painted grey by a friend. The worktop is 40mm- (1¹⁄₂in-) thick birch, with a routed drainer. The units drop down to form a fitted bench-cum-storage cupboard in the living room where the children's toys can be tidied away.

∨ A desk and workspace are fitted along the side wall in the study below the rooflights that extend from the front of the house to the back. The fronts of the divider units are made from birch ply.

⌐ The study-bedroom at the front of the house is visible beyond the divider. The garage's old roller door was removed and the space infilled with glass bricks. The sofa bed is for overnight guests. To the right of the divider, a door with a porthole conceals a separate lavatory.

⌐ On the other side of the divider is more storage space for books and computer equipment.

> The exposed beamed ceiling, roughcast walls and original terracotta tiled floor create a simple background full of original character. The all-white decorative scheme of the main living-dining area makes the most of natural light. Large loft-style pendant lights have a utilitarian look in keeping with the simple style of decoration and furnishing.

∨ The children's bedroom leads off the kitchen and is decorated in pale ice-cream colours. Free-standing wardrobes and chests provide essential storage space that would otherwise be difficult to build in.

ANCIENT AND MODERN

On the face of it, medieval buildings do not make the most promising contexts for contemporary family life, but this traditional house, located in an Italian hill town near Rimini, on the Adriatic coast south of Venice, has been transformed into an easy-going light-filled home for a young family.

When the owners first came across the property it was almost completely derelict inside, although the external walls and roof were in reasonable shape. What convinced them that it was worth undertaking such a major exercise in restoration was the beauty of the location: the house, which dates back to medieval times, is situated in a narrow cobbled street with a castle nearby. Looking out in one direction from the terrace it is possible to see the sea; from the other side there is a view of two neighbouring walled hill towns and their castles.

When converting an old building, there is a fine balance to be struck between preserving historical character and updating for modern convenience. In this case, the owners were determined to respect the quality of the original structure by doing as little to it as possible, while at the same time creating a simple background that they could add to and change whenever they liked. The house would originally have been quite a modest dwelling, never grand, so the idea was to keep everything as basic as possible. Accordingly, the roughcast walls were not replastered perfectly smooth, a decision which greatly surprised their builders, and the original worn terracotta floors were kept intact. The 'terrace', which actually was all that remained

> A Moroccan tiled table and basket chairs create an outdoor eating area on the terrace, with its stunning views of the sea and surrounding landscape. The terrace is actually all that is left of a room bombed during the war and has the same terracotta tiling as the rest of the house.

∨ The owners wanted an easy-going background that they could add to or change when they wanted. Furniture has been accumulated piece by piece over the years. Cushions bought on a trip to Thailand sit on an Indian daybed which they bought several years previously in London.

of another room destroyed by bombing during the Second World War, was also kept as a terrace and not rebuilt.

Like most medieval houses in the vicinity, the house is arranged over several levels, which ruled out a complete change of internal layout. Instead, the challenge was to use every available bit of space to fit everything in. On the ground floor, the main entrance leads to a guest bedroom and small bathroom; on the level below is the children's playroom and a 'grotto' or wine cellar. A typical feature of these type of houses, the cellar was discovered under layers of rubble during the process of excavation to inspect the state of the foundations.

The main living area is located on the level above the ground floor. A big open living and dining area leads out onto the terrace with its sweeping views, while on the other side is the kitchen. Two bedrooms and two bathrooms are located on opposite sides of this main space.

The principal modern insertion was the metal staircase that connects all three levels and provides access to a mezzanine slotted into the double-height living area. Decorated in fresh light colours, and simply furnished, the overall result is a well-judged meeting of old and new.

⌐ The main bedroom is very simply furnished and decorated. The narrow steps along one wall lead up to a small bathroom tucked in under the roof. Fitting everything into the relatively restricted space was the main challenge of the conversion.

‹ The house has seen several decorative schemes come and go, with the main living area painted first pink, then green before its present all-white look. Colour remains a feature of the children's bedrooms: the wooden floorboards are painted a soothing pale blue, in harmonious contrast to the colours used on the walls and pieces of furniture.

⌄ The terrace dramatically increases the useable living area when the weather is warm, which is about half of the year. Sliding glass doors dissolve the boundary between indoors and out. An awning suspended over the terrace provides shade and moderates the blistering heat of summer – without it the terrace would be too hot to sit on in the day.

⟨ In the girls' bathroom the shower is tiled in pink mosaic and has soft, curved contours rather than the more usual angular planes. The colour was inspired by a family trip to the Little Mermaid's grotto at Disneyland.

⌃ The main living area extends from the original fireplace on the back wall right through to the dining area and out onto the terrace. A modern steel spiral staircase links all three levels and the mezzanine.

⟩ A stainless steel kitchen occupies half of one wall of the main living area. The industrial-style aesthetic works well with the rugged simplicity of the building's structure.

< Island retreat

A cluster of five log cabins forms a family summer retreat on an island in Lake Saimaa, Finland's largest lake, just 30km (18 miles) from the Russian border. With no electricity, no mains water and the nearest small town a 10km (6 mile) boat ride away, holidays are a chance to experience the simple pleasures – swimming, fishing, taking saunas and eating outdoors.

The compound has grown with the family; the first cabin was built in 1965 when the three children, now grown men with their own families, were small. The cabin was built close to the water's edge, so close that the children could fish from the house and be watched over while they swam in the lake. It now serves as the main sleeping area where grandchildren can be tucked up in bunks while the adults talk around the fire.

In the succeeding years, further cabins have been built, one housing the kitchen, which was made out of fallen timber, another the sauna. Two houses on the mainland, one of which belonged to the owner's mother, were painstakingly taken apart, the timbers ferried across the lake and rebuilt on the island to provide more living accommodation for family members and guests. The owner, a textile collector and designer, has a studio in one of them.

Fireplaces, indoors and out, provide heating when the summer evenings grow too chilly. Bottled gas is used to power a freezer and an oven. Drinking water and provisions – with the exception of fish caught in the lake or bought from neighbours – have to be brought in by boat.

Extensive terraces and decked areas around the cabins provide space for sitting out and eating. One of the terraces has a gap in it to accommodate a tree growing through. Secluded and screened by the trees, the cabins have been designed and built to blend with the forest, an ideal way to enjoy a sense of connection with the natural landscape.

HOLIDAY HOME

Getting away from it all from time to time is essential if you lead a hectic urban life. Holidays, however, can in themselves be sources of stress, particularly holidays to previously unknown destinations that turn out to be not quite what you had bargained for. One solution is to put down weekend or summer roots in a holiday home situated in an area that you know and love well.

The holiday home is far from a recent phenomenon. But while second homes used to imply privilege and serious wealth, more and more people these days are finding it a practical and affordable way to unwind. In the case of some young professionals, the holiday home is where real living takes place, as opposed to the flats or apartments they maintain in the city as a base for the working week. There are those who only manage to cope with the pace of urban life by leaving it behind every weekend for saner, more peaceful surroundings.

If holiday homes act as a safety valve, they can also teach us lessons about how to live our daily lives in a less complicated fashion. Where furnishings and fittings are uncomplicated and basic, irrelevant household clutter has not had the chance to accumulate and there is easy contact with the simple pleasures offered by a rural, seaside or mountain location, there is a real opportunity to reassess priorities. When your holiday home is the place where you feel you can be truly yourself, why not re-evaluate the way you live the rest of the time?

LOCATION

As estate agents can confirm, emotion plays a large part in the decision to buy any sort of property; where holiday homes are concerned, people are even more susceptible to sudden romantic impulses. As smitten as you might be by a location, country, or particular house, you need to think long and hard about the respective pros and cons before signing on the dotted line.

Distance is a key factor, and not just distance as the crow flies, but ease of travel. If you are intending to use a holiday home at every opportunity, preferably every weekend, getting there should not be a gruelling exercise. When you've sat for hours in gridlocked motorway traffic there and back, any benefits you may have gained from time away will seem minor in comparison. High-speed rail travel and budget flights are making far-flung areas more accessible than ever before; it may be quicker, cheaper and less stressful, for example, to commute to a holiday home that is actually more distant but is well served by such links.

It may sound obvious, but make sure that you actually like the area enough to relish the prospect of spending most of your free time there for the foreseeable future. A place in a particular part of the world that draws you back time and again is one thing; a place that just happens to be in the country may quickly lose its appeal. If you have had a blissful holiday in an idyllic spot and immediately decide you want to spend every summer there, make sure that you do some thorough research first. What is the area like out of season or in less-than-perfect weather? If you are attracted by the idea of a holiday home abroad, how proficient are you in the language and how at ease are you with local customs and food?

What is the attitude of the local community to summer visitors or weekenders? Do other people in your household or family share your preferences? Are there other activities or amenities in the area to provide a little variety or a source of alternative excursions when the weather is bad? And if you plan to finance your second home by renting it out for part of the time, is the location popular with other holidaymakers or tourists?

When it comes to choosing an actual property, rather than a location, questions of scale and workability come into play. As any casual student of the property pages can tell you, the price of a one-bedroom flat in a dense urban area such as London or New York can translate into a seventeen-bedroom Scottish baronial castle with its own loch, an eighteenth-century French manoir or a ranch in Montana. But the vagaries of the market should not allow you to be seduced into buying a holiday home that is larger than you need or that requires more upkeep and maintenance than you are prepared to provide.

The same is true in reverse. Many people who would not otherwise consider taking on a property with obvious structural problems acquire a kind of blinkered optimism when it comes to buying a holiday home, particularly one that is offered at a bargain price. If you do steam ahead and buy a ruin, you should be realistic about the time, money and effort it will take to put it right. Running an extensive programme of building works is complicated enough; if you do not understand the language, have no reliable recommendations for building firms or are ignorant of local codes and regulations, you may be in for a few unpleasant surprises.

PRACTICALITIES

Unless you are in the type of income bracket where owning multiple homes is the norm, financing a second home will be a prime concern. The expense of a holiday home does not begin and end with the purchase price, the necessary building work or even fitting out and furnishing. Two homes mean two sets of bills, local rates and taxes. When you are buying abroad, make sure you investigate any hidden costs of the transaction – in France, Spain and Italy, for example, notary and legal fees add ten per cent to the basic selling price of a property.

One way of coping with the steady trickle of brown envelopes is to let out the holiday home part of the time so that it is self-financing. Alternatively, you could enter into some form of contract, joint purchase or time-share arrangement with other people who are keen to have a bolthole in the same area. Make sure you check the financial position in detail with an accountant or legal adviser. Income generated by a holiday home is usually liable for tax; if you purchase a holiday home through your own business it might count as a company asset, which may also adversely affect your tax position. Conversely, you may be able to claim tax relief on any mortgage you have taken out, as well as allowances for maintenance work, repairs and management. In areas where second homes or holiday homes are a source of resentment among the local community, particularly in places where prices have been driven up by outsiders, there may be some form of local surcharge or premium to pay. Legalities also vary. In France, for example, under the Napoleonic code, any property is automatically inherited by the children of the owner, upon the owner's decease.

Letting out a holiday home may help with the financing, but there are other practical factors to consider. Holiday lets are in greatest demand and therefore

⌄ Holiday homes offer the opportunity to experience the simple life. A circus caravan dating from the 1930s, which was originally horse-drawn, has come to rest half-an-hour's cycle ride from Amsterdam where it now serves as a holiday home for a young couple.

> With a romantic view over expanses of water and snowy forests, this Scandinavian cabin makes the perfect winter retreat. If you intend to use your holiday home year-round it is important to make sure that it's accessible when weather conditions are less than ideal.

>> Australian architect Sean Godsell's design for a holiday retreat features slatted wooden panels that flap up to screen the interior from strong light. When the panels are dropped and fixed in position, the property is secured when unoccupied.

⌐ Easy transitions between indoors and out promote a relaxed mood. A covered veranda provides a shady outdoor area for eating or relaxing, just a few steps away from the pool.

∨ Environmental factors play a part if you are building a new house in an unspoiled natural landscape. Sited on an isolated stretch of coastline, this timber house is supported on stilts made of treated eucalyptus to reduce its impact on the beach.

˄ In hot climates, there is the opportunity to enjoy outdoor living to its fullest extent. This shaded veranda has room for a dining table, sofa and bed screened with mosquito netting.

˥ With old properties, a sense of place is in-built. Houses that typify the architectural character of a particular region supply an additional cultural dimension to the experience of being on holiday. If you buy a house abroad with the intention of renovating or converting it, make sure you are fully acquainted with local codes and building procedures.

˥˩ Location matters just as much for a weekend or holiday home as it does for the home you live in most of the time. Simply buying a place out of town won't necessarily deliver what you want in the long term. Look out for places where there are a range of activities or amenities in the vicinity so that you can vary your holiday experiences.

attract the best rates during high season and school holidays, which may well be the time when you are most likely to want to use the place yourself. Keeping the house occupied for enough time to cover your costs for the rest of the year is not always easy. When it comes to organizing the letting, one option is to employ an agent to handle the bookings and cope with the day-to-day practicalities of making sure that appliances are serviced and kept in working order and that basic supplies are kept in stock. If you decide to go it alone, it is usually a good idea to pre-select your tenants in some fashion. You could either advertise in a publication with limited circulation – an in-house office newsletter or alumni bulletin, for example – or restrict lettings to those you know or to those who have been recommended by people you trust. Even so, be prepared for damage and make sure you are fully insured.

Security is another practical issue you should take into consideration from the outset. Even if your holiday home is regularly inhabited at the weekend or fully booked during high season, there will be protracted periods of time, often in the darker months, when it will be empty. Make sure that the property is fully secured when there is no one at home and, if possible, ask a friendly neighbour to keep an eye out for intruders.

One of the ways in which a second home can complicate rather than simplify life is in the area of routine maintenance and upkeep. You do not want to begin your weekend or fortnight's break confronted with a raft of problems – a leaking roof, a blocked drain, a broken washing machine – or spend time that could be devoted to relaxing hacking away at the undergrowth that has sprung up since your last visit. Don't invest in a place that has a high-maintenance garden unless your idea of unwinding is cutting the grass or unless you can afford to hire a gardener. Similarly, it can also be a good idea to employ someone to come in from time to time and troubleshoot potential domestic hitches, so that any problems can be sorted out on the phone before you get there.

DESIGN AND CONTEXT

Holiday homes provide the opportunity to express a sense of place. In many cases, that rootedness is in-built. Traditional vernacular houses and cottages constructed from local materials, such as stone, brick and flint, cob or timber, have a natural affinity with the landscapes in which they are set; the same is often true of old redundant agricultural buildings such as barns and stables. If you are restoring or converting such a property, sourcing appropriate materials locally and employing craftspeople or builders proficient in traditional construction methods helps to preserve the integrity of the original fabric. In any case, you may well find that local codes and planning regulations set strict limits on what you can and cannot do, particularly where your alterations affect the external appearance of the building. Follow the same strategy internally by exposing original features or surfaces and choosing appropriate materials for new finishes or floors.

What most people want from a holiday home is not so much creature comforts but the chance to connect with the natural world, which means easy boundaries between inside and out, sweeping views and good natural light. Many older cottages or country houses, however, have relatively small window openings, which can make interiors dim and inward looking. Enlarging existing windows is often not an option and can, in any case, result in an uncomfortable-looking architectural hybrid. One solution is to remove a few internal partitions so that light is not blocked unnecessarily; another is to add a porch, veranda or sunroom to the side or rear of the building to serve as a more open transitional space where views and light can be enjoyed under cover.

Barns, agricultural sheds and other outbuildings offer the greatest potential for flexible spatial planning. Such structures, essentially countryside versions of the urban loft, can be similarly planned and fitted out, preserving both expansive indoor spaces and rugged original features such as beams, trusses and other structural elements. If you intend to build a holiday home on a site you have acquired, taking inspiration in terms of both design and materials from such vernacular working buildings can help to preserve the sense of place.

∨ Exposed wooden walls, beams and rafters have a rustic appeal in this South American ranch house. Basic decor and fittings require little in the way of maintenance or upkeep.

⌐ A home that you do not live in all the time or that you let out to other people should be uncomplicated and simple to run. Facing window walls flood the interior with natural light. A wood-burning stove provides a cosy focus on chilly evenings. The open layout and functional detailing of shelves and storage means it's easy to pick up where you left off.

FURNISHINGS AND FITTINGS

A holiday home should be the epitome of easy living, which means installing basic furnishings and fittings that promote a sense of relaxation and require little in the way of maintenance. This is all the more important when you are letting out the property on a regular basis. A simple approach to decoration and furnishing means that other people will also be at ease when they arrive and less likely to feel as if they are intruding in someone else's home.

Light, airy colours, natural surfaces and finishes, washable loose covers, basic folding chairs or stacking stools and a minimum of clutter add up to a much more liveable environment than a self-consciously countrified or rustic look, or a collection of oddments and cast-offs from your other home. If you are on a very tight budget, it is often cheaper to source secondhand furniture and fittings in a country area; such local finds can add a sense of character and playfulness, which reinforce the feeling of informality.

For some people, a weekend or holiday home is a private refuge or retreat. For others, it is the excuse for sociable get-togethers. If your holiday home is to be the centre of your social life, you will need to provide as much flexibility in terms of sleeping arrangements as possible: bedrooms fitted out as mini dormitories can accommodate extra children and overnight guests can be put up on sofa beds, pull-out beds or futons.

Getting away from it all often enhances our sensory appreciation of everyday activities such as bathing, cooking and eating. An ideal holiday home should feature some form of outdoor eating area, barbecue or outdoor cooking area, or even an outdoor shower or hot tub. Kitchens can be kept very simple, even spartan, provided they are workable. Avoid unnecessary gadgetry and focus on essentials, such as a decent set of knives and pans, a good preparation or chopping surface and a cooker that really works, not a clapped-out model that has to be coaxed into producing even the simplest meal.

⌄ An outdoor shower where you can sluice off salt and sand or simply refresh yourself on a hot day, makes practical sense if your holiday home is in a hot place or located by the sea.

⌐ This wet room, with a pebbled floor and exposed concrete walls, shelves and bench, puts the focus on the elemental pleasures of bathing.

⌐ The traditional sauna, heated by a wood fire, has long been an established means of relaxation in Scandinavian countries. On holiday there is time to enjoy the benefits of steaming or soaking in a hot tub.

⌃ A generous terrace with built-in bench seating and a table on castors provides plenty of flexibility for entertaining friends and family. If you like your holidays to be social occasions, you may need extra beds and bedding to accommodate guests.

⌃ State-of-the-art kitchens are not necessary. A simple workable layout, a basic range of equipment and utensils, and decent appliances will provide years of serviceable use.

⌐ Creative improvisation using found objects or items picked up for a song in local markets and junk shops add a quirky sense of character. This indoor hammock strung from the rafters has been fashioned from a salvaged boat filled with a mattress and cushions.

ORGANIZATION

Weekends away are not much fun if they begin with a frantic dash round the house, scooping up essential items of kit and stuffing them in the car; too much to-ing and fro-ing of belongings inevitably results in what you need being in the wrong place at the wrong time. The ideal should be to cart as little as possible from one home to the next, which means you will have to accept that you need two of everything. This need not entail huge expense; basic, inexpensive tableware, cookware and utensils are widely available and will not cause an emotional wrench or financial dismay if they get damaged or go astray.

Anything specifically relating to activities you enjoy at your second home should be kept there. This includes outdoor wear, boots and Wellingtons, kites, buckets and spades or any other sporting equipment or paraphernalia.

Keep your holiday home well stocked. A freezer can minimize the amount of time you need to spend food shopping. If the property is relatively remote, it is a good idea to buy light bulbs, refuse bags, toilet rolls and other everyday necessities in bulk so you or your tenants are not caught short.

If you let the house out from time to time, or even if you simply lend it to friends or family, provide clear information and instructions. Make sure you spell out what is included in the rental and what is not. A notice board can be a good way of organizing essential local data: shop opening hours, train timetables, nearest doctor's surgery, day of garbage collection, local sights and amenities. Keep appliance manuals and instruction books in an obvious location. A visitor's book can serve as a useful forum for sharing experiences and recommendations.

OPEN TO THE ELEMENTS

Holidays are not merely about unwinding from everyday stresses, but should also provide the opportunity to enjoy a sense of place. This simple summerhouse at Punta del Este in Uruguay has an elemental quality that creates the ideal environment for relaxation, but also perfectly expresses its spectacular setting.

The house is located in a little valley surrounded by green hills with the sea in the near distance. When the owner bought the site with the intention of building a holiday home for his family, one of his priorities was to keep the new building as compact as possible, thus maximizing the extent of the grounds and maintaining a sense of freedom and connection with nature. Another key factor in the design was the owner's preference for the work of the Mexican architect Luis Barragán. Accordingly, the result is a compact L-shaped structure, some 400sqm (4300sqft) including terraces, where openings in successive horizontal planes frame stunning panoramas of the countryside and sea. The Barragán/Mexican aesthetic, which is evident in the strong geometric lines, is also emphasized by the use of simple building materials. External walls plastered in cement are colourwashed with warm earth pigments that help to blend the house with its setting.

⌐ A simple rustic table and bench, made from reclaimed boards and timber posts, forms an eating area adjoining the kitchen. A built-in concrete bench, painted white and with upholstered cushions, provides extra seating that merges with the structure of the house.

‹ In the children's bedroom, white painted concrete provides the framework for four bunkbeds. The integral central ladder has rustic timber rungs. White walls, navy blinds and blue-and-white striped bedlinen create a fresh, cool effect; the individual bedside lights are shaded with parchment.

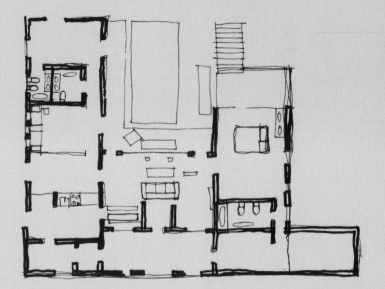

< An enclosed patio, open to the sky, serves as an intermediary entranceway that leads into the main living area. Flooring, both inside and out, is polished travertine. The doors and ironmongery are reclaimed.

∨ The living room leads directly to a terrace, shaded by a trellis of eucalyptus branches, and from there to the centre point of the layout – the pool. Simple modern sofas and chairs, upholstered in white, create a sense of easy informality; natural light spills down through two skylights.

> The L-shaped layout of the summerhouse, with the pool in the centre, reinforces the connections between indoors and out.

The centrepiece of the layout, framed by the L-shaped plan, is the pool, which due to the sloping nature of the site forms a cascade that drops away in the direction of the sea. As the focus of the house's design, the pool is surrounded by a terrace that is accessible from all the main rooms. On the principal axis, the entrance to the house leads directly into the living room, which is open to the shaded terrace and the pool. To one side of the living room is the kitchen, service areas, the children's room, guest room and their bathrooms; on the other side is the main bedroom and bathroom. The easy connections between indoors and out are emphasized by skylights in the living area which provide natural lighting.

Surfaces and furnishings combine rustic, organic elements with a clean-lined easy-going modernity. Floors in the main living areas are polished travertine; in the bedrooms, bleached and stained pine boards. Simple upholstered sofas and benches provide comfortable seating, while more rugged touches are evident in the built-in concrete frameworks – one of which houses the kitchen fittings – and in the dining table which is fashioned from reclaimed timber boards.

∧ A stunning feature of the main bedroom is the sunken slate bath, which is made possible by the sloping nature of the site. The flooring is bleached and stained pine. A fireplace provides a welcome boost of heat on chilly nights. The contemporary metal four-poster bed is hung with white cotton netting.

> In the kitchen, a robust concrete framework houses the cooker and sink and provides space for under-counter storage. The worktops are marble; marble is also used to clad the wall behind the cooker.

>> Because the land drops away from the front of the house to the rear, the pool could be constructed in the form of a waterfall, cascading over one end so that from the house it appears to merge with the distant view of the sea.

EMPTY NEST

In real life, very few nests ever empty completely. And some nests – where grown children or stepchildren come and go – may be empty most of the time, but alarmingly full at others; divorce and remarriage bring their own additional levels of complexity to domestic arrangements.

At the same time, the empty nest is less a clearly defined cut-off point than a protracted transitional period, defined just as much by mixed feelings – on both sides – as by competing demands on space. Although the transitional nature of this stage can make it difficult to decide when to inaugurate change, it is nevertheless a natural time for reassessment. At the very least, this might mean clearing out some of the detritus of family life, or redecorating or upgrading fittings and fixtures. More radically, it can mean moving to an entirely different type of home in a new location.

On the face of it, an empty nest should feel roomier and present more opportunities for you to take up all those activities that, up until now, family life has put on hold. But it isn't always as straightforward as that. Just at the time when you think your grown-up children have finally let go of their old bedrooms and got themselves a place of their own, they're back – this time with grandchildren in tow. Instead of caring for your offspring you may find yourself in the position of caring for an elderly relative who can no longer live independently. Similarly, a house that has operated as an evening and weekend base for partners who work full time, will have to serve rather different functions when you both retire. Flexibility is no less required at this juncture than at other times of life.

ASSESSMENT

As with any period of transition, it is important to take the opportunity to assess future needs and requirements and to reconsider the spatial status quo. We live longer and fuller lives these days and making the most of what is coyly termed the 'third age' means recognizing the fact that the type of domestic arrangements necessitated by family life is past its sell-by date when that family has dispersed.

Timing is a critical issue. Otherwise grown-up and independent offspring can be surprisingly sensitive to radical changes made to their family home. It is well to accept that there may be a period when you find yourself acting as caretaker to the bedrooms of children who don't really live in them anymore. It can be frustrating to postpone taking over a bedroom that is only occupied on infrequent, whirlwind visits home from university, but it is a good idea either to instigate changes gradually or to wait until your son or daughter has established a more permanent base of their own before you act. Some people only fully let go of their childhood room when they have a child of their own, but there is nothing to say you shouldn't hurry the process along a little.

'Empty nest' has a wistful ring to it. These days, for every parent nostalgic for the good old days of lost sports kit and eardrum-shattering decibel levels, there are others who wonder if they are ever going to have the place to themselves. As property prices soar, there is a growing trend for 'children' to live at home well

> Light box

When children grow up and start leaving home, it is a natural time for reassessment. In this case, the owners of a traditional Victorian terraced house in London have opted for radical change, commissioning architect David Mikhail to design a new extension that has transformed the main living areas and introduced a new quality of natural light and air.

Previously, the dining area had been cramped and the kitchen quite dark, lit only by a fanlight giving onto a side passage. The architect's solution was to demolish the existing two-storey rear extension and rebuild, absorbing the redundant side passage to create a dramatic glass box in which the kitchen is sited. Because the new extension did not add more than 10 per cent in volume, the scheme fell within permitted development rights and did not require planning permission.

The long thin kitchen that takes up the area where the side passage used to be has a roof made of a single sheet of double-glazing to enhance the indoor/outdoor feeling. Folding doors connect the kitchen with a light, bright dining area. The line of kitchen units continues beyond the glass box along the length of the garden wall; the external units are used to store the barbecue and other garden items.

Extensions can adversely affect the quality of light and air in existing areas. To prevent this, between the glass box and the living room is a tiny courtyard which is open to the sky and accessed by a pivoting door. The 'bonsai' courtyard space not only sets up cross-ventilation and draws in light, but also provides an unusual focus for the living area.

Equally striking is the pebble flooring that extends from the kitchen into the internal courtyard and garden. Consisting of white marble pebbles set in resin, the material was half the cost of limestone or solid timber. It is kept clean by straightforward vacuuming, or bleach solution if there is a stain.

into their late twenties: 56 per cent of American men between 18 and 24 and 42.5 per cent of women still live in their parents' home. If you find yourself in this position, make it plain that the rules have changed: charge rent, even if it is only a nominal amount, and insist on a contribution to household costs, particularly food and bills. Do not make things too comfortable by providing meals and doing their laundry – they may never leave.

Financial circumstances might not change the instant your children leave home, but it is a good idea to take this opportunity to think about what will happen when you are living on pensions and investments rather than a salary or salaries. Selling a family home and moving somewhere cheaper and smaller will release equity that can be used to supplement a pension. At the same time, a smaller and more efficiently run home should have lower day-to-day running costs, which will help ease pressures on your budget.

If you do consider moving at this juncture, think very carefully about how and where you want to live. In recent years, many active people on the brink of retirement are reversing the stereotype and, instead of moving to a cottage in the country or beside the sea, are swapping suburban family homes for apartments in the heart of the city where they are near museums, galleries, restaurants and all the other cultural attractions that enrich leisure time. Others take the opportunity to explore an entirely different way of living: when you've been battling for years to keep a period property from falling down around your ears, a modern house or flat can seem very appealing.

RECONFIGURING SPACE

When children finally leave home, the average family will find itself with two-point-something more rooms to spare – a spatial embarrassment of riches where most people are concerned. Rather than simply appropriating the space as it is, it can be well worth thinking about how to reorganize your home generally, particularly if you plan to stay put for a while.

⌄ When family life shifts into a different gear and children start to leave home, redecoration can be a positive way of signalling the transition. You may wish to invest in surfaces or materials that were formerly ruled out on grounds of practicality or maintenance. In this Amsterdam apartment glazed doors providing access to the library slide back into the thickness of the wall; chocolate-brown walls are offset by crisp white detailing and woodwork.

⌐ Many people on the brink of retirement are now opting to relocate to the heart of the city, rather than retreat to a quiet village or seaside town. Contemporary open layouts and modern detailing are easy to look after and can make a refreshing change if you have been living in an older property.

Make a list of all those activities you would like to accommodate, taking note of any areas in your home where you feel particularly pressed for space. Your wish list may include, for example, separate studies or workrooms, another or bigger bathroom-shower room or a fitted storage room or dressing room. You will undoubtedly want to ensure that there is at least one room or area where your children can stay the night when they come to visit. You may well have to consider the possibility of fitting out an area for an elderly relative.

If you have formerly partitioned a bigger room to create two smaller bedrooms, it may make sense at this stage to remove the partition and use the room more as a dual-purpose space. It could serve as a workroom or study area most of the time, perhaps, and a place for overnight guests once in a while. Or you may wish to move bedrooms yourself, if it frees up an area with a better aspect for daytime use.

Fitting everything in is more of a challenge when you are downsizing to a smaller home or apartment. In such cases, it is a question of going back to the type of flexible strategies applicable for first homes. Built-in furniture, such as pull-down beds and flap-down tables; sliding partitions and screens; and other architectural ways of articulating space, can resolve space issues in circumstances where children may only live with you part of the time.

In a recent cartoon in the *New Yorker*, an interior designer, presenting a makeover scheme to his client, explains that he sees the empty nest as 'a place where an apartment can finally grow up'. The punch line neatly encapsulates what many people feel at this stage of the game. After years of putting the needs of the children and the household in general above personal preferences and, in some cases, taste, here at last is the opportunity to shift gears and embark on a completely different sort of adult life.

Redecoration is a positive way of signalling this transition. The hard wear and tear of family life is over and you can indulge in attractive finishes or materials that you may have avoided thus far because they would have posed a serious maintenance headache. In decoration terms, familiarity breeds not so much contempt as indifference and it can be worryingly easy to ignore encroaching tattiness, chipped paintwork and scuffed flooring. Making everything fresh again, trying out new colours, finishes or furnishings, will give an erstwhile family home an entirely new atmosphere, which can help you come to terms with the shift from one role to another.

At the same time, investing in new appliances and servicing can also make sense at this stage. Updating and upgrading domestic equipment can bring a new level of labour saving to routine chores and free up time for leisure interests. When you don't have a horde of children to feed or a mountain of dirty laundry to wash, you do not need family-sized refrigerators or washing machines. Switching to more compact energy-efficient models can be very cost-effective.

Perhaps the most critical aspect of this particular rite of passage is the opportunity it provides for de-junking. Paradoxically, the empty nest feels emptiest when it is full of things – when your home is littered with leftover paraphernalia you will constantly be reminded of the way things were. When children leave home, often what parents dread most and find the hardest to come to terms with is the way the house seems suddenly to lose all vitality. Hanging on to a lot of baggage from the past will only serve to reinforce this sense of stagnation, whereby the home becomes little more than a museum. This is not to advocate obliterating all traces of family life, merely to point out that by

⌄ A thoroughly grown-up home, the rectilinear planes, glass walls and smooth finishes of this Scottish house make a surprisingly sympathetic context for the owner's eclectic collection of modern and antique furniture. The drawing room is furnished with classic pieces of modern design, along with a piano and a telescope designed by Ludwig Mies van der Rohe.

⌐ Built to replace a crumbling Georgian mansion, the house is arranged in classical fashion with the main living areas on the first floor and bedrooms below. A sculptural spiral staircase sweeps upstairs from the entrance hall.

⌐ Huge plate-glass windows provide contemplative views of the surrounding countryside and an old stone tower – all that remains of the original house.

≫ The wood-panelled library has a cosier, more enclosed feeling than the other living spaces and is an ideal place for relaxing with a book or perusing the newspaper.

⌃⌃ At a stage in life when many prefer to keep it simple, living on one level has real practical advantages.

⌃ Pure white decor makes the most of light and enhances a sense of space. Maintenance is less of a headache when the family has grown.

⌐ Reversing the trend, one professional couple moved from a traditional Victorian house to a modern townhouse they built themselves. An architectural practice came up with the open-plan design, featuring a huge conservatory courtyard that links with the main living space. The owners then split the tasks of sourcing materials and and construction between them, aided by a team of builders.

clearing out clutter and making room for new activities and interests, you can infuse your surroundings with a new spirit of liveliness and relevance.

A certain level of diplomacy is no less called for when disposing of grown-up children's belongings than it was years back when you were trying to coax them to part with a few old toys. In some senses, a family home will always remain a family home to those who lived there and one way in which children who have long since flown the nest tend to keep an emotional marker in place is to leave some of their stuff behind. Important memorabilia – letters, photo albums, old school work and so on – can go into deep storage in boxes or tea chests; the same is true of treasured childhood possessions that someday your children may want to pass on to their children. Everything else is probably redundant. Once they have a proper place of their own, instigate a few joint sorting sessions and if necessary issue a mild ultimatum or two.

UNIVERSAL DESIGN

The ageing process affects each of us differently. Universal design, or multi-generational design, is a way of accommodating a range of needs and abilities and is applicable equally to those with a specific impairment as to the elderly. By focusing on improving independence and prolonging activity, universal design can make life easier for everyone concerned.

Kitchens

Cooking entails much physical work – bending, stretching, lifting – as well as contact with heat sources and a number of other potential hazards. Concentrated U- or L-shaped layouts avoid unnecessary lifting and walking back and forth between sink, refrigerator and cooker (see page 139). Separate hobs and ovens minimize bending. Electric appliances are easier to operate than gas, and side-by-side hobs avoid the need to reach over burners. Front controls are preferable; side-hung doors provide easier access to oven interiors. Similarly, shallow sinks are more accessible and lever taps that can be operated by the elbow are good for those with impaired grip.

Bathrooms

Like kitchens, bathrooms are another potential danger area and may require adaptation. Those who are finding stairs increasingly difficult to manage may need a lavatory to be installed on the ground floor. Seats and grab rails can be fitted with minimal disruption in either showers or bathtubs. Non-slip mats are a good idea for tubs and shower stalls.

Flooring

Materials used for flooring should minimize the risk of tumbles. Matt-textured tiles and dense low-pile carpeting provide better grip underfoot than smooth surfaces. Make sure that any stair covering is securely anchored, that junctions between flooring materials are flush and that all rugs are laid over non-slip mats.

Lighting

Changes in eyesight are a common feature of ageing and existing light levels may need a boost. The aim should not only be to increase overall levels, but to avoid glare, which tires the eyes unnecessarily and can create a visually confusing environment. Uplighting is a good way of achieving glare-free background light. Dimmer switches and other forms of lighting control enable levels to be set according to the needs of different people.

Accessibility

The prime consideration for wheelchair users is accessibility. In the home, this means ramped steps and entrances, widened doorways and lowered kneehole worktops that a wheelchair can be manoeuvred beneath.

Outdoors

Many people find gardening a hugely satisfying pursuit in later life and an excellent way of remaining active. After retirement age and when children have left home, there is plenty of time for the patient nurturing a garden requires and equal time to savour its rewards. There may come a point, however, when routine garden maintenance becomes physically more difficult.

Raised flowerbeds and borders minimize the need for bending and ease the strain on the back and joints. Container gardening can be a good way of enjoying colourful or scented displays and can be grouped so that they can be appreciated from indoor vantage points. Keep paths, patios and terraced levels clear of weeds and moss to prevent tumbles. Steps or changes in level may need to be ramped.

∨ Hard surfacing, such as decking and pebbled areas, along with raised beds arranged in a formal layout, makes for easy maintenance.

VIEW OF THE STARS

Location always matters, whether you are setting up home for the first time or deciding where you would like to retire. In the case of this retirement house built in the southern Arizona desert close to the Mexican border, the location was chosen for a specific reason. The owners, who were frequent visitors to this part of the southwestern United States, actually bought the land seven years before the house was even commissioned. What attracted them, aside from the rugged beauty of the natural landscape, was the crystal clear night skies. The husband, formerly a radio astronomer, remains a passionate star-gazer. Located outside a small town and with few houses nearby, the site offered an ideal spot to pursue his astronomical studies.

Accordingly, a platform for an optical telescope was one of the first requirements of the brief when the house was eventually commissioned. Others included the provision for two studies, guest rooms and entertainment areas, all on a single level if possible. The hot desert climate and the spectacular scenery also reinforced a desire to connect the interior with the exterior in a free flow of space.

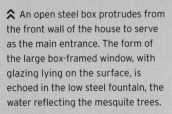

⌃ An open steel box protrudes from the front wall of the house to serve as the main entrance. The form of the large box-framed window, with glazing lying on the surface, is echoed in the low steel fountain, the water reflecting the mesquite trees.

⌃ The two shed-like structures that comprise the house are inclined towards each other. The structures sit on a shelf carved into the hill so that from the road only the glazed ends are visible above ground.

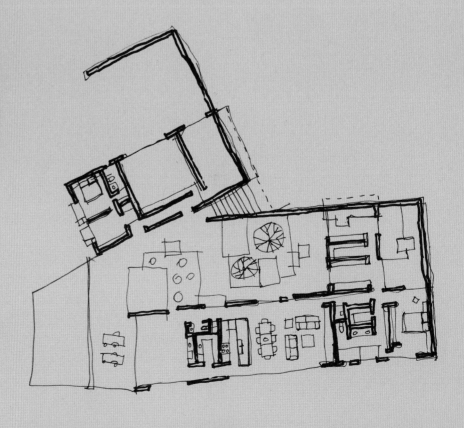

∧ On the southwest side an enclosed porch leads directly to the swimming pool deck. The porch has an outdoor kitchen at the rear; an open cut-out frames the spectacular panorama of distant mountain ranges.

‹ The unusual placement of windows both captures views from a variety of angles and helps to set up currents of cross-ventilation.

› The weathered steel cladding contrasts with sleek white plastered interior walls. Because the Arizonan climate is so dry, expensive oxidized steel was not required.

The house takes the form of two angular sheds, one large and one small, which are inclined towards one another and enclose an open courtyard and pool. The smaller structure contains guest accommodation, the telescope platform and a garage, while the larger contains all the main living spaces as well as the two studies: one for the husband and all his books and the other where the wife engages in quilt-making.

In the extremely dry climate, steel weathers quickly but does not rust through completely, so it was not necessary to opt for a more expensive oxidized steel cladding. The warm rust-red tones of the weathered steel blend naturally with the desert setting, minimizing the structure's intrusion in the landscape. A series of openings, glazed and unglazed, frame panoramic views and set up intriguing internal vistas.

In contrast to the rugged exterior, interior surfaces and finishes are refined and beautifully detailed to create an appropriate context for the owners' extensive art collection. Pristine white plasterwork, maple panelling, stainless steel, sandblasted glass and black polished-concrete floors provide a crisp, graphic background.

Aside from the main courtyard and pool, there is another smaller and more enclosed courtyard behind the two studies. At the main entrance, a hollow steel box protrudes from the plane of the wall to form an open vestibule or lobby. In the same vein, some of the windows also protrude box-like from the walls, with glazing either recessed within the frame or forming its outer skin.

┏ The kitchen and dining area seen from the courtyard. Kitchen units are made of stainless steel; the floor is black polished concrete which absorbs heat in the day and releases it slowly overnight, when desert temperatures can drop dramatically.

❮ Slivers of views captured by the windows are enhanced by the open layout of living spaces; sliding glass panels form transparent dividers.

^ The small courtyard is accessible from both studies and is enclosed by the retaining wall where the site is cut back into the hill.

^ The main bedroom, with its exposed concrete wall creating an evocative contrast to the polished floor, has a large square window overlooking the more enclosed courtyard to the northeast end.

> A long horizontal window runs the length of the living area to the southeast. The kitchen wall is panelled in maple. On the other side is an open kitchen and the enclosed porch leading to the swimming pool.

PART 2

HOME WORK

This hard-working, practical section details the options for change, from decorative facelifts to full-scale building projects, and gives you all the information you need to get on with the job. Essential checklists and breakdowns of key elements are provided to enable you to turn your plans into reality, whether you intend to install a new bathroom or convert a loft, and whether you are doing-it-yourself or employing a team of professionals.

THE BASICS

Any decision you might make regarding how and where you live has significant implications for your financial status as well as for your emotional and physical wellbeing. Buying a home is the biggest investment most people undertake in their lifetime, but even renting property ties up a large portion of income on a regular basis. Carrying out alterations to a home you already own or one that you rent brings a wide range of issues into play, not merely in terms of financing, but also in terms of structural, legal and practical considerations.

The conditions and charges imposed by financial institutions such as banks and other mortgage lenders vary from country to country, as do the legalities and procedures governing the purchase or alteration of property. Such rules are also subject to changes. Wherever you live or whatever you are planning to do, make sure that you get up-to-date information and advice from the relevant professional(s): financial advisers, solicitors, brokers, surveyors, architects and accountants. In every case, success means doing your homework thoroughly first.

You should not be deterred by all of this, however. Altering your home to make it a place that you really enjoy living in is one of the most worthwhile things you can do and should make a significant difference to the quality of your life. It may not feel like it while work is in progress, but when it is finished your efforts will be rewarded.

BUDGETING

First things first: how much can you afford? Setting a financial limit before you begin to investigate options will help to prevent expenditure from spiralling out of control once you set things in motion. If you haven't done so already, work out a detailed monthly break-down of your outgoings – food, bills, travel, clothing, holidays, leisure, car repairs and running costs, and any other routine expenditure, such as loans, credit card or mortgage repayments – and set this against all forms of income (salary, dividends, the interest earned by savings or investments) to enable you to get a clear picture of your financial circumstances. You will then be in a position to consider various options for funding.

Income

Unless there is a very great differential between what you spend and what you earn, you are only likely to be able to fund small projects, such as redecoration, minor repairs and the odd one-off purchase, directly out of your own pocket. If you decide to cut back other areas of expenditure to ease the financial squeeze – by doing without a holiday, for example, or limiting what you spend on other leisure pursuits – make sure that you won't regret the decision later. There may be others in your household who have views on the matter, too.

Savings

Savings or investments can provide greater financial scope – either for a deposit on a new home or for a more extensive programme of improvements. Value for money issues, however, come into play here. If what you are planning to do will add less to the future worth of your home than your savings or investments might have earned over the same period, you may be better off not going ahead.

Short-term credit

Spending on credit cards, or buying on hire-purchase or other forms of credit arrangements (including overdrafts) can be very tempting. However, as many can testify, such debts can be difficult to clear. Short-term credit is one of the most expensive ways of borrowing: the real cost of what you buy is the price plus the interest you pay monthly to borrow the money. If you do decide to buy on credit, take a close look at different options and compare interest rates: an overdraft, for example, may be cheaper than using a credit card or in-store credit arrangement.

Loans

For larger home improvement projects, you might consider taking out a loan from a bank or building society. Loans are repaid at a fixed rate of interest over a considerable period of time. Again, the true cost of the project will be the amount you will pay in interest over the term of the loan plus the amount you borrowed in the first place to carry out the works. If you are taking out a personal loan, the amount you will be able to borrow will be determined by your income and expenditure. Financial institutions may be prepared to lend larger sums in the form of a loan secured against any property that you own. Secured loans, however, can put your home at risk if you are unable to keep up with repayments and may be more expensive in the long run than remortgaging.

Mortgaging and remortgaging

There are many types of mortgage available, all with different rates and conditions attached, so it is important to research the market thoroughly and get expert advice. Some lenders offer mortgages with discounted rates for a fixed period of two to five years, or fixed rates over the mortgage term, as well as standard variable rate products. New types of flexible mortgage allow borrowers to take repayment holidays of up to six months or to make lump sum repayments, which can be both cheaper in the long run than standard mortgages and better for those who are self-employed or whose income varies. Current account mortgages, which roll mortgage, credit and checking or current accounts into a single account are also cost-effective and flexible. If you already own your home and there is sufficient equity – the difference between what you originally borrowed to buy it and what it is now worth – remortgaging can be an extremely cost-effective way of funding large-scale improvements.

BUYING

Buying a home is a huge step. It is important to get the timing right, particularly in areas where property prices tend to fluctuate. Property is normally considered a sound investment but the best returns may only be guaranteed over the longer term. Buying at the peak of a housing price boom, for example, may land you in negative equity when the market takes a nose dive, and if interest rates rise you could be seriously out of pocket. In general terms, buying makes sense if the market is not wildly overheated, if you yourself are at a fairly stable stage of your career with a steady income, and if mortgage repayments would be lower or equivalent to renting a similar property.

In dense urban areas or in parts of the world where property commands premium prices, it can be difficult for single people to get onto the property ladder. At the same time, where prices are escalating well beyond rises in pay, buying a first home may only become more difficult as the years go by. Ways round this problem include opting for joint ownership with friends or relatives, or buying with the intention of renting out a room or rooms to tenants to help cover the mortgage.

> **Do your sums right** The true cost of buying a home is the purchase price plus a number of additional expenses: moving, storage, insurance (life, buildings and contents), professional fees (surveyor's, solicitor's), valuation costs, legal searches and taxes. In Britain, stamp duty, which is paid on a sliding scale according to the value of the property, is a significant extra expense. These additional costs can amount to between three and four per cent of the price of the property. In France and other parts of Europe, notarial charges add ten per cent to the price of the property.

> **Know what you are buying** If you are buying a 'shell' (an unfitted loft space with service connections but no fixtures) or if you are buying 'off plan' into a new development, be sure you know exactly what you are getting for your money and how much extra it will cost to turn the space into a habitable home. Mortgage lenders are generally unwilling to advance more than 80 per cent of the cost of a shell, so you will need more money up front than if you were buying a conventional property.

> **Research the market** Get a feel for what you can expect to achieve for your money in a given location. Sources of information include estate agents and realtors, internet property services, listings of private sales in the local press, property auctions and home search agents.

> **Know what you want** A key decision is location. Do you want to be near shops, transport links, good schools? Do you mind noise and vibrant street life or are you looking for somewhere more sedate? Have you a specific type of home in mind or are you prepared to be flexible in terms of age, character and layout? Do you want a garden? A parking space? How many bedrooms? What is your price range? The more specific you can be about your requirements, the easier it will be to brief agents and the less likely you are to fall head over heels for a property that won't deliver what you really need.

> **Be prepared to compromise** Estate agents estimate than only five per cent of house buyers find exactly what they are looking for. Most of the rest of us are forced to compromise, which is where having a clear set of priorities comes in useful.

> **Trust your instincts** If you have done your homework, it may not take you very long to make up your mind about a particular property. Many purchasers know immediately when a potential home 'feels' right; if you don't have that gut reaction, keep looking. If you do fall in love with a home at first sight, don't let your body language give the game away or you may compromise

on down the line. Keep your posture relaxed rather than eager and limit expressions of delight.

> **Look beyond superficial decor or styling** In competitive areas, many sellers are adopting sophisticated sales techniques to shift their properties (see Selling), so be on your guard for tantalizing aromas, stacks of fresh linen and vases of flowers that might distract from less-than-perfect structural or decorative conditions. Similarly, don't let eccentric decor or furnishings put you off what you are really buying, which is the structure and space itself. Study the floor plans to make sure your furniture will fit in.

> **Keep an eye out for defects** Check carefully both the property and the immediate vicinity. Signs of underlying problems include: bowed or sagging roofs or walls, serious cracks, peeling paintwork, water staining, musty smells, plasterwork that sounds hollow when tapped, floors with excessive 'give', old-fashioned electrical arrangements. The most commonly overlooked problems are damp and old wiring, both of which can be expensive to put right. Abandoned cars, rubbish, graffiti and untended gardens in the local area may indicate troublesome neighbours.

> **Commission a full structural survey** This costs more than the valuation survey carried out by mortgage lenders but is much more detailed and can provide the basis for price bargaining.

> **Always go back for a second viewing** If possible, take a friend with you for an objective opinion. Arrange the second viewing at a different time of day (or on a rainy day) to get a feel for the neighbourhood.

> **Treat the seller with courtesy** In certain highly sought-after areas in the United States, would-be buyers have resorted to writing personal letters to sellers, explaining why they would be ideal future owners of the property. There may be no need to go this far, but all other things being equal, most owners prefer to sell their property to people they like and respect.

> **Be sure you know what is included** Agree in writing which fittings and fixtures will be left behind. Mean-spirited sellers have been known to strip a property of everything down to the last bathroom fitment and light bulb before moving out, and some people even dig up rosebushes, shrubs and trees in mature gardens to take with them. It can be a good idea to turn up at your new home on the day of completion to make sure what you expect to see is still in place. After completion, your only recourse will be through the courts.

It may seem an obvious point, but do not put your property on the market unless you are sure you want to move. Buyers may be reluctant to put an offer on your home if they sense you haven't made up your mind. The next decision is whether to use an estate agent (or joint agents) or go the private route. Selling through an agent or realtor costs more money but is a more secure option and should entail less bother and disruption if you choose the right agent with expertise of selling in your area.

Developers in certain areas also offer part-exchange schemes. If you are interested in buying into a new development and want to move fast, some developers will guarantee to buy your old home, often for full market value (based on independent valuations), on condition that the property that you purchase from them is worth 30 per cent more. Such deals can take as little as a week to finalize.

The longer a property has been on the market, the less likely it is to attract a buyer, so the ideal is to hit the ground running, presenting your home in the best possible condition right from the outset. Before you put it on the market, it is worth spending a little time and money to repair and redecorate. A dripping tap on its own won't ruin a sale, but a number of such minor defects may put across the wrong message. A lick of paint (in a neutral colour) can revive tired surfaces or rooms that do not get much natural light. Use a tile-grouting pen to refresh bathroom or kitchen tiling and give the whole place a spring clean.

Keeping up appearances for a protracted selling period and trying to fit in household activities around infrequent viewings can be difficult. One answer is to stage an 'open house' for a single weekend, leave the keys with your agent and remove yourself and your family from the picture.

> **No kids, no dogs** Remove traces of children and pets (particularly dogs) as far as possible. During viewings, try to ensure that children and pets are away from home. Don't arrange viewings to coincide with mealtimes.

> **Make a good first impression** Buyers often make up their minds within minutes of entering a property. Pay special attention to the entrance. A substantial front door, or one that is newly painted and has tactile door furniture, sets the tone. Remove boots, outdoor gear and other detritus from the hall.

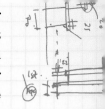

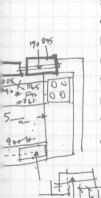

> **Get rid of clutter** Buyers need help to see the potential of a space and to read themselves into the picture. Remove everything that is surplus or that has too strong a sense of personality such as your own personal memorabilia. Strategically placed mirrors can enhance the feeling of space.

> **Appeal to the senses** Eradicate stale cooking, tobacco and pet odours. Stimulating, hospitable smells include: baking bread, brewing coffee, log fires and ambient lavender or citrus scents. Soft background music can help to allay anxieties. Candles, fresh linen and white fluffy towels suggest comfort and ease. Place vases of fresh flowers throughout the home.

> **Use body language** Greet potential buyers at the door with a smile and handshake. Maintain eye contact when you are talking to them. Show the best room downstairs first. Give viewers plenty of room and let them precede you into areas so they don't feel crowded.

> **Be clear what you are leaving** Make sure you state what is included in the price and what you intend to take with you. Put it in writing. On moving day, it is common courtesy to leave behind a few basic essentials such as light bulbs, toilet paper, a towel, soap and a phone, as well as all instructions and warranties regarding existing fittings or services. A welcoming note – and a bottle of champagne – is a truly generous touch.

RENTING

While home ownership undoubtedly offers security, long-term value for money and freedom of expression and lifestyle, there are situations and stages of life when renting is a more preferable option. The chief advantage of renting is flexibility. If you are a student, or just starting out in your career, you probably will not want to be tied to a particular place for very long. Similarly, if you move to a new city or country, renting for a short while gives you the breathing space to get to know a new location and shop around for the right home to buy. Although the rents in many areas can approach or exceed the levels of mortgage repayments for similar properties, renting may still be cheaper overall, when you take into account the hidden costs of home ownership, such as building and life insurance, maintenance and repairs, and property taxes.

In some European countries, many people live in rented homes for a considerable length of time, making their first property purchase in their late 30s or early 40s. Renting has traditionally also been the norm in dense high-rise areas such as Manhattan in New York, where long-standing tenants are further protected by stabilized or controlled rents. Generally, however, unless your rent is low enough for you to save up to buy a property at a later date, or your career prospects are likely to improve dramatically, renting for a protracted period does not represent good value for money. Rent is simply money that is spent; at the end of the day, you will have nothing to show for it.

The legislation governing the relationship between tenants and landlords is often complex, and varies according to locale. In New York, for example, landlords are required to repaint the apartments they let out every three years and in buildings of more than nine units a superintendent must live in; in Britain, tenants are responsible for interior repairs (although there may be restrictions about what type of decoration can be carried out). It is important to know your rights and to check the fine print of any lease or tenancy agreement carefully before you sign on the dotted line.

There are various ways you can rent. Most typical is the single tenancy, where one person signs the lease. Joint tenancies involve two or more people assuming what is known as 'joint and several' responsibility: if one of the co-signers defaults, the others are responsible. Lodging (renting a room in a property with a resident landlord) is the least protected form of tenancy. Notice to quit can be as short as one week if you are a lodger.

> **Assess your needs** The rental market moves quickly, so decide your budget, what you require in terms of accommodation and location before you go looking. Home-search agencies and internet services can take the legwork out of finding the right place.

> **Allocate money for rent** Aim to allow between one-quarter and one-third of net income for rent. You will also need between one month and six weeks' rent as a deposit, plus one month's rent payable in advance. Landlords or managing agencies generally ask for financial and character references.

> **Check the terms of the lease carefully** The lease should specify the amount of rent, the date and intervals at which it should be paid, the length of lease and the notice period on each side, as well as any other specific terms and conditions with respect to pets, subletting, landlord's access, and so on.

> **Check inventories carefully** If you are renting furnished accommodation, there should be a full inventory of the

contents. Make sure the condition of each item tallies with the inventory or you may be charged for pre-existing damage at the end of your lease. Damage, loss or breakage that occurs during your tenancy is generally recouped from your deposit.

> **Ensure everything is in working order** Check that all services, appliances and fixtures are working properly before you move in. Thereafter, it is your landlord's responsibility to replace or repair any faulty appliances and to maintain existing services, as well as to carry out repairs to the structure and external fabric of the property. The lease should clearly specify which running bills and costs are your responsibility and which are your landlord's. In Britain, following cases of carbon monoxide poisoning from faulty gas fires, landlords are legally required to have gas heating appliances inspected once a year.

> **Insure your belongings** Although you do not need buildings insurance if you are renting your home, it is a good idea to take out contents insurance to cover your personal property.

> **Be aware of your landlord's rights** Landlords are entitled to access at any time, with a notice period of 24 hours. Your landlord has the right to evict you if your rent is in arrears. Tenants can also be evicted if the landlord can prove extensive damage to the fabric or contents of the property. Landlords retain the power of sale. Tenants may also be forced to quit if a landlord decides to put the property on the market.

> **Keep documentation** Make a record of all telephone conversations and correspondence with the landlord or managing agent in case of subsequent disputes.

> **Establish what alterations you can make** One of the disadvantages of renting is that it can be difficult to make a place feel like your own home. Most landlords have no objection to superficial decoration, such as painting, although permission may be required. In most cases, however, more extensive changes are not allowed, which can rule out removing existing surfaces or floor coverings or screwing things to walls.

> **Weigh up the pros and cons of sharing** Shared or joint tenancies generally work out cheaper, which means you can afford a better place than you would otherwise. You will also have ready-made company. The downside is putting up with other people's habits and making sure everyone pays their way and does their fair share of the housework. Some shared households run like clockwork; others can descend into near-anarchy.

BUY-TO-LET

A popular form of investment in recent years, buying-to-let is far from a risk- or trouble-free venture. It is vitally important to do your sums properly and to get reliable financial advice, particularly if you are borrowing or mortgaging to purchase a buy-to-let property rather than simply investing a windfall or an inheritance. The buy-to-let market is obviously affected by the supply of rental properties; the more people invest in this sector, the lower the yields. Those who borrow heavily to buy a rental property are most vulnerable; even 'void' periods as short as three months between tenants can result in a net loss.

If you are a private landlord and decide to go it alone, you may find yourself taking on more than you bargained for in terms of dealing with repairs, maintenance, complaints and other routine forms of administration. Managing agents can handle such issues for you, but at a price.

Finding good tenants is not easy. Bank and other financial references may identify potential defaulters or persistent late-payers but are no guarantee of good behaviour. One answer is to seek references from previous landlords who are often able to identify those tenants who leave properties in poor condition or who otherwise behave unacceptably in situ.

LEVELS OF CHANGE

Home improvements come on a sliding scale of expense, difficulty, and impact, ranging from giving your living room a fresh coat of paint, through to installing a new kitchen or bathroom, or adding on an extension or loft conversion. Choosing the appropriate level of change for your home means first assessing what you've got and what you hope to achieve.

Repairs

If you are a homeowner, one type of 'improvement' you cannot afford to neglect is essential repairwork or maintenance. Before you even begin to plan those changes that will make your home more attractive or improve the way it functions, make sure that you are not overlooking any aspect of your home's structure, fabric or general condition that needs urgent attention. Many severe problems start small, so don't be tempted to wait until later, by which time that minor patch of damp, for example, might have led to the infinitely more serious problem of dry rot.

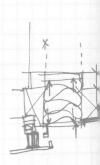

Signs of potential trouble:

> Wide cracks, especially those that continue to widen, may indicate serious problems such as subsidence or the failure of a structural member. Hairline cracks are normal, particularly in new plasterwork.
> Discoloured paintwork, bulging or blown plasterwork, wet patches on brick or stonework, and musty smells all indicate damp penetration or possible leaks. Untreated damp can lead on to more serious problems, such as dry or wet rot.
> Fungal growths, insect boreholes, rotten or powdery wood are signs of wet rot, woodworm and dry rot.
> Pest infestations, such as rodents, can cause havoc, particularly to pipework and cabling.
> Sloping floors may indicate ground subsidence or trouble with the foundations.
> Roof damage, such as sagging and bowing, can indicate serious structural problems; missing tiles or slates can lead to leaks and water damage.

Cosmetic changes

Relatively straightforward, inexpensive and quick compared to many other types of improvement, cosmetic changes such as decoration or installing new surfaces and finishes can have a disproportionately large impact on the way your home looks and feels – which, indeed, is the entire premise of those television makeover programmes. Fresh paintwork can give any room an instant uplift; a good quality material, such as hardwood flooring, conveys an immediate sense of character and quality. Decoration can even make your home feel more spacious by enhancing natural light. What it cannot do, however, is correct poorly planned layouts, fitted areas that don't function properly or other structural or design drawbacks.

Design changes

Various forms of internal rearrangement, from moving partitions and walls to replanning fitted areas such as kitchens and bathrooms, can dramatically improve the way your home functions, a benefit you will enjoy on a daily basis as you carry out routine chores. Such improvements will not necessarily win you more floor area per se, but will make better use of what space you already have. This type of improvement generally involves professional help – if only to establish what you can and cannot do legally and structurally – and may entail moving servicing.

Structural changes

The top end of the scale, as far as expense, disruption and cost are concerned, are improvements that alter the structure of your home; these include changes to load-bearing walls, external walls, roofs and so on. Most loft or basement conversions, extensions and the installation of new openings such as French windows fall into this category. Structural changes may be the only way to gain more space – an additional room or rooms or the enlargement of an existing area, such as a kitchen. They also offer the opportunity to improve both natural light and access to garden areas. Most structural changes involve gaining various forms of official permissions and you will almost certainly require professional advice from a surveyor, architect or structural engineer.

BEFORE YOU BEGIN

After you have come up with an improvements wish list, the next step is to consider a range of additional factors, from cost to legalities, which will give a more definite shape to your plans.

Cost

Set your budget first so that you have at least one parameter in place. Then establish what can be achieved for your money by costing out materials, professional help, design fees, and so on. Remember to include a contingency margin of at least ten per cent to cope with unforeseen circumstances.

If your budget will not stretch far enough to achieve what you want, think again. One way of cutting costs is to opt for cheaper materials – a wooden or laminate worktop instead of one in solid granite, for example – or you can seek out cheaper sources (salvage yards and suppliers of remnants or offcuts are generally much less expensive than custom suppliers or upmarket retailers). Materials often account for a substantial proportion of the cost of any home improvement and provided that you do not compromise on essential practicality, you may be able to make considerable savings here. Another way of avoiding unnecessary expense is to specify standard components that are readily available off-the-peg. Any item or element that has to be custom-made to individual specification – such as a window or door – costs more. Finally, you may be able to save money by taking a lateral leap. If you are desperate for a new kitchen, for example, but cannot afford to rip out the one you've got and start from scratch, you might come close to the effect you are after by leaving the carcass of the original fitted units in place and upgrading drawer and door fronts along with the worktop.

However, there are certain economies that you should never make. It is one thing to opt for a cheaper material, quite another to opt for a substandard one which will not perform as it should and which will degrade quickly so that it needs replacing sooner rather than later. Similarly, don't skimp on preparation or making good underlying surfaces. Finally, do not cut costs by opting to undertake some of the work yourself unless you are fully confident of your abilities and have done similar work before.

Practicalities

Early on in the planning process you should establish whether what you intend to do is structurally feasible. There is often more than one route to the same result, so don't despair if your original idea turns out to be a non-starter. Architectural advice is invaluable for any alterations that entail a complex re-juggling of layout or volumes, or the repositioning of service areas such as kitchens and bathrooms.

Professional help

Many home improvement projects, even the most apparently straightforward ones, require specialist help. This may range from calling in a fitter to lay a new carpet to employing a firm of builders to construct an extension. Although you may be tempted to cut corners in this department, in most circumstances the worst thing you can do is to avoid getting help when you need it. If you tackle a job that you are not really experienced or qualified to do, you run the risk of harming yourself or damaging your property, creating unnecessary wastage or simply taking too long to complete the work, all of which will cost more money in the long run. If you economize by doing without professional advice, you may underestimate the complexity of the work or overlook essential legal or practical factors.

Professional assistance falls into several categories: design and advisory services (surveyors, architects, interior designers and structural engineers); supervisory services (architects, designers and project managers); building work (a wide range of trades from bricklayers to roofers, plumbers, electricians and decorators); and finally specialist services (heating engineers, scaffolders, carpet fitters, and so on).

Legalities

The more radical and extensive alterations generally require official permissions of some type. You may have to submit plans to your local authority for approval before work can begin; work in progress may also need to be inspected and passed at the appropriate stages. If your home is located in a conservation area or is of historic interest, your plans may require the approval of heritage bodies. If you are changing services or installing new ones, you will also need the approval of gas, water or electricity boards and the work will have to be inspected by them.

Broadly speaking, building codes and planning guidelines are designed to ensure that alterations and extensions to property (as well as new-build projects) are structurally sound, healthy, safe and do not have a deleterious effect on either the local architectural context or immediate neighbours. Legislation in this area is constantly changing and up-to-date advice is essential. More detailed information on the type of legal and official restrictions governing different types of alteration is given in the relevant sections.

ORGANIZING THE WORK

Achieving a successful result depends to a large extent on having a grasp of the sequence in which work must be carried out, as well as an appreciation of its complexity so that you can put the appropriate level of assistance in place at the right time. There is always room for manoeuvre, even in the most complicated project; there may well be specific roles that suit your skills and which you can readily assume to save yourself time and money. Most home alterations and improvements, saving the simplest, can be broken down into the following broad stages:

Planning and design

The first stage is to investigate all the potential design options to come up with a solution that delivers what you want and is also in line with practical and budgetary constraints. Design professionals such as architects can be retained for this stage for only a relatively modest fee and will also be able to produce the scale drawings you will need both to commission

> Replacing an old side extension, this striking modern conservatory is made from structural glass panels that are strong enough to walk on. It is supported by glass beams for maximum transparency and visual lightness. The clean lines of the glass roof and smooth white walls form an elegant contrast with the external brickwork of the house, which has also been painted white.

the work and to gain any necessary permissions from planning authorities. If there are structural defects to remedy, or complex structural issues, you may also need advice from a surveyor or structural engineer. There are also specilialist design services available for projects such as kitchen design and loft conversion.

Specification and sourcing materials

A specification is a detailed breakdown of all aspects of the work, including fittings, fixtures and materials. If you leave things open or vague, most builders will take that to mean the lowest common denominator, that is, whatever is cheapest and easiest. Architectural services can include the preparation of a specification and detailed drawings for the builder to work to, which can save headaches and expense further on and remove any potential areas of ambiguity. If you require specialist materials or fixtures, however, it may be worth sourcing these yourself. What you expect the builder to provide and what you intend to organize should be clear from the outset.

Building work

Most projects involve the services of a number of different trades in an overlapping sequence of events (see page 120). If the job is relatively straightforward and you are clear what is required and when, you might consider employing tradespeople directly. The alternative, and one which is strongly recommended for work of a more involved nature, is to engage a contractor. The contractor will then be responsible for subcontracting out any part of the job, such as roofing, for example, or erecting scaffolding, that the firm cannot handle directly, and will coordinate site work so that everything happens in the right order.

Supervision

The day-to-day supervision of work in progress helps to keep things running smoothly. It isn't merely a matter of checking that work is being done to your satisfaction, you may also need to ensure that necessary official inspections are carried out at the right stages. If you are relatively knowledgeable and organized, and the work is not overly complicated, you may well wish to take on the supervisory role yourself. Alternatively, site supervision is another standard architectural service and will include a final inspection for any defects or departures from the brief.

Employing others

Although the professions and trades involved in the building industry are incredibly diverse in terms of skills and expertise, the basic principles of employing them are more or less the same. Do not be intimidated by the sort of horror stories that are regularly aired in the press; there are undoubtedly incompetent and unscrupulous individuals out there, just as there are in any profession or trade, but there are good ones, too, and it is possible to find them.

Bear in mind that if things go wrong, there is often fault on both sides. You can go some way towards avoiding potential pitfalls if you take the trouble to do a little research and get acquainted with basic terms and techniques. Professional mystique is often based on jargon. If you demonstrate a working familiarity with some of the vocabulary, you will find it easier to communicate. At the same time, if you don't understand what someone is talking about, do not let it pass but ask for it to be explained to you in clear language.

> Word of mouth is one of the best ways to find the right person or firm for the job – particularly that elusive being, the affordable, reputable plumber. Ask friends and neighbours who have had similar work done for their personal recommendations. You are more likely to get an honest appraisal this way.

> When choosing an architect or designer, you are more than halfway there if you like their previous work. Look out for projects or schemes featured in magazines or newspapers that appeal to you. That way, you are both on the same wavelength to begin with.

> Make sure that anyone you employ is a member of the appropriate accredited professional body or trade organization. This not only guarantees a standard of competence but also gives you access to a complaints procedure if things do go wrong.

> Always ask for references and take them up. Ask to see examples of previous work if possible or appropriate.

> Shop around, particularly in the case of large, complex jobs. Try to get quotes and a projected schedule from at least three different building firms. If you employ an architect, he or she might be able to come up with a shortlist of suitable contractors to tender for the job. A low quote should set alarm bells ringing as much as an over-inflated one; in most cases, the firm that comes in somewhere around the middle is the realistic and safe choice. A cut-price estimate may be tempting for those

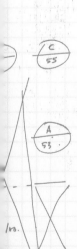

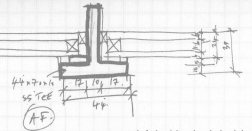

on a restricted budget, but be aware that it can be a sign of an unreliable cowboy outfit. An expensive quote, on the other hand, is not necessarily a potential rip-off, but may indicate that the job may be too small to be cost-effective for the firm in question.

> Put everything in writing and keep records of all conversations, correspondence and any alterations you make to your plans subsequent to the initial commission or brief. An architect may be commissioned on the basis of a letter of agreement; for builders, however, it is advisable to draw up a contract that sets out terms of payment, start and completion dates, and gives a full itemization of the works.

> Never, ever pay the full cost of the work up front. Decide a payment schedule in advance and stick to it. For small jobs, it is usual to pay a percentage up front as a materials float, with the remainder due on satisfactory completion. For longer jobs, you may wish to agree a weekly or fortnightly sum, but you should hold a significant amount back as a final payment to act as an incentive to get the work finished. A flat fee, rather than an hourly or day rate, avoids the risk of the job being spun out to an unnecessary degree.

> Try not to change your mind or revise your plans radically as you go along. There is an understandable element of evolution in every project but if you are constantly chopping and changing your ideas, the work will take longer and cost more – and your builder will lose faith in the project.

> Be reasonable about access to basic kitchen and toilet facilities and tolerant of minor hitches and setbacks. A good working relationship demands an element of trust and respect on both sides.

> Expect the unexpected and be prepared for it. One of your suppliers may go out of business or be unable to deliver the materials you want, your builder may uncover an unforeseen structural defect that needs to be put right, the weather may turn nasty just as the roof comes off – it happens. Allow a generous time margin and a budget contingency so you are covered.

Timing

Much of the stress that tends to accompany home improvement projects could be avoided by getting the timing right. People often wildly underestimate just how long it takes to get even fairly straightforward work carried out and popular television programmes, where whirlwind makeovers are easily achieved over a

weekend, only reinforce this misconception. Then there is the phenomenon whereby faced with an unavoidable deadline of some kind or another, people elect to give themselves another: hence the mad rush to get the attic converted 'by Christmas' or the new bathroom installed 'before the baby arrives'.

> If you are doing the work yourself, make sure you block in protracted periods of free time at weekends or during holidays when you can get on with the job uninterrupted – a stray hour or two after work is not going to do the trick. Being able to see progress at the end of each day is a powerful incentive to finishing the work.

> Plan ahead and be prepared to wait. Usually the best professionals get booked up well in advance. Chase them up nearer to the agreed start date to make sure the schedule doesn't slip. Do not be tempted to employ a second- or third-rate outfit just because you are anxious to get started.

> Avoid scheduling extensive works during already busy or stressful periods, whether you are organizing a major family wedding or celebration, expecting a new baby, moving to a new job or are otherwise preoccupied. Similarly, avoid disruption on the home front during the times when family members are studying for important exams or recovering from illness. It is also worth bearing in mind that during busy times of the year, such as Christmas, suppliers often get backlogged, which can add weeks on to your timetable.

> Investigate the possibility of having the work done out of season. Employing people during quieter winter periods may be a cheaper and faster option, provided that extensive external works are not required, which could result in unacceptable heat loss, lost days due to bad weather and lots of extra mess.

Disruption

For most people 'having the builders in' is shorthand for aggravation and disruption. Most home improvement projects entail at least some interruption of everyday domestic routines. This can be as minimal as the decorator's tools and materials being left overnight or as extensive as the removal of an external wall and the interruption of major services. Establish before work begins what sort of impact it is likely to have on your home, roughly when it will occur and how long it is likely to last, so that you can plan ways of easing the inevitable strain on the household.

> Agree clear rules for working practice at the outset: where tools and materials are to be stored, the standard of tidying up you expect at the end of the day, and protection for existing surfaces and finishes. Remove valuable or breakable items from the area where work will take place. Protect electronic equipment from dust.

> Find out if there will be interruptions of services such as water, electricity or gas supply which could put kitchens, bathrooms or home offices out of use for significant periods of time. If such periods are not extensive or frequent, you can plan round them by eating out, ordering in takeaways, arranging to use a neighbour's bathroom, for example. If not, you may have to consider moving out for a time.

> Know what you are in for. 'Wet' trades such as plastering, bricklaying and concreting are particularly messy. Hacking off old plasterwork, demolishing walls and sanding floors also generate stupendous amounts of dust and debris. Accept the fact that things might have to get worse before they get better.

> Works that expose parts of your home to the elements – for example, those that entail taking off a roof or making openings in external walls – bring the added discomfort of loss of heat, particularly in periods where the weather is not reliable. Make sure that sufficient arrangements are made to keep the fabric of your home secure and weather-tight while such works are carried out. If work requires scaffolding, insist that ladders are removed or locked up at the end of the day to avoid the risk of someone breaking in at an upstairs window.

ORDER OF WORK

Jobs that involve more than a few simple stages, and require the services of more than two or three different trades, need careful planning and coordination. Delay is everyone's worst headache – particularly since it often involves extra expense. Seeing work stretch on indefinitely into the future while you are sitting in what amounts to a bombsite is enough to drive anyone half round the bend with frustration.

Most reasonably extensive building work can be divided into two broad stages, known in the trade as 'first fix' and 'second fix'. First fix embraces all those preliminary stages from demolition and clearing to basic structural work, the moving and laying of service runs and the putting up of new partitions. This is the getting-worse-before-it-gets-better stage, as well as the most disruptive and messiest. Second fix is when the signs of normality begin to creep back into the picture: final finishes, fixtures and fittings and, lastly, decoration and floor coverings.

All building work is less of a rolling sequence and more of a jigsaw, where different trades have to work around each other, which tends to mean a certain amount of to-ing and fro-ing. Hence an electrician may come in early to lay cabling but will then have to wait until walls are plastered before returning to fit sockets and switches. In the interim, they may well be working elsewhere (work which may or may not proceed according to plan). But that is not the only reason why schedules can become stretched: there are also suppliers to take into account. If you are lucky, and the plasterer has finished by the time the plumber returns to fix the radiators on the walls, you will be very lucky indeed if the radiators themselves have been delivered on time.

Assuming that you have obtained the necessary permissions and finalized the design, the following is a general order of events. There may well be parts of the work, though, which require official inspection and approval (such as new drains) and these will need to be signed off before subsequent stages can take place.

First fix:

> Preparation, demolition and clearance: putting up scaffolding; clearing furniture and furnishings; protecting surfaces; propping up structures; demolishing walls; removing plaster.

> Earthworks and service connections: digging foundations and drainage trenches; laying new drains; making external connections to electricity, gas and telephone.

> Structural work: building new walls; laying solid floors; putting up roofing (structure and cover).

> First fix services: laying pipes and cables; installing boilers.

> First fix carpentry: framing doors and windows; making stud partitions; adding floor joists.

> Plastering.

Second Fix:

> Second fix services: installing radiators, sinks and baths; fitting socket covers and switches; connecting appliances.

> Second fix carpentry: hanging doors; fitting mouldings, skirting and architraves; fitting units and built-in features.

> Tiling and some types of floor finishes.

> Decoration.

> Flooring.

Designing fitted areas, such as this compact galley kitchen, demands a high degree of precision to make the most of the available space. Where layouts are essentially open plan, the quality of finish also assumes greater importance, since no areas are hidden behind closed doors. Here the glossy white surfaces emhasize the clean lines of the design and enhance the sense of space.

DECORATION

Decoration is essentially cosmetic. If you are rebuilding or reorganizing your home, decoration comes last in the sequence of events: the fun part after all the mess and disruption of making structural changes. On the other hand, if you are short of time and money, or if circumstances do not permit larger-scale alterations, decoration may be your only recourse when it comes to putting a personal stamp on your surroundings and making it feel like home.

When it comes to decoration, the choice of materials, finishes, colours and patterns on the market today is undoubtably intimidating. Even more intimidating can be the anxiety that you might get it 'wrong' and thus reveal a serious lapse of personal taste or judgement that will have the style police sniggering behind the latest issue of *Wallpaper**. But decorating your home can be fun, creative and fulfilling if you set your worries aside and take the plunge.

The first step is to know what you like. This may present the chronically indecisive with a tall order,

but most of us are able to point to at least some preferences in terms of colours, materials, or, in a more abstract sense, mood and atmosphere. Think about places you have visited in the past that have evoked strong positive responses, places where you could really imagine living, and try to identify the elements that inspired those feelings. A little creative wool-gathering allied with visual research trawling through books, interiors magazines or similar sources can help to bring such tastes into sharper focus. Assemble samples of decorative materials on a board to consider how they work next to each other before making your final decisions. Designers call these mood boards and they do indeed help you visualize the 'mood' you are trying to create.

Successful interiors – on any scale, on any budget – display passion and enjoyment, which means that once you have identified your preferences you should have the courage of your convictions and express them. Subsequently, if a colour doesn't work or if you decide you hate the bathroom flooring, you can always learn from your mistake and change it. But if you take the self-effacement rather than the self-expression route, you rule out any possibility of deriving true pleasure from your surroundings before you even begin. The best interiors are those that really express the personality of the owner.

THE DECORATIVE PALETTE

Colour, pattern and texture are the fundamental elements of the decorative palette. In many materials or surfaces, such elements are indivisible from one another; in others, one may predominate to the apparent exclusion of the others. There is no getting away from the fact that the point of a red wall, for example, is colour: here texture and pattern take a back seat. But in the case of a material such as marble, the striations and mottled patterning that run through the stone, its smooth polished surface and its characteristic tones and shades all contribute to the way we respond to it. For this reason, one of the best ways of coming up with a decorative scheme is to take a leaf out of the professional's book and assemble samples and swatches of all the materials and finishes that appeal to you and assess how they work together. Sample boards encourage you to think in terms of real choices – rather than abstract elements – right from the beginning of the process.

‹ Over-elaborate paint effects are well and truly out of fashion, but there are alternatives to plain single-colour finishes. A simple design of rectangles painted in chalky muted tones demonstrates how colour, texture and pattern can meet successfully to create a backdrop that is subtle yet full of impact.

› Colour can be used as a framing device, accentuating interior views. Here a hallway painted soft pink makes an effective contrast to the vivid yellow walls of the bedroom. Pale-blue painted floorboards provide a unifying element.

< Where colour is virtually absent in an interior, the textural qualities of different materials can provide visual interest and depth. Glass and metal furnishings – along with touches of black – provide graphic definition in an all-white decorative scheme.

∧ A mural of a porthole, marine life, waves and bubbles creates a beguiling ocean illusion on the walls of a child's bedroom.

< In open layouts there is no need to treat all four walls the same. Instead, colour can be used to pick out planes, enclose or define seating areas or simply for graphic effect.

> Every colour has its own emotional signature, inspiring a particular set of feelings and responses. Warm colours such as orange attract attention and are inherently cosy and reassuring.

A decorative scheme is all about the interplay of foreground and background. All schemes need unifying elements, which may be the colour of principal surfaces such as walls, or the main flooring material. But they also need accent and depth. Accent, delivered in small bursts of bright colour, busy pattern or robust texture, brings an interior into focus. Depth, chiefly provided by contrasting surfaces and materials, gives a sense of character and integrity.

Colour

A natural signifier, colour is a crucial means by which we process visual information about our surroundings. It is literally eye-catching: a recent study revealed that adding colour to documents increased the attention span of readers by 80 per cent. From physiological and psychological explorations of the link between colour perception and emotion or mood, to popular rules of thumb regarding the use of certain colours to remedy spatial drawbacks or improve the quality of light, colour has inspired much theorizing. Theory is all very well, but our reactions to colour are also intensely subjective, reflecting not only personal associations and preferences, but also cultural meanings and associations. Colour perception is strongly affected by the quality of both natural and artificial light. Make sure you view paint samples or colour swatches under different light conditions at different times of the day to judge their full impact.

> **'Warm' colours** Red, orange and yellow are 'advancing', which means they leap out at you. This is due to the fact that such colours correspond to the longer wavelengths of light and hence demand maximum adjustment from our eyes, a physical fact we interpret as stimulus or arousal. Warm colours make good accents; in larger doses, they generate a sense of cosiness and enclosure.
> **'Cool' colours** Blue, violet, blue-grey and blue-green are 'distancing'. All such short wavelength colours are inherently soothing. Cool colours enhance the sense of spaciousness but if the quality of natural light is poor they can be a little chilly.
> **Greens** These shades fall in the middle of the spectrum, and are the most restful colours of all because our eyes have to adjust very little to see them.
> **Natural colours** The subtle tones of wood, stone and earth evoke a sense of integrity which derives from their association with the natural world. The neutrals − white,

black and grey − can be used to provide definition and breathing space in colour schemes.

> **Complementary colours** Blue and orange, red and green, yellow and purple are complementary. One of the easiest ways of coming up with a colour scheme is to use complementary pairs in a range of tones from light to dark. The lightest shades can be used for backgrounds; the darkest or strongest for accents.
> **'Tertiary' colours** Terracotta and turquoise, which hover on the cusp between one colour and the next, have an edgy, luminous quality which adds a sense of vitality.

Pattern

Repetition is the essence of pattern and where there is repetition, there is also rhythm and movement. Many patterns, particularly figurative designs, have strong cultural or historic associations that instantly evoke specific periods or styles. Such overtones, which tend to demand an appropriate context, may explain why plain has triumphed over pattern in many modern interiors. Yet even the most reticent surroundings, on closer inspection, reveal patterning of a less deliberate nature − the spines of books on a shelf, for example, shadows of sunlight through a blind or the flecked surface of a granite worktop.

How you use pattern depends to a certain extent on the scale and nature of the repeat. Great pattern designers, such as William Morris, often designed patterns for specific applications. Flowing or branching motifs, for example, were intended for fabric, which hangs in soft folds; more orderly or symmetrical designs were for wallpaper, where pattern is displayed flat. New digital designs, where photographic imagery is transferred to tile, plastic, fabric or paper, display an intriguing tension between the realism of the image and its Warhol-esque use as a repeat.

> **Make pattern a feature** A beautiful rug, a single wall papered in a bold graphic design, a sofa upholstered in a rich print, or a patterned bedcover can provide visual accents in otherwise plain surroundings. Large or striking patterns need a great deal of breathing space.
> **Use pattern to add definition** A small-scale repetitive border can throw an expanse of plain tiling or flooring into relief by creating a focus.
> **Exploit regular geometric patterns** Spots, stripes, checks and plaids work in any kind of setting and also combine well with more figurative designs provided they feature one or more of the same colours.
> **Build up a layered look** Combine patterns that share similar colours or similar themes, but vary the scale of the repeat and complexity of the design.

Texture

Texture brings a physical dimension to decoration. It invites touch. Where much of daily life is experienced visually, if not 'virtually', texture has a powerful role as a means of grounding us in the here and now. It is difficult to think of texture without calling to mind a specific material, which is another way of giving a proposed decorative scheme a reality check.

Different textures not only feel different, they also sound different, look different and reflect the light in different ways. This all-round sensory package is what provides a sense of depth and character. By the same token, because the degree of comfort we feel in our surroundings is often a function of textural qualities such as smoothness, softness, roughness and resilience, textural variety is very important. Relentlessly hard, smooth and reflective surfaces can be noisy, tiring and unforgiving; where surfaces are uniformly soft and padded, on the other hand, the effect can be rather too embracing, if not smothering.

Texture particularly comes into its own in otherwise minimal or neutral schemes, where colour is muted and pattern non-existent. A variety of different textures, expressed in different surfaces and materials, provides the required punch that prevents the result from being bland and insipid. The shift from white painted plastered wall to white painted brickwork, or from sisal to beechwood underfoot, may be subtle but still has considerable impact.

PREPARATION

After you have done your research and come up with ideas that can be translated into tangible choices, there's one further hurdle: preparation. If you watch a professional decorator at work, you'll see how little time is actually spent applying the final coat of paint or sticking up sheets of wallpaper. What makes the difference between a good and bad job is largely down to what happens beforehand. Many people skimp on this stage of decorating because it is time-consuming and dull, but thorough preparation can make all the difference to the final result.

❮ A single wall painted in a simple design of overlapping oblongs demonstrates the use of pattern as an accent or focal point, with surrounding surfaces kept relatively plain.

⌃ Light streaming in through a window picks up the striated surface of a concrete-block wall. Textural variety is essential in otherwise neutral schemes.

⌐ The names of herbs spelled out in pebbles embedded in plaster adds a playful touch to a country kitchen. Natural materials such as wood, stone and terracotta have in-built harmony.

⌐ A contemporary twist on wallpaper: overlapping flaps and folds turn a simple background into something more sculptural.

❯ Digitally transferred photographic imagery is at the cutting edge of new pattern-making. Cork-backed tiles, sealed with vinyl to make them water-resistant, feature a range of images for a *trompe l'oeil* effect underfoot.

❯❯ The essence of pattern is repetition, whether it is of a printed motif, a mark painted directly onto a wall or floor, or more realistic elements, as seen here where copies of the same image have been clipped together to form a screen.

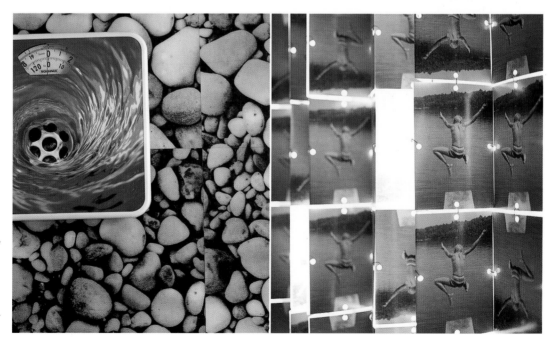

Walls and ceilings

> Clear the room or area as far as possible and cover everything that remains, including the floor.

> Brush down or vacuum surfaces to remove loose debris and cobwebs. Wash with a non-abrasive, non-foaming detergent to cleanse surfaces of grease and grime.

> Fill cracks and other surface imperfections with proprietary filler. Allow to dry, sand down and fill again, repeating the process until walls are level and smooth. If walls are really battered, you can either have them re-plastered, or try cross lining with lining paper: papering horizontally and then vertically to even out the wall.

> If you intend to paint the walls, first apply a thinned layer of undercoat. You may need several layers if you are painting over a strong colour.

Woodwork and floors

> Clear the room or area as before and clean thoroughly.

> If mouldings or other types of woodwork have become clogged with successive layers of paint, you may need to strip these off to restore crispness of detail, either using chemical strippers or a blowtorch.

> Fill holes with woodfiller and sand lightly once dry. If you are renovating or sanding a wooden floor, knock nailheads below the surface with a punch and secure any loose boards.

> Before painting, apply the appropriate primer, in one or two coats, sanding between applications.

PAINT

Paint transforms your living spaces instantly. Modern formulations are easy to apply and provide good coverage and adhesion. You can paint almost any surface, from plaster to wood, from metalwork to tile, but you must choose the right paint for the job and follow manufacturer's recommendations with respect to undercoating and priming. Standard paints broadly fall into two categories: emulsion (or water-based) paints and oil-based paints, which include metal paints, gloss and eggshell. Emulsion paint covers well and dries quickly but is not long-lasting; vinyl emulsion is recommended for kitchens and bathrooms where humidity may be an issue. Oil-based paints are more durable and easier to wipe clean.

Specialist paints are also available. These include milk or casein-based paints, distemper and limewash, which are made according to traditional recipes, as well as paints designed to simulate a specific texture, such as those that produce a 'suede' or 'denim' effect. Traditional paints need careful handling and there may be particular requirements in terms of the preparation of underlying surfaces – distemper, for example, will not adhere to a wall previously painted with a modern emulsion. It is also possible to buy eco paints made from bio-degradable ingredients; these have improved dramatically in recent years, both in terms of colour range and ease of use.

∧ If you choose the right type of paint, you can cover almost any surface. Here paint has been used to suggest the effect of a stair carpet on wooden boards; the distressed quality of the finish adding to the appeal.

< A kitchen wall picked out in a soft matt earth tone makes a subtle backdrop for a sleek modern kitchen with steel sink and appliances.

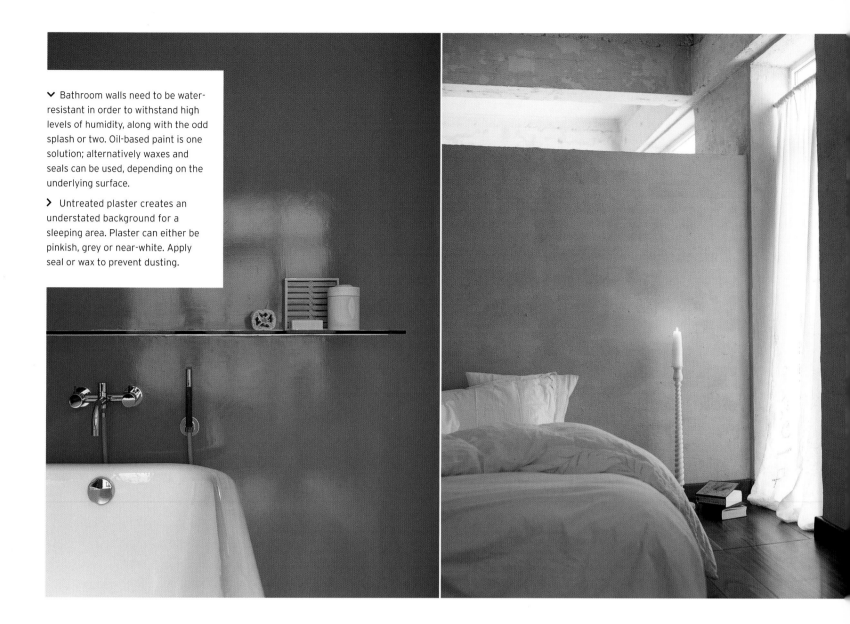

˅ Bathroom walls need to be water-resistant in order to withstand high levels of humidity, along with the odd splash or two. Oil-based paint is one solution; alternatively waxes and seals can be used, depending on the underlying surface.

＞ Untreated plaster creates an understated background for a sleeping area. Plaster can either be pinkish, grey or near-white. Apply seal or wax to prevent dusting.

Paint comes in an incredibly wide range of colours and a variety of finishes, from matt through to gloss. If you are daunted by the choice, the edited or themed palettes produced by manufacturers can be a good starting point. Tone – or the degree of lightness or darkness of a shade – can be difficult to judge. Some colours also have a tendency to 'mount up', or appear stronger and more intense over large areas than they do on paint charts or sample cards. A sample pot in each of your chosen colours is a good way of assessing the final result. It is important to paint patches of colour in different locations – on walls that get direct light and those that do not – and assess how they look at different times of the day.

To paint a room, start with the ceiling, working away from the main source of natural light. Then paint the walls, again working away from natural light, and in vertical sections from top to bottom. Doors, window frames and skirting boards come last.

PLASTER

With the recent rise in appreciation of material quality – effects that go deeper than superficial decorative treatments – plastered surfaces that speak for themselves have become increasingly popular. Bare plastered walls have a basic honesty and lack of pretension that can be very appealing both in clean-lined modern settings and in more rustic or countrified surroundings. Colour varies from a warm mellow pinkish tone reminiscent of old fresco, through pearly grey to near white, depending on the composition. It is also possible to self-colour plaster by adding pigment to the basic mix. Other textural effects can be achieved by scoring or combing the wet surface, by embedding small stones into it, or by rubbing it with metallic or marble powder. Bare plaster should be sealed with varnish or wax to prevent the surface from breaking down into dust and to provide resistance from water penetration and grease stains.

PAPER AND OTHER WALLCOVERINGS

Until recently, wallpaper has had a rather conventional image. Although the market tends to be dominated by traditional patterns with accompanying borders and friezes, an increasing number of chic contemporary designs (some downright tongue-in-cheek) are also available which can provide a graphic backdrop to more modern surroundings. As with paint, before you commit yourself to your final choice (and wallpaper, particularly the better quality wallpapers, can be expensive), it is a good idea, if you can, to get hold of a sufficiently large sample to assess what the pattern will look like on a large scale.

The most expensive wallpaper is hand-blocked. Because it is also hard to hang, you will probably need to call in a professional to tackle the job. Machine-printed papers come in a range of finishes which determine basic practicality; the most robust are vinyl coated which makes them suitable for humid locations. Wallpaper can also embrace those wallcoverings which are thin enough to be pasted to the wall in the same fashion: 'papers' made of wood veneer, woven grass or raffia, foil or metallic papers, thin sheets of cork, and other materials that simulate a fabric finish. All provide interesting textural effects and make good cover-ups for less than perfect walls. In fact, anything that can be stuck on a surface, from posters to construction paper, large photographic enlargements to maps, can be used to create an original collage.

Hanging wallpaper, as opposed to collaging, demands more skill and patience than painting – especially if you are dealing with a large pattern – if you have any doubts about your ability, you should hire a decorator or professional paper-hanger to do the job for you. For best results, the wall should already be covered in lining paper. Use the paste recommended by the manufacturer. Wallpaper expands after pasting, which means it has to be left for a few minutes before it is applied to the wall to ensure a smooth, wrinkle-free result. Some decorators also apply a thin coat of paste to the wall. Begin by hanging the first sheet in the corner of the room nearest the main window and work away from the direction of natural light. If the paper features a large pattern, however, you should centre the first sheet in the middle of the wall or above a fireplace and work towards the corners of the room where interruptions in the design will be more natural and much less noticeable.

FABRIC AND SOFT FURNISHINGS

With a host of applications, fabric literally 'dresses' the interior, in what style – tailored, classic, theatrical – and to what degree will affect overall mood and atmosphere, comfort, sound absorbency and, where window treatments are concerned, quality of natural light. Overly upholstered rooms swathed in drapery can be suffocating (and will hold stale odours for longer than clean-lined interiors) but a space devoid of any soft furnishings at all can be repellantly clinical.

There is a vast range of furnishing materials and equivalent scope for creative borrowing: saris, artist's canvas, sailcloth, suit fabrics and ethnic textiles are but a few of many successful departures that can be made from the soft furnishing norm. Like any other decorative element, practical considerations come into play: different weights, weaves and types of fibre give different results in terms of wear, maintenance and comfort (see pages 226–228).

Quick soft furnishing fixes include loose covers, throws, rugs, bedcovers, cushions, ready-made curtains and blinds, all of which can be obtained or made relatively inexpensively. More effort and/or investment is required for properly lined and headed curtains, tailored blinds and fitted upholstery, particularly where the fabric itself is of high quality.

∟ Modern photographic techniques expand the graphic possibilities of wallpaper. Some companies now provide a service whereby custom photomurals can be created from any image you supply.

︿ A burnished panel of gold leaf adds a luxurious, faintly Eastern touch to a clean-lined contemporary space, contrasting both in colour and texture with the blue panel.

┐ Graphic images and photographs clothes-pinned to lengths of string create an impromptu display in an all-white studio space.

≫ Natural fibres, such as cotton, linen and silk are particularly comfortable next to the skin. There is a huge range of applications for fabric in the interior, ranging from bedlinen to cushion covers.

❯ Familiar materials can gain new impact when used in an unexpected way. Here, sheets of cork have been applied to both walls and ceiling for a warm, textured (and highly sound-absorbent) effect.

⌐ The patina of an old, undecorated plaster wall, set off against the clean surface of white painted floorboards, creates a textured backdrop for an eclectic collection of furniture.

SURFACES AND FINISHES

Changes that entail new surfaces or finishes are technically within the scope of decoration, but are more permanent than simply painting walls or hanging curtains. Panelling a room in tongue-and-groove boarding, tiling a bath surround, installing new flooring, all imply material choices that must be made both in terms of appearance and basic practicality. Detailed information regarding specific materials is given in the Compendium (see pages 176–253).

Combining different materials in the same scheme is a sure way of creating a sense of vitality. Wood and stone, metal and glass, brick and tile are sympathetic pairings, but almost any permutation will work provided the materials in question deliver the appropriate level of practicality for the job they have to do. If you can't afford to install new surfaces, stripping away old finishes to expose underlying materials –

bare brickwork, for example, or sanded floorboards – can deliver the same sense of character and integrity. Where one material or surface meets another, it is important to make sure junctions and edges are neat and properly detailed.

A key surface is the floor. The floor has an immense impact on both the way an interior looks and the way we experience it. Running the same flooring throughout, or at least flooring of the same tone, will make a cramped space look bigger. A change of flooring – from linoleum to hardwood, for example – can announce a shift of activity in a large multipurpose space without the need for further definition. Floors take a beating where there is heavy traffic, such as hallways, entrances, stairs and kitchen preparation areas, and materials here need to be more robust than in bedrooms or living areas where comfort and warmth may be more of a priority.

∧ Orientated strand board (OSB), the cheap manufactured wood used widely to board up windows and shop fronts, makes an economic utilitarian surface behind gleaming stainless steel units and appliances.

< A steel spiral staircase, plastic pod chairs and pristine plasterwork work together to create a strong, futuristic look in this loft. Loft spaces, whose origins are industrial, call for a robust approach to surfaces and finishes.

˥ A hi-tech computer-controlled lighting system can be used to bring colour changes to an all-white house. Concealed blue, red and yellow colour-changing tubes mean that wall and furniture colour can be changed instantly by pushing a button or pre-programmed for a gradual shift from one shade to another.

LIGHTING

One of the simplest, yet most dramatic ways of changing your home is to improve the way it is lit, both artificially and naturally. The quality of light affects the way we feel in a very direct sense; it is also the means by which interior spaces and surfaces are described, revealing texture, accentuating volume and focusing attention on detail. In practical terms, both daylight and artificial sources are necessary for the performance of routine tasks as well as for more specific functions.

The most straightforward way of bringing more natural light into the interior is to avoid screening windows and other glazed openings; where privacy is required during daylight hours, translucent screening with filmy fabric, translucent blinds, etched glass or Perspex shutters will not appreciably lower light levels. Light-coloured decoration and furnishings, reflective surfaces and finishes, including mirror, also help to make the most of whatever direct light an interior space receives.

Improving artificial lighting is not a question of investing in expensive fittings or complicated technical kit; neither is it a case, as many people seem to believe, of making everything as bright as possible. Uniformly lit areas, particularly those that are lit from a single bright overhead source, lack all subtlety and vitality. By contrast, areas which have many different points of light are inherently animated.

Almost all areas in the home require a balance of ambient lighting, which is light we see by, and focused task light, which illuminates areas where work is carried out. Accent or decorative light, including light from fires and candles, enhances overall mood.

> **Create overlapping pools of light and shade** Increase the number of light sources in a given area and vary the heights at which lights are set to draw the eye from place to place.

> **Bounce light off reflective planes** Enhance volume and increase a sense of spaciousness by reflecting light off walls and ceilings. This type of soft, diffused background lighting can be achieved by uplighters, angled spotlights and directional wall-mounted fittings.

> **Avoid glare at all costs** Glare arises when there is too great a contrast between a light source and its surroundings; because it demands maximum adjustment from our eyes glare is both tiring and disturbing to live with. Shade bulbs so that the light source is not directly visible. Remember that three or four relatively dim lights can still deliver the same overall level of illumination as one moderately bright light, but will be more comfortable on the eye and will produce a much more atmospheric effect.

> **Restrict fixed lighting arrangements** Light fittings such as downlights should be kept to those areas where layout and arrangement is also fixed, such as kitchens and bathrooms.

> **Position directional task light with care** The light should be targeted at the tabletop, preparation area, desk or bedside in such a way that you do not work or read in your own shadow.

> **Build in flexibility** Plenty of power points, dimmer switches that enable you to adjust levels, centrally wired control panels, and lighting tracks with moveable spots are all ways of keeping lighting schemes adaptable to possible future needs.

﹀ A raised upstand around a kitchen preparation area screens the view of the counter from the rest of the open-plan space. On the opposite wall, fitted bookshelves constructed around a window opening merge with fitted storage and kitchen units. Accurate measurement, expert construction and attention to detail are essential for a successful result.

DESIGNING FITTED SPACES

There are fixed points in every home, even those that appear entirely organic. These might be appliances or fixtures relating to servicing arrangements, such as sinks, hobs and ovens; or baths, showers, basins and lavatories. At the other end of the scale are homes where not only bathrooms and kitchens are fully fitted, but also most of the storage and some of the furniture.

Designing fitted spaces requires thorough analysis and careful planning. Unlike decoration, where a leap in the dark or a sudden impulse can (sometimes) result in a serendipitous effect, and where mistakes are generally fairly economic and easy to reverse, fitted spaces do not happen by accident. A fitted area that doesn't look right or work properly will be a major vexation and one that is much harder to undo.

There are two sides to the equation. The first is the nature of the space at your disposal (its size, layout and existing features), and the second is what the fitted area is required to house or integrate. Bringing the two together in a coherent and workable whole is what you should try to achieve.

While you might have distinct preferences in this context, how far to fit out a space is not merely a question of taste. Fitted areas are generally more space-saving and space-enhancing than unfitted arrangements. A wall of seamless cupboards housing your entire wardrobe, for example, is potentially calm enough to still read as a wall. Storing clothing in free-standing 'unfitted' storage such as chests of drawers, clothes rails or wardrobes bites obvious chunks out of a room and inevitably makes it seem smaller. Similarly, the fitted route is almost always the best option if kitchen or bathroom areas are cramped.

Drawing a plan

A good starting point is to draw a scale plan of the area. When it comes to designing fitted spaces, most serious mistakes can be traced back to inaccurate measurement: that is, what is supposed to fit, does not. Scale plans allow you to experiment with different layouts until you find the optimum arrangement. They can also form the basis of a brief to retailers, designers, architects, contractors or other professionals.

> **Use one system of measurement throughout** It helps if the system you choose is the one most commonly used by suppliers and retailers. Kitchen units and appliances tend to be designed in modules of 600mm (24in), which makes metric an appropriate choice. But even if you find some elements are sold in imperial, others in metric, you must stick to one system or there is a possibility that mistakes will be made.

> **Start with a rough sketch** Take basic measurements of the area or areas and label your sketch with these dimensions, noting the position of major features such as windows, doors, fireplaces, partitions or alcoves, as well as servicing points.

> **Decide on an appropriate scale** Transfer the measurements to graph paper using a steel rule and a sharp, hard pencil, then decide on a scale you want to work to. For general living areas and bedrooms, a scale of 1:50 is adequate (where 2cm represents 1m or 1/4in represents 1ft). For more intensely fitted areas, such as kitchens and bathrooms, you may need to work at a scale of 1:20. Measure all the features previously noted on your rough sketch and mark these on the scale plan. Include the position of power points, light fittings, radiators and other fixtures.

> **Use templates to visualize alternative layouts** Work to the same scale and using the same system of measurement as you adopted for your scale drawing. Draw shapes of basic units, appliances or fixtures, cut them out and move them about on your drawing to experiment with different arrangements.

> **Draw elevations to assess the full impact** An elevation is a wall seen face on, drawn to scale in the same way as a floor layout. This may be a useful addition to scale plans to assess the overall fitted scheme.

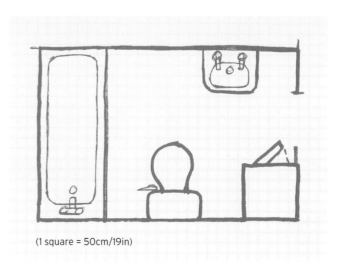

(1 square = 50cm/19in)

KITCHENS

Although bathrooms are fast catching up, kitchens are inevitably a major area of domestic expenditure. It is not simply a question of investing in appliances and equipment; even the simplest kitchen storage (be it fitted or unfitted) costs money, and surfaces and finishes can be very expensive.

Financial commitment is one thing; practicality another. Whatever your level of culinary skill or interest the kitchen must work well, which means that it needs careful planning.

Assessing your needs

The starting point in any planning process has the potential to be complicated. In many households, the kitchen increasingly accommodates a diverse range of activities which may have little to do with cooking; in others, the kitchen may need to be only a slightly more elaborate version of a coffee/microwave station.

> Are you an enthusiastic cook or do you eat out as often as you can? Do you regularly prepare large meals for the rest of the household or entertain frequently? Are you the sole user of the kitchen or is there another cook/helper in the house? The kitchen is defined by its principal function, which is to serve as a place where food is stored, prepared and cooked. But 'cooking' can be anything from pressing a button on a microwave to heat a TV dinner for one to slaving over a three-course sit-down meal for a dozen of your closest friends.

> How much storage space do you need? How often do you shop? Do you need a freezer or extra storage for bulk purchases? Do you need to store cutlery, china and glassware in addition to kitchen utensils, equipment and pots and pans? Do you need a larder?

> Do you want the kitchen to form part of an open cooking-dining-living area or would you prefer a more self-contained arrangement? Do you like everything on view or concealed in cupboards?

> Which other activities would you ideally like to accommodate in the kitchen? Do you need space for a designated eating area or laundry facilities? Does your kitchen serve as a domestic nerve centre, playroom or study area? Where do you do the dishes?

> Is your kitchen sited in the optimum place? How does it relate to other living areas, indoors or out? Is there sufficient natural light? If your existing kitchen feels cramped, is there potential to increase the space by knocking through to adjacent areas or adding an extension? Are there any planning or servicing restrictions which might limit potential changes? (see page 116)

> How long do you expect to stay in your present home? Will money spent on a kitchen be readily recouped in terms of increased sale value? What changes can you anticipate in your lifestyle over the next few years that you may need to cater for?

Kitchen planning

Planning matters far more than size when it comes to creating a functional, workable kitchen. Ever since the 1950s, kitchen planning has been based around the notion of the 'work triangle' – an ergonomic concept originally derived from research into improving industrial efficiency – with the three points of the

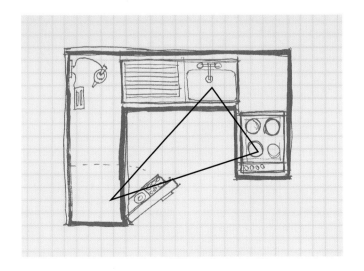

‹ This variation on the in-line kitchen layout features a worktop that spans an opening through to the adjacent living area. The arrangement, providing access to the counter from both sides, also serves to maintain a light, open feeling.

› Kitchens that are arranged along one wall can readily be screened from view. Here a glossy red sliding panel hides the kitchen from sight when not in use; the table doubles up as an additional preparation area.

﹀ Unfitted free-standing kitchen units placed side by side create an island in a large kitchen located in a loft, while a tall storage unit serves as a spatial marker defining the extent of the kitchen-dining area. Island kitchens tend to demand more space than other types of layout.

∧ Galley kitchens are the most space-saving. Here an array of shallow steel shelves provides room to store basic foodstuffs and condiments, an element of display in an otherwise sleek, fitted space.

<< Fitted units raised up on legs and framed by discreet flush-panelled wall cupboards give a kitchen the appearance of a piece of furniture. This type of reticent approach to kitchen design is ideal where the kitchen is sited within a living area.

< Deep custom-built open shelving creates accessible storage for items such as crockery and serving dishes which look good out on view.

> Double sinks and a generous expanse of worktop in this in-line kitchen layout allow two people to work together side by side.

⌐ Toplit by skylights and with a large window, this kitchen is sited to benefit from natural light. Glazed doors provide access to an outdoor eating area and a counter facing the garden also serves as a breakfast bar.

triangle corresponding to the three main kitchen activity zones: sink (or wet area), refrigerator (or cold area) and cooker (or hot area). This gives optimum distances between these three points so that work is carried out not only efficiently but also comfortably. The recommended overall distance, adding up each side of the triangle, is 6m (20ft), with no two points being less than 900mm (35in) apart. Kitchens vary in size, shape and consequently layout, which results in work triangles of different dimensions, but the basic principle can be applied in most situations.

Points to consider:

> If you are not starting from scratch and your kitchen is already plumbed, plan the layout around the position of the sink, as servicing arrangements can be disruptive and expensive to change. Given the opportunity, many people prefer to site a sink in front of a window − or on a counter or island facing outwards − since this eases any feeling of being cramped and provides natural light for the food preparation area. Other plumbed appliances, such as washing machines and dishwashers, should also be sited near the sink to simplify servicing.

> Dishwashing and stacks of dirty dishes can look messy and be noisy; try to screen it off if you eat in the kitchen.

> The main food preparation area − the longest stretch of worktop − should be located between the sink and the cooker. Make sure you plan to include adequate sockets for the type of small appliances − kettle, toaster, mixer,

juicer − which tend to be used in this area. Don't position sinks or cookers in corners − you need elbow room.

> Think about disposal of rubbish, ideally segregating it into organic and inorganic.

> Fridges and freezers should be located away from cookers and ovens or they will not work efficiently. There should be some worktop space nearby so that the fridge door does not have to remain open for long, or be opened frequently, while you transfer food in and out.

> Similarly, you need an area of worktop next to a cooker/ oven so that you are not forced to carry heavy or hot dishes any great distance.

> Take into account the clearance required by appliance doors. While storage units can be fitted with sliding doors to save space, the same is not true of appliances.

> Tall units should be sited at the end of the worktop so as not to interrupt the basic triangle.

> The standard worktop height is 900mm (35in), which is adequate for general food preparation. Although varying worktop height can look visually messy, you may need a lower surface, say 760mm (30in) high, for tasks that require pressure, such as rolling pastry or kneading bread, but a small stool is probably a better solution.

> The top of wall units should be no higher than 1950mm (76in) to minimize stretching, and with a distance of 450mm (18in) between their base and the top of the worktop. Store heavy or bulky items in base units.

> Plan kitchen lighting along with the layout. Fixed lights, such as downlights, should be positioned over the

preparation areas, making sure that you are not working in your own shadow. Lights fitted at the base of wall units can be a good way of lighting a worktop. Make sure there is also background illumination to avoid glare.

Basic layouts

The application of the work triangle results in a number of basic layouts that are suitable for areas of different sizes and shapes.

1 **Single-line** or **in-line layouts** arrange everything along one wall. You need at least 3m (10ft) of wall space; the layout should not be overly extended, however, or it will be tiring to work in. This type of layout works well in narrow or restricted areas.

2 **L-shaped layouts**, arranged on two flanking walls (or with a peninsula counter at right-angles to a wall), are flexible. One arm of the L can serve as a spatial divider in an open-plan area. Carousel units at the right angle avoid dead space.

3 **U-shaped layouts** make use of three walls and offer maximum storage and working area. There should be at least 2m (6 1/2ft) between the arms of the U; in large areas, ensure that the main work areas are grouped in a compact focus so that you do not have to travel far between them.

4 **Galley layouts**, with cupboards on facing walls, suit narrow or confined spaces and are efficient for single cooks. Allow a minimum distance of 1200mm (47in) between facing units for access.

5 **Island layouts** group some of the main kitchen functions at a central workstation; this type of layout requires the most floor area but is ideal for inclusive, sociable kinds of kitchen activity.

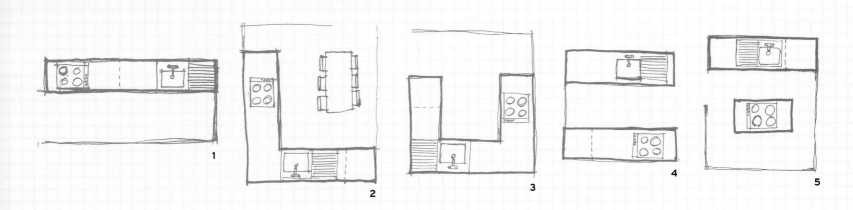

1

2

3

4

5

BATHROOMS

If kitchens are the sociable hub of the home, catering for many and varied activities, then bathrooms can be seen as the ultimate refuge. Today, the 'smallest room' mentality, which tended to result in a rather punitive type of functionalism, has given way to a more sensual, nurturing approach: bathrooms are where we go to look after ourselves and are thus expected to promote a feel-good factor over and above their role serving the necessary practicalities. In some upmarket homes, the bathroom has evolved into a cross between a home spa and private health club, with audio-visual entertainment piped in along with the jacuzzi, power shower and hot tub.

In terms of function, what the bathroom has to provide may be more limited in scope than the kitchen, but planning is no less critical. On the one hand, pressure on space often means that bathrooms and lavatories remain, if not the smallest, at least among the smaller areas of the home. At the same time, while most kitchen elements, from appliances to units, are in convenient and rectilinear modules, bathroom fittings and fixtures come in a wide variety of shapes and sizes, which adds an extra layer of complexity to spatial juggling. Servicing arrangements mean that bathrooms are necessarily fitted spaces: once fixtures are installed, options for change are more limited.

Siting

An early decision in the planning process concerns the siting of bathrooms, shower rooms and/or lavatories. One parameter in this respect will be drainage and plumbing arrangements. Lavatories need to be sited near existing soil stacks, which tend to be located on rear external walls, particularly in older properties. If you wish to move a lavatory to the other side of the house, rerouting drainage will certainly be expensive and difficult; you may also find that it is ruled out if there is insufficient fall for waste pipes. In houses with an upper storey, servicing runs are generally arranged vertically, which makes it both more practical and more economical to install a new bathroom above or below an existing one. In lofts and 'shell' conversions, one solution is to group servicing together at a central point, whereby kitchen, bathroom and shower areas form a service 'core'.

L Bathroom fittings and fixtures now come in a range of sizes, shapes, types and materials. These ceramic basins mounted on top of a fitted unit have a pure, elemental quality.

L Bathtubs made of unexpected materials such as wood, stone and concrete have great sculptural presence. Minimal fittings, such as the angled tap, pursue the elegant pared-back aesthetic.

∧ If you have enough space, siting the bathtub so that it makes a right angle with the wall creates a more dynamic layout than the standard arrangement whereby the long side of the bath is aligned with the wall.

∧ Bathrooms should be designed to promote a mood of relaxation. This ceramic tub is positioned with free space on all sides which creates a sense of calm contemplation.

∨ A natural progression from the en suite bathroom is the open-plan bedroom-bathroom, where the two are at most minimally separated. Here a glass box provides an enclosure for a shower and tub, keeping splashes and humidity away from the bed while retaining a sense of openness.

Another factor to consider is whether bath, basin and lavatory necessarily need to be in the same space. A separate lavatory, or an additional lavatory, can be a very good idea if your bathroom tends to become bottlenecked at busy times of the day; if you have limited space for a bathroom, this strategy can also make bathing or showering a more pleasant experience without taking up more floor area.

Bathrooms are generally used most at the beginning and end of the day, which means they are naturally bracketed with sleeping spaces. The 'en suite' bathroom, leading directly from the bedroom, facilitates the progression from waking to washing, or bathing to sleeping. This can be taken one step further by locating a tub or shower enclosure directly within a sleeping area, either out in the open or minimally screened by a half-height or half-width partition wall.

Planning the layout

All bathrooms – big, small or middling – need careful planning to integrate fixtures and fittings in the optimum way. When space is limited, every centimetre matters. Draw up a scale plan of the area, cut out scale templates of the sanitary fittings you would like to include and move them around on the plan to investigate different options. Bear in mind that it is not only the dimensions of the fittings themselves that you must allow for, but also the necessary clearance. This is the minimum margin of space that is required for comfortable and safe access and use. You also have to consider the water supply and the drainage, which will require a fall.

Typical dimensions:
> Lavatories: standard depth 700mm (27in), plus 600mm (24in) clearance in front.
> Bidets: standard depth 700mm (27in), plus 600mm (24in) in front and space to either side for legs.
> Baths: standard size 1700mm long x 700mm wide (66in long x 27in wide); clearance of 700mm (27in) alongside if sited lengthways.
> Showers: standard size 900mm x 900mm (35in x 35in), plus 700mm (27in) clearance in front.
> Basins: standard depth 400mm (16in), plus 700mm (27in) clearance in front and at least 200mm (8in) to either side.

Points to consider:

> Work out the position of the bathtub first. As the largest fixture, options for siting may be more limited. Basins are best positioned where there is good natural light for shaving and make-up; the lavatory best sited as far away from the bath as possible. Decide whether or not to further build in fittings by housing them in vanity units, or similar forms of boxing-in that incorporate storage. Many modern bathroom fittings have an elegant sculptural quality that invites full exposure – sinks in the form of glass bowls, for example.

> If you can't fit everything in comfortably, you might have to reconsider choice of fittings: forego the bidet or double basins, or substitute a shower for a bath. Smaller size fittings are another option, provided basic practicality is not compromised. Similarly, wall-hung sinks and lavatory pans take up less space than pedestal versions. Sliding or folding doors are a better bet than conventional doors that open inwards, while heated towel rails can provide enough background heat to avoid the need for an additional radiator.

> Where you have a lot of floor area to play with, you have the opportunity to come up with a more dynamic layout. Bathtubs that are centrally placed or positioned so they project at right-angles from the wall into the room mean that you can fully appreciate the spaciousness of your surroundings while soaking. Sunken baths and baths on platforms have similar theatrical impact.

> Many bathrooms are either awkwardly shaped or badly proportioned. Oval or corner baths may help if there are odd angles that have to be accommodated. Bathrooms that have been created by partitioning off a portion of an adjacent room tend to have very high ceilings in proportion to the actual floor area. Lowering the ceiling or part of the ceiling can give a much more comfortable result visually.

Showers

Nothing beats a shower for instant invigoration first thing in the morning or after a long stressful day. Showers are also an eco-friendly alternative to bathing, saving both water and energy. However, the type of shower you can install will depend on your existing water system.

> If the water pressure is low, you may need to install a pumped electric shower that uses water from a storage tank rather than directly from the mains.

> If your hot water supply comes from a combination boiler, there will not be sufficient stored hot water, so you will need an instant electric shower, which heats water from the mains as it is used. This is also the most economic type of shower.

> If you have sufficient stored hot water (a hot water cylinder), then you can choose between mixer showers, which take water from both hot and cold supply, and power showers which work in the same way but incorporate a pump to provide greater force.

Wet rooms

A relatively recent arrival in terms of bathroom design is the wet room, which returns bathing to its most elemental. A wet room is not so much fitted, as de-fitted, with shower heads draining directly to a sink hole in the floor and all surfaces fully waterproofed so there is no need for screens or cubicles.

A wet room layout makes particular sense if space is limited, since apart from the clearances required for lavatory and sink, the rest of the floor area is basically free. Wet rooms can be difficult to construct, though, due to the additional requirements of full water-proofing. Floors must be laid to slope to the main drain so that water does not remain on the surface. Depending on the nature of the underlying structure, you may also need to install additional waterproofing beneath whatever material you choose to clad walls, ceiling and floor to avoid any risk of water penetration.

Service cores

Grouping areas that share the same basic plumbing and drainage requirements into service cores makes practical sense, as well as offering the opportunity for more innovative spatial design. In open-plan spaces, a core comprising a kitchen area on one side and a bathroom or shower on the other is a good option. Such free-form arrangements can be given added impact where partitions are curved rather than rectilinear.

Service cores are a particular feature of contemporary loft design. Many unfitted shells that come on the market offer a choice of service points so you can decide where best to site such areas. With this type of blank slate, the position and design of the service core makes a good starting point for the rest of the spatial layout and can be detailed to include fitted storage areas as well. Remember that your service area may need inspection from time to time.

∧ If you have limited space, a wet room can be a good solution as it avoids the need for separate shower trays or screens. Key elements are fully waterproofed surfaces and a floor that slopes gently to a central drain. Depending on the structure and composition of the underlying walls, additional waterproofing may need to be installed.

⌐ A glass partition screens an open shower from the rest of the bathroom; on the other side a glass door opens onto an outdoor deck. Hardwood flooring gives way to slatted timber in the shower area to facilitate drainage.

❯ White mosaic set off by a green border creates a fresh, practical surface in a wet room. Mosaic is not particularly slippery underfoot due to the small scale of the grid.

❯❯ The type of shower you can install will depend on what type of water system you have. In areas where pressure is low you may need a pump. Power showers use a pump for greater force.

FITTED STORAGE

From basic shelving to entire workstations concealed behind articulated panels, fitted storage provides the organizational back-up that keeps life running smoothly. Not all fitted storage is invisible, but a key purpose, particularly in small spaces, is also to keep visual clutter to a minimum.

Possessions come in all shapes and sizes and there is no one organizational system that is going to work without a high and possibly impractical degree of customization – you cannot, for example file socks or shelve dresses. You need to review what you own, think about what you are likely to acquire more of in the future and consider how accessible such belongings need to be in order to come up with complementary and workable solutions. Ad hoc containers and catch-alls, along with various unfitted types of storage – bins, baskets, boxes, hanging rails, chests and trunks – work well for certain sorts of possessions and at less settled stages of life. Built-in arrangements, however, have a neater, more integrated appearance, offer the opportunity to decant belongings from living areas to between-spaces such as halls and landings, and bring a higher degree of order to everyday routines.

Before you begin to plan fitted storage, take the time to clear out what is redundant. If de-junking is often a painful process, stirring up a raft of emotions ranging from guilt over unsuitable impulse buys to low-level anxiety centred on the conviction that a particular item might come in useful one day, it can also be immensely uplifting. When you get rid of whatever is unused, unworn, unread and unwanted, you not only

free up space but also silence those niggling negative messages that possessions one doesn't really need have a habit of communicating.

The next step is to think about accessibility. While in general terms it makes sense to store like with like, and in close proximity to where such items are going to be needed, frequency of use also plays a key role in determining where things should go. Items used rarely or strictly seasonally, along with those belongings you never use but either must keep or can't bear to part with, can be removed from the picture altogether into some deep-storage arrangement in a loft, cellar or similar out-of-the-way location.

Working walls

Lifting clutter off the floor and other surfaces such as tables and countertops immediately generates a feeling of spaciousness. Working walls of shelving, whether screened or not, can accommodate a surprising number of possessions without impinging on spatial quality. The trick is to make a clear decision and to work within the existing architectural framework of your home. Line alcoves with shelves from top to bottom, or shelve an entire wall and the result will read as a coherent entity. Similarly, a low band of shelving running the length of the entire wall rather like a plinth can have great graphic impact and in itself contribute to the architectural organization of a space.

It may sound an obvious point, but shelves should be dimensioned and spaced according to the size and shape of the things you intend to store on them – it is too late afterwards to discover that half of your books won't fit or that your files cannot be stood upright.

⌐ Shelving looks best when it is conceived wholeheartedly, so that it almost appears to form part of the structure. Neatly integrated into a gable end, these shelves contain books, CDs and a music system.

« In-between spaces, such as the area under the stairs, which would otherwise go unused, are prime candidates for fitted storage. Here deep drawers are seamlessly integrated into a wooden staircase.

‹ Shelving lining the walls of a stair or hallway can decant a great deal of clutter from living areas – and it is easy to reach the upper shelves.

› A fully articulated storage system slotted into a converted Alpine barn comprises roll-out shelving hidden behind flush wooden panels, along with fold-down furniture. A hinged desk folds down from one of the cabinets; a double bed from another.

◀ A high-ceilinged room provides the opportunity to build in tall cupboards concealed behind flush panels. Open shelving integrated below a worktop in the kitchen area is reserved for visually appealing items.

∧ A glass door screens a wardrobe cleverly fitted into the space under a sloping roof. Whether you are buying a storage system off the peg or having one built to your own specification, it is important to know how much space you are going to need for folding, hanging or stacking clothes. Shirts, jackets and skirts can be double-hung to make the most of space.

∟ Wood-framed Perspex panels hide a fitted wardrobe from view. The detailing of fitted storage contributes to the success of the result. Fitted clothes storage is much less obtrusive than free-standing pieces such as chests of drawers.

◀ Storage needs to be readily accessible, otherwise you will tend not to use it and clutter will begin to accumulate elsewhere. Shelves or units that are moveable make it easy to retrieve items or return them to their rightful place. Here books are stored on rotating shelves.

⌐ Losing a certain amount of floor area in order to build in cupboards and concealed shelves can result in a better quality of space, particularly in open-plan areas such as this loft. Sliding panels screen cupboards, drawers and a wall-mounted television In this bedroom area.

It both looks better and is more practical from an access point of view if you design shelving so that larger items are stored lower down.

There is a wide range of shelving systems on the market, including various versions of the popular vertical track and bracket type. Many of these are adjustable so that you can tailor the system to what you're storing – really only an advantage at the outset, since adjustable shelves rarely subsequently get adjusted. All such systems, as well as custom-built shelving, require proper anchorage, preferably into solid walls, as well as shelves of the appropriate material, span and thickness to support the weight of what you put on them without sagging.

A working wall that is screened with sliding partitions, pull-down blinds or flush doors can be the ideal solution for storing not only the items you do not particularly want on view, but also disparate collections of things that lack the visual harmony of a collection of books, for example. Wide hallways and other connecting spaces adjoining main living areas are good locations for such storage.

Fitted clothes storage ranges from relatively simple variations on the working wall theme to highly sophisticated upmarket systems that can be tailored to your individual specification. The average person's wardrobe holds such a diversity of things that such an approach can be far less intrusive and more space-saving than attempting to solve the problem with a number of individual solutions.

Storage rooms

Self-contained areas entirely devoted to storage have an undeniable appeal. Larders and pantries, dressing rooms and linen closets evoke an era when people could afford to be so generous with space they didn't actually have to live in all of it. But such arrangements, scaled down perhaps, can still make practical sense today. Partitioning an existing room in a such a way as to make a separate dressing room may well lose you no more actual floor area than standard free-standing items of clothes storage – wardrobes, chests of drawers, and the like – might otherwise occupy.

Fitted units

Modular or fitted units tend to be produced in standard sizes, both for ease of integration with other elements (in the case of kitchen units, with appliances) and for

efficiency of manufacture. It is important to bear in mind when you are purchasing such units that you are literally buying space, which means you need to consider whether it will best accommodate what you need to store in it. Manufacturers recognize the fact that one size doesn't fit all and many units are available with flexible, adjustable shelves, interior baskets or trays, or other similar means of customizing the basic box. Many contemporary kitchen units don't have 'kitchen' written all over them and can usefully double up as fitted storage in other parts of the home. Robust steel-base and wall units extend the same idea to areas such as home workshops and garages.

Fully-fitted spaces

In open-plan areas where different activities come up against each other, fitting out as much of the space as possible with fold- or flap-down surfaces, shelves, drawers and even foldaway beds concealed behind flush panels can bring an element of flexible shape-shifting to spatial arrangements. Such a high degree of articulation demands custom design and specification. Ease and smoothness of operation is a must if you are going to be reconfiguring space on a daily basis, which means ensuring doors, drawers and panels fit properly and slide or pull out effortlessly without sticking.

< Room for manoeuvre

When the architect-owner moved into this small basement flat with his family, it was only intended to be a stop-gap until they built a new house on a nearby site. But when their new-build plans came to an abrupt halt, he turned his creative attentions closer to home. Through clever structural rearrangement and extending into the outdoor yard, he managed to increase the floor area by half as much again, as well as create an entirely new sense of space.

In its original state the flat was subdivided into a series of small rooms, making it dark and poky. In an arrangement typical of many conversions of Victorian terraces, the corridor alone took up 20 per cent of the available floor area. The owner came up with a scheme that involved a complete overhaul and, to make the whole process easier, the family moved into a rented flat so that the builders had room for manoeuvre.

The entire interior was reconfigured. Most of the internal walls were demolished to open the space up as much as possible and absorb the redundant corridor. At the front, an old coal cellar was turned into a sunken bathroom. At the rear, the property was extended halfway into the outdoor yard to create a new kitchen, now fitted with an electrically operated glass roof so that on summer days this area still feels like it is outside.

Other design strategies maximize the feeling of spaciousness. The opening between the new living-dining area and kitchen runs floor to ceiling so that the plane of the ceiling carries through both spaces. Fitted storage built into every area takes care of clutter and light reflective finishes, including the polished rubber flooring, accentuate the open, airy quality.

Moving internal walls around, reconfiguring patterns of circulation, adding windows or other new openings, carrying out conversions and adding on extensions take home improvement into a new dimension. Many, although not all, of the alterations detailed in this section entail structural change, which always requires professional help. Even if what you are planning does not require outside assistance, you may still need advice to be certain of that fact.

Sketches, scale plans, CAD (computer aided design) diagrams and other visual aids are invaluable when it comes to assessing the impact of any kind of spatial change to your living spaces. Use such drawings to plot circulation routes around your home, marking on the orientation of each area – where natural light is good and where it could be improved – and the relationship of indoor areas to outdoors.

From time to time stories surface in the media of overly enthusiastic home-improvers who find their home teetering on the brink of collapse after removing one wall too many. Knowing the difference between a structural or supporting wall and a non-structural partition, and understanding a little about the different types of construction can help you avoid a similar fate.

Masonry

Many older houses, particularly in Europe, are of masonry construction, either built of bricks and mortar or stone; newer versions use concrete block. The terraced house is a typical example of this building type. In this kind of structure, the weight of the roof rests on the outside or external walls, which also support the floors that span between them. Some internal walls also play a structural role. In turn, the combined weight of roof, walls and floors rests on the foundations. The roof and floors help to brace the entire structure and give it rigidity.

Making any major change to an external wall will entail the substitution of a compensatory element so that the wall can still perform its supporting role. In practice, this means that losing a portion of wall to form a window or doorway or larger opening will require the installation of a beam or lintel above the opening so that the load is still carried.

Internally, the key distinction is between structural or load-bearing walls and partitions that merely serve as spatial dividers. If your house has timber floors, one way of determining which walls are structural and which are not is to look at the direction of the floorboards. In terraced properties, floorboards generally run across the house from side to side, with the joists that support them running from the front of the house to the back. Any wall that is parallel to the direction of the floorboards will be supporting the joists of the floor above and is therefore structural. If you want to remove all or part of this wall you will need to install a beam to carry the floor above.

Timber-frame

A high proportion of houses in North America and an increasing proportion of newer houses in Europe are timber-frame. Many timber-frame houses are clad in other materials – including brick – so it is important to be aware that appearance alone is not necessarily an indication of underlying structural type.

There are many kinds of timber-frame construction. Modern methods generally involve forming external walls out of framed timber panels, with the entire structure covered by a roof system composed of individual trussed rafters. The framed timber panels are often prefabricated off-site which means that they can be assembled quickly, minimizing any possible disruption due to bad weather. In 'platform frame' construction, wall panels are storey-height; those on the ground floor provide a support or platform for the floor above in addition to the upper wall panels. Many prefabricated or kit extensions are of timber-frame construction. Altering a timber-frame structure entails getting advice from an engineer or an architect who specializes in this type of construction. As with masonry construction, making openings in external walls will have a structural impact on your home.

Steel-frame

Modern steel-framing techniques result in very light and minimal structures. With the steel columns and beams doing all the structural work, walls themselves can simply be infills, even fully glazed to provide transparent boundaries between indoors and outdoors. Steel framing creates free internal layouts unimpeded by supporting columns or walls: partitions and other spatial dividers can potentially go anywhere.

SERVICING

Your home's infrastructure – that is, how it is serviced by heating systems, electricity, communication and drainage – is just as important as its structural framework. Many spatial changes also entail changes to servicing arrangements or extension of existing systems to new areas. If you are planning major building works, it can be worth taking the opportunity to upgrade or review existing services at the same time. Both planning the work and carrying it out are jobs for professionals and you may also need to have changes approved by the relevant utilities boards or by a building inspector. Connecting up to a mains supply – whether gas, water or electricity – is always the job of the utility.

How your home is serviced not only has implications for your comfort and wellbeing but also has an impact on the environment as a whole. In Britain, for example, one quarter of total carbon-dioxide emissions is the direct result of domestic energy consumption. Energy and water efficiency helps minimize environmental damage while keeping household running costs to a minimum. New 'smart' forms of technology can play a part in reducing or managing consumption, but low-tech solutions are equally effective and easy to implement whatever your circumstances.

Heating

Most domestic heating systems work by converting fuel into heat in a boiler or furnace and then distributing it throughout the house, either in the form of hot water piped to radiators or hot air ducted to grilles. Alternative or supplementary heating may be supplied by space heaters, gas fires, fireplaces or wood-burning stoves.

Points to consider:

> Upgrading a system and investing in a new energy-efficient boiler can cut expenditure dramatically and improve energy efficiency by ensuring energy is only consumed when required. You may also need a new boiler if you substantially increase the demand on a system by extending it into a new area.

> The most efficient boilers are condensing boilers which reclaim heat from exhaust gases. Combination boilers that heat water from the mains do not require either hot-water cylinders or cold-water cisterns.

> The siting and number of radiators/heat emitters installed is a critical issue. Consult a heating engineer to achieve the optimum arrangement.

> Thermostatic control, either via a central thermostat or individual thermostats fitted to radiators, allows precise control and minimizes wastage. Programmable controls that follow your patterns of use also increase efficiency.

> Improving insulation can cut energy needs by two-thirds. Insulate external walls, roof spaces, ground floors, hot-water cylinders and pipes. You can also weatherstrip doors and windows.

> Underfloor heating can be very efficient, especially when combined with massive flooring materials such as stone that retain heat for longer and release it slowly over a period of time.

> Strict controls regulate the position of meters, the siting and ventilation of boilers, the siting of flues and exhaust vents, and the type, routing and dimension of pipes and wiring.

Electricity

Alterations to existing electrical arrangements should always be carried out by a qualified professional electrician. Electricity is potentially lethal; controls and regulations vary from country to country, as do wiring systems. Generally, power is routed around the home in a number of fused circuits. There will be circuits for power points, others for lighting and single circuits for individual appliances such as cookers. Ideally, wiring systems should be checked every five years; systems more than 15 years old may need replacement. If a fuse blows on a regular basis, this could well be a sign that there is a fault in a particular circuit. Rewiring will entail disruption to walls, ceilings and floors and is best carried out in tandem with other works to minimize disruption. Plan systems so that there are sufficient power points to avoid trailing cables or overloaded sockets.

Ways of saving energy:

> **Save on lighting** Use low-energy light bulbs and switch off lights when you leave the room. Similarly, switch off electronic equipment rather than leaving it on standby.

> **Upgrade appliances to new energy-efficient models** Certain appliances are more power-hungry than others. Fan or radiant heaters, washing machines, cookers, grills, dishwashers, kettles, driers and irons, all of which incorporate heating elements, use more energy than motor-driven appliances such as vacuum cleaners.

> **Switch to a green energy provider** These supply energy from renewable sources such as wind or hydro-power.

> Eco Extension

Building with ecological concerns in mind does not mean you have to sacrifice aesthetics; in fact, the two can and should go hand in hand. The elements that make this extension 'green' also serve to maximize the quality of life – good natural light and air, comfortable heating and a sense of being in touch with nature create a pleasant, optimistic environment.

The entire structure is built as a 'breathing wall' construction, which allows air to permeate through the walls, reducing condensation and creating a healthier interior. Timber stud walls are insulated with recycled newspaper. The ceiling and floor are also heavily insulated, and a new proprietary steel sheeting system used on the roof allows air to trickle through into the ceiling void. The levels of insulation mean that much less energy is needed to keep the whole space warm.

Underfloor heating, combined with the thermal mass of the concrete floor, is both pleasant and energy-efficient. Heating the floor for a couple of hours in the morning and evening is enough to keep the house warm – the concrete absorbs the heat and radiates it slowly when the heat is turned off. Hot water is supplied from an energy-efficient condensing boiler.

A substantial amount of the budget went on high-specification windows, skylight and sliding doors. Low-e argon-filled double-glazed windows with built-in trickle ventilation allow maximum natural light into the interior without heat loss or condensation.

Timber is also used to clad the exterior of the extension, in this case larch, which is highly resinous and can resist weathering for decades without being painted or chemically treated. Kitchen units are made from zero-formaldehyde MDF and all the appliances were chosen for their energy efficiency. Rainwater is used to wash windows or for garden irrigation; low-flush toilets further reduce water use. With kitchen waste recycled into compost via a wormery, this is green living in the round.

> **Consider investing in a solar energy system** New developments mean that systems are now capable of meeting most domestic power needs for water heating and running appliances. Thermal solar energy systems, which use solar collectors to heat water, are ideal for supplying hot water in houses located in warm climates or for heating swimming pools. Photovoltaic collectors, typically available in the form of solar panels or solar roofing slates, work even in cool, cloudy locations. Specialist design and installation is necessary. Such systems are expensive but some lenders now provide solar mortgages so that cost can be spread over time.

Water and drainage

Mains water supply generally enters the home via a rising main which feeds both the cold-water kitchen tap and a storage cistern, typically located in the attic space. All other cold-water taps, the hot-water cylinder (if any) and lavatories are fed by pipes from the cistern. Waste water from sinks, lavatories, baths and basins is drained either to the main sewer or to a septic tank (which requires pumping at regular intervals). Sewage from lavatories on ground level drains directly to the main sewer; waste from upper levels feeds into a vertical ventilated soil stack and thence into the main drains. In order to prevent smells, waste reaches the drains via a trapped gully with a water seal.

Points to consider:

> New drainage arrangements need to be approved by the appropriate inspector.
> There should be a stopcock inside your home so that you can turn off the mains supply in case of a plumbing emergency. There will also be a Water Board stopcock outside between the water main and the rising main. Make sure you know where both are located.

> Simple layouts are best. Blockages are more likely to occur where plumbing is overly complicated, where there is insufficient fall and where there are many branched connections or changes of gradient or direction. There should be access points at various locations to enable blockages to be cleared easily.
> Insulate pipework under the floorboards at ground level and in the attic to reduce the risk of burst pipes. If you leave your home unoccupied during the winter make sure a level of background heat is maintained to prevent pipes from freezing.
> Water is a precious natural resource. Good ways of conserving water include taking showers instead of baths, installing low-flush lavatories, and fitting flow regulators to taps and shower heads. Metering your supply can help you keep track of your water consumption. Don't leave taps running – a running tap sends nine litres of clean water down the drain per minute. Fix all dripping taps, worn washers and faulty valves.

THE SMART HOUSE

Interactive, programmable technology has the potential to transform the entire home into a communicator, with networked appliances, computers, TVs, music, security, lighting, heating – and even curtains – responding to remote commands delivered via mobile phone or keypad. Fridges that know when you are running out of butter and restock via the internet; washing machines that self-diagnose faults and dial up the part and the plumber; heating systems that pay bills via remote metering; curtains that close themselves when you are kept late at the office... are all science fact, not fiction. New housing developments, and not merely those at the luxury end of the market, are increasingly designed to be 'future-proof', with integral cabling systems that facilitate precisely this type of domestic electronic networking.

The networked or blue-toothed home may sound like a futurist's dream but then electrified houses must have appeared no less revolutionary a century and a half ago. The key issue is not feasibility or cost but whether such technology can really deliver both convenience and savings. Internet-linked fridges, for example, still mean that you have to remember to register bar codes as you take food and drink out and there is no point activating a washing machine from the office if you haven't loaded it first. Those who still rely on their school-age children to programme the

video recorder may not necessarily welcome a host of new gadgets into their home, each with its own indecipherable instruction manual. What you really need to consider is if all this complex technology makes your life easier and more pleasant. Also consider its cost and the inconvenience that may be caused by expensive breakdowns. Where networking is proving increasingly popular, however, is in the seamless integration of home entertainment: having the internet, music, video and TV piped into all areas – not merely confined to a single media centre – goes hand in hand with open-plan living and flexible, interchangeable spatial layout.

INTERNAL REARRANGEMENT

Walls are boundaries. They contain or demarcate activities; separate indoors from outdoors, public spaces from private; and shape the routes we take from one area to another. Moving or removing internal walls and partitions may not make your home any bigger, but it can still enhance the sense of space and eliminate wasted or unused space, improve natural light, and simplify both function and circulation.

Designation

The very simplest form of internal rearrangement is simply to change the way you allocate different rooms or areas. Conventional planning of a storeyed house sites the kitchen at the lowest level, living areas at the level above or immediately adjacent, and bedrooms at the top. Turning the layout upside down can make sense if lower ground floor areas are dark – bedrooms are essentially nighttime spaces and the quality of natural light is less critical here. In a family home, as children grow, a certain amount of juggling in terms of who gets which bedroom may be inevitable.

Circulation

Where there is a choice of access to a particular room or area, you may well find that you tend to use one entry or doorway rather than another. Blocking up the under-used entrance can win you additional wall space which, in a living area, might come in useful for siting large pieces of furniture, or in a kitchen for extending a worktop or run of units. Alternatively, you might find that a doorway could be better located to simplify main traffic routes and facilitate routine chores such as unloading shopping or taking out the rubbish.

┌ Solar technology producing free energy from the sun for domestic requirements has improved tremendously in recent years. New photovoltaic collectors, available in the form of panels or roofing slates, are much less obtrusive than previous bolt-on elements. Systems are expensive and require expert installation but environmental benefits are significant.

⌃ Multipurpose spaces, such as this living-dining-kitchen area, need some element of separation between activities. Here a half-height partition screens the kitchen area and provides a focus for the dining table.

⌃ A large internal opening in a dividing wall maintains the spacious feeling of an open layout while keeping a kitchen separate from the living area. Before knocking through or demolishing walls, it is important to get advice from a surveyor or structural engineer.

Open-plan

By far the most common spatial change is to take down internal walls to provide a free flow of spaces. All-embracing, open-plan layouts have grown steadily in popularity along with the sort of lifestyle changes that have spelled the virtual end of formal dining and the promotion of the kitchen to centre stage. Bear in mind, however, that some balance is still required between open areas and more enclosed private spaces: even the most die-hard enthusiasts of loft living feel the need to retreat once in a while. Also remember that open areas are harder to heat and inevitably noisier, which may have implications for your servicing arrangements and choice of finishes. Underfloor heating, for example, can be a better form of heating than using radiators.

There are various options for opening out the layout, from knocking adjoining rooms together to taking down walls that separate living areas from hallways and stairs. The complexity and expense of such changes depends on whether structural walls are involved. It is not always easy to tell which internal walls are structural and which are not: seek advice before calling in the demolition squad. Removing all or part of a structural wall means you will have to restore its load-bearing capacity by installing a beam, steel joist or concrete lintel above to span the new opening (see page 149). You will need professional advice from an architect, engineer or surveyor to ensure that the reinforcing member is the right size for the job. The work may also need approval from a building inspector.

Partitions

Creating new partitions has no structural implications; building work is generally straightforward and no official permissions are required. Here it is more a question of paying attention to siting and access, scale and proportion, and the design of the partition itself.

'Habitable' rooms – all areas except bathrooms, kitchens and circulation areas – must have at least one window, so the position of existing openings will have a bearing on the way you partition space. So, too, will access. Unless the partition serves to divide two areas that are naturally adjoining, such as a bedroom and dressing area or bathroom, you may lose a certain amount of floor area creating separate doorways to the new rooms. Once a large, high room has been subdivided, the new areas may appear proportionately too high and you may need to lower ceilings for a visually comfortable result.

A partition need not be a solid wall. More subtle dividers separate different activities while retaining a sense of openness. Stopping a partition short of the ceiling or short of the walls to either side may be all you need to create privacy and enclosure. Translucent materials such as Perspex, glass and glass block allow light to spill through from area to area; flexible dividers such as free-standing foldable screens, sliding screens or folding doors keep all options open.

Light and air

Internal rearrangement can spread natural light and air to areas of your home that otherwise wouldn't receive it by removing those walls or partitions that stand in the way. But to increase natural light, improve ventilation and forge new connections to outdoor areas, you will need to enlarge existing external openings or create new ones.

Most of these changes are structural and require professional assistance. The exceptions are increasing the size of a window by dropping the sill and losing the portion of wall underneath; and, in most cases, installing skylights or rooflights. All other alterations to external walls entail putting in a structural member (beam, lintel or joist) to span across the new opening.

Orientation is a critical factor. New openings on walls that face the sun will flood the interior with light but may also cause overheating in warm months. Adding a window on a wall at right angles to an existing opening can have a far more dynamic effect

‹ Partitioning space generally has no structural implications, but it is important to site the partition so that the resulting new areas are well proportioned and easy to access. Here a curved glazed wall separates a bedroom and bathroom.

› An electronically controlled glass roof, which can be fully retracted on fine days, brings natural light and fresh air down into the heart of a home. Glazed walls to the upper storey, which wraps around the central atrium, make the most of light and internal views.

⌄ Lofts offer the opportunity to configure space in a variety of ways. The only necessary fixed points are where the services are located. In this case, a box-like structure houses the kitchen area, a variation on the service-pod idea.

than adding one alongside and creates through drafts. Positioning windows and other openings such as toplights in line with prevailing winds will have a positive and invigorating affect on air flow; in hot countries, sensitive siting of windows and doors can obviate the need for air conditioning.

LEVELS

Changes to levels demand a rather different type of spatial thinking. Whereas internal rearrangement is chiefly concerned with layout, changes to levels involve the consideration of what architects term 'volume'. As with internal reorganization, changes to volume won't necessarily win you more space per se, but they can radically alter your experience of it.

You can plot layout changes on a horizontal plan or sketch of floor areas, but assessing volume means thinking about 'section'. A section is a diagrammatic representation of a vertical cut through a building – the same sort of view you get if you take the front off a doll's house. While the difference between a low-ceilinged room and a double-height space can be instantly appreciated, it is difficult to envisage the full impact of changes to volume without architectural or design training, but computer-generated diagrams of your home can help you get to grips with it.

Some changes to levels are structural and hence require professional advice and design; some are not. Any alteration that directly affects the floor (removing or repositioning either all or part of it) has structural implications; the same is true of inserting a new level, such as a mezzanine, because this will increase loads on existing walls. Lowering a ceiling or raising up an area of floor to create a platform, on the other hand, is not structural work because you are merely suspending from or building on to the existing floor.

Most average homes don't have enough square metres going spare to merit the loss of an entire floor merely to create the dramatic uplift that a double-height space delivers. If, however, you have an under-used attic of rather less than head height, you might consider opening a top-floor space right into the roof. The addition of skylights will enhance the overall sense of expansiveness.

Lofts offer the greatest potential for volumetric changes since most have much higher ceilings than conventional domestic homes. High spaces offer the opportunity for vertical subdivision, either by creating a platform or by adding in a mezzanine area or gallery to accommodate those activities such as working or sleeping that require a greater degree of enclosure.

Size and siting of the new level is critical. A simple sleeping platform does not require full head height and may need to be little bigger than a mattress with a little clearance space around the perimeter. A mezzanine or gallery level, however, must be extensive enough to function properly for the use to which it will be put, but not so extensive that you lose the uplifting quality of the space as a whole; neither should it be positioned where it will block light from existing windows. It is also important to think about the area underneath the new level and how best it might be used. Devoting the area underneath a mezzanine to serviced or fitted spaces such as kitchens, bathrooms and fitted storage can help to leave main living spaces clear and unencumbered.

A new level requires a means of access. Minimal but rather challenging options include built-in or pull-down ladders; spiral stairs are less likely to inspire vertigo but are almost as space saving. Open flights of stairs or those cantilevered out from the wall won't interrupt views to any significant extent.

CONVERSIONS

Short of adding on an extension – or moving house – converting an attic or basement area may be the only way of directly increasing the amount of space at your disposal. Although attic or 'loft' conversions are generally simpler and hence less expensive than basement conversions, both require a considerable investment of time and money. Before you go ahead, compare the price of the work with what it would cost to move somewhere bigger. If you are otherwise happy with your home, and there isn't a great deal to choose between the two options in terms of cost, a conversion can be a good solution, particularly as it is bound to add value to your property, but be prepared for the inconvenience that building work will cause.

Attic conversions

One of the most popular forms of home improvement, attic conversions can dramatically ease pressure on space. Roof spaces are inherently quirky, offer the potential for good natural light through rooflights and dormers and are remote enough from the rest of the household to make excellent self-contained retreats.

∧ Double-height spaces can be subdivided vertically without losing their inherent sense of volume. A metal-framed mezzanine level incorporating a glass walkway allows the full height of this space to be read. The kitchen fitted underneath is only partially screened from the main living area, with a large circular window framing internal views. The shift from living to cooking areas is underscored by a change of flooring from hardwood to tile.

❯ A mezzanine makes an ideal location for sleeping or working. In a high-level bedroom, the generous rooflights and curve of the exposed cast-iron structure create a light-filled space with a great sense of character.

Before you begin work on your roof space, think about how you might use the new space you will be gaining. If you need an additional bedroom or a separate area for working, it does not necessarily follow that the converted attic should be put to that purpose: re-juggling rooms or areas throughout the house may suggest different options.

For simple attic conversions you might consider buying a loft conversion kit which will supply all the necessary components, from rooflights to access ladders. If you are after a more finished result, it is a good idea to consult an architect or a building firm specializing in such work, not least because they will be able to negotiate any official planning permissions and approvals on your behalf.

The roof structure will dictate whether an attic conversion is feasible. Older properties generally present few difficulties, but newer homes often have pre-formed roof trusses which effectively rule out this option completely. A related issue is how much usable floor area the attic provides. Floor area is generally calculated as that space at which the roof is a minimum of 1.5m (5ft) above the floor; in some areas, regulations stipulate that at least half of the floor area in the converted space must have a head height of 2.3m (7¹/2ft). You can increase floor area by adding a dormer window, but a certain degree of space will always be lost under the eaves where the roof slopes to meet the walls. If there is insufficient head height, even with the addition of a dormer window, the only option may be to lower the floor, which increases the scope of the work, as well as impinging on the spatial quality of rooms in the storey below.

A key consideration will be to provide access to the new area. Folding loft ladders are fine if you only intend to use the loft occasionally, otherwise a more permanent arrangement is necessary. Fitting in a new staircase, however, can result in the loss of floor area in the storey below or at least a certain amount of reorganization of layout.

In order to count as a habitable room, the converted space must have at least one window. Rooflights that lie in the plane of the roof are a popular option; pivoting designs facilitate cleaning and general maintenance as well as ventilation. If your roof is due for an overhaul anyway, it may be worth installing rooflights at the same time in case you decide to go ahead with an attic conversion in the future.

⌐ A floor-level bed makes the most of restricted height in a converted attic. Whitewashed rafters create a cosy enclosure for the bedhead.

❮ In order to count as a habitable room attic conversions must incorporate at least one window. The simplest way of meeting this requirement is to install a rooflight in the plane of the roof. In some cases, the roof structure may require additional strengthening to bear the weight of the window.

∟ A new window in the gable end provides natural light for a working area in a converted attic. The sloping ceilings are lined in white-painted tongue-and-groove boards, with the existing roof structure left exposed.

❯ The ultimate in toplighting is provided by this fully glazed roof supported by glass beams. Waking up with the sun is not for everyone, however; rooflights or skylights screened with blinds offer the opportunity for flexible light control.

∨ Tucked away from household distractions, attic conversions can be ideal locations for work areas. Permanent stairs are important if the space is in regular use.

< Semi-basements generally offer more scope for conversion than those that are completely underground. In this case, part of the garden has been excavated to create a new kitchen-dining area. This type of conversion requires thorough damp-proofing, usually by installing a damp-proof membrane.

L Sitting on top of the extended basement is a glass box that brings a dramatic quality of light to the new area, an effect heightened by the pristine white walls. In general, it is a good idea to make sure your glass roof is inclined sufficiently or the rain will not run off it and it will get dirty.

∧ Pavement lights set at ground level spill light down into a basement that has been converted into a bathroom. Basement conversions are more difficult, disruptive and expensive than attic conversions.

Building work

The floor joists in an attic are rarely as strong as those on other storeys and will either need replacement or strengthening in order to support new flooring and furniture. Strengthening is usually achieved by bolting on additional joists alongside existing ones. Similarly, roof rafters may also need to be doubled up alongside rooflights to provide extra support for the weight of the window. If you are installing a dormer, a certain area of the roof structure will need to be removed and alternative support put in place. Storage tanks may need to be relocated and soil stacks extended beyond new windows. The new area will also need to be serviced with electricity, heating and possibly water and drainage, depending on use.

Regulations

All structural changes will require building regulations approval. Fire regulations can also be stringent, particularly if your house has more than two storeys. You may need to put in a fire door to seal off the new area and there are certain restrictions regarding means of escape which may affect the design and construction of access ladders or stairs.

If you are simply installing rooflights in the existing plane of the roof and not altering its shape in any way, planning permission is not required. Planning permission is, however, required for dormers that overlook front or side roads, or public spaces, and there are rules that stipulate how big such structures can be. All loft conversions in conservation areas are subject to planning permission. If the works involve building on to a party wall, you will need a party wall agreement with your neighbours.

Basement conversions

Basements lack the immediate appeal of roof spaces. Any area that is sited wholly or partially underground is bound to have a poor quality of natural light and damp may also be an issue. Creating a basement by digging down under the foundations of your house is messy and disruptive work; you will need specialist help from a surveyor, architect, and structural engineer, as well as the services of a building firm experienced in underpinning houses. Costs are also high: certainly twice as much as loft conversions and possibly up to four times more expensive, depending on structural issues. On the plus side, a full basement conversion adds another floor of usable space on to your home; such spaces are energy-efficient and also have good sound insulation. In dense urban areas where property prices are very high and the scope for other forms of extension is limited, this type of conversion can be well worth the effort and expense.

The scope of the work depends chiefly on what you've got in the first place. An existing basement area that has some natural light (perhaps via a lightwell) or a semi-basement on a sloping site offer the greatest potential. In such circumstances conversion might only entail damp-proofing and some excavation of adjoining garden areas to improve light and access.

Creating a completely new basement is rather more complex. You will need to commission a survey into ground conditions and determine the nature of existing foundations. In older properties the ground floor is generally suspended over a shallow void, with floor joists supported by foundations. Excavating that void to create a room with sufficient head height entails digging under existing foundations and underpinning with concrete until the right depth is achieved. Where the floor rests directly on the ground, excavation and underpinning will necessarily put the entire ground floor out of action until work is completed.

New basement walls and floors require damp-proofing, either by constructing them from water-resistant materials or by installing waterproof membranes. You may have to reroute drainage, particularly if you are extending some way out into the garden. You'll also need planning permission and possibly a party wall agreement with neighbours.

EXTENSIONS

Adding on to your existing home can be a cheaper and more effective way of gaining extra space than moving to a larger property, particularly if you take all the associated costs of a move into account (see page 111). If you are more or less happy with the status quo but just need an extra room – or if you want to make an existing room, such as a kitchen, bigger – building an extension is probably the most cost-effective way to do it, and is likely to add value to your property in the long term. At the same time, a properly planned extension can bring other benefits to your home, such as a better quality of natural light and improved spatial arrangement, so that existing areas function better and seem more spacious.

> One of a pair of side extensions to a 1950s house contains a sitting area; the one on the other side contains a kitchen, with a living-dining area in between. The three individual spaces can be opened into one large area or divided into rooms by sliding doors. The side of the extension is solid construction with a low horizontal window to provide a view of a water feature.

⌄ Terraced properties typically have a side passage between the house and the garden wall. This area can be absorbed by knocking through the external wall. Here a side extension was used to create a long in-line kitchen roofed in glass connected via large openings to the dining area.

> Prefabrication is an increasingly popular option for home extensions. The new structure is designed to your specification and constructed in factory conditions, using either custom or standard components; fixtures, fittings and insulation may also be installed at the same time. After delivery to site, the extension can be ready for occupation in less than a day, once basic connections have been made. Minimizing fuss, delay and mess, the prefab solution is ideal for those who might otherwise not consider extending their home.

Extending a house is not simply a question of tacking on extra space where you think you need it: the entire way your home is planned and used should also come into consideration. For this reason, and because most extensions require substantial building work and generally entail structural changes, it is essential to work with an architect. He or she can help you to realize your plans and come up with a solution that is practical, within your budget and legal, as well as one that makes the most of all design possibilities.

In terms of design, it is not always necessary to replicate the architectural style of your existing home: a bold contrast between a traditional house and a sleek modern extension, provided you can get the planners to agree, can be very effective. Structural and material developments now make it possible to create very light, transparent extensions – such as steel-framed structures entirely infilled with glass – which have the advantage of serving as subtle transition areas between indoors and out.

Conservatories have long been a popular add-on, so popular that a wide range of styles is available in kit form. More recently, a number of companies have also begun producing other types of prefabricated extension, which require a minimum of assembly on site. The prefab or 'kit' option may not result in a wildly original design solution, but it is economic, fast and much less disruptive than building from scratch.

Assessing needs

As with attic conversions, before you brief an architect or designer, you should try to determine what functions the extra space should fulfil and think about the impact this will have on the way your home is currently arranged. If you need an extra bedroom or somewhere private to work, it is not necessarily the case that an extension should have that designated function. Making another room or area bigger can free up space elsewhere in the house where the extra bedroom or study can be located. For example, if you extend a kitchen, this may give you the opportunity to create an informal kitchen-dining-living area which can then absorb many everyday activities that are at present taking place elsewhere. In turn, this may release space that was previously devoted to an eating area, for example, and which could now usefully serve as a study or workroom.

Extensions, however, do not always improve the quality of existing spaces. If you extend a ground-floor area further out into the garden, for example, other areas that formerly were well lit by natural light may become darker. By the same token, an extension that accommodates the bulk of everyday activity – such as a large inclusive kitchen – can turn former living areas into little more than ante-rooms. New dividers or sliding partitions may need to be introduced to restore a sense of dynamism; new internal openings can 'borrow' light from adjacent areas.

Siting

Most houses offer at least some choice when it comes to siting an extension. Siting should be very carefully considered with regard to conditions of natural light, relationship with adjoining or neighbouring properties and potential legal or structural complications, as well as impact on interior spaces.

Options include:

> Extending the house at the rear and forming a direct connection with ground-floor areas. As this may entail losing a substantial part of your garden, you must be sure you are prepared to make do with more limited outdoor space.

> Demolishing existing outbuildings or lean-tos to create space for a rear extension.

> Extending over the top of an existing extension.

> Adding on an extra storey at the top of your home.

> Extending the house to the side, either by building on a new wing, or by absorbing a side passage between your house and the property line.

Building work

All extensions require some kind of new connection to be formed with the existing house. In the case of ground-floor extensions, this tends to mean creating a new opening in an external load-bearing wall, which has its own structural implications. For extensions built on top of an existing extension, it may be possible to utilize an existing window to form the connection, removing the portion of wall beneath the lower sill to create a doorway. This is much less disruptive than creating an entirely new opening and does not affect the overall structure of your home.

Extensions on upper levels, however, including those that create an additional storey, may have implications for the house's foundations. You will need expert advice

to determine whether existing foundations can bear the additional load. Ground-floor extensions require their own foundations, which may need to be tied into existing foundations. Building work also entails running new services to the new area: at the very least, electricity, but possibly also gas, water and drainage.

As far as extensions are concerned, size is critical. In Britain, for example, planning permission is not required for small single-storey extensions, provided the extension is under a certain height, within a given distance of the property line and does not increase the volume, or cubic content, of your house by more than ten per cent. This means that the average bolt-on conservatory does not usually require planning permission. By the same token, if you want to construct an outbuilding that will not be used for living purposes – such as a shed, garden pavilion, pool house or garage – planning permission is also not generally required, provided the structure is within certain size limits and is sited appropriately.

Where you will almost certainly need planning permission is for larger extensions: those that back on to party walls shared with neighbours and those that alter the front elevation of your property or the way it appears on its principal frontage. Neighbours are not always best pleased about the prospect of major, lengthy building works next door and may even go so far as to object if they believe that what you propose will have a deleterious affect on their own property. Successful planning challenges generally arise when neighbours can prove that your proposed extension will block natural light from their own property. However, there is no 'right to a view' and challenges made on this basis will not necessarily be successful.

Other requirements, which are not actually covered by planning permission but fall under the jurisdiction of local building regulations, concern the nature of the construction, fire safety and means of escape, and other such factors. For example, it is necessary for large extensions to be built to current insulation standards, although these might not be met in the existing building. The building inspector will need to view the work in progress at specific stages and this should be allowed for in the schedule; if you miss a stage, completed work may have to be torn up to allow the relevant inspection to take place. It is not unknown for inspectors to insist that freshly laid foundations be dug up so that new drainage can be approved.

⌐ Rooftop extensions provide both extra space and spectacular views, both good for relaxing or creative daydreaming. At a high level, privacy is not an issue, so structures can be as transparent as you want.

∧ A two-storey glass extension slots between two terraced houses, occupying what was formerly a redundant yard. Because the house used to be divided into two flats, the stairs to the basement had been removed. The extension allowed room for a new staircase and enough space on the first floor to extend the kitchen. Where the kitchen has been widened, a new strip of flooring made of thick glass panels has been inserted to maintain the overall feeling of lightness and transparency. The new area on the ground floor is used as a recreation room.

‹ A rear extension offers the opportunity to connect with garden areas. Here, the entire rear wall is fitted with sliding glass doors that fold back on each other so that the living area is completely open.

< Weekend retreat

Situated on a peaceful peninsula north of Stockholm in Sweden, this weekend house was designed by a furniture and interior designer for her brother and his family. Their grandfather used to pasture his cattle on the land and the house replaces a small one-roomed cottage where the brother used to spend vacations and weekends until his family outgrew it. When he decided he wanted a new house, he found the off-the-peg selection in builders' catalogues too old-fashioned and his sister decided to help him out with the design.

Permission was granted for a house with a maximum living area of 100sqm (1076sqft), with a 30sqm (323sqft) guesthouse at the side, which is planned for the future. To prevent the design from looking too boxy and to make the planned addition look more natural, the angle of the roof varies, so the house clearly reads as a series of different volumes defined by different functions.

Unlike many Scandinavian summerhouses, which have low ceilings and small windows, the living areas of the house are light and open, forming a connection with nature and the sea views on both sides. Private areas on the 'land' side, where the bedrooms and bathrooms are located, are more enclosed.

Floor-to-ceiling windows form the walls of the largest space, the combined living and dining area, with sliding doors leading to external decking. Separating the kitchen from this large open area is a central structure housing the fireplace on one side, part of the kitchen on the other and a log store at the back.

Like many local buildings, the timber house is raised on piles to avoid damp, but the external 'Falu-black' paintwork is an unusual departure from the standard Swedish country shade of 'Falu-red'. More typical is the luminous white interior, with white-painted spruce wall panelling and whitewashed pine floor making the most of the summer light.

Building your own home may be the ultimate challenge but it is an increasingly popular option. In many parts of the world, the bespoke or one-off house is far from unusual. Over 100,000 new homes a year in the United States, for example, are owner-built. But the trend is accelerating even in densely populated countries like Britain where plots are more difficult to find. According to the Council of Mortgage Lenders, 'self-build' is the fastest growing sector of the British property market, accounting for a third of all new detached houses built every year – bigger than any single commercial developer.

The term 'self-build', which is widely used in this context, can be a little misleading. It does not merely apply to those brave souls who set out to dig their own foundations, source their own materials and otherwise get their hands well and truly dirty in the process of making their dreams come true; it also covers all those projects that are architect-designed and professionally built by contractors working to an individual brief.

Undertaking a new-build project on this type of scale is not for the faint-hearted. Anyone who has had some experience of even minor building works will be aware of the potential risks involved. But incentives are also compelling. Self-build houses can be anywhere from 20 to 50 per cent cheaper to construct than buying an equivalent existing house in the same location. Where property values are sky-rocketing, building your own home may be the only way of obtaining the space you need in the place where you want to live. And where the housing market is split between older properties that need to be adapted to shape contemporary living spaces and new homes in developments built to lowest-common-denominator specification, the opportunity to create your own home can be too tempting to resist. If you don't want to live in someone else's idea of what a home should be, the new-build option may be for you.

THE BRIEF

Building your own home means setting your own brief, which in turn demands significant preparation and research. It isn't necessary to have vast amounts of technical knowledge to successfully run a self-build project and achieve the result you want, but thorough planning and assessment are critical. There are fewer controls in place to prevent you from spending your money unwisely – and you will be spending a great deal of money as a matter of course – so these preliminary stages are vitally important.

The internet is a good source of information and there are also a number of specialist publications that cover a range of issues from sourcing materials to legal and financial matters. Trade fairs featuring self-build show houses can be worth a visit. I suggest you find an architect to hold your hand and who is excited to work with you from the beginning to the end of the project.

BUDGETING

The first step, as with all major domestic undertakings, is to set a budget. This should not necessarily be as much as you could possibly afford. You also have to look at likely values for the type of home you are considering building – spending a fortune building a house in an area that does not achieve high property prices is not a good investment.

Options for self-build financing are much the same as they are for buying an existing house or undertaking major improvements and can be briefly summarized as cash, equity in existing property, and the amount you are able to borrow. Financing has become easier in recent years due to the availability of special self-build mortgage packages. Formerly, lenders generally required that self-builders found the cost of the site themselves, whereupon they would lend the money for construction, repaid in the usual way after completion. Now, lenders are prepared to lend a proportion both of the cost of the land and building costs provided the borrower sells their previous home and repays their existing mortgage first. How much you can borrow will depend, as a standard, on your income. The main difference is that lenders will advance money in a series of payments linked to the completion of various stages of construction.

After you have set a notional budget, the next step is to decide how much space you need or want in order to come up with a rough figure for building costs. These costs will vary depending on how much of the work you tackle yourself, as well as choice of materials and construction method. Self-build magazines publish updated tables of building costs which will enable you to compare different options, such as using sole contractors or subcontractors for all or part of the job.

Overall costs will include:

> Price of the land.
> Building costs.
> Professional fees.
> Insurance and warranty premiums.
> Cost of borrowing.
> Cost of accommodation while the house is being built.

A rule of thumb is that the land cost should be about one-third of the eventual value of the new house, the building costs another third and the remaining third representing equity or profit. But since land values vary widely, the proportion of the total value these costs represent may also vary, from as little as a quarter to as much as half. Building costs may also vary, particularly between urban and rural areas. It is wise to research the market thoroughly both to

establish cost guidelines and to discover what your proposed home might be worth when it is completed.

If likely costs exceed your budget, you will have to look at ways of bringing the figures into line, either by scaling down the size of the project, looking into cheaper construction methods or by reconsidering location. Don't be tempted, however, to cut costs by deciding to take on more of the work yourself than you had originally intended as this may prove a false economy if things go wrong.

PLOT-FINDING

If you already have a plot of land on which to build your home, you are more than halfway there. For those who don't, finding a site can be the hardest part of the whole business, particularly in those areas or parts of the world that are densely populated. In the United States, some companies buy large tracts of land, secure the necessary permissions based on a development proposal, put in access roads and services, and then market individual plots for private sale.

Ways of finding plots:

> **Use the internet** Plot-search lists on the internet provide a good introduction to the availability and cost of plots in specific areas, as well as an indication of which agents deal in land.
> **Contact estate agents** Agents that specialize in land may be helpful, but many prefer to sell to developers rather than self-builders because they will make more money in commission selling on the new property.
> **Scour the press** Local magazines, newspapers and specialist self-build publications may contain details of plots for sale.
> **Check with the council** Local authorities and utilities often have plots of land for disposal.
> **Visit a local planning department** Check schemes that have received outline or preliminary permission with your local authority. The owner of the site might be prepared to sell it on to you.
> **Ask around and tour the area** Word of mouth and legwork are often successful ways of locating potential sites. Don't be put off by dilapidated or overgrown plots.
> **Consider plots with existing houses** Demolishing a derelict house and building a new one can be a good way of getting a site in a dense area.

L Plot-finding can be difficult in dense urban areas and you may face strong competition for any available land. Small sites, though, particularly those that are awkwardly shaped, do come on the market from time to time and are less attractive for commercial builders and developers. This two-storey house a with roof garden makes a neat infill in an old industrial area.

∨ The plot of land on which this house now stands was occupied by a shop at the front and derelict buildings at the rear. The architect-owner has created a two-bedroom house arranged on split levels, which incorporates an internal courtyard and roof terraces. The bedrooms are on the lowest level, the kitchen a level above, with the living room mezzanine connecting to one of the two roof terraces.

∧ An artist's retreat on the northern coast of Denmark includes living quarters and a generous studio. The simple wooden structure (right), reinforced by a steel frame and with a brick service core in the centre housing the kitchen and bathroom, has louvred glass walls that echo the cladding made of narrow larch slats. Sliding doors inside divide the big open space into a north-facing studio and south-facing living area.

Once you have located a site, the next step is to decide whether it is suitable for development. Most people have at least some sense of what to look for when buying a house; buying land is a different proposition and you may require specialist advice.

Points to consider:

> Does the plot already have planning permission for development into a private dwelling? If not, what is the attitude of local authorities?

> Is the site directly accessible? What sort of access is it? How easy will it be to get materials and construction equipment on site?

> Is the site connected to main services and drainage? If not, how easy will it be to make connections?

> Do the physical conditions of the site pose any potential difficulties in terms of gradient, soil type or contamination? Is the area prone to flooding? (If it is you may wish to consider building on stilts.)

> Is the site in a conservation area? Are there trees on the site that may limit design and siting of a building?

> Is the site located in an area that has a history of opposition to new development? What is the attitude of neighbours?

> Is there a prevalent local building style that may influence the attitude of planners with respect to the design or materials? What are the cost implications?

DESIGN-AND-BUILD

There are several different options when it comes to design-and-build. If you engage an architect to oversee the entire project, the full architectural service will include coming up with a design to your individual specification, submitting it for planning permission, appointing a main contractor to handle all the building works on site, and providing supervision and general management thereafter. Alternatively, you might commission an architect to come up with a scheme and detailed drawings and then undertake the managerial or supervisory role yourself. If you are confident about your skills and have the time to do it, you might decide to manage without a main contractor altogether and employ the various trades directly on a subcontract basis. It must be stressed, however, that this approach is not for the faint-hearted. Running a complex building project without some experience or a sound knowledge of construction techniques is foolhardy at best and can be a recipe for delay and cost over-run.

One further option is to opt for a 'package deal'. Package-deal companies produce a range of house plans and designs and also supply structural kits and materials for construction. In most cases such designs can be adapted to suit your needs but this is not the route to choose if you are interested in a wholly original design: the house types offered by such companies are largely traditional. A high proportion of package-deal or kit companies use timber-frame structural systems. Since many of the elements have to be prefabricated weeks before delivery, a significant amount of money is usually required up front.

You may have distinct preferences when it comes to the appearance, design and layout of your new home, but planners will also have an impact on the design process. One of the reasons why 'kit' houses tend to be so conventional is that such schemes are more likely to pass through planning departments without raising too many eyebrows. It is worth a visit to your local council planning department to ascertain if the building you propose is likely to get permission. It is fairly safe to say that anything more unusual and, sadly in some areas, even faintly modern, is more likely to attract objections than more traditional designs. In some cases, a planner's reservations can be worked around by making minor compromises, by changing materials or altering a few significant elevational details. Not all planning authorities are conservative, however, and a truly innovative design – an exciting modern infill in a terraced street, for example – may win unexpected backing.

Another area of potential conflict concerns building regulations. Building regulations or codes cover every aspect of construction and are framed to ensure that what you build is structurally sound, safe and conforms to a wide range of other health and environmental factors. If you are using standard structural systems and have employed a professional designer, there is no real reason why your new home should not pass the necessary inspections. Some people, however, are attracted to self-build because of the opportunities it provides to experiment with different types of structure, form and materials – for example, eco designers intent on building houses out of straw bales or adobe. If you fall into this category, be prepared to fight your corner. Some eco designers have found it necessary to campaign to change building codes before they could win approval for their designs to be built.

> Orientation, a restricted site area, mature trees and overlooking from neighbouring houses dictated the form of this new-build house in an Auckland suburb in New Zealand. On the middle entry level are the main living rooms, with bedrooms above and guest rooms below. The front of the house faces the direction of the sun and has a semi-enclosed deck shaded by trees.

>> An elegant, contemporary reworking of a classical model, this new house occupies a prime site in the heart of London. The design respects rather than replicates its immediate context.

⌄ Building in otherwise unspoilt landscape heightens environmental issues. This modular construction sits lightly on the land on metal legs. Orienting the house towards the sun makes the most of passive solar gain.

L An economical and compact house comprising living and working areas is sited on a narrow piece of land in the middle of Toronto, with houses on one side and workshops on the other. The lower level, where the living areas are located, is clad in softwood boarding; the workspace on the upper level is clad in Douglas fir plywood.

⌄ A long, low house, ending in a storied block reminiscent of a watch-tower, enjoys spectacular sea views. A deep overhang shades a terrace running the length of the long arm of the house.

FLEXIBLE FAMILY HOME

When the owners of this contemporary house in an Essex village decided to move out of London, building their own home was not the first option they considered. The move to the countryside, prompted by the birth of their son, was inspired by a need for greater space and a desire to live closer to family. After searching unsuccessfully for suitable properties to renovate in the area, they decided to take the plunge and build their own home when they came across an affordable site that was large enough for a family house and generous garden. They subsequently chose a London-based architectural practice to come up with the scheme after following up recommendations from friends.

A clear brief is essential for all types of building work, but especially for projects as potentially complex as building an entire house. The owners, who are both professional designers, had very definite ideas about what they wanted, both in terms of accommodation and with respect to overall style and appearance. What they wanted was a house that was modern not pastiche, with plenty of open space for all the family to be together. In addition, they specified three bedrooms, a lavatory and utility area downstairs, a work area if possible – and an open fire.

All this had to be achieved on a strict budget. To cut costs, the owners decided to run the building works themselves, with supervisory assistance from a local architect.

┌ Contrasting views of the house from the rear elevation (top) and front (centre). The front of the house has a plain, discreet appearance with deeply recessed windows and door. The jettied overhang is a reference to local building styles and serves both to provide extra room on the upper level and to shelter a driveway. The rear of the house, entirely clad in black weatherboarding, has a more open appearance.

‹ The light-filled open-plan space downstairs accommodates spacious kitchen, dining and living areas.

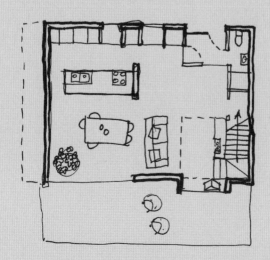

∧ On the rear elevation, large openings make the most of light and views. Glazed doors fold right back to connect the interior directly with the outdoor decked area. From the second storey it is possible to see the estuary in the distance.

❯ Plans of the first (left) and second (right) storeys show the open-plan nature of the layout. On the upper floor, partitions fold back to enable almost the entire space to be used as a playroom or communal family area.

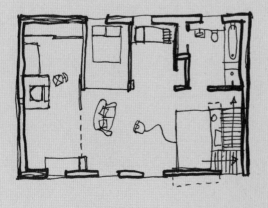

« Appropriately enough for a family home, surfaces and finishes are child-friendly and easy to maintain. An entire wall downstairs is covered floor to ceiling in blackboards.

⌐ Subtle variations in ceiling height and floor level help to demarcate distinct areas within the open-plan space. In the entrance, the ceiling is low to give a more cosy approach to the main space. In the sitting area, part of the ceiling is open to the roof which gives a feeling of volume.

‹ The two children's bedrooms on the upper floor are compact and fitted with folding doors so they can be opened to the generous landing-cum-family room. Oak flooring is used throughout the house.

As is the situation for all new-build projects, planning regulations had an impact on design. In this case, the site was in a conservation area and design guidelines dictated how big the house could be and which materials could be used externally. From the outside, the simple two-storey structure, clad in red brick and black weatherboarding, and with a slate roof, appears to be a modest, if slightly austere variation on the theme of local building styles. The brickwork is in keeping with the existing brick-built village houses and the weatherboarding a reference to sail lofts in the marshes and nearby estuary.

Indoors, facilitated by a complex structural framework, both levels are as open plan as possible, with the lower level essentially one huge space and the upper floor fitted with flexible partitions and sliding doors between rooms. The rear of the house has large box-like bay window and folding glass doors that open straight onto a decked outdoor area, creating an airy, open feel.

Materials throughout are simple, robust and honestly expressed. Exposed concrete blockwork walls, oak flooring with underfloor heating, and an entire wall covered floor to ceiling in blackboards for creative scribbling, make the ideal environment for modern family living.

< Changes of level on the upper floor are also employed to mark out different areas. The bathroom steps up to the main level of family room and children's bedrooms; the parents' room is up another step. Running the full width of the house, the parent's room also incorporates a home office. The openness of the upper storey, with its flexible dividers, means that the parents can keep a watchful eye on the children as they play.

⌐ A contemporary take on a bay window, this large box-like opening protrudes externally, creating a generous window seat indoors. A simple concrete-block wall houses a working fireplace.

> Another exposed concrete-block wall screens the kitchen area from the main living space. The white lacquered finish on the kitchen island and cupboards is easy to wipe clean.

PART 3

COMPENDIUM

On the domestic front, breadth of choice has never been greater, whether it is a case of flooring finishes, storage solutions or light fixtures. This section serves as a buyer's guide to all aspects of interior design and decor; it is a complete source book of materials, architectural elements, interior details, furniture and furnishings, appliances, fittings and lighting – all the practical information you need to make a selection to put your home together the way you want.

MATERIALS DIRECTORY

TEXTURE AND TONE

The materials that form the surfaces of your home stimulate your senses and add an extra dimension to the way you experience your surroundings. When choosing materials, you should consider your home in its entirety before you focus on the details. Ideally, this process should not be undertaken piecemeal. Even if you can only tackle one room at a time, keep your whole home in mind. Your living spaces should flow, allowing you to move from one area to another without jarring dislocations of style.

Natural materials such as wood, stone and slate bring character and depth to your home; the warm glow of wood and the irregular colours and contours of stone help to form living environments that are both sensuous and grounded. Man-made natural materials can be equally appealing: old brick and terracotta, for example, have a lovely time-worn patina, and linoleum, cork and sisal make attractive, tactile flooring. Other manufactured materials such as concrete, metal and glass create interiors with a modern edge. Their surfaces can be rugged or smooth and, when juxtaposed, produce dynamic textural contrasts. Synthetic materials like acrylic, vinyl and polypropylene have recently been given new leases of life as cutting-edge products and add to the sensory experience of the contemporary home.

The impact of materials cannot be overestimated and the palette available to choose from is enormous. Consistency and restraint are perhaps the key factors to achieving a harmonious result: using too much of one type of material causes overload, but combining too many different surfaces ends up in confusion. Something else to consider when making your choices is ecology: whether or not a material comes from a sustainable source, has a long life-span and is recyclable are issues that have become increasingly important and may well influence your decisions.

WOOD

Choosing wood

Wooden surfaces are warm and tactile. The colour, texture, and even the smell of wood, add richness and sensuality to living spaces. Aesthetically, wood is an incredibly versatile material. In the home, you can use it to create the cosy ambience of a country cottage by cladding your walls in old-fashioned tongue-and-groove, or you can install pale birch-ply panels for a modern, minimal look. Wood embodies a connection with nature and placed alongside other natural materials such as slate or stone, it can lend an elemental quality to pared-down contemporary spaces. For furniture, the widely varying colours and qualities of different woods — from smooth ash to densely patterned burr walnut — combined with their inherent workability, means that wood will never be displaced as the ultimate material of choice.

The vast array of woods that exist all have specific properties, and different types are therefore suited to different purposes. If you are planning to lay a wood floor or fit a wooden worktop, you should first consider which wood will be most durable and easy to care for. Oak, for example, makes hardwearing flooring that provides a mellow, warm surface for a family home and one that will mature gracefully and improve with age; though more expensive it may well prove a better investment in the long run than a cheaper, noisier laminate flooring. Oak is a relatively easy wood to care for, but if you have set your heart on a beech worktop for your kitchen, it will need regular oiling and you should ask yourself if you are prepared to put the time into its upkeep before reaching a decision.

Sources

Selecting wood can present a challenge, given the almost infinite variety that exists. It is important not only to choose the right wood for the job, however, but also to consider its environmental impact. As a renewable resource wood is potentially very ecologically friendly, but you need to choose carefully to ensure that you are not contributing to the world's deforestation.

Many of the world's most beautiful woods are now endangered, among them ebony, mahogany and teak. These species should be avoided. Other attractive woods that you might consider using are cedar, gumwoods, chestnut, walnut and lime; although not on the endangered list, they should always be obtained from a sustainable source. The international organization that inspects

and certifies timber across the world is the Forestry Stewardship Council, or FSC. An FSC certification guarantees that the wood comes from a legal, environmentally managed source. The FSC checks timber at every stage from the forest to the retail outlet, along what is know as the 'chain of custody'. To find a responsible supplier, and for information about timbers, visit the FSC website (see page 261).

Softwood

This type of wood generally comes from the fast-growing coniferous trees of northern climes, largely North America, Scandinavia and eastern parts of northern Europe. As its name suggests, it is softer than other timbers; it is also pale in tone and has a close, knotty grain. Softwood is relatively cheap and is most commonly used for construction, cladding and making inexpensive furniture. The best known softwood is pine.

Hardwood

Hardwood comes from slower-growing broadleaf trees that are found in both temperate and tropical regions. Some of its uses include furniture, flooring and external doors. It is harder, denser and longer lasting than softwood and is more expensive. There is more variation between different hardwood timbers than between softwoods: they may be pale or very dark, close-grained or loose. Some tropical hardwoods are under serious threat from over-harvesting.

Manufactured woods

Much of the 'wood' used today in homes is not solid timber but has been manufactured in various ways from wood products that are less expensive compared to real wood.

CHIPBOARD Rough-and-ready chipboard is made from wood fragments crushed together with resin and it is sometimes veneered. The result is inexpensive but not very strong and it is generally used for substructures where it will not be seen.

BLOCKBOARD Formed from blocks of wood sandwiched between veneers, blockboard is used in a similar way to chipboard.

PLYWOOD This highly versatile material consists of several layers of wood glued together with their grain laid at right angles to each other for extra strength; the layers (always an odd number) give plywood its distinctive striped edge. It is widely used for contemporary furniture and fittings. A recent development, 'bendy ply' can be employed to create curved surfaces.

1
2
3

MDF Medium density fibreboard, or MDF, is wood dust bound together with resin, which is dimensionally stable and has a smooth surface that is ideal for painting. MDF is inexpensive and can be an economical material for constructing fitted cupboards. However, it can contain the dangerous chemical formaldehyde and it is important to avoid inhaling the dust; you should always wear a mask when cutting it, and ask for 'E1' MDF which contains less of the chemical.

LAMINATE Used as a cheap alternative to solid wood, laminate can be coloured or printed paper, or a melamine-covered layer of wood veneer bonded to planks to lay as wood-effect flooring. Laminate can be used to face kitchen and other cupboards, or tables.

Wood flooring

The floor is one of the main areas where wood is used in the home, usually in the form of bare floorboards or parquet. Taken throughout one level, a wood floor acts as a unifying element. Chipboard or poor quality floorboards can be used as a base for carpeting or other wall-to-wall flooring.

FLOORBOARDS Laying a fine wood floor can be a considerable investment, but treated well, it could last several generations. Oak, elm, ash, beech and maple are among the best woods for this purpose. The cost will depend largely on the type of timber, and the labour involved in laying it. New boards may need to be finished or may be provided already sealed, which will be reflected in the price.

Alternatively, if they are in good enough condition, you can renovate existing boards, or lay a new floor with reclaimed floorboards from a salvage yard. In either case the wood will probably need to be sanded before applying a finish (see page 211).

PARQUET An attractive alternative to floorboards, parquet consists of strips or blocks of solid hardwood (or, less usually, veneered blocks) varying in dimensions but usually not much more than brick-sized, which are laid in a pattern on a sub-floor. The simplest patterns include plain strips and herringbone, while the most complex involve blocks of different shapes and sizes placed in elaborate designs – as found on the floors of seventeenth- and eighteenth-century French chateaux, for instance. Reclaimed parquet can have a lovely patina, if it has not been milled or sanded away. Parquet can be turned to show a fresh face, but often the bitumen in which the blocks were traditionally bedded must first be cleaned off and sanded.

Wood panelling

In traditional construction, wood panelling was an efficient way to finish walls with the added benefit of cutting out draughts. Panels were slotted into each other, allowing them to move and flex as their moisture content changed in different seasons. Today, panelling is undergoing something of a revival. Walls can be clad in panels finished with sheets of fine veneer, with relatively inexpensive plywood or tongue-and-groove planking. Woods with an attractive grain are oiled or waxed or otherwise sealed to allow the grain to be appreciated; softwoods can be finished with paint. Some cheap manufactured timbers such as MDF can be a positive aesthetic choice when sealed and enjoyed for their raw, industrial appearance. Alternatively, walls and ceilings can be clad in tongue-and-groove planks for a traditional look.

Sealing and finishing wood

If left untreated, wood will absorb dirt and stains unless it is scrubbed regularly. Few people have the time or inclination for such labour-intensive activity, but a range of finishes is available that can protect and, in many cases, enhance wood's natural qualities. Most sealants will darken the colour of the wood and you should read all labels carefully.

PROTECTIVE STAIN This treatment lends wood colour while still allowing the grain to show through. Repairs and old floorboards can be disguised with staining, and cheaper timbers can be given a dark stain to imitate the appearance of more expensive hardwood species. Stains should be applied along the grain using a bristle brush and cloth to achieve an even finish.

BLEACHING Wood bleach removes the pigment in wood and is useful for toning down the orange tints of new pine. After bleaching, wood should be sealed with oil, wax or varnish.

OIL Different types of oil are available with varying degrees of durability. Danish oil is a blend of tung oil with resins for added wear and waterproofing. It is suitable for use on bare wood in all situations, including floors. Boiled linseed oil with five parts of turpentine can be used for surfaces where a waterproof finish is not required, such as on internal doors.

WAX This gives wood an attractive low sheen, but is not waterproof and leaves the wood susceptible to spillages. It is therefore better not to use wax on wood surfaces that will receive a lot of wear and tear. Liming wax adds a white, 'limed' appearance to the wood grain.

1 The beauty of wood grain is powerfully expressed in the sleek variegated finish of this hardwood panelling and cantilevered kitchen shelves. Note the dovetailed joints on the shelves.
2 Dark stained floorboards make a practical and good-looking surface in an eating area.
3 Tactility is an important part of the appeal of wood. A curved handrail, carved from seven pieces of redwood, brings a textural dimension to the sweeping curve of a staircase. **4** Painted wood panelling is a subtle, discreet background.
5 Slatted timber panelling makes a contemporary wall finish that also insulates and sound proofs.

HARDWAX OIL Combining the best qualities of oil and wax, this feeds wood while providing a waterproof finish. Using hardwax oil makes it possible to sand and repair worn spots on a wood floor without having to renovate the entire surface.

VARNISH Forming a thin coat on the top of the wood, varnish can quickly become tatty if its surface is damaged by wear. If you want to varnish a floor, choose a special floor varnish and apply three coats (or as many as the manufacturer recommends) with a bristle brush, allowing them to dry overnight between coats. Many varnishes contain polyurethane, which adds a yellow tint and becomes darker and yellower with time.

ACRYLIC OR ALKYD SEALANT Synthetic sealants have hardwearing properties that resist water and household chemicals and do not turn yellow like polyurethane varnishes.

PAINT Painting wood will conceal the grain and is useful for covering a poor quality surface or one that has been subjected to repairs in wood of different shades. Ordinary paint can be thinned to feed into the grain of the wood for a liming effect, but its protective qualities are likewise diluted. Gloss or semi-gloss paint should be used on floors, but it is a good idea to add several coats of protective varnish. Alternatively, you can apply a special floor paint, which is much tougher (and often shinier) than ordinary paint.

Care

Wood demands care in its initial treatment and its installation, but thereafter it is relatively trouble free. The two main dangers to wood floors are damp and impact. You should avoid dragging objects across a wooden floor and use furniture cups under the feet and castors of tables, chairs and other furniture; stiletto heels will dent the surface.

Do not leave water lying on the surface of wood, and keep it well ventilated so that any damp can dry out. A certain degree of moisture is necessary to prevent wood from contracting too much, but water left soaking into the grain will cause distortion and rot. Cleaning a wooden floor involves little more than sweeping or vacuuming regularly, and an occasional wash with a damp (not wet) mop and, if it is very sticky, a gentle detergent. Waxed floors will need rebuffing with wax at intervals, depending on the product and the wear to which your floor is subjected. Other wooden surfaces simply need regular dusting, and possibly occasional oiling (worktops) or polishing with wax (fine and antique furniture).

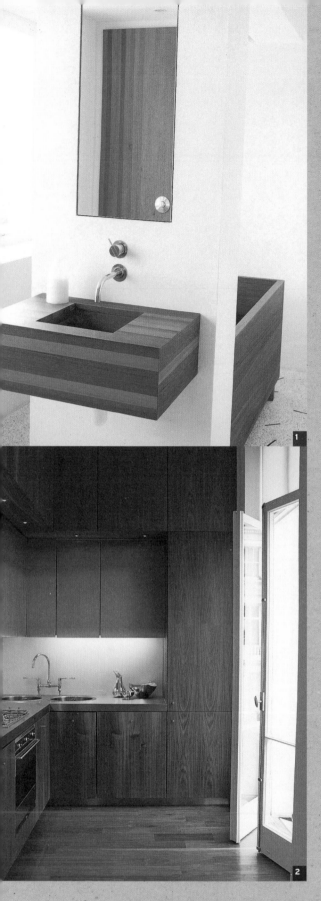

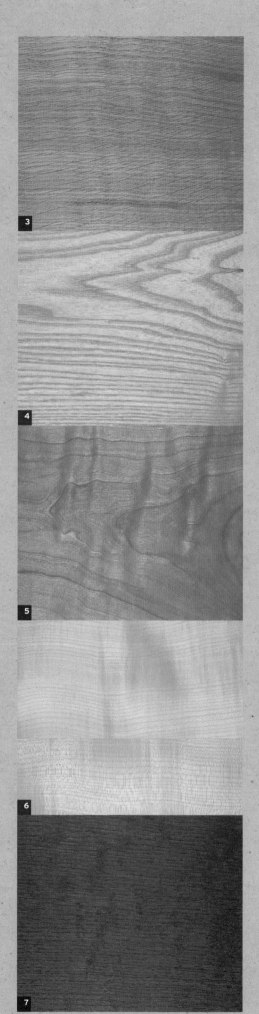

1 One unexpected use of wood in the interior is in the fashioning of contemporary basins and tubs. Cedar is a suitable type of wood for this purpose. **2** Veneered kitchen units echo the dark hardwood used as flooring. Types of wood include: **3** Oak. **4** Ash. **5** Cherry. **6** Sycamore. **7** Dark stained oak. **8** Maple. **9** Pine. **10** Elm. **11** Douglas fir. **12** Beech.

Types of wood

Wood comes in myriad colours and textures – from the deep hues of elm to the blondness of birch and sycamore. Colours change over time when exposed to light: as a general guide, pale woods become darker and yellower while dark woods lighten. Woods also vary in texture: grains can be loose and open like the folds of chestnut, or form tight, delicate streaks such as those of American cherry. While it has a family likeness, the grain of each timber varies from piece to piece, and between heartwood (the harder, older timber at the centre of the trunk) and sapwood (timber from the softer, outer layers). The individual character of a wood also depends on the angles at which the planks were originally cut from the solid trunk.

OAK A hardwood, oak is strong and resilient, and makes some of the finest floors and furniture. It is beautifully grained and has a golden-brown colour that darkens with age and sunlight. Among the well-known varieties of oak are North American white oak (a dense, fine-grained variety), red oak (which is cheaper and less strong), brown oak (naturally stained by the beef-steak fungus) and bog oak (a rare timber found preserved in bogs). Oak takes many interesting treatments well, including fuming (exposure to ammonia, which turns it a smoky brown), charring (blackening the surface with a flame) and bleaching. Oak is stained by contact with iron and all tools and fixings that come into contact with it should be steel, brass or other metals.

ASH Its suppleness, outstanding smoothness and strength mean that ash is an ideal wood from which to make furniture. As well as being robust, it rarely splinters and so is also a popular choice for flooring. Ash can be pale, almost white, in colour and has a pleasingly regular, striated grain.

BEECH With a pale, creamy colour like ash, beech is easily distinguishable from it because its grain has many, darker cross-markings or 'rays' between each line, which creates a more shadowed, mottled tone. Unlike most woods, beech can be worked in any direction – with or across the grain, or at any angle. Its colour, strength and weight make beech popular for furniture, worktops and flooring. It is famously bendable under steam, as every elegant bentwood chair testifies, and it also makes good veneer for plywood.

CHERRY Hard but relatively lightweight, cherry wood has a soft tone with a pinkish or greenish tinge. It can be used as flooring for an entire room, or is sometimes incorporated into a decorative border where it forms an attractive contrast with the tone of other woods. It is often used for furniture.

BIRCH Historically associated with Scandinavian furniture, birch has a cool, pale colour that lends itself particularly well to airy, modern interiors. It supplies much of the veneer that faces plywood, which is widely used for contemporary fitted kitchens and storage.

MAPLE AND SYCAMORE Traditionally used for dance floors because it wears evenly and does not splinter, maple is also a popular flooring material in homes. It has a creamy, biscuity brown colour, a loose, light grain and a lustrous finish. Sycamore is a type of maple that is fine-grained and has a similarly pale colouring to other maples. It is especially suitable for turning and does not pick up the taint of food. For these reasons it is often found on kitchen table tops and is used for food bowls and platters.

ELM This wood has a particularly distinctive grain with multiple, closely arranged lines that are sometimes wavy, and a rich, dark colour that turns silvery when weathered. A tall, broad tree, elm yields wide planks that are traditionally used as weatherboarding on houses. Elm's special quality is its unsplittable strength, even when other timber elements are driven into it, which makes it another valuable, though less common, flooring timber.

CEDAR A finely grained wood, cedar has a rich red colour and is often used for cladding the outsides of houses; it weathers to a silver grey. Traditionally, lebanon cedar, which is paler and has a resinous smell, was used to line wardrobes because it wards off moths.

PINE Real pine comes in a variety of types, all of which share a yellow tone and strong graining. The name 'pine' is also often loosely used as a generic name for other coniferous softwoods with the same practical qualities. Pine is an easily available and inexpensive wood, and has been widely used for centuries for furniture, flooring and construction. The timber tends to become even yellower with age, but it can be toned down with wood bleach or by adding a touch of white paint or pigment to the sealant.

DOUGLAS FIR Also known as 'Oregon pine', Douglas fir is a tall tree (once recorded at 127m/417ft tall). A softwood, it is lightweight and is easy to work with. Douglas fir is used largely as a construction timber and also makes some of the best plywood.

8

9

10

11

12

STONE, SLATE & MARBLE

Choosing stone

Stone is a material that brings a sense of solidity and permanence to its surroundings. Visually, it offers a range of beautiful colours, patterns and textures, which are all the more pleasing for their irregularity. Depending on how it is used, stone can look either very traditional or highly contemporary. It is not a budget option, however, due to the cost of quarrying, transporting and laying it, but if care is taken during its installation, stone will be extremely hardwearing and long-lasting.

There are many different purposes that stone can fulfil in the home – as flooring, most obviously, but also as treads on stairs; as mantelpieces; as kitchen worktops, sinks and splashbacks; and as basins and bathtubs. Which type of stone you choose for any one of these tasks depends partly on aesthetics – the colour, pattern and texture you want – and partly on practical considerations.

Some stone is better suited to a job than others and it is important that you select the correct one. Slate, for example, makes excellent treads for a staircase because of its lateral strength, whereas treads made of sandstone would need careful support to prevent them from cracking under the flexings of the stairs. Polished marble is fine for a basin surround or splashback, but it might prove slippery on a bathroom floor unless it has a honed finish.

SOURCES When choosing stone, you may want to consider which type is traditional in your area. Using local materials wherever possible to build or decorate your home is not only environmentally friendly, but creates a visual and psychological link with your home's surroundings in a way that imported materials, however beautiful, never can. Buying stone from salvage yards – either paving slabs, tiles, or masonry – is another eco-friendly option. Reclaimed stone is also highly desirable because of the patina it has acquired over time, which lends it a certain authenticity. This means that it is not necessarily a cheap alternative, but you may think it worthwhile.

OTHER FORMS It is possible to buy reproduction stone, which nowadays can look very convincing and which costs a fragment of the price of the real thing. Pebbles set into cement or resin are another option; they have a textural, rustic look and can be used for kitchen, bathroom or wet room floors and spashbacks, and also look good outdoors.

Granite

Found mostly in mountain regions of the northern hemisphere, granite is exceptionally hard and strong. Its great density means that it is waterproof and very hardwearing (hence its use for kerbstones), and can be highly polished. Colours of granite vary from black through every shade of grey to yellow and pink tones. Patterning in the stone can include speckles, larger mottled patches and long streaks. Its hard, glossy surface shows little sign of wear and it is popular for kitchen worktops for this reason. Granite with a rough surface gives a good grip as flooring, to which purpose its robust qualities suit it well.

Limestone and sandstone

These are sedimentary rocks formed by the consolidation of crushed shells, minerals, skeletons and other types of matter, and some contain attractive fossils. Many limestones and sandstones are golden, with a variety of tones from pale to rich, but they also come in shades of grey, green, brown, pink and blue. These stones are most familiar as high quality flooring, with good looks that only improve with age. They can be used for other purposes as well, including cladding walls and bath surrounds. Limestones and sandstones are usually softer than other types of rock and are generally porous and susceptible to staining unless they are well sealed.

Famous types include French limestones, which are non-porous and considered the finest for flooring; travertine, a limestone found in Tuscany in Italy; and Yorkstone, an exceptionally tough, frost-resistant sandstone quarried in Yorkshire in the north of England for use as flagstones.

Slate

The geological structure of slate makes it exceptionally strong laterally, so that a properly supported slab, whether in a larder, on a floor or on the tread of a staircase, is unlikely to crack or split. Cheaper than granite and other stones, slate is known for its bluey-grey tinge. Colours range from dark, almost blue-black, to a greeny-grey. Patterns vary from gentle streaking and mottling to distinctive yellow mottling and silver streaks caused by the presence of minerals.

Slate has an interesting quality that distinguishes it from other types of stone popular for use in interiors: it splits naturally into sheets (and can therefore be cut to order relatively inexpensively). This is one reason why historically it has been used for roofing tiles. It has also been used for cladding the outsides of buildings in wet and windy locations because it is waterproof and

hardwearing. This makes it particularly suitable for bathroom and kitchen floors and when combined with underfloor heating, it forms a warm and tactile surface underfoot. Slate can be cut by machine or by hand; the hand-cut variety has a rougher, more robust texture and character.

Marble

For centuries, marble has been valued for the beauty of its colours and striated patterns, and for the fact that it can be polished to a high gloss. It has a repertoire of colours resulting from mineral deposits in the stone: green and yellow tones give way to warm pink, orange and red, and it can also be found in dark shades such as brown and black. The purest white marble comes from Carrara in Italy and is highly prized by sculptors as well as architects and designers.

Marble is an opulent material and in many contemporary homes it is confined to private areas – largely bathrooms – as this is more in keeping with a pared-down modern aesthetic. In hot climates, though, its coolness underfoot is a positive, practical attribute for any room in the house. Marble does not have to be highly polished – in a matt or low-gloss finish it retains its beauty but takes on a more restrained appearance.

Marble comes in slabs or tiles which are available in widely differing sizes, from large flooring pieces to mosaic tiles for surrounds and splashbacks. Basins and bathtubs made from marble create an image of elegant luxury. Cooks, too, appreciate the smooth cool of a marble slab set into a worktop for preparing and rolling pastry, or fitted into a larder cupboard (see page 237).

Stone flooring

Stone, slate and marble slabs are heavy (traditional flagstones are exceptionally so) and they are also fragile during installation. Stone floors should therefore be laid by professionals and on the correct type of base or sub-floor. A solid concrete floor is ideal: the stone should be laid upon a cement bed on top of this. Before buying expensive stone flooring, it is wise to calculate its potential weight and check with a surveyor the load-bearing capacity of your sub-floor.

Tiles are thinner and lighter than slabs, and so are better suited to upstairs flooring. Marble tiles should be laid on a level, solid sub-floor with a cement or sand screed, or any smooth sub-floor with a latex screed. Slate can be laid on floor-grade chipboard, providing there is an intermediate layer of plywood, with a waterproof latex bonding on top; this reduces the likelihood of it bending

or cracking. On all these considerations, take advice from your supplier and/or the professionals you employ to lay your stone.

Sealing and finishing stone

Porous stones such as sandstone need sealing both before and after being laid and grouted: this prevents the grouting material (and indeed any form of grease or dirt) from penetrating the pores and staining the stone. However, sealing can alter the stone's character, for example by changing its colour, so check with your supplier what treatment is recommended. Various sealing and finishing products are available from DIY outlets. Grouts can be bought in a variety of colours and some have added properties such as flexibility or antibacterialism.

1 Natural stone has a certain monumental quality. These large rectangular slabs provide a unifying element linking ground-floor areas. 2 Slate, used here as flooring, is available in a range of dark, moody colours and in honed or riven finishes. 3 A rough-hewn stone sink makes an evocative contrast with smooth tiled walls. 4 Limestone tiles clad bathroom walls, tub and shower enclosure for a clean, crisp look. 5 Fieldstone or rubble stone, used here on walls and hearth, has a pleasing rustic quality, the irregularity of the surface adding textural depth and character. 6 Pebbles set in cement provide a tactile dimension underfoot. 7 White marble chips set in resin make a striking and surprisingly practical floor: maintenance involves vacuuming or washing with a mild bleach solution. 8 White marble has strong connotations of luxury. This shallow bathroom sink, splashback and integral shelf are neatly detailed.

CONCRETE, TERRAZZO & BRICK

Choosing concrete and brick

Concrete has now taken its place alongside glass, metal, wood and plaster in the repertoire of elements that compose the planes of contemporary interiors. The image of concrete has swung like a pendulum from villain of urban brutalism and decay in the second half of the twentieth century, back to that of an honest, unpretentious material that is appreciated for its industrial aesthetic. If you are not ready to embrace the stark, minimal effect of exposed concrete walls or floors, you can achieve a modern look by choosing smaller concrete features to incorporate into your home, such as a cast-concrete sink or fireplace, which can be painted or left bare.

Another manufactured building product, brick has also suffered from a negative image. Industrialized manufacturing processes all but destroyed the link between the character of brick – which was formerly made of clay local to an area – and location. It came to be associated with soulless modern housing developments. Today, however, a renewed appreciation of vernacular buildings and brick-built industrial buildings (which have been given new leases of life as blocks of loft apartments) has led to a new popularity of brick as a warm and versatile material.

There is now a wide range of traditional brick designs and materials to choose from, including handmade brick. Though naturally expensive, this can be used in small quantities to construct a chimney breast, for example, and will bring a warm ambience and sense of authenticity into your home.

Concrete

Made from cement, water and aggregate, the exact recipe of concrete depends on the purpose for which the material is intended and the finish required. Once mixed with water, concrete generates heat and hardens in only a matter of hours, but much longer is needed – possibly a month – before the concrete can be said to have 'cured' or hardened fully. The surface of raw concrete has pits and creases and the texture is affected by the surface of the material pressed against it to mould it into shape. It is grey and mottled, with aggregate possibly showing in places.

Concrete is strong and relatively cheap; it is also fireproof, resistant to moisture and insects, and has high thermal mass, which means that it is effective at keeping heat inside a building. Its strength means that it can be used sparingly in lightweight structures, making it relatively eco-friendly. Concrete is an incredibly versatile building material, readily creating organic, curved surfaces, such as undulating walls; or robust, block-like fittings that lend an industrial look. Various ready-formed concrete items can be incorporated into the structure of an interior.

The simplest way of using concrete in a modern interior is to leave structural members uncovered. A concrete pillar or beam that previously might have been camouflaged with plaster and paint, can be revealed as a bold, heroic element. The austere beauty of concrete interiors can be seen in the houses of Japanese architect Tadao Ando, whose monumental concrete-slab walls are illuminated by strategically placed windows, revealing their textural, irregular surfaces.

CONCRETE BLOCKS Basic concrete blocks can be used to form internal and external walls; they can be left uncovered or have paint applied directly to them. Some blocks have a higher insulation rating than others, making them friendlier to the environment (and reducing your energy bills).

CONCRETE SLABS These can be used indoors as well as out. They can be left in their rugged natural state, or they can be coloured and polished, producing an effect almost indistinguishable from stone.

FINISHES FOR CONCRETE Raw concrete needs to be sealed to prevent its surface from becoming dusty; a proprietory concrete sealant or concrete paint should be used after all loose material has been removed. Alternatively, a wide range of finishes can be applied to concrete to transform its texture and colour. A smooth sandy screed can be laid over it, giving it a matt, napped texture, or it can be polished after curing, giving it a high-sheen elegance. Resin can be applied to it for a wet-look gloss. Pigment can be added to the mixture to give concrete added colour, including strong, rich tones, and photo-etching can introduce graphic patterns and designs, further enhancing its sculptural credentials.

CONCRETE FLOORING Concrete makes a surprisingly good flooring material, and has the advantage of being heat- and scratch-resistant. Once cured it is sealed to make it resistant to oil, food stains and water. For a warmer feel and texture, several heavy coats of commercial paste wax are applied once the sealant has dried, and it is then be buffed with a machine to give a sleek finish.

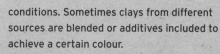

CONCRETE WORKTOPS One of the latest uses of concrete in interiors is as worksurfaces. Fabricated on or off site, a good quality concrete worktop consists of a layer of fibre-reinforced concrete applied to a fibreboard backing, thus reducing the weight of the whole. The concrete is cured in such a way that it is harder, stronger and less porous than ordinary concrete. It is also waterproof, alcohol resistant and anti-microbial, and has good heat tolerance. Standard colours (which are UV stable, and so will not fade) include shades of off-white, yellow, brown and black.

Terrazzo

An aggregate of concrete and marble, glass or granite chippings, terrazzo has been used to clad floors in Mediterranean countries for at least a century, where its smooth, polished coolness is a welcome quality. Now more widely available, terrazzo can be installed as ready-made 'tiles' or mixed and laid on site. It has a characteristically stippled appearance and is available in a vast range of colours from subtle, natural shades to vibrant modern hues. Terrazzo is not a cheap material but is incomparably hardwearing and long-lasting. An environmentally friendly alternative is to buy terrazzo where the stone chips have been replaced with fragments of recycled glass and the concrete with non-toxic resin.

Brick

Brick is one of the world's oldest building materials. Its main ingredient is the same as it has been for thousands of years: fired clay. When baked, different clays produce different colours – some redder, some buff, some blue-black, some glazed white – due to the proportions of iron and lime in the clay. The colour of bricks is also influenced by firing

conditions. Sometimes clays from different sources are blended or additives included to achieve a certain colour.

In an interior, brick (especially red brick) is warm and textured. Colour ranges from brown through ruddy shades to creamy gold. Texture can vary from the satisfying regularity and relative smoothness of newly-built cladding or walling, to the irregularity of old bricks that have been uncovered or left as found.

HANDMADE AND RECLAIMED BRICK

Like stone, handmade brick is beautiful, textural and expensive, but is undoubtedly worth the investment in terms of the qualities it brings to an interior (or exterior). Likewise, reclaimed brick has an attractive mellowness, and is also an eco-friendly option. However, you will have to take a risk in terms of strength and frost resistance, so reclaimed brick is perhaps best used for cladding rather than load-bearing purposes. Another possible disadvantage of reclaimed brick is erratic sizing: this was only standardized in the 1930s, and previously differed between areas and brickworks.

MACHINE-MADE BRICK The wide variety of factory-made brick includes wirecut brick, which is extruded (pushed through a template) in one long piece, then cut into brick-sized sections. Engineering brick is exceptionally strong with low water absorption, and firebrick is designed to withstand exceedingly high temperatures – in the home it is used for firebacks (see page 204). Brick is available pre-whitewashed and even in pre-constructed brickwork panels. One new development is a type of brick that contains air pockets to make it not only lighter but also more thermally efficient. Paviours (also known as 'pammets') are thinner, flat bricks for flooring.

1 Concrete features and fixtures, such as this kitchen sink and counter, can be cast in situ. **2** A concrete wall and cantilevered shelf contrast with a steel chimney breast. **3** A partition constructed out of rugged concrete celebrates the uncompromising nature of the material. **4** Polished concrete makes a surprisingly sleek floor. Because concrete has high thermal mass, it absorbs heat slowly during the day and releases it gradually overnight, which can contribute to energy saving. **5** The regularity of modern brick paviours makes a suitably contemporary floor; the earthy colour adds warmth. **6** A well-worn original brick floor makes a mellow background in a converted barn. **7** Exposed brick walls, suggestive of an industrial aesthetic, have become standard features of lofts and converted warehouses. **8** Terrazzo, commonly used as a flooring material in hot climates, is ideal for unifying outdoor and indoor areas.

TILES

Choosing tiles

Tiles come in so many different shapes, sizes and colours that the choice can seem overwhelming. There are tiles for floors and walls, glazed and unglazed tiles, even tiles made from leather and metal. Some have a coloured finish laid over them and others are the natural colour of the clay from which they were made. Patterned tiles vary hugely in themselves, from medieval-inspired slipware through to the latest photographic designs.

Each choice carries with it practical and aesthetic implications. Floor tiles provide areas that are likely to be wet or subjected to heavy traffic with an extremely hard-working and waterproof surface, but they need a stable, flat sub-floor on which to be laid. Wall tiles do much the same for vertical surfaces but are thinner and lighter.

Large areas of tile look more convincing than small ones, relative to the size and scale of the room and its features. A bathroom tiled floor to ceiling looks elegant whereas a tiled rectangle only the length of the bath is reminiscent of student accommodation.

The success of all tiling in the home depends on thorough preparation, careful calculation and attention to detail. Unlike paint, tiles cannot be slapped up in an afternoon and changed easily and cheaply if the effect is not quite what you intended.

Terracotta

In spite of all the advances in the design and manufacture of tiles, the oldest form in existence still has an enduring appeal. Terracotta is, literally, 'fired earth', a slab of clay out of the ground, dried in the sun and then baked in a fire or kiln. Terracotta tiles have a characteristic warm russet glow and can be square, rectangular, octagonal or lozenge-shaped.

1 Unglazed terracotta tiles have an unpretentious natural charm. After laying they require sealing and light polishing to enhance stain resistance. **2** The gridded pattern of tilework adds rhythm and movement to the interior, demonstrated here by these dark ceramic tiles set off by crisp white grouting. **3** Circle mosaic comes in sheet form to make it easier to apply. **4** Vividly coloured or patterned tiles create a focus of interest. New digital techniques enable photographic imagery to be directly transferred to tile. **5** 'Metro' or bevelled tilework has a retro appeal, given a contemporary twist here by the use of contrasting colour. **6** Mosaic makes an ideal finish for bathroom surfaces. The small scale of the grid provides added grip underfoot. **7** Handmade and hand-glazed tiles have a pleasing irregularity that adds character.

HANDMADE AND RECLAIMED TERRACOTTA TILES The irregularities of a handmade terracotta tile are a strong part of its charm, while reclaimed terracotta has an added element – the patina of age. These tiles make a floor that is ideally suited to a large, homely kitchen, but they also provide a suitable backdrop for more sophisticated furnishings, be they antique furniture and Persian rugs or more contemporary pieces.

MACHINE-MADE TERRACOTTA TILES At the other end of the range are the much cheaper, more regular and smoothly finished terracotta tiles manufactured by machine. These give a more uniform look that accords well with modern furnishings and fittings. New terracotta varies widely in colour from golden through rosy pinks and reds to almost vibrant red and orange; with age it will become more distressed and textural.

SEALING AND FINISHING TERRACOTTA All terracotta tiles are unglazed and require care in handling and finishing in order to get the best service from them over the years. When they arrive they may need drying. Terracotta tiles are porous and so should be sealed before laying (check requirements with your supplier). Spots of adhesive, cement or grout will stain them, and any blobs of these should be removed immediately before sealing. After grouting they will need sealing again, and when they are completely dry and 'cured' they should be lightly polished regularly during the first couple of months – if you use too much polish they will become sticky and collect grime, however. Thereafter terracotta tiles will only need polishing at intervals according to wear.

Quarry tiles

More robust than terracotta, quarry tiles need none of its careful treatment, though they should be treated with respect like any other surface. They are harder, having been fired at a higher temperature, and are already sealed or glazed when you buy them. Quarry tiles do not have quite the same mellowness as terracotta, and their uniformity will not alter with age. However, their warm tones and practicality – and perhaps their association with Victorian houses and old country kitchens – ensure their continued popularity. Quarry tiles are square or rectangular, and colours vary from bright orangey-red through brown to black.

Ceramic tiles

These are tiles made from highly processed clay, which is pressed into moulds, glazed and fired in a kiln. Ceramic tiles are made for both floors and walls. They range from budget, mass-produced varieties to expensive small-production wares.

Pattern on ceramic tiles can be applied in various ways including printing, transferring, embossing, moulding or inlaying. The latter is known as 'encaustic' decoration, where an indented pattern is filled with glaze or clay of another colour. Tile panels have decoration that has been applied in a unified design across a number of tiles – two-by-three or three-by-four are common. Edging tiles are narrow strips for giving tiled panels or areas of wall a finishing flourish.

HANDMADE CERAMIC TILES Ceramic tiles made by craftsmen have the same artisanal appeal as old terracotta tiles, and may be similarly irregular in size and shape. They are generally more substantial than machine-made varieties and are available in glowing, jewel-like glazes or hand-painted designs, either graphic or figurative. Used in a kitchen, a patchwork of handmade tiles in different colours creates a cosy, traditional look.

MACHINE-MADE CERAMIC TILES Mass-produced ceramic tiles may lack the individuality of handmade ones, but they are by no means uninspiring and come in myriad designs, finishes and sizes. The uniformity of machine-made ceramic tiles, along with their reliability, is an asset when you are planning a neat, regular configuration of tiles. In a minimal interior, tiling adds pattern and texture to the overall scheme.

Glass tiles

An increasingly popular choice for kitchens and bathrooms, glass tiles are available in a number of guises, including clear, brightly coloured, rippled and recycled glass. Other effects include glass mosaic in plain, metallic and iridescent finishes; glass that is smooth to the touch with a crystalline embossed pattern within; and glass with a shimmery finish introduced by holograph. When installing glass tiles it is important to use an adhesive that is transparent when dry.

Mosaic tiles

Tiny mosaic tiles are available in an enticing choice of designs, colours and shapes. As well as the usual square ceramic variety, they are available in round and hexagonal shapes (which have a contemporary look), with lustre or iridescent finishes, and in coloured glass.

The simplest and most cost-effective way of using mosaic tiles is in ready-mounted sheets that you apply to walls *en bloc* then grout; 'swimming pool mixes' of different shades

of blue are a particularly popular choice for bathrooms. At the other end of the scale, you can commission a mosaicist to create a bespoke design of your choosing to suit the size and style of your space. Alternatively you can make your own mosaic from individual tiles or from carefully broken plain-colour tiles of your choice. Use tiles of the same thickness for an even finish, and form the mosaic on a plywood panel so that you can take it with you when you move home (or remove it easily when you want a change).

Metallic tiles

These tiles come in two varieties. They can be either wooden blocks (ideally made from marine ply, which repels water) faced with real metal, such as copper, brass, stainless steel or zinc, or they can be made from resin containing chemicals that give the tile a metallic finish when subjected to heat in the firing process. Both wall and floor tiles are available, and also larger panels for cladding walls. Large metal tiles (plain, ridged or patterned) can be used to clad walls and ceilings using a commercial clip-on system. Solid metal inserts are available to punctuate the expanse of a stone or tiled floor.

Light-up tiles

Light emitting diodes, or LEDs, (see page 245) promise a revolution in domestic lighting. One new development is light-up tiles, which are essentially glass panels in which tiny LEDs are embedded. These are available either in single colours or in tiles that pulse through the spectrum. They are relatively complicated and expensive to buy and to install, requiring wiring, transformers and computerized programmers; they are also thicker than regular tiles, so have to be recessed into the wall.

Fibre optics (see page 245) also offer possibilities for light-up tiles (glass and metal tiles are already used in commercial settings in a clip-on format that can be combined with fibre-optic lighting). For outdoor use, solar-powered lighting tiles are both decorative and practical. Alternatively, you can use coloured glass tiles combined with recessed halogen lighting (see page 244) in your own cleverly devised individual scheme.

Leather tiles

Once the preserve of club sofas and armchairs, leather is found on more and more surfaces in the home. It is now available in rectangular tiles of thick, tough buffalo hide, which are attached to walls and floors with tile adhesive in the usual way. These tiles work well in living spaces, bedrooms and studies where they add a warm, textural element.

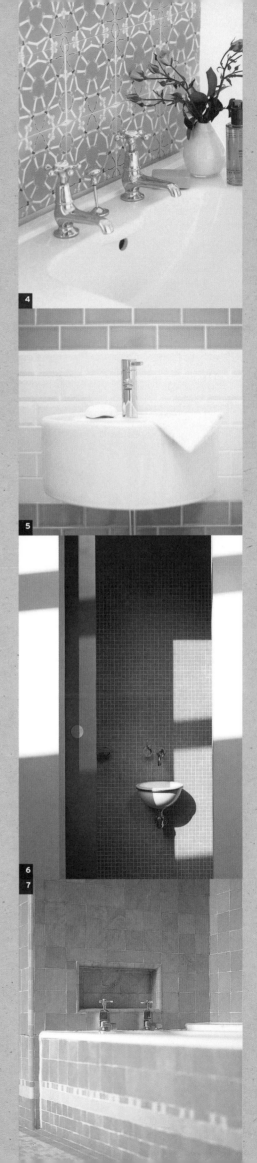

LINOLEUM, CORK, RUBBER, VINYL & PLASTICS

Choosing natural and synthetic materials

The world of materials is ever-changing and there is an increasingly wide selection to choose from. New products are constantly being developed – from natural, synthetic or recycled components – while some traditional materials are being revamped and given new leases of life. Warm, tactile linoleum flooring, for example, has experienced a renaissance in recent years, and cork tiles can now be printed with funky photographic designs to create *trompe l'oeil* effects on your kitchen or bathroom floor. Rubber is another natural material that has been given a modern twist to create striking, contemporary flooring, and plastic in its many forms maintains its status as a versatile cutting-edge design tool.

Linoleum

Once perceived as a boring, old-fashioned flooring option with institutional overtones, linoleum has been 'rediscovered' not only by the environmentally conscious but also by homeowners and designers. Sometimes lumped together with vinyl as an 'artificial' flooring, and often confused with it, linoleum is, in fact, an entirely natural product. It is composed of cork flour, wood flour, ground limestone, rosin, pigments and linseed oil, and is backed with jute. In the most eco-friendly linoleum, the wood flour comes not from tropical hardwoods but from controlled temperate and northern forests, the pigments do not contain heavy metals, and all the ingredients are biodegradable. Linoleum is very hard-wearing; once laid it has a lifespan of between 25 and 40 years, quite possibly longer. It also resists heat, and repels dust, dust mites and bacteria, therefore making it a hygienic choice for kitchens and playrooms, and ideal for asthma sufferers.

Among linoleum's other attractive qualities are its tones and texture. It is available in a wide choice of shades from pale to rich (the nature of its ingredients means that its colours are never bright); it is matt and quiet, warm to the touch and relatively soft – comparable to wood rather than stone. Linoleum is available as sheeting or tiles, which can be laid in a solid block of colour, in a traditional chequerboard design or in a more contemporary random pattern of three or more colours or tones. Apart from flooring, linoleum also works well as a desktop surface.

Cork

This spongy bark is harvested from the cork oak tree, which grows in countries around the Mediterranean. The bark is reduced to granules and compacted with resins before being heated to produce cork flooring. Like linoleum, cork is soft, quiet, warm and has a natural spring. Unlike linoleum, the choice of colours available is limited by the natural material and consists only of variations on brown. Nevertheless, the pale, creamy tones and dark bitter-chocolate shades work well with contemporary interiors. Cork is porous and needs to be sealed before use if it is to withstand wear and repel water.

A recent development is photo-printed cork tiles. Photographic images transferred onto PVC are laminated to the surface of the tiles – some current designs show autumn leaves, swirling water, bubblewrap, pebbles, denim jeans and soap bubbles, which can be used to create witty, waterproof flooring for bathrooms and other areas.

Rubber

Flooring made from rubber is largely synthetic. In its natural state rubber does not have the practical or aesthetic qualities necessary for flooring – it is soft, inflammable and is not colourfast. Rubber flooring, known as 'vulcanized rubber', contains a tiny quantity of real rubber but otherwise consists of petrochemical derivatives (sometimes in the form of recycled car tyres). Rubber is a relatively environmentally friendly product in terms of its manufacture (the vulcanizing process involving high temperatures is brief) and disposal (it is a recyclable material), and because of its longevity.

A rubber floor is waterproof, hard-wearing, antibacterial and non-slip, but it may show stains and can be burnt by hot objects. In terms of interior design, it is particularly versatile because of the range of colours available. These include brilliant saturated blue, green, red, pink, purple and yellow, as well as a range of more subtle tones. Supplied in tile and sheet form, it comes in various textured surfaces. Certain forms can be used outdoors, including special self-draining, grippy rubber surfaces, and in the gym where anti-fatigue cushioning comes into its own. There is even magnetic rubber for laying over metal structures.

Glossy, warm 'poured rubber' flooring has become increasingly popular due to its sleek contemporary finish. The first generation of this type of flooring was expensive and hard to install – the floor had to be completely level, smooth, dry and clean; it took a long time to set; and the weather conditions had

to be almost perfect for it to dry. The latest version is much cheaper and easier to install. It is made from recycled rubber granules (formerly car tyres) which are laid in sheet form off a roll and finished with a high-gloss liquid coating. Like other synthetic rubbers, it is available in a range of colours.

Vinyl
Made from petrochemical derivatives, vinyl has proved a hugely popular product because it can be moulded and printed to imitate natural materials such as wood and stone without the expense of laying the real thing. It is inexpensive, waterproof and hypo-allergenic. As flooring it is relatively warm under foot and comes in tiles or sheets.

Acrylic
A type of thermoplastic, acrylic can often be used as an alternative to glass – for example, as coloured panels in contemporary furniture – because it is rigid, lighter and less likely to break. It is also softer than glass, is highly flammable and scratches easily. Acrylic can be clear or coloured, or clear but with coloured cut edges. As well as forming flat surfaces, it can be used to make whole pieces of furniture, such as the classic nest of tables, each of which is constructed from a length of bent acrylic. The best known acrylic is Perspex and this name is widely used as the generic term for the material.

Corian
Another trademarked product, Corian is the generic name for this tough material. It is made from a mixture of natural minerals and acrylic, which forms a stiff sheet that is ideal for kitchen worksurfaces. Your kitchen worktop and sink can both be moulded as one for a perfect fit, which has practical benefits as well as a sleek, streamlined appearance. Corian is relatively expensive but has distinct advantages: it is heatproof, non-flammable, non-porous, self-coloured so no wear and scratches will show, and is hypo-allergenic. Importantly, Corian is non-toxic and does not passively emit gases like some other plastics.

PVC
One of the most widely used plastics, PVC (polyvinyl chloride) is lightweight and cheap and has countless applications both in the fabric and interior of the modern home. It is, however, also a material that gives cause for concern, both from a health and from an environmental point of view, because it readily gives off gases, which means that chemicals seep out of it into the atmosphere. In houses, PVC is most often used for flooring, windows

and conservatories, guttering and surface water pipes, and damp-proof coursing. It has become practically indispensable and cannot instantly be phased out, but concern and awareness may mean that in future this cheap plastic becomes less ubiquitous.

Polypropylene
Like acrylic and PVC, polypropylene is another strong, versatile thermoplastic. In the 1960s the mass-production of cheap moulded polypropylene furniture and household objects helped to bring modern designs into every home. Most famous, perhaps, is the moulded stacking chair designed by Robin Day. Twenty-first-century designers such as Philippe Starck and Tom Dixon have also turned to polypropylene to create the shells of furniture and fitments. As a translucent material available in many colours it is also used to great effect in contemporary lighting.

Melamine
A laminate applied to chipboard and other surfaces, melamine serves as a plastic surface for furniture and worktops. It is practical and inexpensive and comes in a range of flat colours, abstract patterns or imitations of marble, terrazzo and other materials. Melamine is a thermoset, the family of plastics that is resilient and less flammable than others, but it is prone to scratching.

Recycled plastic
This relatively new material is available in the form of thick sheets, which can then be cut and glued to make worksurfaces and furniture. It usually has a colourful, mottled appearance – the exact tones are dependent on the items that were recycled, which might be anything from toothbrushes to drinking cups or plastic bottles. Plastics can also be recycled to form furnishing fabrics, some of them luxurious in tone and texture.

1 An update on a standard: cork tiles faced in photographic imagery and with a top layer of vinyl to provide wear and water resistance. 2 Linoleum is available in a wide range of colours; striking patterns can be inlaid into sheet formats. 3 Studded rubber creates a hard-working contemporary floor. One particular advantage of the material is the range of bright, strong colours. 4 Acrylic is suitable for many of the same applications as glass, such as these Perspex stair treads and curved panels. 5 Poured rubber has a soft glossy appearance that enhances the effect of natural light. 6 Corian is a proprietary manufactured product that can be moulded and shaped to individual specification to create seamless counters with inset sinks. 7 Lightweight, cheap and translucent ribbed plastic sheeting encloses a kitchen area within an otherwise open space.

GLASS

Choosing glass

Advances in glass technology mean that it is now safe and structurally sound to use large areas of glass in your home for walls, windows (see pages 202–203), partitions and screens, and, on a smaller scale, for fittings and fixtures. It has become one of the key features of contemporary home design, letting in light to create bright, airy spaces and turning planes that were solid and opaque into transparent and luminous surfaces. Used inventively, glass has the ability to transform even the most cramped home environments into places that are a pleasure to live in.

STRUCTURAL ELEMENTS When choosing how much glass to use in the external walls of your home – whether you are building from scratch or adding an extension – it is worth considering issues of privacy as well as how

to achieve greater openness. Not everyone wants their lives to be permanently on display, and if your house is overlooked you may want to keep some areas enclosed or incorporate a semi-transparent element such as a glass-block wall. If your aspect is relatively private, however, a plain glass wall can enhance your living space by dissolving the boundaries between inside and out, encouraging a closer link with the natural world.

Used inside, glass helps to brighten dark areas and create a sense of space. An internal window, for example, can transfer borrowed light to another room, and translucent glass panels and partitions gently diffuse light when illuminated. Apart from vertical elements, almost any horizontal surface in the home can now be made from strengthened glass, including areas of floor such as mezzanine platforms or walkways, and the treads of staircases, all of which enable light to permeate between levels.

Whichever way you choose to use glass in the structure of your home, you will need expert advice to determine the correct size, thickness and type required.

OTHER SURFACES On a lesser scale, glass can be used to transform everyday surfaces into something more elegant – a glass-topped desk or table, for example. Frosted glass shelves are a traditional bathroom accessory, but shelves in clear or coloured glass can add interest to any room in the home. Glass doors on kitchen cupboards look sleek and modern and mean you can display attractive tableware without it becoming grimy. Glass can also be moulded into basins and bathtubs to create striking contemporary bathrooms.

When choosing glass surfaces do not forget the practicality of keeping them clean. Glass bathroom fittings may look glamourous but watermarks will show, especially in hard water areas. Glass demands regular cleaning if the surface is to look its best.

Strengthened glass

There are a number of forms of strengthened glass that can be used for constructing architectural elements. Flooring glass is made of two thick layers of annealed (heat-treated) glass laminated to each other to add strength – this is called annealed float glass. Although it is very tough, this type of glass is most comfortably used in panels no larger than 1sqm (11sqft), which are fully supported around the edges and cushioned with rubber. The panels can be placed edge to edge to create a longer area of glass floor if required.

Other methods of strengthening glass include tempering it by rapid cooling – this

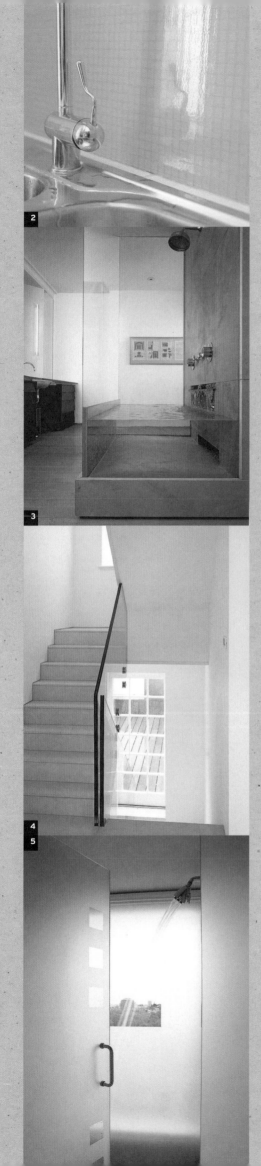

1 A strip of glass floor running alongside a huge plate-glass window, directly beneath a skylight, enhances the effect of openness and light. **2** Wired glass, typically used as a security feature in glazed external doors, can also make a good-looking and practical splashback. **3** A tank-like bath and shower enclosure made of clear glass encourages a sense of spaciousness. **4** Glass guardrails create a bright and airy stairwell. **5** Frosted or etched glass lets in light while providing an element of privacy. **6** Glass blocks and bricks look best when used generously to create entire walls rather than meagre infills. **7** An open glass staircase lets light spill down from the glazed door at the top. **8** A dramatic glass walkway on a mezzanine level is formed out of thick layers of annealed glass set in a metal framework. **9** Alternate strips of frosted and coloured glass make a bath/shower enclosure.

is known as toughened glass – and laminating it with clear plastic between two layers of glass. Toughened glass shatters into tiny fragments rather than the jagged shards that result when ordinary glass is broken. In the home it is used for table tops, shelving and furniture. Laminated glass shatters but is held together by the layer of plastic inside it in the manner of a car windscreen (for which purpose it was developed). It is used for large plate-glass windows and doors.

Double- and triple-glazing

When used for windows, double- or triple-glazing provides increased energy efficiency and sound-proofing, and can reduce indoor condensation. This type of glazing is made from sealed units of two or three layers of toughened glass with a space between them for insulation. Some units have argon gas in the space which further reduces heat conductivity, making these windows even more environmentally friendly.

Low-emissivity glass

Another eco-friendly option, low-emissivity, or low-e, glass has a special insulating coating that allows light through, but not heat. This makes it an ideal choice for large expanses of glass because it prevents the interior from becoming too hot during the day, but stops heat escaping in the cold hours of the night. Low-e glass can be incorporated into double-glazing to make it super energy efficient.

Glass with integral blinds

Either double- or triple-glazed, this type of high performance window unit has Venetian blinds sandwiched between the layers; they are operable by a mechanism on the inner frame. The result is a fully sealed, highly insulated unit with optimum light control.

Patterned and translucent glass

These types of glass are both practical and aesthetically pleasing. Patterned glass is formed by rolling the glass with a textural pattern as it cools; translucent glass is made by sandblasting or acid-etching to create minutely stippled, milky frosting. Traditionally found in bathroom windows and doors, patterned and translucent glass can be used for other areas of the home that require a degree of privacy. To maintain a light, open feel, for example, a translucent glass screen or partition can be installed between a sleeping or bathing area and an open-plan living space. Translucent glass works particularly well when illuminated with coloured light. Thicker forms of patterned or translucent glass can be used for external doors to maximize natural light.

Vision-control glass

Another solution for areas where privacy is needed, but clear glass panels or screens are preferable, vision-control glass offers ultimate flexibility because its transparency can be switched on and off as required. It consists of two sheets of laminated glass with a liquid crystal film between; the crystals can change instantaneously from opaque to transparent.

Coloured glass

Using coloured glass is an effective way of introducing colour into an interior, especially when it is sited where light will shine through it. Plain glass is available in a range of glowing colours, from subtle pastels to rich, deep tones. A coloured window, such as a beautiful stained-glass panel from a reclamation yard, can provide a striking focal point for a room or stairhead, and a traditional doorlight will bring colour into a hallway. You can also commission a glass artist to create a unique design to your own specifications. Densely coloured glass panes can be used to provide a degree of privacy for bathrooms and other places.

Glass blocks

Popular with modern architects and designers, chunky glass blocks are both practical and attractive: they allow light through, but are not entirely transparent, and as a surface they have a pleasing geometrical rhythm. Glass blocks are sufficiently solid to act as structural members, and can be used to construct either flat or curved walls and panels, both inside and out. They have the added practical advantages of acting as sound and heat insulation. Blocks are available in a variety of finishes, including frosted or rippled, and also come in different colours.

Safety and security

Its very invisibility makes glass potentially hazardous, especially for children. In many places in the home it may be more appropriate to use frosted, patterned or coloured glass – which you can see – rather than clear glass. On floors and stair treads, sandblasted dots and ridges provide friction underfoot to help prevent slipping. The unprotected edges of glass tables are usually ground and polished to render them 'soft', but it is important to be aware of jutting corners when children are around. Placing glass partitions near water sources can also be risky as spilt water might cause someone to slip and fall against the glass. From a security point of view, a useful development is alarmed glass for doors. This contains electro-conducting circuits connected to alarms that are activated if the glass is broken.

1 Glossy panels of brushed aluminium clad the walls of a wet room. 2 The sleek utility of a stainless-steel basin and bathtub makes a strong statement in a contemporary bathroom. Types of metal include: 3 Mirrored stainless steel. 4 Steel mesh. 5 Bright polished copper. 6 Satin stainless steel. 7 Dark patinated copper. 8 Satin aluminium. 9 Patinated zinc. 10 Perforated aluminium. 11 Heat-tempered copper. 12 Polished pewter. 13 Stainless-steel kitchen units convey a professional aesthetic, but demand extra upkeep. 14 Metal mesh panels make a semi-transparent staircase.

METAL

Choosing metal

With its industrial connotations and hard, cool surfaces, metal may not seem an obvious choice for the home, but in contemporary interiors it is celebrated for those very qualities. Juxtaposed with other materials, smooth metal finishes can provide a pleasing contrast in terms of colour, texture and temperature, adding to the sensual enjoyment of a space. In loft-style apartments, structural steel girders are often left exposed, their rugged aesthetic now a key feature in this type of interior.

Metals have any number of uses throughout the home, from architectural elements such as windows and staircases to kitchen and bathroom fittings, and all kinds of furniture and lighting. Using metals like steel and aluminium to clad walls, stair risers, doors, units and even ceilings creates a very modern look, or you can choose less commonly used metals such as zinc, copper and pewter to add sheen and texture to countertops or other surfaces and interior details.

From an environmental point of view, metal loses marks because of its high 'embodied energy' – the energy used in its extraction, processing and transport. A redeeming feature, however, is that nearly all metals are recyclable. It is also possible to source some metal features from salvage yards, such as wrought-iron gates and railings, cast-iron fireplaces and brass door furniture. More contemporary reclaimed items such as metal filing cabinets and meat safes can be bought from sale rooms and dealers.

Cast iron

Iron is the metal from which many alloys, including steel, are made and it is now ubiquitous in modern building construction. Cast iron is so-called because the molten iron is cast in moulds. It is strong and more resistant to corrosion than wrought iron. In homes, it is most likely to crop up in the form of period features such as roll-top bathtubs, firebacks and grates, or as stoves, both old and new (see pages 204–205). Traditional ranges such as Agas are also made of cast iron (see page 234), as are some types of heavy-duty pots and pans.

Wrought iron

Instead of being cast, this iron is stretched, hammered and twisted when in a red-hot, semi-molten state. Wrought iron can be used to make gates and gateways and, indoors, banisters and balustrades. It has a traditional, robust image. You can commission a skilled craftsman to produce a unique piece of wrought iron for a specific location.

Steel

A metal alloy, steel is a mixture of iron with a small proportion of other metals added to enhance the iron's performance. There are many different recipes, which vary according to the end use of the steel, and countless different products are made from it. Unlike iron, which to date has a strongly traditional image, steel is a self-consciously modern material: strong, light steel frames form the basis of much modern architecture.

So long as it is in a dry environment, steel should not corrode and does not therefore need any special finish. It can, however, be coated with paint, lacquer or oil (beware of making surfaces on which you are going to walk slippery) to seal it and exclude air that might be damp. Steel can also be galvanized – hot-dipped in or electroplated with zinc – to pre-empt corrosion, or coated with a mixture of elements including carbon and copper, which create a superficial rusty layer and thereby protect the steel beneath.

Steel mesh or sheets can be used on walls, stair treads and risers, and to form walkways and clad areas of floor, especially where there is heavy traffic; sheeting can be ridged, gridded, brushed or perforated. Usually found in a commercial environment, steel diamond-plate flooring brings a modern, industrial quality to living spaces.

Stainless steel

Of all metals, stainless steel is the most popular for use in interiors as it doesn't rust. An alloy containing as much as 20 per cent nickel and chromium, it has a smooth, shiny finish that is immensely appealing. The area of the home in which stainless steel is most widely used is the kitchen. Inspired by the streamlined, utilitarian appearance of professional kitchens, designers have created a sleek modern look for domestic ones that has become mainstream. At the centre of the contemporary kitchen stands the ultra-desirable stainless-steel range; it can be surrounded by a whole battery of stainless-steel appliances and fittings from dishwashers, fridges and microwaves to units, sinks and splashbacks (see pages 234–239).

So long as it has a satin rather than mirror-polished finish (the latter is harder to maintain with a flawless finish and the former is therefore more practical), as a material, stainless steel is almost maintenance free, any stains or marks quickly disappearing under the friction of a scrub with a kitchen

scourer. Bathroom basins and bathtubs have followed kitchen sinks and units, though these are still expensive, exclusive items.

Choosing stainless-steel kitchen and bathroom fittings from utility outlets can sometimes prove less expensive than buying those designed for domestic use.

Aluminium

This lightweight metal is associated with aircraft and the wheels of sports cars. In its anodized form aluminium is porous and can be stained with coloured dyes – an effect demonstrated by housewares such as salad bowls of the 1950s and 1960s. Unlike steel or iron, aluminium resists rusting and is therefore a useful material for windows. Its light weight makes it ideal for cladding surfaces both horizontal and vertical; sheeting can have a simple brushed finish or be embossed with geometric patterns. Both tiles and sheets can be used to make a lightweight floor covering, which lends an element of modernity to an interior. It is a good idea to stick aluminium flooring into position rather than simply screw it down, otherwise the floor will rattle. There are also a number of designs for lightweight chairs and tables, and most door furniture is made from aluminium.

Pewter

A metal that is unusually warm to the touch, pewter has an attractive bluish-grey tone that is deeper than the silver colour of other metals such as zinc and stainless steel. Historically, pewter had a dangerously high lead content (possibly 70 per cent), but today it consists of around 93 per cent tin mixed with about five per cent copper and two per cent antimony (a non-toxic by-product of smelting lead) and is completely safe to use. In homes, pewter tends to be found in decorative items such as bowls or details such as handles.

Zinc

A malleable, food-safe metal, in sheet form zinc traditionally lined the inside of butchers' vans and the counters of French bars. This metal is soft and abraded by use and so develops an attractive clouded patina over time. When it is new, zinc sheet is bright and silvery, with countless minute striations caused by the rolling process. If so desired, a patina can be almost instantly reproduced by applying a cocktail of chemicals to create a darker, more practical surface that will not show daily wear and tear. Its softness means that zinc can easily be folded, soldered and pinned or glued over the surfaces and around the contours of tables, countertops, splash-backs and the doors of kitchen units.

Copper

When it is new, copper has a distinctive reddish-orange glow. The metal has a long life, is easy to work with, and has practical uses such as wiring and piping. Copper's main contribution to interiors, though, is on a purely aesthetic level: in kitchens, copper sheeting can be applied to the fronts of kitchen units in the same way as other metals, and an array of copper pans hanging from a rack has a striking visual appeal. Perhaps a more familiar use for copper in the home is in the form of beaten fireplace hoods, coal scuttles and similar rustic details. Outdoors, copper reacts over time with carbonic acid in rain to acquire the distinctive green corrosion-resistant patina known as verdigris, which looks attractive on cladding and roofing; indoors, however, there is no reason why copper should not retain its bright colour and lustre.

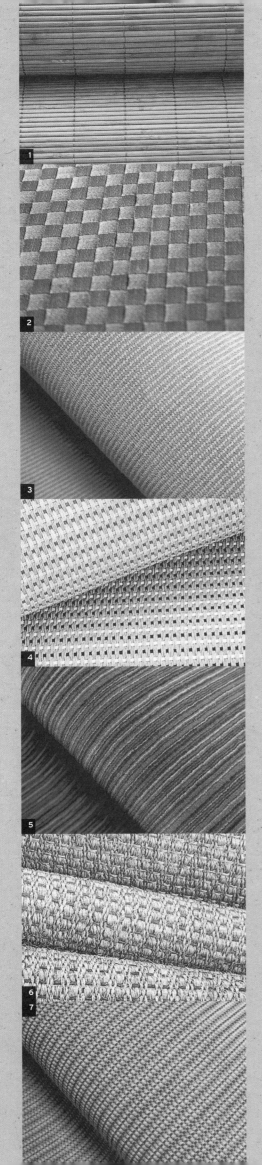

CARPET & NATURAL FIBRES

Choosing soft flooring

The floor is one of the key parts of an interior. It is constantly touched, and so forms an important sensual element as well as one that is subject to a considerable amount of wear and tear. From a visual point of view, the floor often covers a large area and it will therefore have a huge impact on the look of a room, setting the whole tone of the space.

The choice of soft flooring is essentially between three types: natural-fibre, carpet or rugs (although leather is a less-common option). Both natural fibres and carpets can be fitted, or you can lay a 'rug' of the same material – a large piece with bound edges.

Colourful tribal or modern rugs are a distinctive and flexible option. You can use a single beautiful rug as a striking decorative feature, or scatter several rugs casually over a stone or wood floor.

Natural-fibre floor coverings

Made from the grasses and leaves of plants (or wood pulp, in the case of paper), natural-fibre floor coverings are flat-woven (in other words without pile) in a variety of designs. They often have a latex backing and can be fitted like carpet or bought as mats. Derived from natural, renewable sources they are an environmentally friendly choice. Of the most popular natural floorings, jute is the softest, seagrass the most resistant to staining, coir generally the cheapest and sisal probably the most versatile. Apart from rush matting, all can be kept clean with vacuuming. Most natural-fibre floorings – with the exceptions of rush and seagrass – are not suitable for damp rooms such as bathrooms and kitchens.

SISAL Made from the decorticated leaves of the agave plant, sisal is tough but not too rough, which makes it suitable for most locations in the home, although it does not like damp. Sisal is available in bright colours (which may eventually fade if exposed to sunlight) as well as in its natural state.

SEAGRASS Like sisal, seagrass has a soft texture and can be used throughout the home. Grown in paddy fields, it has smooth, hard fibres that are fairly resistant to spills and water (although prolonged damp will eventually cause it to rot) and consequently it works well as a bathroom flooring. Seagrass is impermeable to dyes and so is only available in its natural sandy tones.

JUTE Soft underfoot, but less hardwearing than sisal or seagrass, jute can be woven with cotton to add colour.

ABACA Also known as Manila hemp, abaca fibre comes from a species of the banana family and is traditionally used for making rope and matting.

RUSH An ancient form of floor covering, rush matting is made from hand-plaited strips of rush which are sewn together with no backing. It actually needs to be damp to stay supple and it should be sprayed or sprinkled with water once a week.

COIR This is made from coconut husks and is the least comfortable fibre against bare skin. It is cheap and very hardwearing, however, and is available in mats, tiles and strips. Coir is susceptible to damp and should be kept dry.

PAPER Woven paper yarn makes an attractive, durable floor covering. Made from softwood pulp, the spun paper has added resin for increased water-resistance.

Carpet

Few things feel as luxurious as a closely woven woollen carpet underfoot and it remains a popular choice of floor covering, especially for bedrooms. Luxury wool carpet has a price tag to match, but the huge choice of carpet types and qualities means that there is something for nearly all budgets. Poor quality, though, will give correspondingly poor performance and, ultimately, poor value for money.

Carpet is available in different materials, pile weights and constructions. Materials include wool, nylon (mixed 1:4 with wool, this makes probably the hardest-wearing, good-quality carpet at a manageable price) and other man-made fibres including polyester and polypropylene. Pile weight refers to the weight of fibre in any given area of carpet – this will be higher where the pile is closely woven, giving a thicker covering that is more springy and resilient than less densely woven types.

WOVEN CARPET In a woven carpet, the weft and pile are woven into the warp at the same time, resulting in a short pile. This is the usual substructure for pile carpet, and it is generally better quality than tufted. The tighter the weave, the more likely the carpet is to last.

TUFTED CARPET For tufted carpet, the pile is injected into a ready-woven backing. The tufts can be cut for a softer finish or left looped (or a mix of both). It is cheaper than woven but can still be hardwearing.

CORDED CARPET A type of woven carpet, the pile of corded carpet is arranged in ridges in a similar manner to corduroy.

SHAG-PILE CARPET Recently fashionable again, shag-pile carpet has an exceptionally long pile and is suitable for bedrooms and living areas where you want to introduce an element of luxury. It should be avoided for stairs and bathrooms.

NON-WOVEN CARPET Tending to be cheap, thin and less hardwearing, a non-woven carpet has fibres glued to the backing.

CARPET TILES Originally designed for commercial use, carpet tiles are now available in interesting colours and designs suited to the home. They are generally hardwearing and individual tiles can be replaced when worn.

Rugs

Buying a good quality rug can represent a real investment and it is worth looking at a great many before you choose. You should also give yourself time to respond to a rug's colours and designs; some dealers will allow you to take a rug home to see how it works in the space where you want to put it before you buy it. Apart from being placed on the floor, any top-quality rug can be hung on the wall to be enjoyed as a superb piece of craftsmanship.

FLAT-WEAVE RUGS These are smooth, thin rugs, many of which are good value for money. Patterned kilims are made of coarse wool and generally come from the Middle East. Dhurries are constructed from woven cotton and come from India. With their colourful, often geometric designs both of these types of rug can have a dynamic, modern appearance even though such weavings have been part of tribal life for centuries. They can be laid on the floor or, as they are so supple, over tables or beds.

PILE RUGS Unlike flat-weaves, pile rugs have upstanding tufts of fibre that form a thick, 'furry' surface. The best known and most coveted pile rugs over the centuries have been Persian tribal rugs, which are made of knotted wool and come in a stunning array of colours and patterns. There are many other types of pile rug, however. These include bold and bright gabbehs, which do not follow traditional designs and often incorporate small figures on a plain background.

An alternative to a tribal pile rug can be a contemporary rug. Available in interesting textures, bold patterns or cool minimalist designs in muted shades, these can be more in sympathy with some modern interiors.

Fitting and underlay

Laying and fitting soft flooring is generally a job for a professional. To be truly comfortable and hardwearing, carpet requires an underlay, and so do some natural-fibre floor coverings if the floor underneath is uneven or in poor condition. The latter also need time to adjust to their new environment and should be unrolled in situ and allowed to dry and acclimatize for 48 hours before laying. If a rug is laid on bare floorboards, it should have a rubberized underlay both to protect it and to prevent it from slipping. The best quality underlay is made from hair and jute topped with felt or rubber which is resistant to mildew.

Types of natural flooring: **1** Bamboo matting. **2** Abaca matting. **3** Woven wool carpet combining cut and looped pile. **4** Paper matting. **5** Woven wool carpet with cut pile. **6** Sisal matting. **7** Plain woven wool carpet. **8** Leather tiles make a luxurious natural flooring. **9** Contemporary rugs come in a wide range of colours, designs and prices. **10** Shag-pile carpet in a bedroom has retro chic and a certain sensual appeal. **11** A simple felt mat works well in a pared-down interior. **12** A fine woven rug from Marrakesh contributes subtle colour and pattern in this interior.

ARCHITECTURAL ELEMENTS & DETAILS

FORM AND FUNCTION

Architectural details, both major and minor, can transform a space and are therefore key elements in any interior scheme. Everything that is discussed in this section is functional, but function is not enough on its own – the aesthetic appeal of forms and finishes is equally important. If you put time and effort into choosing the right structural features and details, your trouble will be repaid.

Some elements dominate by virtue of scale. Staircases and fireplaces, for example, set the tone of an entire room or living space and, once installed, are costly and inconvenient to replace. As well as being beautifully designed, they must also be safe and are therefore items generally only suitable for expert construction and installation. Other, smaller details, such as door handles, are less expensive or difficult to change and it is possible to update or subtly alter the look of an interior simply by replacing them with new ones.

Windows and doors not only take up a significant part of the walls of each room but they also have a unique function in the home – they create a relationship with the world outside, both from outdoors and in, and between one room and another. Windows and doors original to a house are a treasure and should be replaced with identical ones in order to retain your home's architectural integrity (and you may damage the value if you do otherwise). If you are building an extension to a period building, you might find interesting compatible windows and doors at an architectural reclamation yard, or have them specially made in either a historical or simple modern style sympathetic in scale. Doors in particular are one of many features that give a home a sense of history, or contemporaneity. If you are building from scratch, the choice of these structural elements is a huge and exciting issue. Today, it is possible to install vast expanses of glass that blur the boundaries between windows, walls and doors to create modern interiors that are filled with light and air.

DOORS

Choosing doors

A number of factors should be taken into consideration when choosing a door: whether it is for internal or external use, the style and size of your home, and how important it is to let in light. The front door is usually wider and taller than other doors in the house and is made from solid timber or other substantial materials. It needs protection from the elements and also needs to fit well to avoid draughts. Security is an additional and important issue. Internal doors offer more flexibility of both materials and styles, but need to be chosen to fit harmoniously within an overall decorative scheme.

Wooden doors

Doors have been made of wood for centuries, and this is still the most commonly used material. For an external door, hardwood is the best choice because of its strength (see page 180). An outside wooden door needs to be protected from the elements, and should be prepared with primer and undercoat before gloss paint is applied. For a natural look, bare hardwood can be varnished or given a finish of wood preservative.

Interior wooden doors can be either painted or left natural. A half-and-half mixture of linseed oil and button polish feeds bare softwood and helps it to glow. Hardwood doors can be finished with furniture wax; dissolving a little turpentine in it will help the wax soak in better but will reduce the sheen.

Wooden doors of all types are available from builder's merchants; or try salvage yards for original examples (see page 211).

LEDGED-AND-BRACED DOORS The most basic of wooden doors, this consists of a row of vertical planks secured with battens set in a zig-zag shape. This type of door is best suited to simple, traditional houses.

RECESSED-PANEL DOORS This style dates back to the eighteenth century, and is probably the most common form of wooden door. There are usually three to four panels, the proportions of which vary according to the period and style.

FLUSH DOORS In the twentieth century, the hollow-frame flush door became popular, its smooth planes in keeping with a less formal modern style. White-painted plywood flush doors tend to lack character, but more stylish doors are now available in a range of interesting woods and veneers.

1 Flush doors are reticent and contemporary. Here, shallow circular cutouts applied to the door introduce a subtle note of interest. **2** This robust metal door is suspended on tracks and slides back to reveal a utilitarian bathroom. **3** The proportions of the traditional panelled door reflect the architectural styles of the eighteenth and nineteenth centuries. Such doors are usually painted and set within an architrave.

Glass doors

The ideal medium for creating light, airy interiors, glass doors are a common feature of many contemporary homes. Technological advances in manufacture mean that it is now possible to use large expanses of glass, but you will need to consult a professional regarding the numerous safety regulations relating to thickness, strength and type of tempering (as well as energy efficiency). For an external glass door it is best to choose toughened or laminated glass for reasons of safety and security (see pages 192–193).

Doors can be made entirely of glass, with just a few metal fittings, or contain glass panels of various sizes. Inside, glass doors allow borrowed light into underlit areas or rooms. Where privacy is not an issue, they can also be used to draw the eye from one space to another, thereby creating an open, friendly atmosphere without losing the advantage of being able to close the door on a room. Coloured and patterned glass adds interest to a door, and draws attention to the presence of a solid barrier.

Metal doors

Solid metal doors have an industrial aesthetic in keeping with converted loft spaces and work best when they can slide along a track. Lighter metal-frame doors can support large sheets of glass and are suitable for most types of door. An aluminium frame is light and malleable, with a good strength-to-weight ratio, but steel is stronger overall. The longest-lasting type of metal frame is steel galvanized with zinc which is finished with a powder coating to make it rust-proof. This kind of finish is almost maintenance-free; coatings are available in a wide choice of colours and are suitable for either internal or external use.

Pivoting doors

This type of door balances the weight on one side of the pivot against the weight on the other, giving it a structural advantage over hinges. This is a good idea for a very large door – such as a floor-to-ceiling glass door leading to a garden – where the weight might pull hinges away from the wall or cause distortion. A door can pivot at any point along its length, provided the pivot can bear the extra weight of the larger portion of door.

Sliding and folding doors

Sliding doors are useful because they require no space to swing open. Smooth wood, metal and glass are the most common materials. A sliding door can either be set into the thickness of the wall or be suspended from a runner on the wall's surface (in which case

4 Doors that extend from floor to ceiling, like this framed glass door, enhance the sense of space by doing away with the visual break of the door head. **5** A huge pivoting panel of metal-framed glass demonstrates where door meets window meets wall. **6** Stained-glass panels in double entrance doors provide a focal point in a hallway. Salvage yards are good sources of such traditional features. **7** A door made of translucent etched glass allows light through from area to area. **8** Pivoting doors that fold back out of the way are ideal for interconnecting areas. **9** A custom-made door blends with an overall scheme and expresses a sense of thoughtful detail.

it will stand proud of the wall). If it is set into the wall, door furniture has to be flush with the door so that it does not catch. A sliding all-glass external door is often called a 'patio door' (see page 203). For very wide openings or interconnecting spaces, doors that fold back neatly in a concertina to one or both sides are a good solution (see page 165).

Double doors

A pair of wide double doors between one room and another looks elegant and expansive, both open and closed. Narrow double doors, which together add up to the width of a single door (or a bit more), are useful where space is too tight to allow an ordinary door to swing open and where a sliding door is not an option. Double doors can of course be sliding.

Covered doors

A flush door can be covered with sheet metal, fabric, leather, collage or any other material, provided it does not interfere with its opening and closing action. Any of these treatments will make a strong decorative statement and can complement or throw into relief the overall decor of a room or space.

French doors

Originally introduced in late Georgian houses to allow easier access to balconies, French doors are a cross between doors and windows. They are full-height, glazed (either in one large panel each or subdivided) and hung in pairs that open together. Their combined width can be that of a single door, or each can be as wide as a single door. French doors can be used either between two rooms or, as traditionally, giving on to an outside space such as a balcony or garden, or perhaps a conservatory. They have one potential weakness, which is security, since there is no fixed element at the centre where their edges meet.

Security

While you do not necessarily want your home to become a fortress, it is sensible to take precautions against break-ins. An external door should be as sturdy as possible – as should the frame – and fitted with appropriate locks. The most secure is a five-lever mortise deadlock. Side and rear doors should be reinforced with strong bolts (preferably key-operated) at the top and bottom. Remember, however, that you must be able to leave your home quickly and easily in the event of fire, so keys should be stored within easy reach and always in the same place so you know where they are. Many insurance companies impose minimum security requirements, so consult your home policy with regard to these.

WINDOWS

Choosing windows

Windows let in light and air to your home. They are also an integral part of any building's overall style and structure, so their design and material should be in keeping with this.

Wooden windows are generally a sympathetic choice for most homes built before 1920, and are the best choice all round in terms of the environment. For long-lasting windows specify tannalized timber and use a microporous paint that allows any damp in the wood to evaporate. Some types of paint are guaranteed for six or eight years.

Metal windows look clean-lined and contemporary, and were one of the archetypal features of modernist architecture. Hence they are suitable for apartments, houses and converted industrial buildings built in this style from the 1920s onwards, and remain a key element in today's home design.

While plastic (PVC) windows are becoming ubiquitous in many new homes, they can seem out of character in buildings that are more than a few years old. Moreover, PVC should be avoided as far as possible as it is a significant source of dioxins, which are harmful both to people and the environment (see page 191).

Casement windows

A casement window swings open like a door, usually either sideways (with hinges at the left or right) or upwards (with hinges at the top). Such windows are generally found on small houses and cottages of all periods. Metal casements that open inwards and downwards are a feature of many converted industrial buildings, as are windows that pivot on a central horizontal access.

Sash windows

In a sash window, one section of framed glass slides across another to create an opening. In a vertical sash, the weight of the moving section is counterbalanced by weights and pulleys hidden in a box at the side of the window or, in more modern versions, by a spring concealed in the vertical stile (part of the frame holding the glass). Tall sash windows divided into many smaller sections by wooden glazing bars are an elegant feature of much eighteenth-century architecture. Side-sliding sashes are more commonly found in cottages.

If properly made and fitted, a sash window should be as secure and draught-free as any other type of window. Small, single-paned sash windows may be double-glazed if required, but for larger windows the weight may well prove a prohibiting factor.

1 Outstanding original details, such as this roundel of circular windows, provide immense architectural character and are often a feature of buildings with a non-domestic history. **2** Toplighting is a vitalizing way of bringing natural light into the interior. Here the rooflight is positioned over a void so that light reaches the lower level. **3** In hot tropical climates air flow is an important means of cooling the interior. These louvred windows can be angled to catch the breezes. **4** Modern glass technology now makes it possible to create virtually frameless openings. **5** Continuous horizontal strip windows wrap round a corner and appear to raise the roof. **6** A sandblasted panel of glass lets in the light but maintains privacy. **7** Modern windows protrude from the exterior wall like light boxes. **8** Panels of tinted glass add a subtle touch of colour to an all-white bathroom.

Round and oval windows

'Oculi' or 'ox-eye' windows were a feature of houses in the seventeenth and early eighteenth centuries, sometimes set into a dormer or gable. Porthole-style windows can be used to make an interesting and sometimes witty contribution to a building's façade.

Sliding windows

The simplest sliding window is the so-called 'patio door' which gives access to a garden, terrace or decking in countless modern homes (originally a patio was an inner courtyard open to the sky in Spanish and Spanish-American houses). Patio doors usually consist of a large area of glass divided into two parts, one of which slides across the other – a descendant of the traditional sliding sash window. Just like every other window in the house, they can be made of timber, plastic or metal.

Some modern architecture challenges the traditional definitions of window, wall and door by combining all three functions in one large expanse of glass. Contemporary engineering means that (location permitting) a wall of glass can disappear completely, sliding into the ground so that indoors and outdoors become one, or sliding aside or upwards provided there is sufficient height or wall-width around the opening.

Continuous fenestration

This is the term for windows that form a strip along an external wall and sometimes wrap around the corner of a building, as opposed to individual windows set into a wall. It is a feature of modernist and later architecture as typified by the buildings of Le Corbusier and others. As with sliding windows and glass doors (see page 200), this type of window is usually set into a thin metal frame. Continuous fenestration is possible where the structure of the building is provided not by the external walls, but by steel or concrete pillars and girders. These create a supporting skeleton onto which the external walls are hung, and with modern technology, an entire wall of glass can be used to flood the building with light.

Louvred windows

These windows have panels of glass that can be tilted open, offering variable ventilation in hot weather and the possibility of a through-draught. In hot climates, there may be parts of the house that do not need glass windows at all, merely ventilation and protection from the sun as it rises in the sky. The solution is to install louvred wooden window panels where the louvres are fixed in a horizontal position so that they provide shade without impeding the movement of air.

Pivoting windows

The pivoting skylight in a sloping roof is a familiar feature of many attic conversions (see pages 156–158), but in fact pivoting windows can be used anywhere in the home. A window can pivot horizontally or vertically, or it can pivot up-and-over style, in the manner of a garage door. A pivoting window has the advantage that both sides of the glass can be cleaned from indoors

Rooflights

A rooflight is a window set into a roof and is a useful way of illuminating top floors or single-storey homes. This type of window allows views of the sky and also a closer relationship with the elements. The sound of rain pattering on the glass can be an added charm, but in a bedroom it might feel more like a hammering alarm call if it wakes you in the middle of the night. For this reason rooflights are perhaps best installed in bathrooms, living rooms, kitchens and attic conversions. Some roof-lights can be opened by remote control, or there are automatic versions with built-in sensors that detect rainfall and changes in temperature, closing the rooflight when it rains or drawing across a blind when the sun's rays become too strong.

Internal windows

Besides the rooflight, another effective method of bringing light into the home is by opening up internal windows. These borrow light from other windows or spaces, thereby transforming otherwise dingy corners. Internal windows can be made in walls, doors and partitions; if necessary privacy can be ensured by using sandblasted or etched glass. Coloured glass or gels (thin sheets of coloured plastic stuck to the glass) can be used to reduce the level of brightness if need be.

Security

Like doors, windows can give unwanted intruders access to your home. It is therefore always worth considering security when making decisions about windows. If you are having windows made, unobtrusive locks and bolts – including ones that allow you to lock the window slightly open for ventilation – can be installed at the manufacturing stage. These can alternatively be fixed at a later date. Many windows that can be bought off-the-peg from suppliers come with built-in locks. Toughened or wired glass is a good security feature for ground-floor windows or glazed doors. You can also increase your security by thinking about the way you use windows: a large proportion of burglaries are opportunistic and are the result of doors and windows left open.

Choosing fireplaces and stoves

A fire is a focal point in any room. Not only does it make a visual statement, drawing the eye and setting the room's tone in aesthetic terms, but it also provides movement, colour and warmth when the fire is alight. This effect is the result of two components: the type of fire, and the setting or surround. These should be in harmony – choose a simple, plain setting for a wood-burning stove, for example, rather than an elaborate marble fireplace.

Your choice of real fuel (and which type) or real-effect gas fire will depend on your lifestyle and the availability of different fuels. A real-effect fire is clean and trouble-free. In either case, you should use a professional to check that your flue and chimney are in working order before installation – an old flue may need cleaning or repair.

Fireplace components

Whether you are fitting an open fire or a real-effect one, the components are essentially the same. Wood-burning stoves obviously do not require a basket or grate, but still need a fireproof hearth area, a chimney and a flue.

CHIMNEY AND FLUE The chimney and its internal passageway, the flue, are an integral element of any fire. In an open fire or stove, the gases inside the chimney are hotter and less dense than the air in the room, so the air is drawn from the room and up the flue along with any smoke and combustion gases. From here they then pass to the outside air via the chimney. A gas fire also needs a flue to allow the fumes to escape.

HEARTH There are two main elements to a hearth: the back hearth (the area immediately under the fire) and the front hearth, which extends into the room. The back hearth should be of firebrick or heatproof screed – never use natural stone, marble or tiles, as these can shatter or explode. The front hearth comprises a constructional hearth, built into the floor (usually of concrete) and a decorative hearth on top of it; this must be of a non-combustible material such as stone, marble, tile or slate.

BASKET OR GRATE This is where the open or real-effect gas fire is lit. It can be a stand-alone item within the recess, or part of a larger insert made of cast iron or steel. Baskets are available in a wide range of designs, from traditional to contemporary.

in an open fire, which protects the masonry and reflects heat back into the room. It sits behind the basket or grate and is usually made of cast iron or refractory firebrick.

LINTEL The weight of the chimney is carried by the lintel. It can be made of any strong, non-combustible material; in older houses it often takes the form of a brick-built arch.

MANTEL This is the decorative frame to an open fire and might be of wood, stone, tile, marble or slate. Adding two legs to the shelf creates a classic mantelpiece. Modern materials such as fibreglass, fibrous plaster or resins can also be used.

Safety and preparation

Before you light your fire make sure you carry out a few safety checks:
1 Check ventilation. All appliances, whatever fuel they burn, need an adequate flow of air for combustion and a working flue. If your home has draught proofing or double-glazing you may need an air-vent or airbricks in an exterior wall of the room.
2 Is the chimney lined? If it is unlined, that is, rendered with cement or exposed brick, corrosive elements in the gases can eat into the mortar and weaken the structure.
3 Has the chimney been swept? Chimneys need to be clear of all obstructions such as birds' nests, building debris and soot and tar build-up. Even if you have a gas fire or are burning smokeless fuel, you should have your chimney swept regularly as it will help prevent chimney fires and reduce the risk of dangerous fume emissions from blocked appliances.
4 If you have an open fire, pre-warm the chimney before lighting your first fire of the year. Do this by lighting a piece of newspaper or a firelighter and placing it in the chimney for a few minutes. This kickstarts the flue and enables combustion gases to vent more easily.
5 Always use a fireguard if there are children or infirm people around. An open fire should never be left unattended unless a fireguard is in position to catch flying sparks.
6 Battery-operated smoke alarms are an invaluable safety item. Alarms are also now available for detecting flammable gas and carbon monoxide leaks.

Buying and fitting

Specialist fireplace companies usually offer a range of options – from restored antique fireplaces to contemporary surrounds, from real-effect to solid fuel – and can provide a full installation service. Renovated eighteenth- and nineteenth-century fireplaces can be

1 A contemporary steel fireplace incorporating hearth and flue provides a modernist reinterpretation of a traditional focal point. **2** A circular hearth half-lined in bricks is seamlessly integrated into the plane of the wall. **3** Wood-burning stoves are more efficient than open hearths and are ideal in areas where there is a good supply of timber. **4** As hot air rises, this contemporary hearth sited at high level is not the most efficient, but it still provides the psychological comfort of a real fire. **5** A minimal vertical hearth reduces the fireplace to its most elemental. **6** A classically proportioned fire surround with simple detailing blends old and new. **7** A Zen-inspired take on a gas fire: stone chips in a sleek stone hearth.

adapted to use with gas fires. Salvage yards (see page 211) are a good source for antique pieces, but you will need to arrange your own specialist fitter. When buying an antique fireplace check for cracks as these will widen with the heat of a fire. You should also make sure the grate and front bars are intact as cast iron is not malleable, so it will be difficult to get a replacement grate fitted.

Wood and solid-fuel fires

A 'real' fire provides the ultimate in homely comfort – but you need to be prepared to spend time lighting it as well as cleaning out the ash. The choice is between an open-fronted fire and a stove.

STOVES Wood-burning stoves have long been a popular way of heating the home in heavily forested areas such as Scandinavia and North America. Stoves are considerably more efficient than open-fronted fires and many have now been developed to burn both wood and solid fuels (generally known as multi-fuel stoves). With the addition of a back-boiler, a stove can provide domestic hot water and even heat several radiators.

Stoves can be either free-standing on the hearth or inset into the fireplace recess, and constructed of cast iron, sheet steel or a combination of both. Cast iron has many advantages – it is more durable, tends to hold the heat longer and can be cast into a huge range of shapes and mouldings. However, sheet-steel stoves, made by folding and welding the seams, have an airtight design, and can be cheaper than cast iron.

OPEN-FRONTED FIRES At its simplest an open fire comprises hearth, fire basket and flue; at the other end of the scale are built-in fireplaces with ornamental surrounds and fitted grates. The 'draw' of a fire is the key to its success; this depends on the relationship between the width, height and air-tightness of the flue on the one hand, and the size of the hearth opening on the other. This ratio can be manipulated by installing a metal hood or simple flat panel to decrease the size of the hearth opening. A professional fireplace specialist can calculate the size and type of fireplace that will work best for your room.

BURNING SOLID FUEL It is an offence to burn bituminous house coal in a smoke-control area unless on a special burner. Most urban areas are smoke-control zones but check with the environmental health department at your local council. If you do live in a smoke-control zone, try a natural smokeless fuel such as anthracite cobbles; these are best suited to closed appliances such as stoves. Anthracite is a purer carbon compound than household coal, resulting in fewer waste products and less smoke. Otherwise, man-made smokeless fuels are manufactured from selected coals and processed into briquettes using binders, or 'coked', which means they are pre-burned to get rid of smoke.

BURNING WOOD Fire logs need to be properly seasoned and dried, as unseasoned wood contains high levels of moisture, making it extremely difficult to burn. For open fires, burn hardwoods (deciduous trees); softwood is better used for kindling and in closed stoves as it 'spits' a lot. Wood burning produces tar, which can build up within the flue and cause internal problems as well as the possibility of chimney fires or structural damage. Open fires usually have enough oxygen to burn off most of these gases, but in a woodstove, each time fresh fuel is added, open the draught controls and run the stove hot until the flames die down. It is environmentally acceptable to burn wood provided it comes from a local source and would otherwise be wasted or left to rot.

Gas fires

Many new flame-effect gas fires are very convincing, giving the effect of a 'real' fire with none of the fuss. Another advantage of gas is that it can be more economical than solid fuel. Some types give out more heat than others: if your concern is heat as well as aesthetics, ensure that you choose a model with a heat exchanger. If you do not have an existing flue and chimney, the fire can be fitted with a flue leading to an outside wall. An electrically powered fan wafts the fumes out of the flue. All gas fires should have a pilot light that shuts down if the oxygen in the room drops to a dangerously low level. They should be installed by a qualified gas installer and serviced once a year.

Fire alternatives

Gas-flame grates are now breaking away from the 'coal-effect' aesthetic with innovative new designs incorporating ceramic pebbles and other materials. In addition, new fuels are being developed that produce a warming glow without harmful emissions. These include fire gel, a gooey substance that you place in a suitable container in a fireplace or elsewhere. It does not require a flue, which makes it extremely versatile. The gel is made from a waste product of sugar cane manufacturing and gives off only water vapour and a small amount of carbon dioxide. Eco-charcoal, made from crushed olive stones, is another new product currently being developed.

Choosing a heating system

There are three vital elements to choosing a heating system, setting aside the technical issues of boiler and power source (see page 150). First is the issue of matching the output of radiators or heating units to room size; second, the question of how to control your heating system for maximum efficiency; and third, the matter of style and materials. Take advice from professionals on all of the above.

Materials

Which is best: cast iron or aluminium? Cast-iron radiators retain their heat for longer, but they also take longer to heat up, so you have less control over the heating of your home. Aluminium, pressed steel and stainless-steel radiators are better thermal conductors. Radiators are now being made from relatively unfamiliar materials – glass and stone – with a translucent chemical element bonded onto their surfaces. This is heated with electricity and in turn heats the material, which radiates 80 per cent or more of the heat out into the room. The appeal of these radiators, however, is their appearance rather than their energy efficiency because electric heating is more expensive than other forms.

Radiator designs

Radiators now come in a wide range of sizes, shapes and finishes. Some are designed to be enjoyed as sculptural features, while others will blend in with the rest of the decor. If your budget will not stretch to replacing old radiators you can make them less prominent by painting them the same colour as the wall.

CLASSIC RADIATORS Traditional radiators have a solid, physical aesthetic that works well in both period homes and contemporary interiors. Classic-style radiators made from steel can be bought new or second-hand and cast-iron ones can be bought from salvage companies (see page 211). Reclaimed cast-iron radiators need to be adapted to modern plumbing and it is sometimes difficult to calculate their heat output. Do not buy salvaged radiators unless their insides have had old silt flushed out chemically and the outsides have had ancient paint removed.

VERTICAL RADIATORS Tall, wall-mounted radiators are a good solution where space is at a premium as they fit conveniently between architectural elements such as doors and

arranged either vertically or horizontally to geometric grids and sleek spirals. Vertical radiators can be used anywhere in the home, but work particularly well in bathrooms and kitchens. Designed to be seen rather than blend into the background, these highly contemporary radiators come in a range of finishes including white, black and chrome.

Standard slimline radiators can also be positioned upright rather than horizontally, and some manufacturers will custom-make them to fit your wall space.

LOW-LEVEL RADIATORS There are various types of radiator with a very low profile which are ideal for fitting beneath tall windows, for example. Some have a boxy form with a single or double row of convection fins, and others take the form of a long coil. Another form is the tubular finned radiator, which is a long tube with disc-like fins projecting along its length; these provide a large surface area for heating the air.

UNDERFLOOR RADIATORS As with conventional radiators, underfloor radiators heat a room by convection but they are almost invisible. Set below floor level with a grille across the top, they are ideal for minimalist interiors or for areas where wall space is limited but underfloor heating is not an option.

Radiator cases

To incorporate traditional radiators into architectural features they can be concealed inside fitted cases. Radiator cases have grilles or holes in the top and/or sides and front to allow heat to rise and circulate, but they will also absorb some of the heat.

Underfloor heating

Suitable for most floor surfaces, underfloor heating is ideal for contemporary homes that have large expanses of floor, glass walls and room dividers, and consequently fewer solid walls against which to place radiators. It is also a good system for heating smaller spaces as it leaves walls free.

When underfloor heating is installed, pipes or cables are laid in the solid floor, on top of insulation, or just under the floor if it is suspended. These heat the floor, which acts as a huge radiator. Because of the large surface area, the temperature does not need to be high in order to create an even heat throughout the living space, making this a highly energy efficient alternative. Each room has its own thermostat to control the temperature. An underfloor heating system can be either water-heated or electric, and

1 Contemporary radiators are now available in a variety of sculptural forms, transforming what was formerly a solely utilitarian element. **2** Low-level tubular finned radiators heat air by convection. **3** The 'Hot Hoop' radiator is suitable for all round heating and makes a strong design statement.

complements eco-friendly installations such as condensing boilers, heat pumps and solar panels as well as traditional energy sources such as gas, oil and electricity. The water system is currently the most common, with warm water travelling through a pattern of plastic pipes. As the water is warm rather than hot, it cannot be linked directly to a conventional central heating boiler, but has to be adjusted by a distribution manifold, water pump and blending valve. An electric system is also available, which has cables in the floor rather than pipes.

Choosing a cooling system

If you are deciding whether or not to have an air-conditioning system or unit, first consider other ways in which to keep rooms cool without using chemicals and machinery. Simple options include keeping blinds and curtains closed or having shutters fitted to your windows to keep out sun during the day; installing louvred windows that can be left open for ventilation (see page 203); putting in low-emissivity glass windows that allow in light but not heat (see page 193); or installing a fan. Air conditioning is undeniably the most effective solution in tropical climates, however, and for those with serious pollen allergies.

Air conditioning

An air-conditioning system works in the same way as a fridge, drawing heat from the air by means of a coil filled with cold, low-pressure gas and releasing it outdoors (or within a stand-alone condensing unit that will need emptying periodically). Homes are generally cooled either by a central system that works through ducts and vents or by individual room air conditioners.

The formula for establishing the size and power of an air-conditioning system or unit is complicated (a supplier will do this calculation for you). It depends not only on the dimensions of your home or room but also on other factors including, for example, whether there are south-facing windows (in the northern hemisphere). You should also consider how many hours you will be running your system or unit and over how many months of the year. It is worth doing these calculations carefully, as an over-large, over-powered machine will be inefficient and constantly turning itself on and off, while a too-small unit will struggle to give the required performance.

Fans

Available in various different forms, fans can be floor-standing sealed units, floor-standing standard fans, table-top fans, and those attached to and wired into the ceiling. A floor-standing sealed unit gives general movement of air through a room while standard and table-top fans can be directed more precisely at a particular point. A ceiling fan should be fitted by an electrician and generally only in rooms with at least 3m (10ft) clearance. Fans do not actually cool the air, but give a cooling sensation by blowing air across the surface of the skin, causing evaporation. In other words, a fan provides a muted wind-chill factor.

Heat-exchange units

A heat exchanger allows you to ventilate your home without losing the heat that is already inside. It works by drawing dusty, damp 'used' air from each room and expelling it through a vent, while at the same time drawing in fresh air from outdoors. The two bodies of air pass each other with only a fine membrane separating them, so the heat passes from the warmer to the cooler, thus saving the energy that would otherwise have to be generated anew. The ceiling in each room has a discreet vent attached to piping (slim enough to fit in a partition wall), which leads to the exchange unit in an attic or other void.

A heat-exchange unit can filter the fresh air for pollen, so is of benefit to those suffering from allergies. It is an eco-friendly alternative to air conditioning and extractor fans.

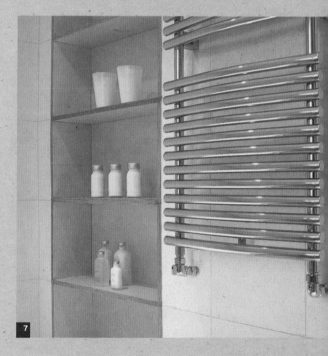

4 Old-fashioned cast-iron radiators have retro appeal. Salvage yards are good sources for reclaimed versions. **5** A warm-air system, where heat is vented through grilles set flush with the floor, does away with the need for radiators completely. **6** An electric ceiling fan boosts natural ventilation. Air is more cooling when it is moving. **7** Vertical radiators, such as this ladder-like design, double up as heated towel rails and are ideal for kitchens and bathrooms.

STAIRS & STAIRCASES

Choosing stairs and staircases

A staircase is a complex piece of engineering and is integral to the structure of any building of two or more floors. If you are carrying out any large-scale home improvement, you may wish to modify an existing staircase or construct an entirely new one – to lead to a mezzanine or an attic conversion, for example. You will need to discuss your plans with an architect to decide which style will be most appropriate. It is useful to know the names of the following constituent parts.

TREADS All staircases have treads: these are the steps on which you place your feet as you walk up. The upright surface at the back of each tread is the riser.

HANDRAILS AND BANISTERS A handrail is self-explanatory, giving you something to hold on to while ascending and descending the stairs. Supporting it are wooden or metal uprights called banisters or balusters. In many staircases, the handrail is an integral part of the design and construction. In others, such as in some spiral or enclosed staircases, or built-in ladders, the handrail may be added separately. A handrail might be made from wood or metal (well polished or painted for smoothness) or can take the form of a length of rope, knotted at the ends and strung through loops that secure it to the wall.

GUARDRAILS Rather than handrails, more contemporary staircases have guardrails to prevent you falling off the edge of the staircase. They are often made of glass or metal. Glass can be clear, frosted or etched and must be strong enough for the task (see pages 192–193). A wire tensioned between surfaces at the top and bottom of the staircase can serve as a guardrail, but must be strong enough to resist a weight falling against it.

INNER AND OUTER STRINGS On a conventional staircase, the sloping vertical side pieces of timber that slot onto the treads and risers, one against the wall and one on the outer edge below the banisters, are called the inner and outer string respectively. Stairs more than about a metre (3ft) wide may need a third string running up the centre of the steps underneath to support them.

LANDING The landing is a wide, flat section where a staircase turns a corner.

NEWEL POST The newel or newel post is the substantial timber upright at the bottom and top of the handrail and banisters. It gives them structural rigidity and directs the weight and stresses of the staircase into the floor.

Safety considerations

There are numerous safety regulations relating to the construction of stairs and staircases. Foremost are the rules concerning handrails and guardrails, which are required by law in most circumstances and countries. (Unfortunately, in several homes illustrated in this and other books these have been omitted.) Other regulations include the design of the treads themselves – their depth, shape and number – as well as the height of the steps, the width of landings, the pitch of the entire staircase and the clearance height above it. Even the space between banisters is regulated

1 Circulation spaces, which includes stairways, tend to be particularly generous in older properties. This beautifully detailed wooden staircase is a dominant architectural feature. 2 Wide, shallow concrete steps sweep elegantly around a curve. 3 Pristine white paintwork accentuates the rhythmic quality of the banisters. 4 Spiral staircases make good use of restricted space and have innate appeal. 5 A glass stairway provides the ultimate in visual lightness. Friction spots sandblasted on the treads reduce slipperiness. 6 Staggered steps up to a platform bed are very space-saving. 7 A curved staircase descending into the centre of an open-plan space provides an element of theatricality. 8 A sheet of clear glass encloses a minimal stone staircase.

(you would not want a child's head wedged between them). A qualified architect should be aware of safety regulations or you can apply to your local council for advice.

Materials

Staircases in period homes are generally made of wood. In grander houses, and in apartment buildings with a public stairwell, stone is often used for treads and risers and their supporting structure, while the banisters might be wrought iron. Stairs in many contemporary homes are made of wood, but glass, metal and concrete are also part of the modern repertoire (see pages 178–197), as they are in other parts of the building. Stairs may be left bare, to celebrate the material of which they are made, or they can be covered with carpet or natural-fibre flooring (see pages 196–197).

Shape and space

Deciding where a staircase should go and what form is should take is like fitting together the pieces of a jigsaw puzzle. Some staircases are slotted neatly into a space up the centre or side of an interior, with landings and rooms opening off them in the conventional manner. Others are conceived as grand, theatrical gestures, their sculptural forms serving as the central feature of an interior plan. Glass or cantilevered staircases are often the most dramatic because of the dizzying sense of insubstantiality they convey. The following are some of the interesting routes that can be taken by staircases.

Curved staircases

A curved staircase may undulate gently downwards or wind tightly around a central support to form a spiral stair. This latter type of staircase is useful where space is limited but may present difficulties, however, when you need to take large objects, such as pieces of furniture, upstairs. A staircase that winds in a tight circle, almost spiral but without the central support, is known as 'helical'.

A curved staircase sweeping around an open hallway, with radiating tapered steps, is known as a 'winding' staircase. The curve might be a circle or an ellipse.

Quarter- and half-turn staircases

A quarter-turn staircase is one that rises straight up to a landing from where it turns at a right angle. On a half-turn staircase, the landing is more than double the width of the stair, with the second flight of stairs turning back on the first and running parallel to it. Both types are useful where the space for a staircase is wide rather than long and narrow. Unlike most other forms of stairway the eye is

not led to the top – indeed it may not even be possible to see the top of the stairs from the floor below. This can add a sense of mystery.

Dogleg staircases

This is a form of tight half-turn staircase, with the inside edge of the upper flight of steps running directly above the edge of the lower flight. In this way the dogleg staircase demands the minimum possible width that a half-turn can occupy in a building.

Flying staircases

A staircase that shoots up the centre of an open space is 'flying': unsupported on either side and open underneath. This makes a dramatic impact, both in the room as a whole and on the person ascending or descending the stairs. This type of staircase is also known as a 'gallery' staircase.

Enclosed staircases

Old cottages and small workers' houses often have a staircase that rises between two walls in an entirely enclosed space, without a balustrade. This design deprives the stairs of the opportunity to make an architectural statement or offer any sort of visual interest, unless at least one wall of the stairwell is glass. In a previous age, however, this design performed an essential function: it prevented the staircase from being a channel for draughts, by means of a door closing it off at the bottom. This was a serious consideration when the stairs rose directly out of the kitchen or living room and the only heating was provided by a single fire or stove.

Cantilevered staircases

In a cantilevered staircase, the weight and stresses of the structure are directed into the wall, so that it appears to rise up the wall without any visible means of support. This can create a dramatic visual effect, especially when the staircase can be seen from some distance rather than being enclosed by solid walls in a stairwell.

Steep and laddered staircases

Despite the stringent regulations governing the design of staircases in new houses, it is sometimes possible to construct a staircase that is almost more of a ladder. This is a useful option for providing access to a sleeping gallery, a library or other type of space with specific rather than general use, and where space is limited. Stairs have been designed with only half a tread on each alternate side, or with wedge-shaped treads, for example. Both of these are strategies for making a steep staircase more comfortable to use.

HANDLES

Choosing handles

It is a classic piece of advice to those on a budget that the quickest and cheapest way of updating your kitchen cupboards is simply to change the handles. Replace elaborate antiqued-brass drop-handles with simple stainless-steel handles and the look is at once fresher, cleaner and more contemporary.

Remember when choosing replacement door and window furniture that the new knobs and handles need to fit where the old were for the sake of simplicity. This means, for example, that you need to replace lever-action handles with the same because they are set closer to the edge of a door than knobs; if you replace them with knobs you may find you grate your knuckles when you open and close the door.

Most knobs and handles are made of metal or wood, though glass, china and acrylic are becoming increasingly popular.

Metal knobs and handles

For a contemporary look choose silvery metal handles rather than yellow brass ones. There is a huge choice available, from basic and inexpensive DIY store models to elegant designer fins. Knobs can be cylindrical, spherical or elliptical, or geometric shapes that fold flat into recesses; handles can be arched or severely angular; long bars for pulling open unlatched doors and cupboards can be rectilinear or curved, with flat or rounded surfaces. The quarter-round handle – a sort of bulge under which you fit your fingers to pull – is an example of a traditional form (associated with old-fashioned emporia) that has survived and been updated in polished chrome or nickel. For old houses, thumb latches and rim locks can still be bought to complement the original doors.

Wooden knobs

Wood can be stained, varnished or painted, or rubbed with old olive oil or a mixture of beeswax and turpentine. This will soak into the grain and prevent it from being stained by the natural oils in the human hand through use. Old wooden door knobs, sometimes with prettily shaped or decorated collars, can sometimes be picked up cheaply in junk shops. If there is no mechanism, match the old knobs to basic modern mortise or rim latches.

Glass, china and acrylic knobs

In period homes, white china knobs (which can still be bought in ironmongers) are appropriate for bedrooms and bathrooms; reception rooms would have had brass or copper knobs or

handles. In contemporary interiors, glass, china and acrylic knobs offer the opportunity to introduce some colour and pattern.

Ties, pulls and cut-outs

There are other ways of opening drawers and cupboards besides knobs and handles. Ties and pulls can be made from flexible materials such as leather or rope, while cut-out shapes enable you to pull out a lightweight drawer with a single finger. Chamfered drawer edges provide a finger grip while maintaining a plain finish. Some cupboards are designed so that you simply push them at the hinge to open.

1 Stainless-steel bar handles are an elongated version of the classic contemporary 'D' handle. **2** Simple circular cut-out finger-pulls. **3** Small crystal knobs complement the period style of an old cabinet. **4** Drawers with chamfered bottom edges to provide a finger grip obviate the need for handles altogether. **5** Metal bar handles look good with wood cabinets. **6** U-shaped metal handles. **7** An easy-going collection of retro furniture and junk-shop finds pairs Fifties-style chairs and kitchen table with Victorian architectural details. Stripped and varnished floorboards provide another area of contrast. **8** A generous reclaimed free-standing double-ended bathtub provides an elegant focal point in this airy bathroom. **9** A pair of old barber's chairs sits in front of an Art Deco mirror.

SALVAGE

Choosing salvage

Using materials, objects and architectural features that have been saved from older buildings is a form of recycling and one of the most environmentally friendly ways of fitting and furnishing a home. The craftsmanship and elegance of old fittings are often appealing, and their very age can endow them with a sense of authenticity and continuity. While the attractions of salvage are many, there are also potential problems: some items need repair or at least major cleaning, and the proportions of old pieces may be out of kilter with modern homes, so choose carefully.

Wood flooring

This is one of the most popular forms of recycling, and the most inexpensive timber floor to salvage is the one already in your home. Sanding is a possibility, especially if you want a paler, more contemporary looking floor. One of the great charms of salvaged materials, however, is their warm, lived-in glow. If your floor is in good condition, renovating without stripping will retain this patina. Scrub and scrape the floor clean, hammer down loose nails and make any necessary repairs before applying a finish such as stain, oil, varnish and paint (see pages 181–182).

If you buy a reclaimed timber floor, it may already have been resawn or remilled, or it may be in its found condition in which case you will have to decide whether to sand it after laying. Parquet blocks may have a hardwood veneer which, if already worn down, it may not be possible to sand.

Tiles

Antique and vintage decorative tiles can be incorporated into splashbacks for sinks, cookers, baths and basins. The other most common tiles found in salvage yards and specialist shops (or, if you are lucky, under old carpet or linoleum in your own home) are terracotta, quarry and encaustic floor tiles. Very often, simply scrubbing them with hot water and soda crystals will remove decades of grime; specialist tile shops will advise on how best to lay and seal them.

Doors, windows and shutters

Old doors found in salvage yards are often better quality than new doors that have been mass produced for joinery outlets and DIY stores. They are not necessarily the same sizes as modern door openings, however, and it is not advisable to cut more than a few millimetres off a door as this both alters the proportions and weakens the structure. If you choose doors before the construction stage of a wall, you can have the opening made to fit (or enlarge the existing opening if you must have that door). Doors with their original coloured or decorated glass are an attractive salvage possibility, as are handsome, sturdy front doors and pairs of double doors and shutters.

Reclaimed windows present the same difficulty of matching the shape and size to existing openings. For this reason it is best to incorporate them as one-off special features or as part of a new extension. Coloured and patterned glass can be found in a wide range of styles, from Art Deco to Gothic Revival.

Fireplaces

The trend for stripping out period detail in the post-war decades of the twentieth century has filled salvage yards with old grates and fireplaces – in fact there are now numerous specialist companies dealing in nothing else. It should therefore be relatively easy to find a fireplace to suit the style of your home. If you have a period property in need of updating, you may be lucky enough to find original fireplaces preserved behind boarding.

A little rust on an old fireplace is not a problem – you can clean it using a wire brush and finish it off with grate blackener – but avoid fireplaces that are cracked or broken. It is important to make sure that your chimney and flues are in order before installation (see page 204). Marble and stone fire surrounds are heavy and will need specialist fitting.

Kitchens and bathrooms

Sinks, basins, lavatories and baths can often be found cheaply in salvage yards and by advertising in a local paper. Remember that old cast-iron baths can be extremely heavy to move, and the bathroom floor must be robust enough to bear the weight. Entire ceramic bathroom suites in unfashionable colours like turquoise or yellow offer a quirky, enlivening alternative to ubiquitous plain white, and may even be more authentic than white in some later twentieth-century buildings. Stains can be difficult to remove from old baths, and the tub may need to be resurfaced professionally.

Materials and *objets trouvés*

Most salvage yards stock a wide range of structural materials from demolished buildings; these might include stone lintels, bricks and old timbers. Other smaller items range from mirrors, garden ornaments, indoor and outdoor furniture, to bizarre *objets trouvés*. With some creative imagination your salvage-yard find might become the starting point for an entire decorative scheme.

7

8
9

FURNITURE & FURNISHINGS

QUALITY AND TASTE

Furniture and furnishings are the things that make your home functional, comfortable and a pleasure to live in. At the same time, it is through such choices that you can make your home truly your own. Before you begin, though, you need to ask yourself some questions. How much do you want to spend? What exactly do you need? Do you want to invest in classic furniture that will last for years or will something cheap and cheerful do for now?

Quality and value for money vary widely – with furniture and furnishings, the adage 'you get what you pay for' largely holds true, although bargains can be found in sales, sale rooms and second-hand shops. It is generally the case that the better the quality in terms of design and construction, the more comfortable a piece of furniture such as a bed or sofa will be, the longer it will last and the more gracefully it will age. This also applies to soft furnishings such as curtains or upholstery, although these are usually less expensive to change. However, if longevity is not required – as with storage for children's toys or loose covers for a chair, for example – inexpensive options may be more suitable.

With the parameters of your budget in mind, you need to determine the specific function an item will fulfil. If your kitchen is the hub of your home, a large, robust kitchen table is a good idea; if your living room or children's playroom is also where occasional visitors will sleep, your choice of seating should clearly include a sofa or day bed that will usefully convert. Flexible furnishings, such as folding chairs and tables, stools that serve as side tables, and beds that disappear under one another, are now widely available and offer a range of practical solutions. If in doubt, choose a minimum quantity of better quality pieces, and let simplicity and functionality be your guides.

BEDS & SOFA BEDS

Choosing mattresses

The importance of your choice of mattress cannot be over-estimated. You may spend as much as a third of your life sleeping, and the health of your back in both the short and long term can be affected by your mattress. When you are lying on your side, your shoulder and hip should create indentations that allow your spine to remain horizontal. A mattress that is too soft for your weight or too hard will not support your spine correctly, and you will not sleep well. A lighter person needs a mattress of light or medium support; a heavier person needs firmer support (mattresses can be bought with different support on either side). Most mattresses should be turned regularly depending on their type (take advice from your mattress supplier), and should be replaced after seven to ten years.

Types of mattress

Besides different degrees of firmness, mattresses may be either sprung or unsprung. The latter includes foam and natural-fibre mattresses and futons.

SPRUNG MATTRESSES These come in a variety of formations. Open springs comprise a honeycomb of metal coils wired to each other with air in between. Pocketed springs each have a fabric sheath – traditionally made of cotton calico – and act independently of each other, responding locally to the weight of your body. Nested-spring and double-spring constructions have two separate springs (for added support) at any given point on the mattress, each with its own cover. Nested springs consist of a smaller inside a larger, double springs of one on top of the other. Non-turn mattresses have a substantial fabric base and heat-tempered springs, which will retain their shape for longer.

UNSPRUNG MATTRESSES Foam mattresses include latex and slow-recovery foam, both of which are hypoallergenic. Latex is a form of rubber that has been expanded by vacuum to make a thick, springy block. Slow-recovery foam (also called 'memory' foam) responds to the warmth of the human body by softening and moulding itself around you.

Unsprung mattresses can be made up of various natural fibres such as coir (coconut fibre), horsehair or cotton wadding. Many different combinations are possible: latex or horsehair sandwiched between layers of coir and wool, for example, or coir sandwiched between wool and/or cotton.

Futons consist of two or more layers of felted cotton and wool fibres, sometimes mixed with other materials. The most luxurious futons have between five and nine layers. A two-layer futon is suitable only for occasional use by children or lighter adults.

Another form of unsprung mattress is the water bed. A water-filled vinyl mattress is supported either by a firm frame or by soft sides of foam. Water beds support the weight of your body evenly, eliminate pressure points, and are good for allergy sufferers.

Divans

A divan is a fabric-covered bed base that supports the mattress. A well-sprung divan can substantially alter the feel of the mattress lying on it, making it feel softer and more luxurious than the same mattress laid on a slatted wooden base. Some divans have deep drawers built into them and are consequently sprung only around the edges of the drawers. Some single divans lock and zip together to make a double bed – a good solution if two people sharing a bed require different degrees of mattress support. A divan is a bulky item, so remember to check that it will fit around corners and up stairs to reach your bedroom.

Slatted bases

The most likely alternative to a divan on a modern bed, a slatted wooden base sits in a frame that has legs or feet. The gap between slats should ideally be not more than 6cm (2 1/4in) in order to support the mattress effectively. The advantages of a slatted base include being able to see the floor beneath the bed for a clean, uncluttered look; the open space also allows air to circulate to keep your mattress fresh. Solid softwood slats give a harder base; sprung beech (or other type of hardwood) slats have more 'give' and hence can improve both softness and the lifespan of the mattress. An electric adjustment facility in some slatted bases allows you to move the mattress into semi-upright position.

Frames

Before divans, a bed was traditionally constructed from a substantial head and foot that locked together with strong metal side pieces. Over the frame lay a flat, heavy base made of wood and upholstery, or metal mesh, on which the mattress lay. An antique or reproduction bed is likely to follow this pattern. Most frame beds can be dismantled into their constituent parts, meaning that an apparently huge model can be navigated through relatively small doorways and passages and reconstructed in situ. In this situation it helps if the base folds in half.

1 A versatile arrangement combines a bunkbed with a divan that can double up either as a seating or sleeping area. Drawers under the divan provide storage space for bedding. 2 The long, low lines of this contemporary wooden bedstead have an Eastern appeal. 3 A modern take on the four-poster features a minimal black lacquered-metal framework draped with muslin. 4 High-level or platform beds are good for saving space, with the area beneath fitted out for storage. 5 Antique beds have a certain theatrical flair. 6 Old paints often contain lead, so it is a good idea to strip off existing finishes on an old bed if a child will be using it. 7 Contemporary metal bed frames are widely available in different styles and finishes.

Bedheads

A quick way to change the appearance of a bed, and indeed of the entire bedroom, is by switching bedheads. Replace modernist birch or chrome with a smooth leather panel or velvet upholstery for a glamourous, luxurious look. Or vice versa. When deciding on the style of a bedhead, consider issues such as comfort (do you like to sit up in bed to read or watch television?) and practicality (a white linen cover should be removable, secured in place with Velcro or zips, and washable).

Four-poster beds

There is no bed so romantic as a four-poster. It adds height and importance to the bed, creating a dramatic centrepiece for a bedroom. A four-poster need not be antique or historical – there are many sleek modern designs available in metal or wood. These can be left entirely bare for a pared-down look or the frame can be dressed with fabrics, either translucent and floating or warm and heavily textured. Either way, the introduction of fabric lends added sensuality to the bed.

Half-tester beds

With a tall head like a four-poster, a half-tester has only half the canopy. This can be round or square, and acts as a vehicle for decorative drapes or mosquito netting. Some antique beds have a half-tester that can either be removed or attached depending on the height of the bedroom ceiling.

Beds for small children

A good-quality mattress is as important for a child as it is for an adult to provide proper support for the spine. A low bed is easier for a small child to climb into and out of safely, but even a low bed may need an added side piece if the child is likely to fall out in their sleep. Otherwise, the design can be utilitarian, colourful and fun.

Beds for older children

Any adult bed is suitable for older children and teenagers, but a type that wins particular favour is a mattress placed on a raised platform that is accessed by a ladder, leaving room for a desk, storage or folding sofa bed underneath. This arrangement has the fun of a tree house combined with maximum use of floor space. Where children share a bedroom, traditional bunkbeds free up floor space for toys, games and computer tables.

Stash-away beds

A spare bed that neatly slides away under another is a useful space-saving expedient. It also allows versatility – you can use the

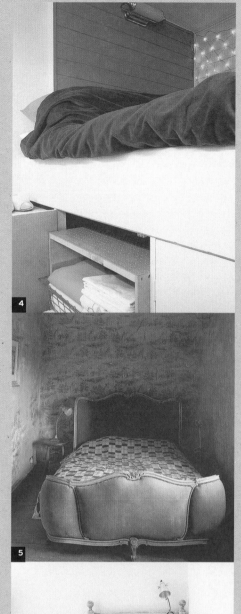

'parent' bed as a single or as a day bed or sofa, placed against a wall with cushions along its length, or pull out the companion bed to make two singles, or place them together to form a double. The pull-out bed should have sturdy legs that bring it up to the same height as the parent, preferably with locks or catches that will prevent them from collapsing or trapping little fingers. Remember, however, that it will be slightly shorter in length and probably a bit narrower than the parent bed beneath which it has to fit. One advantage of the pull-out bed is that the quality of the mattress is usually equal to the parent, whereas the folding bed, another flexible option, usually has a thinner mattress that will fold double.

Sofa beds

Always a versatile addition to your household, sofa beds vary from the expensive to the very simple, such as the basic arrangement of fabric-covered slabs of foam that unfold to accommodate your children's friends sleeping over. The lightest-weight sofa beds, suitable for the occasional adult visitor, consist of a foam mattress on a mesh support, which folds away neatly into the seat of the sofa.

An 'everynight' sofa bed is sufficiently heavy-duty to survive regular use should it be necessary. These higher-specification sofa beds are more comfortable because they have a more substantial, interior-sprung or latex mattress that will properly support your spine and give you a decent night's sleep. One consequence of this is that the sofa itself will necessarily be bulkier. Before you buy one, you should experiment in the showroom to determine how sturdy the foot support for the bed is, and how easily you can open and fold away the mechanism.

Futons

A futon mattress is very useful for the occasional overnight visitor and for children's sleepovers. It can be folded up and stored in a cupboard in the Japanese style when you do not need it or, when supported by a slatted wooden framework, a futon can double up as a sofa during the day. Single futons are available that fold into a zip-up cover to transform them into solid floor cushions.

Foldaway beds

The ultimate space-saving bed is one that tilts up in its entirety, flat into the wall. Whereas these once had a somewhat shoddy, bedsit image, now the foldaway bed is incorporated into the smartest city mini-pads. You need to tuck your bedding in properly, however (or stash it away in a cupboard), or it will fall down when you tilt the bed.

SOFAS & ARMCHAIRS

Choosing sofas and armchairs

Once the almost exclusive preserve of the three-piece suite, the living room is now a far more individualized space, and sofas and armchairs have become something of a design statement. We all need a comfortable place to sit and relax – whether watching television, curling up with a book or chatting with friends and family. The solution might be a contemporary modular seating system, an eclectic selection of old and new pieces, or anything in between. Your living space is an important focus, and how you furnish it will set the tone for your whole home.

Sofas and armchairs exist in a vast array of shapes, sizes, fabrics and fillings – the possible combinations are almost endless. When choosing shapes, think about how different elements will work together and where the sofa or armchair is likely be situated. If you want to place it in the centre of a room, for example, does it look good from behind? Apart from looks, it is important to try out a range of different styles to see which you find most comfortable. Although most people like to 'sink' into a sofa or armchair, remember that it must provide enough lumbar support to be comfortable for extended periods.

FABRICS The supplier of your sofa or armchair will explain the fabric options available with that model, and also tell you which types of fabric are suitable if you are supplying your own. They should advise you on matters such as colour-fastness (some dyed fabrics are susceptible to sunlight) and dry cleaning, and whether fixed upholstery or loose covers would be more appropriate. Any fabric used as upholstery must comply with current fire regulations, and some fabrics can have an extra fire-resistant coating applied.

The range of fabrics suitable for upholstery and loose covers is huge (see page 227). Popular choices include textured and pile fabrics such as bouclé, chenille and velvet; plain woven fabrics including linen and linen union; and heavier fabrics like wool mixes and tapestry. Leather is still one of the most enduring and popular materials for covering sofas and armchairs and gets better with age.

When the fabric does wear out or you want to update your furniture, it may well work out cheaper (but not cheap) to have a sofa or armchair re-upholstered or even resprung. It is also the more environmentally friendly option. Bear this in mind when making your original

choice; a simple or classic design may age better than something more *avant-garde*.

FILLINGS As with fabrics, so with cushion fillings – there may be several options for any given model, and your supplier will advise you. Fillings can be pure feather, which quite quickly becomes squashed and needs plumping every day (and therefore may be a better option for back cushions rather than seats); or fibre; or a mixture of the two for a combination of support and softness. Bouncy foam can be used on its own or wrapped in fabric or feathers for added 'give' and a softer appearance. Whichever you choose, turn your cushions regularly and plump up feathers and fibre by punching the cushion on all sides.

MANOEUVRABILITY When buying a sofa or large armchair do not forget that it has to fit into your house or flat. Take a plan of your home and all relevant measurements with you to make sure you choose something that will not only pass through your front door, but also your hall and living room door. If you want to buy a very large sofa, you might consider bringing it in through a window or French doors. Some specialist sofa companies offer their models with bolt-off arms (which costs a little more) for extra manoeuvrability.

Sofas

An expensive sofa is an investment, so once you have decided on your budget, consider whether size is your priority, or would you rather have a smaller sofa of better quality that is more comfortable and will last longer? It is useful to think ahead to the sort of home you hope to have in the future – a larger family house or a chic city apartment, perhaps. How does the sofa you want now fit into this future picture? There are other places, besides a living room, where you might want a sofa – a playroom, kitchen-living area or bedroom, for instance. A day bed might be a flexible alternative in these rooms.

LARGE SOFAS No living space is really welcoming and comfortable without a sofa to offer sociable seating, and a big, squashy sofa is many people's ideal. A big sofa is likely to be the largest piece of furniture in the room and makes an important statement. It can be the starting point for the entire scheme of your living space, or you may need to choose a sofa to fit in with your existing decor. A modern sofa made of tubular steel and foam will look good in a sparse, contemporary interior, while a battered leather club sofa will suit a more traditional living room or a robust industrial space such as a loft. A large sofa can

be used effectively to organize space in a long room, placed widthways to demarcate sitting and eating areas, perhaps, or to separate a messy children's area from a more civilized grown-up space. Perhaps it is obvious, but it is worth stopping to think just how large you want your sofa to be – you do not want it to completely dominate your living room so that there is no space left for other furniture.

SMALL SOFAS A small sofa is useful in a small room but may look lost in a large one. A pair of small sofas, however, can be used in place of a larger model with or without armchairs: set at right angles to each other with a table in between, two small sofas can virtually furnish a living room. A small sofa can also be placed across the foot of a bed or in a children's room, or slotted into a kitchen or even a spacious bathroom.

Modular seating

A modular seating system is one that you buy in pieces – in any number or configuration – to suit the shape and size of your room. You can choose from end units, middle units, corners, and sometimes day beds and footstools. This type of seating was once the preserve of waiting rooms and corporate foyers, but it has recently been rehabilitated as a stylish, practical arrangement that sits well in contemporary interiors.

Armchairs

After the sofa, the armchair is a priority in any 'comfort zone' living room. A deep, comfortable armchair embraces you when you sit in it – a well-designed model should support your legs to the knee as well as your head and neck. This sort of armchair is a large piece of furniture – as deep as a sofa from back to front – and as with a sofa, you should consider how it will fit through your doors.

More contemporary armchairs include modernist classics (available from furniture specialists) such as Le Corbusier's 'Grand Confort' club chair made of tubular steel and leather; and Alvar Aalto's 'Paimio' armchair, a collection of organic curves in bent plywood. Charles Eames's famous lounge chair and ottoman from the Fifties, with its rosewood shell and leather upholstery, is still the epitome of elegance and comfort.

Day beds

A chic modern day bed has a long body and a back to lean against at one end. The ultimate in luxury (few people have space for one), it can be a place to read or write letters during the day. However, a day bed can double as a sofa, ranged along a wall with extra cushions

to lean back against, or as a spare bed if the back folds down or the overall dimensions are sufficiently generous.

Chaises longues

A chaise longue is not unlike a day bed; the difference lies in the fact that the chaise longue has an arm stretching half its length from the headrest. A far cry from the curvy boudoir furniture of popular imagination, modern chaise longues now come in a range of designs from elegant oblongs supported on metal legs to airy frames made from wood, plastic or tubular steel, with either webbed fabric, cane or leather seating. This style may incline backwards and forwards for added comfort. The chrome and leather chaise longue created in the 1920s by Le Corbusier and Charlotte Perriand, called 'B306', has become an icon of chic modernist design.

1 A contemporary chaise longue provides flexible seating and lounging space. **2** An L-shaped sofa arrangement supplies all the necessary seating in a living area, keeping the rest of the space clear of incidental furniture. **3** Sectional or modular seating is a good way of accommodating different spatial layouts. **4** Sofas dominate by virtue of their size, and can set the whole mood of a living space – in this case one that is relaxed and modern. **5** Classic sofa designs make good investments; loose covers make for easy maintenance. **6** Matthew Hilton's 'Balzac' chair updates the traditional leather club chair. **7** Steel-framed upholstered armchairs have a spare, modern look.

TABLES & CHAIRS

Choosing tables and chairs

Tables and chairs can be main features in a room, or folding or stacking items that you stash away until they are needed. In between is a whole variety of extendable or dual-purpose furniture, reflecting the flexibility that has come to be the essence of the contemporary home. Materials used to make tables and chairs range from traditional solid hardwoods, such as oak or beech, to more modern materials like plywood, aluminium, tubular steel, glass and plastic. Your choice will depend not only on your preferred style and budget, but also on how much wear and tear your furniture is likely to receive.

Kitchen/dining tables

The main table of the home can be the focus of a whole range of activities, from family meals or celebratory dinners to book-keeping or letter-writing and children's homework. Your choice of table will depend to an extent on how you intend to use it. A multi-function table, especially one in a kitchen (where it is also likely to act as a culinary workstation), needs to be sturdy, resilient and accommodating. If your table will be used almost exclusively for dining, however, you can afford to let aesthetics have the upper hand. The choice between traditional or modern, polished or scrubbed, sealed or laminated, round, oval, square or rectangular, is otherwise a matter of taste and style (and available space) — there are good examples of every type of table obtainable in both top-end retailers and cheap-and-cheerful flat-pack outlets.

Extending tables

The extending table has always been a mainstay of many homes. One traditional form is the draw-leaf table, where an extra leaf is stored under each end and drawn out when required, nearly doubling the table's length. Others have separate leaves that are inserted into the middle of the table and are stored elsewhere between uses. Some contemporary designs have a spare leaf concealed beneath the centre of the table, which pops up when the ends are drawn apart.

A variation on the extending table is the false top. This is a cut-out square, rectangle or circle of wood that is larger than your usual table, and which can be placed over the table and covered with a cloth for entertaining. It is secured in place by batons screwed to its underside so that it will not slip from side to side. A possible drawback of having a false table top is finding somewhere to store it.

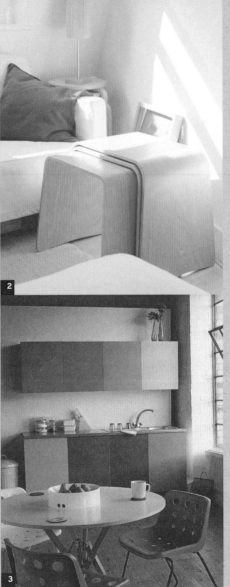

1 A scrubbed and planked table with bench seating brings a rustic character to this kitchen. **2** A nest of bent-plywood occasional tables is space-saving and multi-functional. **3** The ultimate in unpretentious living, lightweight stackable polypropylene chairs surround a simple circular table. **4** Eero Saarinen's classic modernist designs of the 1950s, the 'Tulip' chair and table, have enduring contemporary appeal.

Folding tables

Another useful standby for large gatherings, folding tables can be brought out for a party where they can fulfil the functions of serving table, occasional table or as an extension to the dining table.

The trestle table with folding legs and detachable rectangular top can be stored in an attic, garage or basement between uses.

The gate-leg table provides a large dining surface that folds away to a sliver of its full size and can be stored against a wall.

A table top can be fitted to fold up or down from the wall, usually supported by a swinging leg in the same manner as a free-standing gate-leg table. This is useful in a small kitchen or workroom but because of its permanent position it is perhaps not as versatile as a free-standing folding table.

Side tables

In most living spaces, one or two side tables are necessary as places to put drinks. They can also be used for holding lamps, plants and flowers, or for displaying photographs and ornaments. Some side tables contain useful storage in the form of shelves or drawers. Traditionally side tables came in matching pairs — one for each side of the fireplace, window or sofa — but today any handy-sized piece of furniture can serve the purpose. A stool, a metal trolley, a garden table, a stainless-steel kitchen buffet or a leather-covered console are all options.

CONSOLES A console — a narrow table designed to fit against a wall — is a useful side table for narrow spaces such as hallways or behind sofas. In a hallway, the console's slenderness prevents it obstructing free passage whilst offering a home for the day's post, keys, diary and other vital items.

STACKING TABLES A simple idea, stacking tables are identical to each other except that each is slightly smaller than the last and fits underneath it. The 'nest' of tables was once subject to stylistic ridicule, but has been reinstated as a space-saving necessity by modernist designs in bent acrylic and plywood.

SIDEBOARDS AND BUFFETS These are both variations on the side table, originally designed for serving food. They can be invaluable in a busy kitchen, so that a meal can be presented separately from the clutter of preparation. The sideboard is also a useful place to store tablemats and napkins, salt and pepper, candlesticks and other items for laying and dressing the table, as well as some glassware or china if there is sufficient space.

Folding and stacking chairs

Essential items for every home where space is an issue, or simply where you want to keep the floor clear of furniture, folding and stacking chairs offer maximum flexibility. Folding chairs come in wood, metal or plastic, or a combination of these. Others comprise a fabric seat with a wooden or metal frame – such as the 'director's' chair and 'butterfly' chair, both of which work equally well indoors and out. Some fold completely flat while others are bulkier when closed. Inevitably, folding chairs are not as sturdy as others and it can be worth looking at garden furniture for more robust wooden folding chairs.

Modern stackable chairs often have a metal frame supporting a moulded one-piece seat in either plastic or plywood. Robin Day's original 1960s moulded polypropylene chair on tubular steel legs is the classic example.

Stools

Good-looking stools, such as Alvar Aalto's three-legged plywood stacking stools, can double as occasional or bedside tables. When not in use stools can easily be tucked away or stacked which makes them space-efficient. By contrast, the ottoman is a large, solid form of stool, often with storage space beneath a hinged lid. The pouffe – a cross between a cushion and a stool – has lately regained favour; the contemporary leather-covered cube is its modern interpretation.

Benches

Being long and narrow, a bench is a useful form of seating for a hall or passage or along one side of a table, especially where the table is against a wall. As well as saving space, a bench does not clutter the table visually as it cannot be seen above table height.

Iconic chairs

The last decade has witnessed a great surge of interest in the design classics of the twentieth century, and chairs in particular have been celebrated for the way they balance form and function. In contemporary interiors, chairs are often displayed as sculptural pieces in their own right, serving as focal points for an overall scheme. Some of the originals have never been out of production, while others have come back into manufacture or can be found in sale rooms and specialist shops. Chairs that have found favour again in recent years are Mies van der Rohe's perfectly proportioned leather-and-steel 'Barcelona' chairs (1929), Charles Eames's 'cat's cradle' wire chairs (1952), Arne Jacobsen's curvy 'Egg' and 'Swan' chairs (1958) and Verner Panton's moulded-plastic one-piece stacking chairs (1960).

Dining chairs

Besides choosing between old and new, rustic, contemporary or antique, other choices in dining chairs concern scale, colour and material, and degrees of comfort. Tall-backed upholstered chairs look sophisticated and formal, and can be covered in a fabric to match your decor; the classic café chair with a bentwood frame is stylish and unpretentious, as is the simple wooden ladder-back chair. If you want to splash out on cool, contemporary dining chairs, you could opt for Fifties classics such as Arne Jacobsen's 'Series 7' or 'Ant' chairs in bent plywood, which come in a range of bright colours, or Eero Saarinen's moulded-fibreglass 'Tulip' chairs. When considering size, always check that not only the seats but the legs, which often splay out to add balance, will fit under your table.

The least expensive choice is a collection of old non-matching chairs from a junk shop or auction room; these can be stripped back to bare wood and finished with wax or sealant or painted one colour to create a sense of unity.

5 Bentwood chairs have resilient, flexible backs that make for comfortable dining. Beautiful colour and grain are features of the clean-lined hardwood table. **6** Canvas sling or 'butterfly' chairs are foldable and portable, ideal for outdoor eating. **7** The form of the chair has been a focus of interest for designers and architects; the strong sculptural shapes of these different designs complement each other. **8** Classic simplicity: ladder-back chairs and a plain wooden table.

1 A flexible ergonomic office system, 'Cube Station', in birch ply, provides surfaces at different heights for screens and keyboards. 2 Modular mobile storage units on castors slide neatly under the worktops when not in use. 3 The nesting arrangement means that the entire office can be demounted and neatly packed away. 4 Good-looking home-office furniture is widely available and need not break the bank. An ergonomic desk chair is essential to prevent back strain.

DESKS & WORKSTATIONS

Choosing home-office furniture

Most homes need somewhere to file papers and deal with domestic administration, but as increasing numbers of people work from home, the need for a workspace set aside from domestic activities has become a necessity in many households. Whether you want a clever office-in-a-cupboard to fit into a small flat, a smart modern desk and storage system for a complete home office, or a computer table for the kids, there are now many flexible options to choose from. When you are deciding what to buy, it is worth bearing in mind your future needs, especially in terms of storage.

Ergonomics

It is important when planning a workstation or home office to bear in mind your physical parameters. This means considering not only how far you can reach for items without having to get up from your seat when working at your desk, but also seating posture. You can injure your back if you do not sit and use a keyboard in the correct manner.

A keyboard should be low enough and close enough to you so that your hands are below your elbows and you have to reach forward as little as possible. For this reason, modern desks usually have an extra shelf or drawer below desk height, which slides out for a keyboard or laptop. Raising your arms to type at desk height may cause you health problems in the medium and long term. The screen of a computer should be in front of you so that you do not have to bend your neck up or down, or twist it to one side.

Even if your desk and chair fulfil all these requirements, you should still stand up and walk about regularly while working in order to flex your muscles and release tension.

Office chairs

An adjustable office chair is vital so that you can be at the right height to look at a screen without arching your neck. Your hips should be above your knees and the slight arch in your back (known as 'lordosis') maintained and supported by the padded back of the chair. The back, too, should be adjustable so that it fits you personally. An adjustable chair will also allow you to rise to a good height for your desk so that you do not have to lift your arms more than a few degrees in order to use the surface. If you choose to sit on an 'ordinary' chair at your desk, have a small cushion for the small of your back to keep it concave.

Adjustable stools are useful where space is an issue, as they can slide under the desk when not in use. Useful as short-term seating, stools are not advisable for extensive office use as they do not support the back.

Designed to prevent back strain, kneelers promote good posture and support. If you use a kneeler, however, remember to maintain lordosis rather than allowing your back to curve outwards.

Computer tables

These are specially designed to hold a monitor, hard drive, keyboard and printer, and often have additional space for peripherals such as a scanner or CD burner. Compact, ergonomic and fairly transportable, they provide a useful solution in a family home where the computer is likely to be used by several different people.

Classic desks

The traditional rectangular wooden desk with drawers ranged to either side combines elegance with functionality. While this may be ideal for domestic administration and letter writing, it is not necessarily well suited to computer work. One solution is to stand a discreet computer table alongside or to have the desk fitted with a keyboard shelf. Office furniture stores now sell more flexible and ergonomic styles of classic desk – arranged in an 'L' shape, for example, or incorporating a raised monitor stand.

Trestle tables

Comprising simply a rectangular, removable top and two trestle legs, this is an inexpensive and flexible option. Trestles are increasingly sophisticated, with adjustable height and sometimes incorporating drawers. Trestle tops are available in wood, toughened glass or linoleum-covered particleboard.

Office-in-a-cupboard

In many homes there simply is not the space to devote an entire room to the function of an office, especially when it would only be in active use for a limited part of each day. The solution is to combine your home office with another function – occasional spare bedroom, for example – or tuck it into part of a room that is generally only used in the evenings or overnight. In these cases the ideal way to hide the unsightly clutter is to fit the office into a cupboard that is arranged to accommodate the special requirements of computer, filing, telephone and reference material.

Many such cupboards are now available, across the spectrum of cost and style. Mass-market retail furniture stores offer them at reasonable prices, some in pleasingly plain

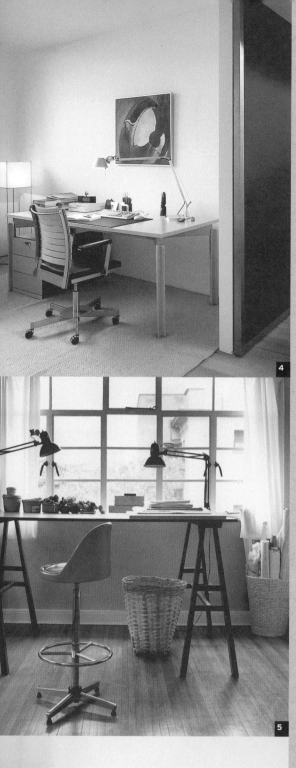

forms, and in varying sizes. There are also desks that swing open or pull out to reveal office equipment inside. At the other end of the price scale is discreet hi-tech furniture, from which drawers, shelves and screens glide out as required.

Custom-made workstations

Office furniture fitted to your specifications may give you greatest flexibility. Everything can be hidden in drawers and behind doors that swing or slide, sideways or up and over, to suit the design. Fitted office furniture can make the best use of a small room and a wasted or awkward space like an alcove under the stairs – although it is obviously much more expensive than buying a ready-made workstation cupboard.

A joiner or cabinet-maker could construct your fitted workstation for you, or you can buy an ensemble from a fitted furniture company. Make a list of all the equipment and storage you want to incorporate and make a note of your current configuration and what it is that you like and dislike about it. Having an office specially made is like having a suit tailored – it should fit you and your needs exactly, from the height of the desk, to the space between bookshelves to accommodate your type of reference material, to the drawers or cubby holes for everything you use in your particular household or line of work.

Lighting

The most important factors to consider when lighting your work area are first, to avoid glare – a light should not shine directly in your face or reflect off your computer screen – and second, to avoid the light casting a shadow over your work. If you are right-handed, this generally means the light should be on your left and slightly in front of you. The classic desk lamp is the anglepoise, which can be angled, lowered or raised to illuminate whatever you are doing. Clip-on spots or carefully positioned overhead lights also provide good task lighting (see page 249).

Storage

One way of reducing the amount of workspace you need is to rethink the way you organize and store your office paraphernalia. Many items that might once have been filed in an ugly metal filing cabinet can instead be stored on shelves in storage boxes: all sorts of designs are now available, made from plastic, plywood, cardboard, leather or covered with fabric. Longer-term filing (your accounts for past years, for example) that you store in this way need not be in the same room as the workstation or office cupboard. Research and

reference material in book and leaflet form can be stored in magazine boxes if necessary, which will keep them upright and orderly without reducing their accessibility. Likewise there are storage boxes in all shapes and sizes – designed for computer disks, CDs, and other items – that will accommodate everything from bulky stationery supplies to paper clips and postage stamps.

When office space is limited, the ideal is to keep to hand only items that you are currently using. To achieve this you need to be aware of a build-up of clutter and regularly re-allocate and file material, a tedious business but one that will produce liberating results.

Filing cabinets

Vital elements of office storage, filing cabinets can fit under your desk or slot into a corner of your work area. They do not have to be dull shades of grey or brown: you can have old metal cabinets stripped and/or lacquered, or spray-painted in the finish of your choice. Alternatively, you can repaint a filing cabinet yourself in a hard-wearing or enamel paint; remember to wash it well first and sand it down to help the paint stick. If you prefer, you can now buy new filing cabinets in various colours to suit the decor of your workspace.

5 The standard trestle table makes a good surface for concentrated work. An adjustable stool allows you to vary the working height. **6** An antique knee-hole partner's desk is combined with a gleaming steel filing cabinet for a sense of personal style. **7** An extended shelf makes a simple working area and accessible storage keeps the space clutter-free.

STORAGE

Choosing storage

Before you begin to think about storage, there are three things you should do. Firstly: edit your possessions. Sort through your belongings, consigning as much as is reasonable to the charity shop or dustbin. Secondly: get stuff off surfaces. Shift the clutter from the floor, kitchen worktops, side tables and anywhere else it has settled and replace only the few items that really belong there. Just this simple process can transform the appearance of your home. Thirdly: organize your possessions and choose suitable storage for them, making sure that the things you use daily are easily accessible. To keep general clutter under control, a flexible modular system combining shelving with cupboard/drawer space is very useful, as is furniture that contains storage spaces. If you are short of floor space, hanging storage is a good solution, and crates, boxes and baskets of all kinds are always invaluable.

Bookshelves

Nearly every home accumulates books over the years, and as their numbers grow their storage can become an issue. Paperbacks can be accommodated in slim bookshelves that will not obstruct passages, and small bookshelves can be hung on walls above other furniture. When deciding where to put shelves, look beyond the obvious locations and consider spaces that are often redundant – such as over windows and doors, around the tops of rooms and on walls opposite the tops of stairs.

Sometimes space is wasted if the vertical gap between shelves is much greater than the height of the books. A cantilevered shelving system on wall-mounted brackets, allowing you to adjust the distance between the shelves, can help save this space, as will custom-made timber bookshelves designed specifically to the dimensions of your library (see pages 144–147). A free-standing book shelving unit will probably have to be attached to the wall at or near the top, to avoid any danger of it toppling over.

Room dividers

A shelving unit organized into cubby holes that are accessible from both sides makes a useful room divider. It has the advantage of not entirely blocking light and vision, at the same time as providing storage for books and objects – both useful and decorative. If the unit has wheels it can be moved aside for a party or other event when you want the space to be uninterrupted, or when you want to experiment with a different room layout.

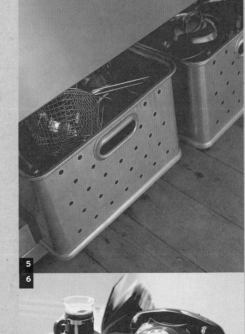

1 Modular open shelving cubes partition space and provide room for the display of favourite objects. **2** This flip-top coffee table provides a place to keep tapes, CDs and DVDs right where they will be needed. **3** Storage containers and boxes can house a great deal of everyday clutter discreetly. If you tend to forget where you put things, a labelling system can be a good idea. **4** Open box shelves provide a display case for crockery. **5** Steel containers serve as useful catch-alls for kitchen utensils and equipment.

Modular storage

This is shelving that you buy in sections that either attach to each other or stack together to make a coherent unit of whatever overall size and configuration suits your living space. Some of the units might be subdivided into shallower shelving, or have doors creating small cupboards for concealing clutter. This type of system is also available for wardrobes and other types of storage. A modular system gives you maximum flexibility and has a clean-lined contemporary look. As well as wood, modular units are available in plastic, metal and other materials. The modules may be all the same colour, which creates a unified effect, or you can experiment with back and side panels of different colours, for example, to create a modernist Bauhaus-inspired pattern.

Chests of drawers

These come in all shapes and sizes to suit every type of storage requirement. Deep drawers are useful for bulky winter jumpers in the bedroom, or for pots and pans in an unfitted kitchen. In general, though, shallower drawers are less likely to result in objects getting lost underneath others.

HANDMADE DRAWERS A chest of drawers made by a professional cabinet-maker should embody a harmonious combination of form and function. For beauty and durability, it should be made of good-quality hardwood, have smooth-running drawers that glide open effortlessly, and be perfectly finished with dove-tailed joints; tongue-and-groove boards inside the drawers allow for natural expansion of the wood. Whether ultra-modern or antique, a well-crafted chest of drawers is something to be valued and can be displayed as a feature in your bedroom or living space.

BUDGET DRAWERS At the opposite end of the scale is the utilitarian flat-pack version, which generally comes in basic softwood. Some self-assembly furniture now comes in smart modern designs and can be varnished, stained or painted to give it a better finish.

Another budget option is a drawer system consisting of a rack or box with runners, into which slot 'drawers' that are essentially wicker or plastic baskets, or plastic or fabric boxes. These are ideal for children's playrooms, utility rooms and garages, and also for inside wardrobes to make use of space beneath short hanging clothes.

SALVAGE DRAWERS Other options are reclaimed drawers that were formerly designed for a specific use. The plan chest is one such example, its wide, deep and shallow drawers originally intended for architectural plans or drawings but now useful for a range of storage functions. Other interesting configurations include old shop fittings with glass-backed drawers and the miniature chests with shallow drawers designed for cotton reels.

Chests and trunks

These provide useful storage for items that lie flat, such as books or magazines, or which can be jumbled together, such as children's toys. Chests, trunks and old leather suitcases can be bought in junk shops and sale rooms. Good-looking metal or wooden trunks and chests work well as occasional or bedside tables. Painted and lacquered fabric and leather cannot take weight and heat, however, so trunks made from these materials should be topped with a tray or sheet of heat-proof acrylic if they are to be used as tables.

Crates and boxes

The ubiquitous brightly coloured plastic crate can be found in almost everyone's garage, storage cupboards and child's playroom. Plastic crates are useful for storing anything to which you want regular, easy access, and for creating a recycling system – glass, plastic, tins or newspapers can be stored in them, they are easy to transport and, if necessary, the boxes can be washed out after each visit to the recycling centre (or doorstep collection). Several identical crates look effective when ranged alongside each other on a shelf (high or low) and smarter versions in leather, heavy-duty cardboard with reinforced metal corners, wood and translucent white plastic are all designed to be on view.

Baskets and hampers

The tactile materials and natural colours from which baskets and hampers are made makes them highly attractive storage containers: they look good in almost every room in the house and in almost every style of interior. Often handmade in their countries of origin, they come in a variety of materials, from woven banana leaf and hyacinth to bamboo, wicker and rattan. They can be soft, organic shapes or stiff, lidded boxes.

Baskets – either open or lidded – can be used for numerous purposes, such as wash-baskets and bins in the bathroom; containers for bread rolls and fresh vegetables in the kitchen; storage for CDs, videos and DVDs in the living room, or holders for logs by the fire. Due to their open structure which allows air to circulate, wicker hampers are a good choice for storing duvets and blankets over the summer months. A hamper also makes a sturdy and capacious toy-box.

6 An old metal trunk, stripped and polished, doubles up as storage space and side table. **7** There is a wide variety of storage systems on the market. This metal-framed system combines open shelves with drawer space. **8** Ron Arad's witty 'Bookworm' design is a sculptural modern twist on shelving.

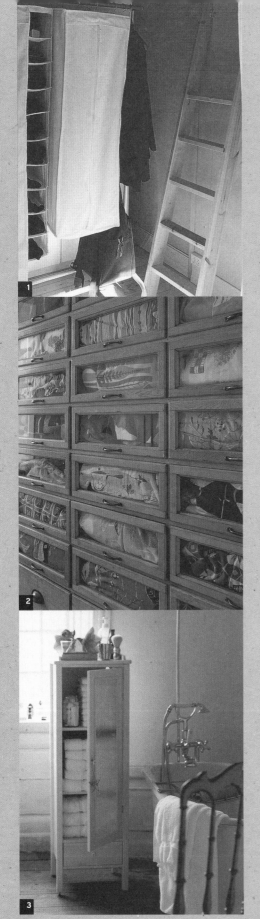

Hooks and racks

Invaluable 'up-storage' devices for getting things off surfaces, hooks and racks are useful in every room for items that are in regular use. Almost every bedroom and bathroom door needs a hook on the back, while cup-hooks organize mugs and jugs in the kitchen, and a paper rack keeps your paper and envelopes in order. A row of coat hooks near the door is vital in any home, as well as perhaps a rack for boots and outdoor shoes so that they do not become a hazard.

In the kitchen, racks and hooks keep utensils, colanders, sieves and pans accessible but clear of the worksurface. A rail for light-to medium-weight items can be fixed to a ceiling if it is low, or across a window. Heavy-duty hanging racks are available in various materials including wood and wrought iron, or you could have one custom-made by a joiner or blacksmith. Ensure that the fixings into the wall or ceiling are secure – if attaching to a ceiling make sure you screw into timbers rather than plasterwork.

It is not only small items that can be hung up – the Shakers, renowned for their functional and organized approach, used to hang their chairs on the wall and this is still a good solution in smaller kitchen and dining areas. Bicycles can also be hung up in a hall using a pulley, and ladders can be stored on garage walls. DIY stores sell various types of hook designed for hanging heavy items.

Cupboards

A cupboard protects the objects inside it and organizes them so that they are accessible. More importantly, perhaps, it hides the detritus of everyday life, allowing the space around it to look clean and simple, a key characteristic of modern interiors. Many small, urban homes in Japan have a huge cupboard for all the family's possessions, including futons and bedding, and this system can offer a useful solution to anyone short of space. Extra-large cupboards for home assembly can be bought at furniture stores.

Cupboards should be in proportion not only to the items stored inside but also to the spaces in which they stand, where they can make a bold statement as a feature or be discreet and inconspicuous.

FREE-STANDING CUPBOARDS These can be pieces of fine furniture – inlaid antiques and corner cupboards, for example, made from rare hardwoods. At the other end of the spectrum, cupboards that were once seen as mere utility items – such as meat safes – are now appreciated for exactly that utilitarian aesthetic. Industrial lockers and metal

1 A cheap and effective way of storing clothes: cloth bags and tidies suspended from a simple rail. Clothes hung on rails without some form of protection are vulnerable to fading and dust. 2 Reclaimed shop fixtures and fittings, like these glass-fronted cubbyholes, make appealing places to stow away belongings. 3 An old free-standing cabinet organizes bathroom accessories. 4 Wardrobes and other pieces of free-standing storage furniture need not be overly intrusive, as this discreet modern design indicates.

5 A modular mobile storage unit on castors houses items that must be stored flat. 6 A bedframe folds up to reveal useful storage space for bedding underneath. 7 Stools stack away neatly within the framework of this kitchen counter. 8 Folding chairs can be hung up out of the way when not required. 9 A mobile kitchen storage unit slots underneath the counter. 10 The solution for those with a serious shoe collection: fold-down trays in vivid metal units.

stationery cupboards have now joined the domestic interior repertoire. Heavy cupboards, or those that store heavy items (pans and china, for example), may need to be fixed to the wall for safety.

WALL-MOUNTED CUPBOARDS From the bathroom cabinet to the key cupboard, small storage units fixed to the wall can be useful in any room. They present their contents at eye level so you do not need to bend, the items are well out of reach of small fingers, and they do not take up floor space. Wall-mounted cupboards are best for storing a number of small items rather than a few larger, heavier ones, so that the weight of the contents does not pull the cupboard off the wall. It is nonetheless important to ensure that a wall cupboard is securely fixed, allowing for the weight that it is likely to hold.

Wardrobe storage

Free-standing wardrobes come in every shape, size and price bracket, from the huge, valuable antique armoire to the budget-conscious softwood framework with polypropylene panels. Some of the latest designs are soft – like the nylon zip-up curvy pod or the tented canvas wardrobe. Others are designed for an occasional visitor's weekend wardrobe – the folding all-in-one hanging rail and shoe rack, for example, or the full-height mounted mirror that conceals pegs, a shelf and a short rail that holds just a few garments. The most basic wardrobe storage, which is useful for temporary situations such as student digs, is the hanging rail, available in different heights (often adjustable) and varying degrees of sturdiness from almost any interiors outlet. Some have an optional plastic or fabric hood or cover to keep the dust off your clothes.

The interior of an ordinary wardrobe can be subdivided by installing a clothing rack – a set of shelves made from plastic or tough canvas stiffened with cardboard on which you place your garments.

Shoe cupboards

Shoe storage is a perennial problem. Few wardrobes offer perfect-sized pigeon holes or have room for more than a few pairs. The solution is either to introduce a system of clear or cardboard boxes or a rack, or to buy separate, purpose-designed footwear storage. Shoe cupboards take various forms from the low, bench-like model to the tall cabinet that has several tip-out storeys that can accommodate tens of pairs of shoes. An antique trunk is another alternative, though inside it will need further organization to protect your shoes and boots.

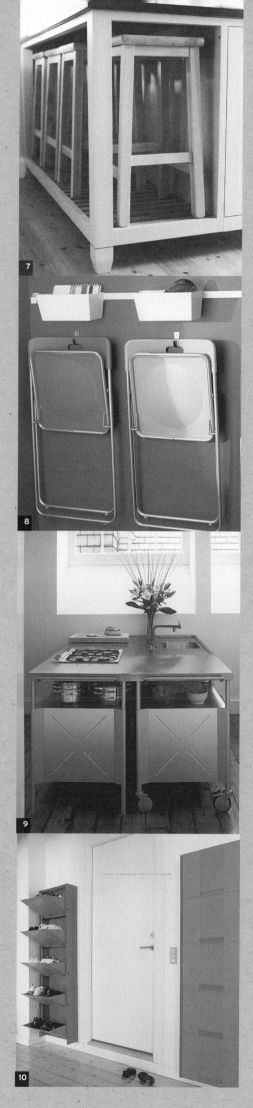

Underbed storage

The spaces underneath beds can easily be put to work for storage. In general, it is better to use fewer, larger containers rather than a number of smaller ones, as these might get lost. Each container should have a lid – zip-up, see-through plastic lids on breathing, cotton bags are an ideal option – to prevent dust falling on the contents. You should regularly remove your bags or boxes and clean under the bed. This way you will be reminded what you have there, at the same time as removing the fluff that inevitably accumulates. Do not jam too much under the bed as this will prevent air from circulating.

Alternatively, choose a bed that has storage built in – many divans and children's beds have drawers designed into the base. If the bed is to be placed against a wall, check that the drawers pull out on the appropriate side. Some beds have different configurations of drawers – none near the head, for example, where a bedside table would get in the way.

Deep storage

Efficient long-term storage demands more than basic cardboard boxes that will crumple or cheap suitcases that will buckle over time. As long as the space is dry, heavy-duty cardboard boxes secured with string or strong parcel tape will survive well, as will better quality suitcases (which can be picked up cheaply in department store sales, sale rooms and junk shops). Smaller-sized containers will be easier to move about and transport in the future, but you will need large ones if you want to lie clothes or other items reasonably flat. It is a good idea to use acid-free tissue paper and moth repellent when storing clothes, and bubble wrap for fragile items.

Rather obviously, the key to successful longer-term storage is labelling. It is worth writing a brief description or list of the contents on each side of a box, and on the top. If you do not bother, you can be sure the lack of easily visible information will prove a serious irritant in the future. For easy legibility in gloomy places, use a thick black marker pen and write in large letters. For labelling the contents of suitcases, old-fashioned reinforced-card luggage labels fastened to the handles are useful. If you are testing whether you can live without the contents, add the date of consignment so you will know how long they have been put away.

Store items that you need annually (for Christmas, or for beach, camping or skiing holidays, for example) near the door or access hatch to your long-term storage space, and return them to that spot after use so you will always know where to locate them.

FABRIC & SOFT FURNISHINGS

Choosing fabrics

Selecting fabric and soft furnishings can be a fraught business: you need to consider not only how the colour, texture and possibly pattern will work in your interior, but also whether the material is suited to its intended purpose. The wide choice of available fabrics can be daunting, but this is also an area where you can have a lot of fun, and where even a small change can bring about a major transformation in a room.

Textured fabrics

An important part of any interior scheme, the textures of soft furnishings are a necessary complement to the hard surfaces of structural components such as stone, brick, wood and glass. Fabric brings softness and comfort to an interior and adds a sensuous element. Some fabrics are rich and warming while others are cool and slippery, offering changes of mood as well as textural contrasts.

ROUGH Shaggy, rough, dense fabrics such as faux furs, felt, tweed, chenille and velvet bring warmth into an interior and are particularly effective when set against a minimal scheme. The softest natural fibres such as angora and cashmere add an element of luxury, while less expensive fabrics such as cotton waffle, knit or flannel, and polyester fleece can be equally warm and textural. Wool blankets and rugs create a cosy, embracing environment.

SMOOTH The textures of shiny, reflective fabrics and materials, and gauzy, translucent sheers can be used to create cool, sensual contrasts with other fabrics and furnishings. Satin, organdie, taffeta, mercerized cotton, polished leather, nylon and a whole range of man-made textiles can be used sparingly to accent contrasting, matt fabrics such as mohair or slubby silk, or used in quantity to create a sense of opulence.

Coloured fabrics

Besides texture, colour is the most vital feature to consider when furnishing your home. It is perhaps the key element to creating the character of an interior and establishing its mood – whether via calming neutrals or vivid, intense shades.

NEUTRALS The most soothing, least assertive colours are neutrals. These are soft shades of cream and grey, beige and taupe, which provide a restful, safe background to almost any decorating scheme. Neutral shades are associated with natural fibres in an almost natural state – unbleached calico, cottons and linens – though the most luxurious and sophisticated fabrics such as silk, satin and velvet are of course also available in these tones, as are faux and real suede and other leathers. Neutrals can be dreary if not enlivened with dashes of brilliant white and/ or definite colour, provided by accessories like cushions and throws, or a band of colour added at the top or bottom of curtains.

BRIGHT COLOURS Fabrics and textiles in bright, saturated hues – such as fuchsia pink, Mediterranean blue, emerald green, sunshine yellow and burnt orange – are vibrant and exciting, with a strong presence. They work well in warm places and bring an enlivening element into homes in temperate climates. Bright colours can be used in small amounts in a careless, uncoordinated way for an easy look, such as a single chair upholstered in scarlet; or over a large area for powerful impact – tall windows curtained in acid green set against brilliant blue walls, for example. Clashing, brightly coloured cushions on a plain sofa look particularly effective. Before using a fabric in a vibrant colour, test for fastness both to light and to washing (or reconcile yourself to dry cleaning).

DEEP COLOURS Navy blue, plum, brown and other deep colours – including black – have a heavy, masculine image. They can be dramatic if used carefully on curtains and covers, either *en masse* or leavened with white, neutrals, pale tones or bright colour. Like neutrals, fabrics in deep colours tend to show every mark and are therefore not particularly practical. Check all fabrics for colour-fastness.

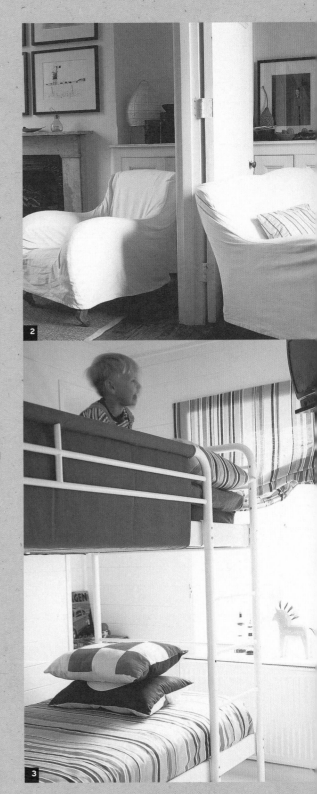

1 Sturdy sailcloth hung from wire threaded through eyelets makes a simple and economic way of concealing open kitchen shelving. 2 Loose covers for seat furniture allow you to ring the changes. White cotton provides an instant summery mood. 3 Bright striped cotton fabric doubles up as blind and bedcover for an easy-going coordination in a children's bedroom. 4 Soft-textured fabrics such as velvet, as well as leather and suede, contribute an important sense of tactility and comfort. 5 Close covering emphasizes the sleek lines of this modern sofa. 6 Sheer, vividly coloured fabric hung against a window accentuates the enlivening effect of natural light.

Patterned fabrics

Pattern brings life and movement into a space. For example, a Mexican rug on a plain wooden floor provides a graphic focus to a room, and a patterned border on a simple pair of curtains creates rhythm and movement.

WOVEN Traditional woven fabrics and textiles, such as Madras checked cotton or silk sari borders, have beautiful patterns in different colours which can be made into decorative features. The weaving technique can also give a fabric a distinctive patterned texture, as with twills (which have fine diagonal ridges), jacquard (a complex pattern made on a special loom), herringbone or seersucker. These types of fabric add interest in a more subtle way.

PRINTED Patterns that are printed onto fabric vary widely, from traditional flowers or Fifties-style leaf designs to modern geometrics and barcode stripes. With the latest fabric technology it is also now possible to transfer photographic images onto curtains and bedspreads. Use patterned fabric sparingly at first, building it up gradually, as too much can be fussy or overpowering. But as with textured and coloured fabrics, interesting juxtapositions, such as chintz roses and bright checks, create a witty and dynamic effect.

Classic fabrics

However wonderful the new fibres and manufacturing technologies may be, certain natural fabrics never lose their appeal and have become categorized as classics. Linen, cotton, wool and silk are used in fabrics both traditional and modern, often combined with man-made fibres to lend them additional strength. It is in their pure forms, however, that they are perhaps most attractive.

LINEN This is one of the most versatile fabrics. Linen has a delicious texture as well as superb practical qualities: it is absorbent, dries easily, is hypo-allergenic, anti-static and hard-wearing; hence it is a good choice for sheets, pillow cases and table napkins. Linen takes dye well, giving cloth a beautiful depth of colour, yet as the colour fades with repeated washings it takes on an equally lovely relaxed appearance which is enhanced by the fact that linen crushes distinctively. Alternatively, linen can be transformed into paper-sharp crispness by using a hot iron when damp.

COTTON Second only to pure linen as the finest of fabrics for both table and bedlinen, the finest cotton is not much less expensive than linen. Man-made fibres (primarily polyester) mixed with cotton reduce the

price and the perceived labour in maintaining natural fabrics, but also their sensual qualities and absorbency. Glazed cotton is treated with a chemical finish that gives it a glossy surface (which must be dry cleaned). Waffle is a geometric weave that gives the fabric a raised, squared-off texture.

WOOL Traditionally used to make tartan fabrics and suitings, wool has a multitude of uses. It is usually dyed before being woven into cloth, with the combination of colour and weave forming the pattern — whether it be checks, stripes or geometric repeats. Boiled wool is a matted, felty fabric that has been shrunk by boiling.

SILK The fibres of silk take dye beautifully, resulting in fabulous glowing, glossy cloths — an effect that is increased when the fabric is 'shot' (when the warp and weft threads are different colours). Silk of different grades is woven into cloths of great variety, from crisp, lightweight taffeta to heavy slubbed silks. This delicate fabric is vulnerable to sunlight and dust, both of which eventually fade and rot it.

Upholstery fabrics

The hardest work to which any fabric is subjected in the home is as upholstery on a chair or sofa. Good upholstery fabrics include tapestry (a heavy fabric with a textured, ribbed weave); velvet; jacquards, suitings and other tightly woven woollens; linen union (a blend of linen and cotton); moquette (similar to velvet, but with uncut pile); damask and brocade (sumptuous pattern-woven fabrics). Some fabrics are simply not tough enough in terms of either fibre or structure to withstand wear and tear. Interior designers of public spaces are guided by the 'rub test' which is measured in thousands and indicates how much wear a fabric can withstand. Fabrics used for upholstery in Britain also have to pass the cigarette test to be legal.

Lightweight fabrics

These fabrics are almost purely decorative — their attraction lies in their delicate, floaty quality. They filter light rather than block it out, and if they are loose-woven, have a cut-out pattern, are embroidered, or are dyed bright colours, they create patterns and colour when light shines through them.

Ready-made lightweight curtains in muslin or voile made from cotton, linen or man-made fibres are available in a huge range of colours and styles. Topped with tab loops or metal-rimmed holes, these can be hung instantly from a wire or lightweight pole across a window or door, around a bed or as a room divider. Stiffer lightweight fabrics such as organdie have a gauzy sophistication which can be used to good effect as crumpled curtains, glamourous bedcovers and even as decorative covers for chairs and tables. Medium-weight fabrics such as silks, taffeta and utility cottons can be used on their own as unlined curtains, screens and occasional loose covers, or lined to make more substantial curtains, blinds and bed and cushion covers.

Care and cleaning

Fabrics vary widely in the care that is needed to keep them clean and looking their best. Many luxury fabrics and those with piles have to be dry cleaned, though a pile can sometimes be kept fresh simply by vacuuming. Some can be washed but will shrink (linen, for example), and these should be washed before sewing. Many washable fabrics need ironing – unless the crumpled look is what you are aiming for. Blinds and curtains made with linings and interlining will probably have to be dry cleaned because of the different properties of the various fabrics used in a single construction. When you choose a fabric, ask about cleaning it and, if in doubt, take a small piece to test. If washing it, remove a piece to match the colour after washing, and measure the piece you are going to wash first to check shrinkage afterwards.

Accessories

While practical issues such as cost and durability may to an extent dictate your choice of upholstery material, accessories are an area where you can afford to express yourself.

LOOSE COVERS On sofas, chairs and stools, loose covers offer you versatility. You can change them without the expense of having the furniture re-upholstered, whether to update existing furniture, or to alter the mood according to the seasons or occasion. Having a spare set of covers, in washable fabric, means that you can clean them regularly.

CUSHIONS Few things beat the luxury of sinking into a pile of soft cushions. As well as the comfort factor, cushions provide an opportunity to use fabulous colourful fabrics in small quantities for maximum effect. You can also play around with different sizes and shapes including cylindrical, oblong and round.

THROWS A throw tossed over the back of a sofa or chair creates a single sweep of colour – a quick and easy way of ringing the changes in an interior. In a tactile, sensual fabric such as mohair, faux fur or quilted silk it can also provide textural contrast.

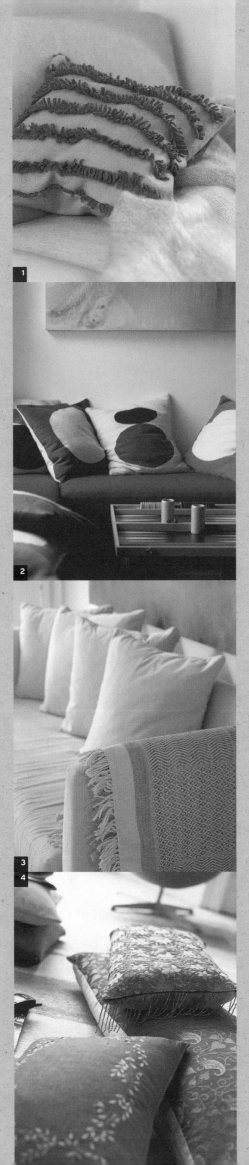

BEDLINEN

Choosing bedlinen

Climbing into a bed made up with clean, crisp sheets is one of life's great pleasures. Combine this with a good mattress (see page 214), a comfortable pillow and a duvet or blankets of the right warmth, and you have everything you need for a perfect night's sleep.

Pillows

Fillings for pillows can be either feathers or man-made fibres. The latter are ideal for anyone with an allergy or asthma, the best quality can be machine washed without it becoming lumpy. The filling that feels most like down is probably siliconized cluster-fibre, but you should feel various types in a shop before choosing the one with a bulk and weight that suits you. Feather fillings vary from utilitarian duck to the finest down from Siberian geese (rather like the difference between ordinary wool and cashmere). Some feather pillows are machine washable, and addicts to feather may find that they can use them in spite of allergies if the pillow is regularly frozen to kill any dust mites.

Pillows vary in construction – a duck-feather core can improve the bulk and hence the support a pillow gives your neck when you sleep, while the rest of the pillow is filled with goose down for luxurious softness. Orthopaedic pillows are specially designed to provide additional neck support. Feather pillows should be cased in downproof cambric, and piping increases the strength of the seams.

Pillow cases

Check the size of your pillows when buying pillow cases – different qualities often vary in size, as do pillows from different countries. Shapes vary, too: the square pillow is now increasingly popular. Pillow cases are either plain slips or 'Oxford' – the latter having a flange (an extra piece of doubled-over fabric) around the edge. A significant detail on pillow cases is the size of the inside overlap which conceals the pillow at the open end. A well-designed pillow case has a deep, generous overlap; a poor pillow case has a mean overlap, which will gape and expose the pillow during use. Before putting on a pillow case, cover the pillow with a plain slip in heavy cotton to protect it from staining during use.

Sheets

Some people prefer traditional sheets and blankets, and even with a duvet a sheet is necessary on the mattress. At one end of the range available is the classic pure-linen sheet,

which is cool in summer and warm in winter, with the additional benefit of being absorbent but quickly refreshed. At the other end is the ultra-glamourous satin sheet, once a cliché but now in vogue again. In between is a vast choice, including pure cotton of various grades (Egyptian is the finest), densities (measured in threads per square inch) and weaves (percale is smooth and closely woven; flannel is a cosy brushed cotton). Some cotton sheets have a special 'non-iron' treatment. Cotton may also be mixed with other fibres, such as linen or polyester; the latter lacks the crisp, pure feel of natural fibres. As a guideline, sheet sizes are as follows: single 275cm x 180cm (108in x 71in); double 275cm x 230cm (108in x 91in); king/superking 275cm x 290cm (108in x 114in); emperor 290cm x 310cm (114in x 122in).

Mattress covers

A cover can give added comfort to your mattress (with a degree of padding) or be purely practical (easily removed and washable) to protect or relieve the wear and tear on the fabric and help your investment last longer.

Duvets

These could be said to have transformed the daily household routine more than any other non-mechanical item – a quick shake and the bed is made. Duvets come in various weights giving different degrees of warmth to match the seasons, from 4.5 tog (cool) to 13.5 tog (warm); versatile combination duvets are available whereby a light and medium duvet can be poppered together to form a very warm one. Like pillows, duvets are available in various hypo-allergenic man-made fibres, and in feathers of varying degrees of luxury, some of which are washable. Quite apart from their warmth, different fillings have different weights – feel the difference in a shop before finally deciding. As a guideline, duvet sizes are as follows: single 200cm x 140cm (79in x 55in); double 200cm x 200cm (79in x 79in); king 220cm x 225cm (87in x 89in); superking 220cm x 260cm (87in x 102in); emperor 240cm x 300cm (94in x 118in).

Blankets

No longer the utilitarian items they once were, blankets have become highly desirable additions to contemporary bedrooms and something of an art form in themselves. They are available in various woven and knitted forms, and come in different types of fibre, the perennial favourites being wool and cotton. Modern blankets may feature classic tartans in bright shades, minimalist designer patterns or muted natural colours. Heated underblankets can give extra warmth on cold nights.

Bedcovers

A duvet is very practical, but some people prefer their bed to have a more tailored appearance for the hours of the day when it is made up. A large throw or bedspread will do the job, as will a fitted cover that lies squarely over the corners. Eiderdowns in pastel silks or traditional floral designs are currently undergoing a revival, as are patchwork quilts and hand-embroidered bedcovers, which can be mixed and mismatched for interest and texture. A faux-fur bedspread will add an element of James Bond-style sophistication.

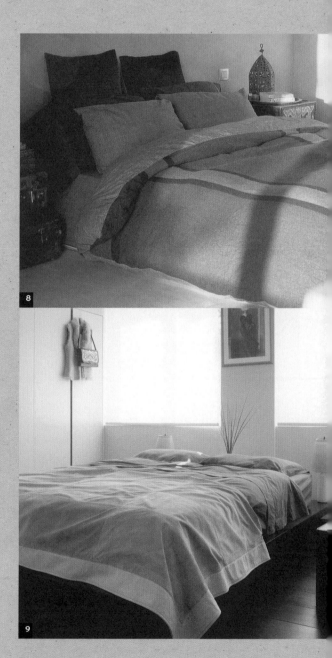

1 Bands of soft fringing applied to a cushion cover add textural interest. 2 Variations on a theme: cushions covered in bold geometric designs. 3 In neutral or all-white decorative schemes, varying textures provide depth of interest. 4 Details and accessories such as cushions, pillows and bolsters offer the opportunity to experiment with colour and pattern. 5 Quilted satin bedcovers pile on the comfort. 6 A crisp white linen valance gives a tailored look.

7 A wool blanket in a bold contemporary pattern makes a striking bedcover. 8 A floor-level bed heaped with pillows invites relaxation. 9 Natural fabrics, such as cotton and linen, are the most comfortable fabrics to have next to the skin because they absorb moisture and allow air to circulate.

& SHUTTERS

Choosing window treatments

Central heating and advanced forms of glazing, together with the drive towards a simpler, pared-down aesthetic, have liberated windows from the sort of 'dressing' that was formerly popular. If a window has architectural merit or looks out onto a fantastic view, then there is arguably no reason to festoon it with draperies for their own sake. You may wish to cover the windows of a bedroom, however, for privacy, in order to keep out early morning light or to create a more intimate atmosphere.

If some type of window covering is necessary or desirable, simple treatments work best in contemporary interiors. Loosely hung fabric can be more easily seen and appreciated for its colour and pattern rather than fabric that is bunched up into elaborate swags. Blinds may be preferable to curtains, especially where you do not want fabric falling below the level of a window sill, and shutters are another elegant option.

Roman blinds

A Roman blind pulls up into a concertina of deep, flat folds. Because of the way it draws up, the blind needs a certain depth of window recess in which to hang, the depth depending on the height of the blind and how substantial both the fabric and the lining is. Wide Roman blinds can also become very heavy. Given these constraints, though, the Roman blind is a versatile form of window covering with a smart, tailored look. Any fabric apart from fragile or diaphanous types can be used to make a Roman blind, but the tighter the weave and heavier the fabric, the more substantial the blind and the crisper the folds.

Roller blinds

The simple roller blind is an inexpensive, effective way of shading a window. Roller blinds are made from stiffened fabric – ordinary fabric can be transformed for the purpose by using a special spray. Some are simple rectangles, others have shaped bottom edges or cut-out shapes. The white roller blind is the fall-back of modernism, utterly simple and discreet. Roller blinds made from black-out material will shut out the light completely – useful in a bedroom where you want darkness at night but do not want to sacrifice floaty, translucent curtains. Roller blinds can also be used as alternative cupboard fronts and partitions, dividing space and hiding the clutter of a home office or mini kitchen.

On a tall window, or as an alternative to net curtains if you front onto a street, pull-up roller blinds are an attractive option. They are simple roller blinds, fixed to the bottom of the window instead of the top and fastened with a hook each side of the frame at the appropriate height (or several, if you want a choice). The advantage over blinds rolling downwards is that you do not cut out all the light and view from the upper part of the window, only the bottom where people would see you if they looked in. This is also an option where your window is round or pointed at the top.

Venetian blinds

This type of blind has horizontal slats that can be tilted up or down – depending on how much light you want to exclude and the direction of the sun – or pulled up in their entirety. Besides offering a greater degree of control than any other blind, Venetians appeal on other counts as well. Usually made of wood or of metal – which can be shiny, matt or coloured – they have a strong contemporary image. The slats can be wider or narrower, increasing the choice of look. A Venetian blind is also useful for a window that is wide because you simply increase the number of vertical strings that support the slats along its length – in contrast to a roller blind, for example, which is supported only at the ends.

Conservatory blinds

These are a possibility for windows that have an awkward shape or are in unusual places, such as a triangular window or a skylight, as well as in a real conservatory. Their design means they can pull out from the side or the bottom of the frame – whatever meets the need of that particular window. They will be made to order and require careful measuring, but offer a straightforward solution to the problem of how to treat difficult windows.

Other types of blind

Blinds are made in a variety of materials for various effects both practical and aesthetic. Split-cane and bamboo blinds have a pronounced texture and natural colour. They do not entirely exclude the light, which casts interesting patterns when it shines through them (likewise they are not entirely private). Pleated blinds are made from paper or man-made fibres, some with concertina air pockets that provide a measure of insulation at the window. Alternatively, blinds can be specially made in a material to match your room's decorative scheme – velvet or suede, for example – by one of the many companies that specialize in custom-made blinds.

1 Floor-to-ceiling panels of plain white fabric make over-scaled blinds to screen strong light. 2 Venetian blinds in metal or wood provide flexible light control. 3 Filmy cotton curtains enclose a sleeping area. 4 Hinged wooden shutters fold back into the window recess. 5 Curtains suspended well above the window opening and allowed to trail on the floor accentuate the height of the room. 6 Sliding slatted panels create interesting patterns of light and shade. 7 Perspex shutters provide an element of privacy without blocking light. 8 Irregularly toothed shutters give an interesting jigsaw effect.

Sheer and unlined curtains

A flat panel of material, which may or may not be hemmed around the edges, can be fixed across the top of a window and hitched up to one side during the day. This is the simplest form of window treatment, with the advantage that the fabric is seen ungathered, its colour and pattern or texture fully revealed. Similarly, a finished curtain of unlined fabric can be strung on a wire threaded through eyelets, or hung with clip rings from a wire or slender pole for an equally uncluttered look, hardly gathered at all. Extra-long curtains made from light or translucent materials filter light rather than exclude it and will be easily lifted by a breeze at the window. In the city, where furnishings inevitably become grimy, these lightweight curtains are also easy to remove and clean regularly. Because they do not demand great financial investment, you could have more than one set and change them according to the seasons – white for summer, for instance, with a bright or rich, warming colour for winter.

Heavy curtains

When draped elegantly onto the floor, heavy curtains are the epitome of luxury. Both figuratively and literally, they give a room a warm, cosy feel. Lining lends extra weight to the curtains and protects the fabric from light, while interlining – a layer of padding between the fabric and the lining – provides an even more substantial barrier to light and draughts. Interlined curtains, or those made from thick fabrics such as velvet, can be extremely heavy, and the pole or rail from which they hang must be both substantial and suitably attached to the wall. Heavy curtains are expensive to make – in terms of both time and materials – and you will want them to last. It is therefore worth using the best materials you can afford – and then be prepared for the cost of dry cleaning them when necessary.

Poles and tracks

A curtain pole with rings or a concealed track makes a strong, simple support for curtains of all weights. Lightweight unlined curtains can be sustained on a wire or very slim pole – even one contrived from wooden dowelling or copper pipe. Running a wax candle along the top of the pole eases the movement of the rings along it. A pole or track should be wider than the window to allow the curtains to pull back from it completely to maximize light – unless you are fitting voile or other lightweight curtains inside the window embrasure in order to leave their architectural details uncluttered.

Traditional shutters

When closed across the window at night, shutters give complete darkness, considerable insulation and some sound-proofing. In period houses, traditional panelled wooden shutters fold back into a box at each side of the window embrasure. Similar shutters, or more modern-looking plain ones, can be made from wood to fit almost any window, but you need to consider how the shutters will fold, and into what space; they should have flush-fitting bolts that will not obstruct the folds. Louvred shutters (which have horizontal parallel slats that slope outwards) will let in fresh air, but keep out the sun during the day.

Cut-out shutters

Flush-surfaced shutters can have shapes cut out of them for added interest, though it does mean that they lose their insulating properties to some extent. During the day, light shines through the holes, casting ever-changing shapes around the room. Alternatively, the cut-out shape can come along the shutter's leading edge, with corresponding shapes on the edge of its pair, so that when closed they fit into each other like pieces of a jigsaw.

Pivot shutters

Rather than being attached to the wall or window at the outside edges, shutters can be fixed in place and pivot on a rod fitted down the length of the shutter from top to bottom. Each shutter can be controlled separately according to the position of the sun. This arrangement is useful where you want to conceal an ugly view but still want to have access to daylight and sunshine. An alternative to pivot shutters is to fit coloured glass, frosted or patterned glass in your windows, thus partially obscuring the view but still letting in precious daylight.

DOMESTIC APPLIANCES & FITTINGS

PRACTICALITY AND STYLE

There are some fundamental questions to ask before you can enjoy the business of choosing appliances and fittings for your kitchen and bathroom. Some are more obvious than others, but they come down to four key factors: the space available to you, your budget, the kind of look you prefer and the level of technology appropriate to your requirements.

In your kitchen, selecting the right appliances and equipment should be the result of a realistic appraisal of your lifestyle and needs. Do you really have to have a vast and costly stainless-steel range, for example, or will a neat fitted hob and oven suffice? When it comes to smaller kitchen appliances, finding the right level of technology is a question of balance – choosing equipment whose special features will regularly save you time without taking away the pleasure of cooking (or vital space on your worktop). These essentials should include gadgets appropriate to your style of cooking and your family's preferences – a mixer if you like to bake cakes and puddings, for instance, or a juicer if you make fresh juice daily, alongside the ubiquitous food processor. The amount of storage space you have in your kitchen and elsewhere may also influence the level of technology you can accommodate. Household appliances are not insubstantial, but there are various ways of compacting – such as having a washer-dryer instead of two separate machines.

In the bathroom, space can also be a pressing issue – if it is limited, deciding whether to splash out on an expensive roll-top bath may not be one of your options, but this does not mean that aesthetics need to be compromised. There are many stylish ways of fitting out smaller bathrooms, from creating a simple wet room using elemental materials such as wood and stone, to installing a modern wall-mounted lavatory that leaves the floor free and creates an illusion of space. As the bathroom is seen increasingly as a place of relaxation and refuge, the choice of luxurious, beautifully designed fittings now available is vast. The bathroom has become an area where, like the kitchen, the combination of form and function can result in an inspiring contemporary interior.

KITCHEN APPLIANCES

Choosing kitchen appliances

Most kitchen appliances and fittings represent a major investment, and should last for a number of years. It is important, therefore, to think carefully and consider all the options before you buy. Remember, your kitchen does not need to look like that of a television cook (unless you want it to): it should suit your own requirements, not somebody else's.

Cookers

The appliance that is central to a kitchen's function is the cooker or hob and oven. There are three initial considerations to bear in mind when making your choice: the combination of equipment, the location of your cooker, and its heat source. For example, do you want an all-in-one cooker or range, a separate hob and fitted oven, one oven or two (or more), an integral or an eye-level grill, and so on? If there is more than one element here, where are these going to be located in relation to each other and to other elements such as the sink and the refrigerator (see pages 136–139)? How will they be powered – is the heat source to be gas, electricity or oil?

The influences on your choice will include available space, cost, mobility, experience, cooking style and fuel availability. You may prefer to have a separate hob and oven, with the oven at counter height so that you do not have to bend down when lifting heavy pans. You may not have mains or tanked gas, but it may be possible to fit bottled gas (liquid petroleum gas, or LPG) to power your hob if gas is what you have set your heart on. Or you may choose to have a combination of two gas rings and two electric rings.

The all-in-one cooker, be it a basic model or a professional-looking range, is the simplest choice. As a single unit, it can be disconnected and taken with you should you decide to move house. The basic model is around 60cm (24in) wide, the same width as a standard kitchen unit; cookers then become larger and more multi-featured with a price tag to match. The basic all-in-one cooker has one or two ovens with an integral grill and four rings on top.

Ranges

At the other end of the scale from the basic stand-alone cooker is the range. This might be a gleaming stainless-steel model of the type used by professional cooks or an old-fashioned cast-iron Aga or Rayburn finished in coloured enamel. Any of these is a major investment,

a heavy piece of kit that takes up a fair amount of space, and a focus for your kitchen, setting the tone for everything surrounding it.

With a modern stainless-steel range, the possibilities in terms of ovens, rings and special features vary considerably from model to model. A traditional range such as an Aga, meanwhile, usually consists of a hot ring and a cooler ring over a hot and a cooler oven; larger models have an extra, warming oven and hotplate above. There is no grill, but it is possible to cook certain things such as chapattis, drop scones and toast directly on the rings. These rings and ovens are powered constantly so that they are always available for cooking, and the range gives out continuous gentle heat – as warming psychologically as it is physically. Agas can be powered by oil, mains gas, LPG or electricity, but solid fuel ones are no longer made; Rayburns, however, are still fired by solid fuel. In summer the continuous heat from a traditional range may prove too warm. Many owners switch off their range and revert to other cooking methods during the summer months – not a realistic option, however, in a kitchen short of space.

Hobs

A set of rings installed into or on your worktop, hobs usually come in pairs or in groups of four. A set of four is either all gas powered or all electric. With two sets of two you can, if you wish, choose to have two of each, giving you maximum versatility in cooking methods. Most people, however, tend to prefer one heat source or the other. Single rings can also be fitted to a worksurface in any configuration you choose, for the ultimate customized hob.

GAS This is a popular choice for hobs, even where the oven is electric, because it gives immediate heat that is instantly controlled by the turn of a knob. Compared with electric, a gas hob is more complicated to keep clean and gleaming; the pan stands are proud of the hob's surface and must be removed to clean underneath. The overall look is rather more industrial than that of an electric hob.

ELECTRIC Compared with gas, electric rings take slightly longer to heat and retain the heat afterwards to some extent. Halogen and induction rings heat faster than conventional thermostatic ones. Induction rings give a performance nearest to gas and are the most efficient form of ring, but they are expensive and only certain types of pan will work with them. The rings of an electric hob can be different sizes, and it is possible to combine different types – two halogen and

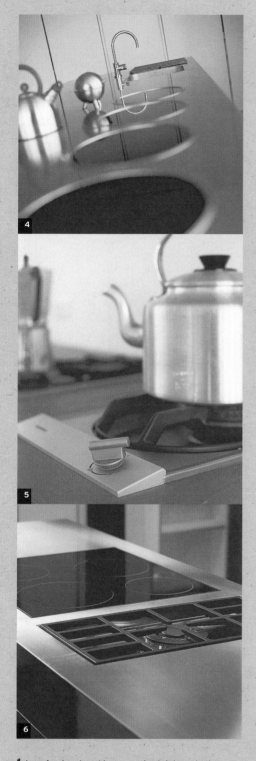

two thermostatic, for example, and possibly one ring that has a core and additional outer band for smaller and larger pans. The overall look of an electric hob is more streamlined than gas, with no crevices in which food can lodge. The sleekest design is the flat ceramic hob – cleaned lightly but often, a ceramic hob will keep its looks for years with minimum effort.

SPECIAL FEATURES Among the special types of surface-mounted cooking devices available on a hob is the tepan, a circular stainless-steel plate on which you can stir-fry directly, without needing a wok; a gas-powered wok ring (more powerful than average, with two or three concentric burners); deep-fat fryer; long fish kettle burner; griddle; barbecue grill; and domino rings which flip up off the worksurface, leaving it free for other use when you are not cooking.

Ovens

As with hobs, for ovens of both stand-alone cookers and fitted models the choice is between cooking by gas or electricity, though some ranges can be oil-fired. There are also a number of specialist options for specific types of cooking or dish, including the pressure or steam oven, the wood-burning pizza oven and the tandoor. Electric ovens are popular, especially fan ovens which circulate the heat and produce an even temperature quickly, so cooking food through evenly and saving on energy. By contrast, a conventional electric oven, like a gas oven, is hotter at the top and cooler at the bottom. An electric multi-function oven, with both conventional and fan settings, offers the maximum choice; some even include rotisserie (or the same effect, using hot air) and defrosting (cold air) functions. A second, smaller oven above the main oven is often a conventional type, with the grill built into the top. Fan gas ovens are also now available.

Two other considerations to bear in mind when buying an oven are its capacity and its cleaning. To check whether the size is right, take your regular roasting tin or large oven dish with you when you shop. Alternatively, compare the figures – capacity is measured in litres, with the oven of an average 60cm- (24in-) wide cooker offering around 55 litres (12 gallons). Smooth enamel is easier to keep clean than a matt, porous oven surface, but easiest of all is a self-cleaning system. This is likely to consist of panels on some of the oven's surfaces that burn off accumulated grease when you use the oven at a high temperature. An alternative system locks the door and heats the entire oven interior until all deposits are incinerated at an extremely high temperature over several hours.

1 A professional cooking range in stainless steel with double oven announces serious culinary intent. 2 The classic Aga can be powered by gas, electricity or oil. Radiant heat preserves the flavour of food and provides constant background warmth for the kitchen. 3 Ranges that sit up on raised feet are space enhancing. 4 Individual ceramic hobs inset into a stainless-steel worktop. 5 Gas rings with robust cast-iron pan rests. 6 This black ceramic hob is seamlessly integrated into a steel worktop.

7 A mobile oven on castors slots neatly under a counter top. 8 Steam ovens cook food quickly and healthily, retaining vitamins and minerals better than other cooking methods. They can be expensive however. 9 An indoor grill provides an appealingly simple and direct way of cooking.

Microwaves

The microwave oven is an invaluable tool in the kitchen, and not only for heating food from packets and cans for snacking children (and adults) or for defrosting frozen foods. Milk can be infused or simmered for sauces and hot drinks, stock can be heated in a jug, fish cooks to perfection, and countless dishes can be made without their colour and vitamins leaching away in the process. You can even heat serving dishes instantly.

Models vary from the smallest and most basic, which can sit neatly on a shelf above the worksurface, to larger ones with additional features. These might include a fan or grill for browning, a steamer facility, and a mass of programming options, including memory and speaking control panels. With a small model, check that you can fit a decent-sized dish into it and that it will turn with the turntable. Microwaves that are designed to be built into a fitted kitchen have vents for air circulation to prevent overheating.

Extractors

Cooking creates steam, grease and smells that will cool and deposit on every available surface in your kitchen if they do not have an outlet. An extractor hood with a fan will carry them to the outside world through a duct. In some locations a ducted system is not possible, in which case a recirculating system with renewable filters (which need to be changed on average every three months) will help. Manufacturers recommend the ideal distance above the hob to be between 50 and 65cm (20 and 25in); make sure the hood is situated where you will not knock your head. Noise is also an issue, as is drawing power – ten times the volume of your kitchen is usually adequate. Most models have variable settings and integral lighting. Looks vary from square and chunky to streamlined glass and steel.

Energy efficiency

Retailers and manufacturers of refrigerators, freezers, dishwashers and washing machines, are required by European law to label their appliances, identifying them as 'more efficient' (A grade) or 'less efficient' (G grade) energy users, or somewhere in between. Different products offer different information, relating to their function. Washing machines, for example, carry information not only about energy consumption but also spin-drying performance. The water consumption will also be indicated, a 40-litre-per-wash (9-gallon) machine being more efficient than a 90-litre (20-gallon) machine. The European Ecolabel is awarded to products considered to be the most ecologically friendly.

1 Combination microwave ovens incorporate a fan or grill for browning food. Built-in models must have air vents to prevent overheating. **2** Microwaves vary greatly in size, function and power. Some have talking programmes, which is an aid for the visually impaired. **3** A hob set in a kitchen island makes an accessible cooking area. An extractor hood removes unwanted cooking smells and steam. **4** This sleek stainless-steel refrigerator incorporates a cold-water and ice dispenser.

Refrigerators

The massive larder fridge has become something of a cult object, especially as it is now available in bright colours and hip vintage styles. With their massive scale, larder fridges represent in-your-face technology – some 'smart fridges' even incorporate an internet connection so that your food can be automatically reordered. At the other end of the scale, an under-counter fridge with a door-front matching the rest of the kitchen is almost invisible. In between is a range of free-standing models, and others that are capacious but slip neatly into a fitted kitchen. Special designs include cold drawers for bread or salads fitted into your kitchen units.

There are certain checks to make before buying a fridge. The first concerns energy consumption: an A-grade fridge will be cheaper to run, and kinder to the environment, than one lower down the scale. Next, consider the internal organization and flexibility of shelving and racking. Are the compartments in the door sufficiently deep for your needs? Are there separate chiller departments for storing salads and raw meats or fish with their own temperature settings? Are the shelves sturdy and can they easily be moved to your own configuration? An important final consideration: will your choice fit in through the door or window of your kitchen?

Freezers

Most household freezers come as part of a single fridge-freezer unit and, with larger fridges, can comprise anywhere between a quarter to half of the unit. A kitchen fridge with a small freezer section can be backed up by a large chest freezer in a garage or utility room if necessary. As with refrigerators, check the energy efficiency rating before purchasing.

Larder cupboards

A larder cupboard offers an alternative cool area for storing food. Sited against an outside wall, it is ventilated to keep it cool. Inside it, you can keep dishes you are about to serve up at around room temperature, cheeses and anything else for which the fridge is too cold. You can also store food in packets and jars, and bottles of squash and ketchup, for example. A good larder cupboard has a slate or marble slab for added coolness.

Dishwashers

Once criticized for their high levels of energy and water consumption, today's dishwashers are far more efficient. Additional features to consider on a dishwasher are the arrangement and versatility of the inside space, and the choice of programmes. Useful programmes include a short cycle, a low-temperature glass cycle and an intensive setting for washing pans and baked-on food. The interior organization of the dishwasher can include a cutlery rack at the top, in place of a cutlery basket, plate racks that fold down, and an upper shelf that can be raised or lowered to accommodate different sizes and shapes of china and cookware. Look for a revolving spray arm at the top and bottom of the interior – this arrangement gives the best wash – and check whether the element is exposed or concealed. An exposed element presents the possible danger of plastic items being melted. It is also important to check the noise level of the dishwasher when running.

Dishwasher models are either free-standing or will slot into a fitted kitchen. Alternatives to the conventional full-size dishwasher are a slimmer version with a capacity of about two thirds, or a dishwasher with drawers, one of which can be run on its own when there are fewer people present for meals.

Washing machines

The ideal washing machine has a short programme, a heavy programme and one for delicates or woollens, in addition to the standard cycles. Front-loading machines are more convenient where you want to use the top for storage – slip the machine under a counter or stack machines on top of each other. Some top-loading machines have greater capacity, but you lose the useful workspace on top. European washing machines generally have a capacity of between 3 and 7kgs (6 and 15lbs), the latter being compact models. The way you use your washing machine influences its eco-performance: it is inefficient to run the machine with anything less than a full load.

Dryers

The clothes dryer elicits widely differing opinions: many people would not be without one, while to others it is a superfluous piece of equipment. Dryers do consume a large amount of energy, but they can be invaluable if you have a family or no outdoor space in which to hang out clothes to dry. Some fabrics shrink in a dryer, so always check the label. A washer-dryer is a good solution if you do not have the space for an extra machine; however, the drying clothes need more space in the drum so you will not be able to dry an entire washing load in one go. Dryers work by two methods, either extracting and expelling hot wet air through a duct to the outdoors, or by condensing the moisture that has been extracted (this machine does not have to be fitted to an outside wall). The water from a condensing dryer needs to be emptied regularly.

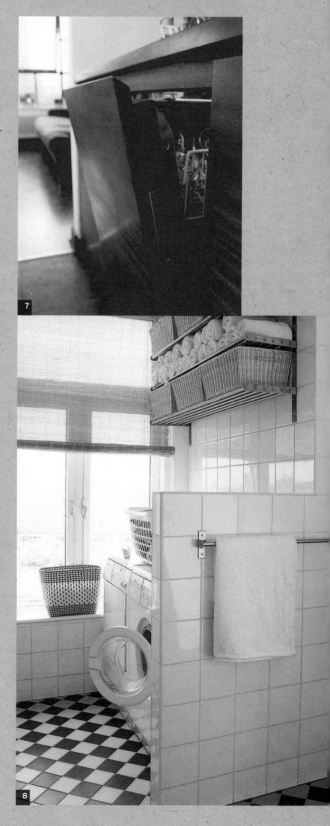

5 Curvy retro styling transforms the fridge into a kitchen icon. **6** Glass-fronted chill cabinets allow you to take stock at a glance. **7** A dishwasher is discreetly concealed behind a fitted panel. **8** A half-height tiled wall screens a laundry area, complete with washer, drier and linen storage.

There are many refinements to the form. Some, for instance, have a guage up one or both sides that shows how full of water the kettle is, others for use in areas with hard water have a gold-plated element to which the calcium carbonate build-up cannot adhere.

TOASTERS The quickest way to grill bread, pitta bread, bagels or teacakes is to drop them into a toaster. Before choosing a toaster check its heating power, lifting mechanism and versatility of slot arrangements. Toasters with four slots are ideal for large families.

COFFEE MACHINES These come in two types: a machine that percolates the coffee (meaning that the hot water seeps through the coffee grounds into a jug), or one that jets hot water through the coffee under pressure. A percolator may have extra features such as a timer, which allows you to come down to fresh coffee each morning, a heated or insulated jug, and a removable water reservoir that is easy to refill at the tap. Espresso machines vary from those with average water pressure (10-12 bar) to high pressure (17 bar). Some make espresso only, others have a steam wand that is used to make hot frothy milk, transforming espresso into cappuccino. Some can have water plumbed in, some have a water tank conveniently at the back or the top, while on others the tank is at the front and is fiddly to fill. Some coffee machines have extras like a cup warmer on top, an anti-drip valve and a removable drip tray. Take your time exploring the options.

Small appliances

Dozens of kitchen appliances and gadgets are now available to perform a multitude of tasks. One or two items are absolutely essential, arguably a kettle and a toaster, depending on your requirements. Others are genuinely useful and labour saving, such as, perhaps, a food processor or liquidizer. Your choice of appliances will depend on the size of your household, your tastes in food and style of cooking. Enticing as they may be, think carefully before you buy as you do not want to clutter up the worktop or cupboards with things you don't ever use. Some functions overlap, so you are unlikely to need them all.

KETTLES A kettle can be stove-top (with or without a whistle); plug-in electric; or electric but cordless, with the kettle sitting on the power-supply base unit which is plugged into the wall. Some shapes are low and bulbous, others taller and cylindrical (the narrower the base, the less worktop the kettle occupies).

FOOD PROCESSORS Many people find a food processor invaluable for fast slicing, grating, chopping, mixing, blending and liquidizing. With the right attachments you can use a food processor to make mayonnaise, batter or pastry; chop herbs; whip eggs; knead dough, and far more. Useful add-ons include heat-resistant bowls for hot liquids such as soup, mini inner bowls for preparing small quantities and juicer attachments. It is possible to have a food processor built into your worktop.

ELECTRIC MIXERS These are useful if you like to make a lot of cakes and bread. An electric mixer can quickly beat mixtures for cakes and puddings, or whip up cream or egg whites and (with a hook attachment) knead dough for bread. Some mixers also have a socket on top for a liquidizer fitment.

LIQUIDIZERS/BLENDERS If you feel you do not require all the facilities of a food processor or mixer, a liquidizer is perhaps one of the few essential items you may need. It can be used

for blending large quantities of soup, purees for sauces, houmous or smoothies. Some models also have chopping and stirring modes or special blades for crushing ice.

HAND-HELD BLENDERS For whisking, blending and liquidizing directly in the pan or jug, a hand-held blender can be very efficient: it saves you having to take the food to the liquidizer, saves on washing-up, and is especially good for small quantities.

JUICERS When choosing a juicer, consider not only its performance at producing fruit and vegetable juices but also how easily you can remove the fruit or vegetable residue between batches, how easily it comes apart afterwards, and which parts are machine washable.

SCALES There are three types of scales to choose between: traditional, electronic and digital. With digital scales you can weigh everything in the same mixing bowl, switching the scale to zero for each ingredient.

BREAD-MAKING MACHINES Baking bread at home can be a sensual pleasure, but it does demand the cook's presence and attention at several different stages. A bread machine eliminates almost all the labour but allows you to enjoy good freshly made bread even when there is no high-class bakery nearby. If you prefer, it can be used to knead the dough only, taking away the hard work but leaving the shaping, the timing of proving or second rising and the oven baking to the cook.

STEAMERS Using a tiered electric steamer is an easy way to cook a healthy meal, especially of fish and vegetables.

DEEP-FAT FRYERS A plug-in deep-fat fryer can be used to make everything from chips and doughnuts to tempura and whitebait. Some have more sophisticated temperature controls than others, so check before you buy.

ICE-CREAM MAKERS These can be used to create desserts with truly fresh flavours using combinations of fruit, cream or yoghurt.

YOGHURT MAKERS A yoghurt maker is ideal for making sugar-free fruit yoghurts as well as fresh plain yoghurt which is good for cooking.

FIZZY DRINKS MACHINES A worktop fizzy drinks machine turns tap water into sparkling water at the touch of a button; a small gas cylinder produces about 30 litres (6 gallons). Different essences can be added to produce tonic water, cola and various fruity drinks.

Kitchen sinks

The sink is not only a practical necessity, it is also a highly visible element of the kitchen and the colour and finish should be sympathetic to the overall style. Sinks are now made in a vast range of materials from wood, stone or porcelain-coated fireclay to Corian, resin or coloured enamel laid over cast iron. The most common material for kitchen sinks, however, is stainless steel, which is easy to keep clean, relatively inexpensive and available in numerous finishes and thicknesses (thicker generally being better quality). Sinks can be inset into the worktop, moulded with it, for example as part of a Corian worktop (see page 191), or set beneath the worksurface.

Your choice of size, shape and configuration in a sink are practical considerations and depend on your own requirements. A simple combination of one main bowl and one half-size alongside is convenient for washing-up and rinsing. Alternatives include a large, deep catering sink; full-sized double or triple bowls; the circular sink, which is not capacious but useful for vegetables; and the L-shaped corner sink. Drainers are another factor to consider: do you want one or two, how large, and on which side? A large sink or sinks with drainers each side will occupy a considerable length of kitchen counter: do you have the space, and are you prepared to walk that much farther to your cooker, fridge and worksurface?

Kitchen taps

As with sinks, a combination of practical and aesthetic considerations will influence your choice of taps. The most common designs are dual-control or single-lever mixer taps. In terms of practicalities, long lever-arm mixer taps are worth considering – they are useful for operating with greasy or full hands, and are easy to use if you are old or disabled. If space is short, wall-mounted taps free up more of the sink area. They have an added advantage, too: the channel behind counter-mounted taps tends to gather water and debris and wall-mounting prevents this. A useful addition to a kitchen tap is an extending hose, which emerges either from the end of the mixer tap or from the side of the sink, with a spray at the end to help speed washing-up and rinsing.

Specialist companies offer various finishes for kitchen taps including nickel and copper in addition to shiny chrome. For those on a more restricted budget, high-street suppliers offer a good range of possibilities. These include good-looking utilitarian models, and some with smooth, undecorated china heads. Pairs of antique taps from salvage companies can be used in conjunction with, for example, a Belfast sink for a more traditional look.

1 For coffee afficionados, a professional coffee machine can be worth the house room. 2 Pull-down tambour shutters screen small appliances from view when not in use. 3 A stainless-steel sink under-mounted in a worktop is neat and unobtrusive. 4 A reclaimed stone sink sits on top of a counter. 5 This under-mounted Corian sink has a lever-controlled contemporary tap. 6 The deep Belfast porcelain sink is still a kitchen classic. 7 A spray hose fitted to a tap speeds up rinsing and washing. 8 A wall-mounted swan-neck tap spout and pillar taps.

BATHROOM FITTINGS

Choosing bathroom fittings

Even in mass-market outlets there is now a wide choice of bathroom fittings – the days of the obligatory avocado bathroom suite are well and truly over. Although functional, the bathroom is still a place where you can use your imagination: invest in some special taps, for instance, to transform a standard suite, or consider installing baths or basins in cutting edge materials if you have money to spend.

Materials

Standard bathtubs tend to be made from either moulded acrylic or pressed steel. Acrylic is warmer to the touch and does not absorb heat to the same extent as steel, so the bath water remains marginally hotter for longer. It has a somewhat undeserved reputation for scratching easily; should scratches appear it can be polished with car-wax polish. Moreover, acrylic has shed its image as a substitute for cast iron and is the standard material for even some of the most expensive baths. Typically, shower bases are also likely to be pressed steel or acrylic, while everyday basins are usually ceramic.

Beyond the standard, a bathtub, basin or shower base can be made of any practicable material. Increasingly, more adventurous bathroom fittings are available from specialist firms, and others can be custom made. Your bath or basin could be made of wood, stainless steel, glass, fibreglass, resin, tiled mosaic, copper, marble and limestone. Basins can be made from all of the above and other materials such as silver and hand-beaten copper. When it comes to shower sides, these can be flat or curved glass, and the partition wall covered with any waterproof material, including sheet stainless steel, or made from glass blocks.

Bathtubs

It might seem that the most desirable bath is a huge, luxurious one in which you can stretch out and float, but in fact this is not likely to be the most practical or comfortable choice. It is possible for a bath to be too long, so that you will slip down unless you hold the sides. The ideal tub is long enough for you to rest your head on one end and your feet against the other with your legs straight but not stretched. If you like sharing, the most comfortable is a double-ended bath, with the plug and taps at the side and with sloping head ends at the top and bottom. Always sit or lie in a bath to test it for size before buying.

The usual rounded rectangle is only one of many possible fitted bath shapes. For very small bathrooms there are extra-short, extra-deep tubs, which allow you be completely immersed even with knees bent. If you are installing a shower above the bath, consider a combination bath: this has a larger, flatter area at the shower end, together with a fitted glass shower screen, and narrows to the usual bath width at the other. A large triangular corner tub provides extra space for companionable bathing or for children's bathtime and can be fitted with a spa or whirlpool function.

An elegant stand-alone bathtub takes up more room than a fitted bath and should have space around it so that its form can be enjoyed rather than crowded out. It is the best type for a large bathroom where a fitted bath would look mean, crammed against one wall. If you are installing a renovated cast-iron bath (see page 211), make sure that your bathroom floor is sturdy enough to take the weight.

Basins

As well as the conventional ceramic wall-mounted basin supported by a pedestal, there is now a great variety of designs available, including pedestal-free basins, washstands that incorporate storage and top-mounted basins that sit on the bathroom counter. The latter two types have the advantage that they offer you space around the basin on which to put bathroom kit. Some small basins for cloakrooms are designed to be recessed into the wall. When planning the type and position of a basin in a bathroom, consider how it will look from below, the angle you will see it from when lying in the bath.

Bath and basin taps

Taps for baths and basins can be mounted on the wall or set into the bathtub or basin itself. Some mixer bath taps incorporate a lever or knob so that water can be directed either to the bath or to the shower above (or the shower may have separate controls). Even if you have a stand-alone shower cubicle or wet room, a shower head on a flexible hose is useful in the bath for rinsing hair and washing the bath out after use.

The standard finish for bathroom taps is shiny chrome. Even high street suppliers, however, are now offering a more varied choice, including a modern matt steel finish. Specialist companies offer more alternatives, including matt chrome, nickel, brass, antiqued brass, a dark-brown matt bronze and even silver.

Probably the most sophisticated type of bath tap available is the thermostatic tap. This incorporates a dial, which allows you to set the exact temperature before running the water.

Showers

Trays for showers can be square, rectangular (which provides more room for manoeuvre), round or quadrant. A quadrant has three squared corners but the forth corner is cut off in an arc. As well as presenting an attractive curved glass front, the quadrant is a useful shape for fitting into a corner; the interior space for the person showering is still perfectly adequate. An alternative is the complete shower cubicle, which can have extra jets to give you an all-round shower. A fully waterproofed wet room (see page 142), where an open shower drains into the floor, is an increasingly popular option. Showers above a bath can be closed off either with a shower curtain (the design of which can provide a dynamic feature), with glass folding panels, or a single large panel hinged at the wall.

Shower taps and heads

Shower taps offer the same variety as bath taps; many mixer taps are thermostatically controlled so that the water is always the right temperature when you turn on the shower. Heads vary from the traditional 'rose' spray to ultra-powerful jet heads that pummel you with water. The latter only work with the requisite water flow and pressure, so you may have to install a pump before you get the expected performance (see page 142). It is important to consult a qualified professional before choosing your shower to find out what is possible in the way of water engineering in your area, as local pressures tend to vary.

Lavatories

A lavatory can be either floor or wall mounted. The advantage of the former is that its weight is borne and supported by the floor; the advantage of the latter is that it can be set at any height off the floor to suit you – higher than usual for a tall or elderly person, for example. In addition, the floor beneath is free which is helpful both for cleaning and for creating a sense of spaciousness in a small bathroom. Environmental concern about water consumption has encouraged the development of lavatories that use less water than formerly, or have a choice of shorter or longer flushes, and these are now required fitments in new bathrooms in many countries.

Bidets

As with lavatories, bidets can also be floor or wall mounted. The water supply to a bidet is either by tap and plug as in a basin, or by spray. In many countries a spray fitment in a bidet legally requires the fitting of a non-return valve, to ensure that none of the water finds its way back into the system.

1 A tub completely tiled in mosaic blends in with the basic structure of the bathroom. **2** A free-standing roll-top bathtub in a central position makes a dynamic focal point. **3** A wet room is an ideal solution where space is tight. **4** A deep trough sink with double taps provides generous room for washing. **5** A porcelain basin mounted on a storage cabinet is neat and unobtrusive. **6** Basins and baths come in a range of materials, shapes and sizes. These double sinks are set in individual cabinets that provide bathroom storage. **7** A circular stone basin set on a plinth has sculptural presence. **8** A wall-hung lavatory and small wall-hung sink make the most of confined space. **9** A deep basin made of tinted glass adds a splash of colour.

LIGHTING

LIGHT AND MOOD

More than any other element in the interior, lighting is responsible for generating atmosphere and hence has a considerable impact on the way you feel about a living space. Every home needs a mixture of different types of light: ambient background lighting, task light and information light. It is therefore important that a lighting scheme is carefully planned and not left to last-minute decision making. Once the basic system is established, there is a mesmerising variety of lighting to choose from – both hi- and low-tech – which, as well as offering practical solutions, presents a whole host of decorative possibilities.

Of all forms of contemporary fittings and furnishings, lighting is probably the one that is changing most rapidly. It is developing so fast that it may take little more than a generation for the fundamentals with which we are familiar – the traditional light bulb and wall switch – to be all but redundant in new homes. The ordinary tungsten light bulb is already outmoded in terms of its inefficient energy consumption and long-term cost, although its warm glow is reassuringly familiar and consequently it continues to be widely used. Long-lasting, low-energy mini-fluorescents are more efficient and adaptable to the practical and aesthetic requirements of modern lighting, both as a result of their small size and because of the tonal quality of the light they emit. Another exciting new development are tiny light emitting diodes (LEDs); controlled by computerized microprocessors they offer wide-ranging flexibility of colour and performance.

New technologies, aside, however, it is possible to improve the existing lighting in your home relatively easily. By changing the types of bulbs and fittings you already have, by installing dimmer switches, or by replacing or moving free-standing and table lamps, you will be able to achieve a much more functional and life-enhancing environment.

1 Small wall-mounted halogen spotlights provide crisp white light in a bathroom, augmenting natural light from a rooflight. **2** A combination of light sources generates a mood of tranquillity. Recessed wall lights provide background illumination, while a pair of angled lights on either side of the bed provides directional task lighting. **3** Downlights highlight a display in a hallway. **4** Fixed lighting arrangements, such as downlights, work best with fitted layouts. **5** A backlit glass shelf makes a glowing focus of interest.

TYPES OF LIGHT SOURCE

Choosing light sources

Different types of light source create varying qualities of light, which in turn are suited to particular tasks and functions in the home. Light quality has a direct impact on the look of a room, affecting the colours of wall finishes, curtains and upholstery. A wide selection of artificial lighting is now available, giving you a choice illumination that ranges from subtle to bright, diffused to focused.

Natural light

The most precious lighting resource is undoubtedly natural light and it should always be considered before planning a scheme for artificial light. Where does it enter your home, and how does it fall at different times of day? How can windows maximize the amount of light entering a room (see pages 202–203)? Can borrowed light be extended inside the home by replacing solid structures with glass or apertures (see page 203)? Are there any fabrics or artworks in the room that should be protected from direct sunlight?

Coloured or frosted glass, gauzy curtains (see pages 227–228), Venetian blinds and pivoting shutters (see pages 230–231) all offer possibilities for using daylight to create colour, pattern and movement in a room.

Tungsten

Since its introduction in 1907, the tungsten-filament incandescent lamp has established itself as the universal household light bulb. Until recently, lighting fitments sold in the high street were almost invariably designed for use with tungsten bulbs. Only in the late twentieth century did the low-voltage halogen lamp start to challenge the tungsten bulb's pre-eminence.

Besides being familiar and widely available, the tungsten bulb retains its popularity because it casts an attractively warm light, not unlike bright candlelight and with none of the 'spikes' in the spectrum that made old-fashioned fluorescent light so unappealing. The tungsten bulb has other advantages, too: it is cheaply made and sold, it runs directly off mains electricity without the need for a transformer, its light switches on instantly (unlike some fluorescent lamps, which need time to warm up) and, unlike fluorescents (and others), the glass bulb contains only a vacuum or inert gases, which are non-toxic to dispose of and therefore more eco-friendly.

The great disadvantage of the tungsten bulb is not immediately apparent: its astonishing inefficiency. The filament burns at more than 2,482 degrees centigrade (4,500 degrees farenheit) using only five per cent of the energy it demands – the other 95 per cent is wasted, transformed into heat. This heat can be dangerous, burning fingers and scorching shades that are too close. Over a period of some 1,000 hours the tungsten filament gradually evaporates until it is too fragile to carry the electric current, and so the lamp dies. By contrast, a low-energy fluorescent lamp lasts many times longer, gives off far less heat and uses much less energy to produce the same amount of light. This cost implication, both financial and environmental, has influenced the increasing demand for and availability of alternatives to the tungsten-filament incandescent lamp in recent years.

Halogen

Halogen-tungsten (commonly known simply as 'halogen') lights burn brighter and whiter than ordinary tungsten bulbs, giving a fresh, clean light that is similar to morning daylight and which complements the bright interiors of modern homes. This sparkling light is made possible by introducing halogen into the gases in a tungsten bulb. Low-voltage halogen is cooler, more energy-efficient and cheaper to run than tungsten.

MAINS-VOLTAGE HALOGEN These small bulbs and small tubes run directly off the mains power supply and require no transformers. They are available in a range of wattages and are dimmable. Like tungsten, however, mains-voltage halogen generates a great deal of heat. This light source works well in track lights, uplights and downlights.

LOW-VOLTAGE HALOGEN These compact bulbs, often with integral dichroic reflectors, deliver bright, focused, sparkling light. Unlike mains-voltage halogen, they do not run directly off the mains supply but require a transformer to step down the power. The transformers are increasingly small and light, however, and are easily accommodated either in the light fitting itself or in the wall or ceiling. Due to the small size of the bulb and fitting, and the clarity of the light, low-voltage halogens are particularly good for spots, downlights and recessed wall lights of all kinds. The weak voltage also means that these halogens can be used on 'bare-wire' tracks stretched across the ceiling.

Mini-fluorescents

Also known as low-energy compact fluorescents, these energy-saving bulbs can be found in a variety of sizes and wattages

to fit a wide range of domestic lighting fittings. The miniature offspring of the old-fashioned fluorescent strip that once flooded garages and kitchens with an unflattering, greenish light (and is still useful in garages, workshops and outbuildings), mini-fluorescents have undergone major developments in recent years. Lamps are now available that give a warmer light, more acceptable in living rooms and bedrooms. The familiar long, cylindrical tube is also available in many sizes and has been adopted by lighting designers for a variety of architectural effects, fitted into alcoves, in rebates, behind shutters and diffusing glass baffles.

Fluorescent light is produced at lower temperatures than incandescent, demanding less energy, which makes the lamps more environmentally friendly. They also last longer – up to eight times as long as a tungsten bulb. Besides the colour tone of the light it emits (which manufacturers continue to address with ever greater success), the potential disadvantages of a fluorescent lamp include the fact that it needs to warm up before giving full light, and the fact that it cannot easily be dimmed. However, a new type of lampshade has made it possible to dim fluorescents to some extent. This is a polyurethane globe with a cylinder in the centre, in which the bulb hangs. As you twist the cylinder from below the thread gradually shutters the light, effectively dimming it. Mini-fluorescent bulbs may seem expensive, but they work out cheaper than tungsten once their extended life and low power use is taken into account.

Fibre optics

These are fine strands of fibre, usually acrylic or fibreglass, along which light is directed. When the fibres have been given a special coating that reflects the light internally along their length, the light emerges at the ends of the fibres or, when this coating is omitted, the light can shine all along their length. Fibre optics have various advantages: they generate no heat except at the light source which can be several metres away from the end of the fibre, therefore making them suitable for use in water; they can be bent and twisted; and the light's low temperature and low ultraviolet (UV) content makes it ideal for illuminating fragile objects. Currently expensive, fibre optics are most often used for displays in galleries and museums, and for special effects in hotels and clubs, where they can be seen tangled, woven or knitted, or simply presented as cascading curtains of light. However, with some imagination, fibre optics can also be used to great effect as decorative lighting in the home (see page 251).

Light emitting diodes (LEDs)

Tiny semi-conductor devices that translate electricity directly into a single colour of light, light emmitting diodes, or LEDs, are usually found in the form of displays on car dashboards, calculators and stereos. Now, enormous advances in technology have produced LEDs bright enough to provide positive illumination (rather than just displays) in every colour – including the whole range of white light from cool to warm. LEDs are organized into small, rectangular units and are controlled by microprocessors that can digitally manipulate colour, timing and the speed of change in a lighting scheme.

The possibilities for lighting design using LEDs are exciting, and include ambient light that increases gradually in response to failing natural light, or that changes tone during the day; light that changes brightness or colour according to a pre-set plan or by manual control according to your mood; and light that responds to sound, movement or heat levels. LEDs have been dubbed the 'holy grail' of the lighting industry on account of their tonal performance, longevity, energy efficiency, low heat, lack of UV rays, ruggedness and controllability (and hence visual versatility), but like fibre optics they are currently expensive for domestic use.

Candlelight and imitations

Always flattering to the human complexion, candlelight has maintained its appeal long after the advent of electricity, not for the quantity of light it gives but for its quality. The warm-toned, flickering flame of a candle is romantic, ephemeral and lively. It can be used to light a dinner table indoors or out after dark, or the bathroom for a peaceful, atmospheric soak. For a party, tealights ranged along windowsills or mantel shelves contribute to the sparkling look of a room, and candles can be used in unconverted chandeliers for a dramatic, authentic effect. Massed candles give off a great deal of heat, however, and all candles pose a fire risk.

For modern or converted chandeliers and wall sconces, there are various forms of bulb and fitting that imitate candles. The most successful of these is the recent 'flickering candle' technology, which uses two tiny sensors alongside each bulb to detect the air movements that would cause a live candle to waver. The result has proved virtually indistinguishable from the real thing when installed in chandeliers in historic buildings, where fire hazard is a public safety issue. As the technology becomes better known and the cost falls this type of bulb will no doubt be seen more frequently in private homes.

1 Tiny halogen downlights accentuate the curve of a partition wall. 2 These wall-mounted fittings combine uplighting and wall-washing within the same design. 3 Sparkling halogen spots on trapeze-like supports incorporate stems for easy repositioning. Halogen bulbs must not be handled directly, even when switched off. 4 Recessed wall lights at low level create a lit pathway.

LIGHT FITTINGS

Choosing light fittings

As with light sources, your choice of light fitting will depend on the level of illumination you want to achieve – whether task lighting or ambient glow, for example – and the kind of look you are after. Flexibility is another consideration: will lights need to be dimmed or repositioned for different situations? From a design perspective, you can choose a striking centrepiece that will make a bold statement, or select unobtrusive lamps that will complement and enhance your decor with their subtle light – either way, light fittings play an integral role in any interior scheme.

Downlights

Discreet and modern in appearance, these fitments recessed into the ceiling give bright general light throughout the home and in circulation areas such as halls, passages and stairwells. They also provide task lighting in areas with fixed activities such as kitchens and bathrooms, and can be positioned to shine directly onto a special object or feature. Halogen bulbs are most often used for downlights because of their compact size and the clean white light they emit.

Downlights vary in size; some can give directional light, and the beam varies from wide to narrow, but apart from these variables downlights are essentially inflexible (although some can swivel in their casings). They are fitted by cutting a hole to a depth of 12.5cm (5in) or more, depending on the size of the fitment, so you need to have a ceiling cavity that is sufficiently deep. For safety reasons downlights should be fitted by an electrician.

Recessed wall lights

Lights recessed into a surface are not confined to ceilings – they can just as well be set into walls. At eye level this would produce an unacceptable amount of glare, but positioned close to floor level, recessed spots can effectively light stairs, halls and passages, acting as information and ambient light.

Spotlights

First used in the theatre and in shops, spotlights have become a standard part of the contemporary home lighting repertoire. Different types can be placed almost anywhere to provide targeted light, and spotlighting therefore presents versatile solutions to numerous lighting requirements. Spotlights make ideal task lights but, used thoughtfully, they can also serve as accent lighting to enhance a room's architecture or decoration.

FIXED SPOTS Spotlights that are fixed to the wall or ceiling can be used to direct light onto worksurfaces, pictures or structural details. Like all spots they have a functional appearance: some have metal cup shades in a range of sizes, colours and finishes, while others have multiple heads to provide omni-directional light from one source.

CLIP-ON SPOTS These are inexpensive and versatile: uses vary from bedside and desk lamps to kitchen worktop lighting, or indeed any circumstance where a strong beam is needed locally, and where there is an available structure onto which they can be attached. Clip-on spots need to be lightweight and usually have aluminium shades or simply consist of a large reflector bulb. One of their advantages is that they leave the surface below free and they can be easily unclipped and moved elsewhere if needed.

FREE-STANDING SPOTS Equally versatile light features, free-standing spots can be placed anywhere in a living area and the light directed accordingly. A free-standing spot can be placed inconspicuously behind furniture or used as a design element in itself. On many designs the lamp can be raised or lowered to give the right angle for the job.

Track lights

Positioning individual light fittings along a length of track is useful for picking out specific items, washing walls with light or serving as fixed task lighting.

FIXED TRACKS Similar in appearance to ordinary spotlights, tracks with fixed lamps are arranged in a row and attached to the ceiling (or a wall). This is a versatile lighting option, as the individual spots can be swivelled to point in any direction required, and it is the least expensive of the various types of track lighting available.

BUS-BAR TRACKS This type of track has a current running along its length into which individual lamps can be plugged at any point. This allows greater flexibility than fixed tracks, both in terms of light quality and the appearance of the fittings, as a combination of styles can be used (so long as they are compatible). The track itself can be arranged in straight runs or curved across the ceiling (or indeed a wall).

BARE-WIRE TRACKS With this relatively new track lighting, slender cables carry current at such a low voltage that it will not harm you if you touch it. A pair of cables is

drawn tight between walls, or between floor and ceiling, and small low-voltage halogens are hung along their length. Bare-wire tracks and fittings are small and delicate at the same time as providing copious light, sufficient for the open spaces of even large contemporary interiors. They do not have the flexible options of bus-bar tracks, however.

Wall lights

Like pendant lights, wall lights are fixed and therefore should be positioned carefully as part of an overall lighting scheme: once in place they cannot be moved without some disruption to the wall. Unlike pendant lights, however, wall lights can be used to diffuse light to the very edges of a living space, creating a pleasant, open atmosphere. This makes them ideal choices for hallways and circulation areas where pools of brightness and shadow, which may be the result of installing pendant lights or spots, would be undesirable. As well as providing ambient light, different designs of wall light allow you to direct light upwards or downwards (or both).

Wall lights can be made from most materials – cut and moulded glass, brass, resin, plaster, aluminium, stainless steel, plastics and plywood – and their designs offer numerous decorative possibilities (in contrast to the anonymous, almost invisible recessed downlight or industrial spotlight). A simple style of wall light is one with a curved glass shade, which is often white and translucent. Ceramic wall lights are another possibility: designed to be painted the same colour as the wall, they can blend almost seamlessly into the background while providing discreet illumination. The swing-arm wall light is ideal for a bedside light or next to a sofa or armchair where there is no room for a table lamp, as it can be drawn away from the wall to the most convenient position for reading. When placed in pairs on either side of a door, window, sofa or bed, matching wall lights also contribute to a sense of order and purpose in a room's decoration.

Wall and ceiling washes

Wide-beamed wall and ceiling lights can be directed onto or across an adjacent surface to create a diffused wash of light. In contrast to a spotlight, which illuminates specific areas, a wash is more expansive and subtle. Smooth, flat walls are ideal subjects for this treatment. The best tones to use on the surfaces you are illuminating are either pale or saturated colours (dark colours will simply absorb the light); the palest reflect the most light while saturated colour will spring dramatically to life. Alternatively, a plain white wall or ceiling

can be washed in colour by the light itself, an option that leaves you free to alter look and mood whenever you choose. Architectural tungsten strip-lights are the best fitting for wall or ceiling washes.

Uplights

Either wall-mounted or free-standing, uplights can be used to provide both ambient light or directed light to illuminate specific features. Bouncing an uplight's beams off a pale ceiling will 'lift the lid' of a room to create a feeling of spaciousness, or you may want to highlight an architectural element such as cornicing or exposed brick. When focusing a light upwards, it is wise to remember that any imperfections in the walls or ceiling will be exposed fully, as will cobwebs and any scars from DIY or Christmas decorations.

Free-standing cylindrical uplights are available in various sizes and are one of the most inexpensive methods of introducing dramatic lighting into an interior: you can direct light up into a large plant, for example, and the shadows of its leaves will decorate your ceiling and walls with beguiling patterns; or you can light a handmade wallhanging or rug from below to accentuate its colour and fully appreciate its irregular texture. Some free-standing uplights are tall, like standard lamps, and come in sleek metal and glass designs that can form one of the integral decorative elements of your interior.

5 Uplighting, in this case from floor lights, is a good way of enhancing the sense of volume; coloured light creates a tranquil atmosphere around a sleeping area. **6** A glowing ball provides diffused illumination at a bedside, combined with concealed lighting behind the headboard. **7** Side lighting or uplighting is more comfortable in a bedroom than an overhead fitting, which tends to cause glare.

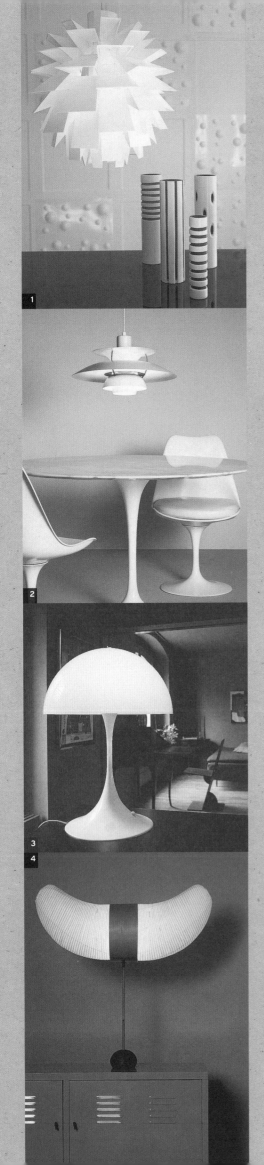

Pendant lights

In the twentieth century, the single bulb and shade hanging in the centre of the ceiling became something of a cliché – the epitome of unimaginative decoration, emitting a predictable and rather deadening glow. The pendant light has now come into its own again, however, not so much as the sole source of light in a room but rather as part of an overall, varied lighting scheme, and to fulfill specific tasks. Practical functions might include providing overhead lighting for a kitchen or dining table, or bringing light into tall, narrow spaces such as passages or the stairwell.

The increasing choice of lighting designs of all types – from classic twentieth-century models such the 'PH' pendant light by Poul Henningsen, to innovative contemporary interpretations like Claire Norcross's 'Eight Fifty' light – means that there is now a much greater and more interesting selection of shades available than ever before. It is worth bearing in mind that a pendant light can serve not only as a light source but also as a sculptural centrepiece.

The simplest forms of pendant light are probably the glass globe and the paper lantern. Globes are an ideal choice for the bathroom, where a fully enclosed form is necessary for safety reasons. Paper lanterns are a versatile and inexpensive option and are available in a vast array of shapes, sizes and colours to suit most interior locations.

The familiar cone-shaped pendant shade now comes in a variety of materials including glass, ceramic and fabric, while drum-shaped shades can be found in a wide range of finishes from coloured silk to semi-transparent paper. Most shades specify the maximum power of bulb suitable to avoid causing a fire hazard.

Table lamps

After the pendant light, the most familiar form of traditional lighting is the table lamp. Derived from generations of oil and gas lamps, the table lamp is portable (provided you have somewhere to plug it in) and cosy. It creates a pool of light (usually directed downwards) that is intimate and atmospheric. Lamps of this type provide the foreground in a room's lighting scheme, while forms of ambient light are the background. They have a reassuringly human dimension, whereas ambient light is more expansive, placing the emphasis on the space. A lamp focuses attention on a spot in the room, and several in different positions can create a tension that describes the boundaries of an area of security or activity. Bases and shades – and lamps that do not conform to this conventional combination, such as minimal glass spheres, for example –

1 Pendants are good sources of omni-directional lighting and provide a focus of interest. 2 'PH' pendant light by Danish designer Poul Henningsen, a design that dates back to the 1920s, features metal 'leaves' that diffuse the light. 3 'Panthella' table lamp by Verner Panton, designed in 1970. The shade is made of acrylic. 4 Horn-shaped paper table lamp by Isamu Noguchi, designed in the 1950s. 5 This conical floor-standing lamp has a clear base through which the wiring is clearly visible. 6 Directional floor lamps provide focused lighting for reading or study.

are available in a fantastic choice of forms and materials such as wood, stone, glass and ceramic. You can choose individual lamps that will complement your decor or use them to introduce an unexpected element in terms of design or colour (see page 251). If you are after a more co-ordinated scheme, you can create a sense of visual connection by using two lamps that are the same, but with different coloured or textured shades (or vice versa); table lamps arranged in pairs either side of a bed or sofa also provide a sense of unity for a more traditional effect.

Floor lamps

Like the pendant lamp, the floor lamp has progressed a long way from its twentieth-century suburban cliché – the turned and varnished wooden upright with fringed fabric shade. Many contemporary floor lamps are more akin to illuminated sculptures, whether made from wicker, paper or pleated plastics. Other free-standing lamps follow a more minimal aesthetic and may be formed from a thin metal stem topped by a geometric shade or elegant sphere, or may simply consist of a tall polycarbonate tube.

Task lights

These are the practical lamps that enable you to see to work without straining your eyes. In order to achieve this, a task light must be bright but without glare. It is often adjustable so that you can position the beam exactly to suit your personal requirements (and alter it as these change) and so that you will not be working in your own shadow. A task light can be an adjustable table lamp such as an anglepoise, which is the ideal desk lamp (see page 221); or a floor lamp, pendant lamp or recessed light (set into the underside of wall cupboards above a kitchen surface, for example) – any type of light that is fit for the job. In cases where a task light is also part of the room's overall lighting scheme – as it is in a kitchen – it is a good idea to make it dimmable (see page 250). Clip-on spots make good task lights in a room that serves more than one function, as they can easily be moved away when the room takes on another guise.

Exterior lights

Every home with its own entrance needs some form of outdoor lighting, at the front door if nowhere else, so that you can see to unlock the door. A light at the entrance not only serves a practical purpose, however, it also makes the place welcoming both for the householder and for visitors. Added to which, when someone comes to your door you can see from inside who is there. Lights that are

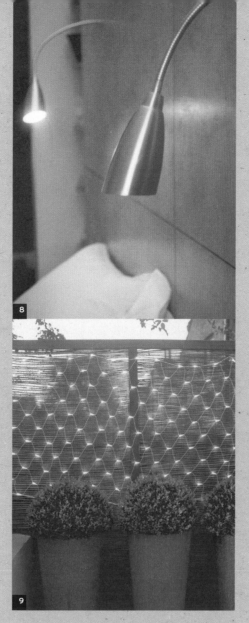

activated by movement or heat are useful in drives or parking areas, not only for your own and visitors' convenience but also to deter intruders. A light outside the back door is similarly practical.

Garden lights

Lighting your garden enables you to enjoy it all year round, and use it to the full in fine weather. Close to the house, borrowed light from rooms indoors, combined with flares, candles and lanterns, can be sufficient to light a terrace or table for meals and parties. Fairy lights, in strings or nets, can add sparkle to the occasion (make sure you buy a type that is for exterior use) and solar-powered lamps can provide economical and ecological illumination for pathways and patios.

To light the garden on a permanent basis requires the services of a qualified electrician who knows the regulations and can lay conduits and cables that will withstand cold and wet weather, and will not be in danger from digging (by animals or humans) and other gardening activities. Lights can be used to highlight interesting textures and surfaces or architectural plants, trees and features, adding drama and definition to a garden after dark. As in a room, creating pools of light in different areas of an outside space will provide a sense of depth. With a programmable system, you can create different moods with various combinations of coloured lights.

An effective overall lighting scheme is not glaringly bright (which would be a nuisance to your neighbours) but is subtle and thoughtful, creating atmosphere and mystery. Small, ground-level lights placed in a border or a garland of twinkling fairy lights festooned in the branches of a tree are far more attractive than the harsh, flattening effect of a floodlight.

7 An elegant, minimal floor lamp, designed by Serge Mouille in 1953, with thin metal stem and tripod support. **8** Adjustable task lights on either side of the bed are directly mounted to the wall, obviating the need for bedside tables. **9** A net of fairy lights strung over a fence creates atmospheric garden lighting. **10** Garden uplights set in planted borders around a deck throw intriguing shadows on the wall.

SWITCHES, DIMMERS & CONTROLS

Choosing lighting controls

Switches are essentially a means of completing an electrical circuit which provides power to turn on the light. Dimmers, sensors and computer controls are now added to the standard repertoire of on/off switches – and even the latter can now be found in some interesting and stylish designs.

Wall switches

These are usually positioned just outside or just inside the door to a room. Traditionally, wall switches control the room's main light source, but it is possible to switch table and floor lamps on and off at the wall as well by means of a separate circuit. This will have different plugs and sockets to the normal fittings so that you cannot confuse the two and plug an appliance into the wrong circuit. You will also be able to switch the lamps on and off locally in the usual way.

The ubiquitous wall switch is made of inexpensive white plastic in various subtly different forms. A variety of metal wall switches is also available, some in stylish

1

2

modern designs. Some toggle switches, where you flick a little finger rather than tipping a rocker, come with clear acrylic or glass finger plates which render them all but invisible, and also with finger plates in various other materials and finishes. Most switches differ little in principle from those of 50 years ago, but there have been some advances. One of these is the 'soft' switch, which is made from silicon in simple, sensuous designs.

Lamp switches

Table and floor lamps are usually controlled by a switch located on the bulb holder, on the flex or on the floor (which is designed to be tapped on and off with the foot). In some countries a twisting switch is also available, which (from off) gives you a dimmed light on the first twist and full light on the second. One recent development is the table lamp that can be switched on and off by tapping the base of the lamp itself: successive taps give a brighter (or dimmer) light.

Dimmers

A dimmer usually consists of a wall-mounted rotary barrel that gradually increases the amount of power to a light and also switches it on and off. Alternatively, a sliding mechanism may be used. Dimmers cannot be used with some types of lamp, so check bulbs before buying. Most fluorescents are not dimmable.

Timer controls

Timers are useful for security, giving an impression that the house is occupied, and they also make a pleasant welcome to come home to at night. They can consist of a simple, inexpensive plug-in device, or a more complex and costly computerized system into which you can programme different times for any day of the week or month. It is also possible to have a light sensor as part of this system, to trigger lights as it gets dark.

Movement activation

Lights can be fitted with sensors that detect movement and switch on illumination for a set period of time. The technology is familiar mainly in the form of outdoor security lights, but there is no reason why it cannot be applied indoors – in a bathroom used by children at night, for example. Other types of sensor can detect heat or sound and use these as the trigger for switching on.

Open-door switches

This is a simple system, free from computer wizardry or indeed any complicated form of technology. When the door closes – be it a fridge door or the door of a coat or utility

cupboard – it presses a switch in the jamb that extinguishes the light within. When the door is opened the switch is released and the light comes on.

Remote manual controls

With a gadget like the television remote control, combined with the necessary technology wired into your lighting and other systems, you can sit relaxing on your sofa and alter lighting levels (alongside music and curtains) without lifting more than a finger. Such a level of control may seem overly self-indulgent or even pointless to the able-bodied, but so, once, did the television remote that we now take for granted. And for those without ease of mobility, such a system offers freedom of choice and control.

Computer controls

Even more advanced than the manual remote control described above, the long-distance computer control for all the home's electronic functions – including, potentially, lighting – has been launched in Japan and will no doubt be available in due course across the globe.

Tiny transponders are attached to appliances throughout the house, which communicate with the base-control system, a unit the size of a book. By using your mobile telephone you can give instructions from afar to heating, cooking and audiovisual appliances as well as computer-controlled lighting systems. All this is made possible by the relative cheapness of computer chips and digital networks and the inventiveness of electronics companies who are looking for new markets. Whether such a degree of automation is desirable or not is a matter of personal taste.

Flexes

The flex leading from a lamp to a plug and socket should comply with safety regulations; check regularly for signs of damage or decay, and replace immediately if necessary. You should make sure that a flex does not drape across gaps between furniture where it could trip someone up or be pulled by a child; it should be trailed behind furniture on the floor or, even better, you could have additional sockets installed so that the lamp and socket are near each other.

There is a surprising choice in styles of flex – they do not have to be boring white or black plastic. Flex covered in woven silk is available in vibrant colours which make a positive contribution to a lamp's appearance and look particularly good on table lamps. On the other hand, white flex can be less obvious if it is secured to the edge of a skirting board with small white plastic hooks.

DECORATIVE LIGHT

Choosing decorative light

Light draws the eye, sets the mood and provides a point of focus in a room, and so is an ideal way to make a decorative statement. You can choose an old-fashioned glittering chandelier to make a grand statement or incorporate a witty sculptural piece by a new designer or, perhaps, a quirky arrangement of fibre-optic strands. Making a feature of your light need not entail vast expense: simple fairy lights, coloured lamps and lanterns can all be effective options.

Fairy lights

A string of tiny bulbs that plugs into the wall, fairy lights were once associated exclusively with Christmas decorations and gaudy colours. Now they are available not only in plain white but in a myriad guises, some of which can be used outdoors (make sure you check first). Modern fairy lights can have delicate fronds, each with a tiny bulb at the end; or they may consist of a snaking coil of lights encased in plastic (with long-lasting but non-replaceable bulbs); some have individual shades which may be plain or coloured, or shaped like tiny flowers to resemble a glowing garland.

Fairy lights can be used to decorate your home for special occasions at any time of year, or used as an addition to a room's everyday decorations: little 'bunches' of lights can be wound into the leaves of a houseplant or amongst the flowers in an arrangement on the dining table; larger strings can decorate your mantlepiece or pictures on the walls for special occasions, or you can wind plastic coils around architectural features such as banisters. Always beware of the danger of the fragile bulbs being trodden on, especially at parties, and as with flexes, keep them out of the reach of small children.

Star lights

These are similar to fairy lights, but are permanently wired into one location rather than being something you bring out for special occasions. Their tiny halogen lamps can be dotted around a ceiling (or indeed a wall), where they will be all but invisible until switched on. When lit up they create the impression of a multitude of stars in the sky.

Fibre-optic lights

These are acrylic or fibreglass strands that carry light from a source to their many tiny tips (see page 245). They are most familiar in the form of the 'fountain of light' lamp in which the ends of a spray of these acrylic strands gradually changes colour. Fun for a child's room, nowadays these have otherwise become something of a stylistic joke since they first appeared in the 1970s, along with Lava lamps. Fibre optics can have more sophisticated uses, however. Architects and designers have used them to light water – more specifically the spray of water jetting from a shower head – and create sparkling starlight effects. Fibre optics are undoubtedly decorative and dramatic, and their possible uses in the home have hardly begun to be exploited, but until their cost drops equally dramatically they will continue to be an expensive lighting option.

Sculptural lights

This is an umbrella term for the many other types of decorative lighting that have sprung into being in recent years. Lighting has attracted the talents of some of the world's

1 New silicon switches bring an element of sensuality to a practical necessity. **2** Toggle switches, with a dimmer control in the centre, are neater than the more standard rocker switches. **3** A fibre-optic display in a wet room. Because the actual light source can be remote, fibre optics are safe in locations that other types of exposed lighting would not be. **4** Fairy lights piled in a grate stand in for a real fire. **5** A string of fairy lights shaded with Japanese paper lanterns makes a decorative display. **6** Tom Dixon's famous 'Jack' light is part light, part seat, part sculpture.

most original and creative designers, among them Philippe Starck, Caterina Fadda, Bowles and Linares, Sharon Marston, Antonio Citterio, Jasper Morrison and Tom Dixon. Many lighting emporia are akin to toy shops or art galleries as a result. Coloured light-up glass spikes emerging in rows from a solid wall plate, nets of twinkling lights that can be draped or hung flat in a panel, chunky floor lights in the form of jacks that can be used singly or stacked in a column – these are just a few of the striking sculptural forms taken by contemporary lighting installations.

Many contemporary floor lights, table lamps and chandeliers resemble sculptural installations because they defy traditional forms and extend the boundaries of which materials can be used to make a 'light'. The wicker creations of designer Michael Sodeau, for example, use a familiar craft in a new way, to form lights that are texturally appealing as well as attractive in shape. Prandina uses washable knitted polyester microfibre fabric that is stretched over lightweight metal frames in softly geometric shapes to create lights that are simple and glowing. Bloxam De Matteis have taken the structure of the myoglobin molecule (which carries oxygen to muscles in the human body) and based their 'Mb' ceiling light/chandelier upon it.

Chandeliers

A chandelier has always created drama, not only because of the beauty of its glass forms but also because of the beguiling way in which it fragments the light. A delicate, whimsical chandelier makes a romantic addition to a bedroom; in a larger room, something more imposing should be used as a focus – a smaller version may look lost and out of place – or you can hang several chandeliers in a row. It isn't necessary to place a chandelier in the middle of a room unless, perhaps, you have a period house with a plasterwork ceiling rose. Where you can see through from one adjoining room to another, from living to dining room perhaps, choose chandeliers that complement each other in terms of materials and scale. Putting a mirror on a wall nearby will double the impact of a chandelier's glinting glass drops.

TRADITIONAL CHANDELIERS The historic chandelier – a branched, ornate lighting fixture of sparkling crystal drops found in wealthy homes – is a form of lighting whose appeal has endured for centuries. Reinterpretations and reproductions of historical styles are widely available today in traditional materials such as metal and glass. They can be fitted with candle-like bulbs (see page 245) and some are still designed to take wax candles. If you buy

an old chandelier from a sale room (or even inherit one), you can have missing glass pieces replaced by a specialist company.

CONTEMPORARY CHANDELIERS A classic form that inspires reinterpretation, today chandeliers are made of metals, wire, plastics, ceramic, glass – indeed any material that has caught the imagination of a designer. Two of the best known makers of modern chandeliers are Dale Chihuly, who creates organic, twisting masses of blown glass forms, and Ingo Maurer, whose witty, tongue-in-cheek designs are much sought after. Examples of his work include a collection of white china fragments that appear to have shattered in mid-air, and a group of separate bulbs on wires, each of which has a pair of little white feather wings.

Period lights

A period light fitting might be anything from an ornate eighteenth-century wall sconce to a twentieth-century modernist design classic. All types of period light, including chandeliers, table lamps, standard lamps and pendants, are available from specialist stores and antique shops as both reconditioned and reproduction pieces. If you buy a period light fitting at a market or sale room and want it rewired or converted to electricity, it is safest (as with everything electrical) to employ a qualified professional to do the job. Metal light fittings can be polished; lacquered and gilded finishes, and glass, can be gently wiped clean with a damp cloth. If this is not sufficient to get the glass clean, the light fitting should be removed and dismantled (keep a sketch of how the pieces fit together) and each piece carefully washed and dried before reassembling. There are no short cuts to a sparklingly clean antique (or modern) glass light fitting and you may prefer a specialist company to do the job.

As with furniture, some of the best lighting designs of the twentieth century have never gone out of production and it is still possible to buy an authentic period light, such as the hip 1960s 'Arco' floor lamp by Achille and Pier Giacomo Castiglioni, whose arched stem and bulbous metal shade still features widely in today's style magazines. Many of the Bauhaus light fittings and other Twenties designs are also now reproduced at affordable prices, and Fifties designs like Arne Jacobsen's 'AJ Visor' lamp – a functional but elegant metal floor lamp with an oval base and cone shade – have a minimal appeal that is highly contemporary.

Lanterns

A lantern comprises a flame or bulb (which can be dimmable) enclosed within a glass case, which may be transparent or translucent.

1 Ambient atmospheric light is provided by this prop-up, moveable light wand, designed by Michael Young. **2** This striking ceiling light by Dutch design group Droog comprises 85 bulbs grouped together in an organic mass. **3** Light as sculpture: the spectacular 'Glitterbox' by Georg Baldele.

Traditionally, a lantern was used for lighting entrances and hallways, where its glass sides protected its flame from being extinguished by draughts. Lanterns still work well in these and other settings (although you will want to avoid the suburban cliché of orange-tinted carriage lights outside your front door) and they can serve as attractive garden lights for barbecues and outdoor parties. Lanterns can be functional and modern in appearance or highly decorative, sometimes with coloured or patterned glass. Popular Moroccan-style lanterns are made of metal, and pierced with attractive patterns to let through the light.

Coloured light

This is an area of domestic lighting that has hardly begun to be used to the full for its decorative potential. In the future, light emitting diodes, or LEDs (see page 245), combined with microprocessors in a computer-controlled system, may make it possible to use coloured light as freely as coloured paint – or indeed more freely, as it can be changed according to mood – to alter effortlessly the look of your interiors. Retail outlets, clubs and hotels, art galleries and museums already use LED lighting because of its versatility and impact. In due course this form of lighting will no doubt move from the commercial to the domestic sphere, as has been the case with halogen lighting and spotlights (which it is now impossible to imagine living without).

In the meantime, coloured gels (sheets of tinted plastic that you place over the light source) and bulbs of different shades (which are readily available) can be used creatively to wash walls with coloured light from 'ordinary' light fittings; white walls reflect coloured light the best. Other ways of introducing coloured light are to choose a chandelier that is made from coloured glass, or lampshades made from coloured translucent materials such as silk or plastic, or to fix coloured glass (or sticky-back plastic gels) in small windows.

Kinetic light

This is light that moves, forming changing washes and patterns on the planes of ceilings, walls and furniture. A simple way of creating pretty, mobile reflections is by suspending an acrylic or glass beaded curtain above a tall window or doorway, or by hanging faceted glass drops at a window that catches the sun. Kinetic light can also be introduced with a projector or a motorized light mobile – the latter will create a magical effect in younger children's rooms. A more sophisticated approach for modern interiors is to install a programmable lighting system that will pattern your walls with ever-changing colours.

4 Chandeliers, with their many points of light reflected in glass beads and faceted drops, are a gentle and romantic form of overhead lighting. **5** A modern take on the chandelier, this opulent centrepiece was designed by Verner Panton. **6** and **7** A pure white minimal interior makes the perfect backdrop for a programmable coloured lighting system.

USEFUL ADDRESSES

FLOORS

Blenheim Carpets
41 Pimlico Road
London SW1W 8NE
Tel: 020 7823 5215
www.blenheim-carpets.co.uk
design and fitting of body and border carpets; natural matting dyed to order

Christopher Farr Contemporary Rugs & Carpets
6 Burnsall Street
London SW3 3ST
Tel: 020 7349 0888
www.cfarr.co.uk
specifiers and design commissioners of contemporary handmade rugs and carpets

Crucial Trading
PO Box 11, Duke Place
Kidderminster
Worcestershire DY10 2JR
Tel: 01562 825656 (for brochures)
www.crucial-trading.com
natural floor coverings (sisal, seagrass, coir, jute, paper and bamboo) and woven wool carpets

Dalsouple
PO Box 140
Bridgwater
Somerset TA5 1HT
Tel: 01984 667233
www.dalsouple.com
rubber flooring

Decorum
North's Estate
Piddington
Buckinghamshire HP14 3BE
Tel: 01494 882299

134 Walcot Street
Bath BA1 5BG
Tel: 01225 334434
www.decorum-ceramics.co.uk
ceramic floor and wall tiles

Delabole Slate
Pengelly
Delabole
Cornwall PL33 9AZ
Tel: 01840 212242
www.delaboleslate.co.uk
slate floor and wall tiles

Dovecote Studios
Donaldson's College
West Coates
Edinburgh EH12 5JJ
Tel: 0131 347 5547
www.dovecotestudios.co.uk
hand-tufted rugs and tapestries

Fired Earth
Warmington Mill
Eaglethorpe
Warmington
Peterborough
Northamptonshire PE8 6TJ
Tel: 01832 280088
and branches nationwide
www.firedearth.com
floor and wall tiles; natural and wood flooring; paints, rugs, furniture and bathrooms

Forbo-Nairn
PO Box 1
Kirkaldy
Fife
Scotland KY1 2SB
Tel: 01592 643111
www.forbo-nairn.co.uk
linoleum flooring

Gordon Reece Gallery
16 Clifford Street
London W1X 1RG
Tel: 020 7439 0007
www.gordonreecegalleries.com
oriental rugs and antiques

The Hardwood Flooring Company
146 West End Lane
London NW6 1SD
Tel: 020 7328 0481
www.hardwoodflooringcompany.com
hardwood flooring and worktops

Harvey Maria
Unit 17, Riverside Business Park
16 Lyon Road
London SW19 2RL
Tel: 020 8542 0088
vinyl floor tiles with photographic designs

Junckers
1A Wheaton Road
Witham
Essex CM8 3UJ
Tel: 01376 534700
www.junckers.co.uk
wood flooring

Kährs UK
Unit 2 West, 68 Bognor Road
Chichester
West Sussex PO19 8NS
Tel: 01243 778747
www.kahrs.se
real-wood laminated flooring

Marley Floors
Dickley Lane
Lenham, Maidstone
Kent ME17 2DE
Tel: 01622 854040
www.marleyfloors.com
vinyl flooring

Paris Ceramics
583 Kings Road
London SW6 9DU
Tel: 020 7371 7778
www.parisceramics.com
limestone, antique stone and terracotta, hand-cut mosaics and decorative tiles

Plyboo (UK)
55–57 Main Street
Alford
Aberdeenshire AB33 8AA
Tel: 01975 563388
www.plyboo.nl
bamboo flooring and panelling

J Preedy and Sons
Lamb Works
North Road
London N7 9DP
Tel: 020 7700 0377
www.preedyglass.com
design and installation of glass flooring

Quiligotti Terrazzo Tiles
PO Box 4
Clifton Junction
Manchester M27 8LP
Tel: 0161 727 1000
www.pilkingtons.com
terrazzo flooring

Roger Oates Design
The Long Barn
Eastnor, Ledbury
Herefordshire HR8 1EL
Tel: 01531 632718

1 Munro Terrace
Cheyne Walk
London SW10 0DL
Tel: 020 7351 2288
www.rogeroates.com
hand-woven rugs, carpets and stair runners

Scotch Floor
91–93 Great Western Road
Glasgow G4 9AH
Tel: 0141 331 2791

28 Haddington Place
Edinburgh EH7 4AF
Tel: 0131 556 3359
www.solidfloor.co.uk
wood flooring

Siesta Cork Tile Company
Unit 21, Tait Road
Gloucester Road,
Croydon
Surrey CR0 2DP
Tel: 020 8683 4055
cork tiles

Sinclair Till
793 Wandsworth Road
London SW8 3JQ
Tel: 020 7720 0031
linoleum flooring

Solid Floor
53 Pembridge Road
London W11 3HG
Tel: 020 7221 9166
and other branches
www.solidfloor.co.uk
wood flooring

Stonell
Forstall House
Bettring
Paddock Wood
Kent TN12 6PY
Tel: 01892 833500
www.stonell.com
natural stone and slate floor tiles

Swedecor
Manchester Street
Hull HU3 4TX
Tel: 01482 329691
www.swedecor.com
ceramic and mosaic floor and wall tiles

Wicanders
Amorium Flooring UK
Suite 1EA, Bishop's Weald House
Albion Way
Horsham
West Sussex RH12 1AH
Tel: 01403 710001
www.amorium.co.uk
cork flooring

WALLS

Cole & Son
Unit G10, Chelsea Harbour Design Centre
London SW10 0XE
Tel: 020 7604 4288
www.cole-and-son.co.uk
wallpaper

Colefax & Fowler
Unit G2, Chelsea Harbour Design Centre
London SW10 0XE
Tel: 020 7351 0666
wallpaper and fabrics

Craig & Rose
Unit 8, Halbeath Industrial Estate
Cross Gates Road
Dunfirmline
Fife KY11 7EG
Tel: 01383 740000
historic paints

Crown Berger
PO Box 37
Crown House
Hollins Road
Darwen
Lancashire BB3 0BG
Tel: 0870 2401127
for suppliers nationwide
www.crownpaint.co.uk
extensive range of paints

Digitile
15 Redchurch Street
London E2 7DJ
Tel: 020 7613 2783
www.digitile.co.uk
digitally printed ceramic tiles

Donghia
23 Chelsea Harbour Design Centre
London SW10 0XE
Tel: 020 7823 3456
www.donghia.com
wallpaper

Dulux Decorator Centres
Manchester Road
Altrincham
Cheshire WA14 5PG
Tel: 0845 600 2400
for suppliers nationwide
www.duluxdecoratorcentres.co.uk
extensive range of paints

Farrow & Ball
Uddens Estate
Wimborne
Dorset BH21 7NL
Tel: 01202 876141 (home delivery service)
www.farrow-ball.com
*traditional paints, including the National
Trust range, and wallpapers*

John Oliver
33 Pembridge Road
London W11 3HG
Tel: 020 7221 6466
www.johnoliver.co.uk
*an eclectic range of wallpaper, fabrics and
paints; colour-matching service*

Natural Tile
150 Church Road
Redfield
Bristol BS5 9HN
Tel: 0117 941 3707
www.naturaltile.co.uk
handmade tiles in metal, glass and resin

Osborne & Little
304 Kings Road
London SW3 5UH
Tel: 020 7352 1456
www.osborneandlittle.com
wallpaper and fabrics

Papers and Paints
4 Park Walk
London SW10 0AD
Tel: 020 7352 8626
www.colourman.com
*extensive range of paints; colour-matching
service; specialists in the use of paint and
colour in historic buildings*

Sanderson, Arthur & Son
Sanderson Store
233 Kings Road
London SW3 5EJ

Tel: 020 7351 7728
www.sanderson-online.co.uk
paints, wallpaper and carpets

Zoffany
Talbot House
17 Church Street
Rickmansworth
Hertfordshire WD3 1DE
Tel: 08708 300350 for stockists
www.zoffany.co.uk
wallpaper and fabrics

WINDOWS & DOORS

Crittall Windows
Springwood Drive
Braintree
Essex CM7 2YN
Tel: 01376 324106
www.crittall-windows.co.uk
metal-frame windows

Holdsworth Windows
Darlingscote Road
Shipston-on-Stour
Warwickshire CV36 4PR
Tel: 01608 661883
www.holdsworthwindows.co.uk
steel windows and leaded lights

Levolux
1 Forward Drive
Harrow
Middlesex HA3 8NT
Tel: 020 8863 9111
(London & South East)
Tel: 01452 500007
(rest of UK and international)
www.levolux.com
shading solutions

The Mosaic Workshop
1a Princeton Street
London WC1R 4AX
Tel: 020 7831 0889
www.mosaicworkshop.com
mosaic tiles and bespoke mosaic designs

The Original Box Sash Window Company
29–30 The Arches
Alma Road
Windsor
Berkshire SL4 1QZ
Tel: 0500 783 4053
www.boxsash.com
traditional timber windows and doors

Rationel Windows UK
7 Avonbury Business Park
Howes Lane
Bicester
Oxon OX26 2UA
Tel: 01869 248181
www.rationel.com
windows and external doors

The Shutter Shop
Units 2–8
Chelsea Harbour Design Centre
London SW10 0XE
Tel: 020 7351 4204
www.shuttershop.co.uk
bespoke hardwood shutters

Swedish Windows
Old Maltings House
Hall Street
Long Melford
Suffolk CO10 9JB
Tel: 01787 467297
www.swedishwindows.com
*timber windows and doors, including
triple-glazed units*

Ventrolla
11 Hornbeam Square South
Harrogate
North Yorkshire HG2 8NB
Tel: 0800 378278
www.ventrolla.co.uk
sash window renovation

FURNITURE &
FURNISHINGS

The Conran Shop
Michelin House
81 Fulham Road
London SW3 6RD
Tel: 020 7589 7401

55 Marylebone High Street
London W1U 5HS
Tel: 020 7723 2223

12 Conduit Street
London W1S 2XQ
Tel: 020 7399 0710
www.conran.co.uk
*furniture, lighting, homewares and
accessories*

Content by Conran
Tel: 01773 606 782
for stockists nationwide
www.contentbyconran.com
*intelligently designed and affordable
contemporary furniture by Terence
Conran; available at The Conran Shop,
House of Fraser and other outlets*

Couverture
310 Kings Road
London SW3 5UH
Tel: 020 7795 1200
www.couverture.co.uk
bedlinen

David Mellor Design
4 Sloane Square
London SW1 8EE
Tel: 020 7730 4259
www.davidmellordesign.com
cutlery and tableware

Designers Guild
267–271 & 275–277 Kings Road
London SW3 5EN
Tel: 020 7351 5775
www.designersguild.com
*fabrics, wallpaper, furniture and
homewares*

Divertimenti
139–141 Fulham Road
London SW3 6SD
Tel: 020 7581 8065
www.divertimenti.co.uk
tableware and cookware

The Futon Shop
168–170 Devonshire Street
Sheffield S3 7BG
Tel: 0114 272 1984
www.futonshop.co.uk
futons and accessories

The General Trading Company
2 Symons Street
Sloane Square
London SW3 2TJ
Tel: 020 7730 0411
www.general-trading.co.uk
*furniture, antiques, lighting, homewares
and accessories*

Habitat
The Heals Building
196 Tottenham Court Road
London W1T 7LD
Tel: 020 7631 3880
and branches nationwide
www.habitat.net
*furniture (including kitchen and bathroom),
lighting, homewares and accessories*

Heals
The Heals Building
196 Tottenham Court Road
London W1T 7LD
Tel: 020 7636 1666
and other branches
www.heals.co.uk
*furniture (including kitchen and bathroom
design), lighting, homewares and accessories*

The Healthy House
The Old Co-op, Lower Street
Ruscombe
Stroud
Gloucestershire GL6 6BU
Tel: 01453 752216
www.healthy-house.co.uk
*homewares and products for allergy
sufferers*

Hypnos
Station Road
Princes Risborough
Buckinghamshire HP27 9DN
Tel: 01844 348200
www.hypnos.ltd.uk
beds and mattresses

IKEA
255 North Circular Road
London NW13 0QJ
Tel: 0845 355 1144
and branches nationwide
www.ikea.com
*furniture (including kitchen and bathroom),
lighting, homewares and accessories;
extensive flat-pack furniture range*

Inhouse
28 Howe Street
Edinburgh EH3 6TG
Tel: 0131 225 2888

24–26 Wilson Street
Glasgow G1 1SS
Tel: 0141 552 5902
www.inhousenet.co.uk
*contemporary furniture, lighting, homewares
and accessories*

John Lewis
Oxford Street
London W1A 1EX
Tel: 08456 049 049
and branches nationwide
www.johnlewis.com
*comprehensive range of products including
furniture, lighting, homewares, accessories,
electrical goods and appliances*

Liberty
210–220 Regent Street
London W1R 6AH
Tel: 020 7734 1234
www.liberty.co.uk
*extensive range of fabrics; furniture
and homewares*

Lloyd Davies
14 John Dalton Street
Manchester M2 6JR
Tel: 0161 832 3700
*classic twentieth-century and
contemporary furniture, lighting,
homewares and accessories*

Loft
24–28 Dock Street
Leeds LS10 1JF
Tel: 0113 305 1515
www.loftloft.com
*classic twentieth-century and
contemporary furniture, lighting,
homewares and accessories*

Muji
41 Carnaby Street
London W1V 1PD
Tel: 020 7287 7323
and branches nationwide
www.mujionline.com
*'no-brand' Japanese homewares,
furniture and accessories*

SCP
135–139 Curtain Road
London EC2A 3BX

Tel: 020 7739 1869
www.scp.co.uk
classic twentieth-century and contemporary furniture, lighting and homewares

The Shaker Shop
72–73 Marylebone High Street
London W1U 5JW
Tel: 020 7935 9461
www.shaker.co.uk
Shaker furniture and accessories

Skandium
72 Wigmore Street
London W1H 9DL
Tel: 020 7935 2077
www.skandium.com
classic twentieth-century and contemporary Scandinavian furniture and homewares

Slumberland
Salmon Fields
Oldham
Lancashire OL2 6SB
Tel: 0161 628 4886
www.slumberland.co.uk
beds and mattresses

Sofa Workshop
Lords Wood Barn
Lodsworth
Petworth
West Sussex GU28 9BS
Tel: 01798 343400
and branches nationwide
www.sofaworkshop.com
sofas and sofa beds

Thomas Goode
19 South Audley Street
London W1K 2BN
Tel: 020 7499 2822
www.thomasgoode.co.uk
tableware

Twentytwentyone
274 Upper Street
London N1 2UA
Tel: 020 7288 1996
www.twentytwentyone.co.uk
classic twentieth-century furniture

Vi-Spring
Ernesettle Lane
Ernesettle
Plymouth PL5 2TT
Tel: 01752 366311
www.vi-spring.co.uk
beds and mattresses

Wade Smith Apartment Store
Matthew Street
Liverpool L2 6RE
Tel: 0151 224 7617
www.wadesmith.co.uk
furniture (including kitchen and bathroom), lighting, homewares and accessories

LIGHTING

Artemide
Showroom
90–92 Great Portland Street
London W1W 7JY
Tel: 020 7631 5200
www.artemide.com
contemporary lighting

Caz Systems
18–19 Church Street
Brighton BN1 1RB
Tel: 01273 326 471
contemporary lighting

Christopher Wray Lighting
591–593 Kings Road
London SW6 2YW
Tel: 020 7751 8701
and branches nationwide
www.christopher-wray.com
contemporary, traditional, antique and reproduction lighting

Flos
at McInnes Cook
31 Lisson Grove
London NW1 6UB
Tel: 020 7723 7005
and stockists nationwide
www.flos.net
contemporary lighting including outdoor lighting

Forbes & Lomax
205a St Johns Hill
London SW11 1TH
Tel: 020 7738 0202
www.forbesandlomax.co.uk
sockets, switches and dimmers

Gusto
6 Townmead Business Centre
William Morris Way
London SW6 2SZ
Tel: 020 7736 8828
www.gusto.co.uk
bespoke contemporary lighting

John Cullen Lighting
585 Kings Road
London SW6 2EH
Tel: 020 7371 5400
www.johncullenlighting.co.uk
low-voltage lighting

The London Lighting Company
135 Fulham Road
London SW3 6RT
Tel: 020 7589 3612
contemporary lighting

McCloud Lighting
19–20, 3rd Floor
Chelsea Harbour Design Centre
Lots Road
London SW10 0XE

Tel: 020 7352 1533
www.mccloud.co.uk
bespoke contemporary lighting

Quo-Vadis
3 Roundwood Lane
Harpenden
Hertfordshire AL5 3BW
Tel: 07779 286472
www.quo-vadis.com
coloured lighting systems

SKK
34 Lexington Street
London W1R 3HR
Tel: 020 7434 4095
www.skk.net
spots, tracks, uplights and downlights

The Stiffkey Lamp Shop
Stiffkey
Wells-next-the-Sea
Norfolk NR23 1AJ
Tel: 01328 830460
www.thestiffkeylampshop.co.uk
antique lighting

KITCHENS

Aga
The Aga Shop
10 Upper High Street
Thame
Oxon OX9 3ER
Tel: 01844 214214
Tel: 01952 642000 (head office)
also suppliers nationwide
www.aga-rayburn.co.uk
traditional cast-iron ranges

Alno
Unit 10, Hampton Farm Industrial Estate
Hampton Road West
Hanworth
Middlesex TW13 6DB
Tel: 020 8898 4781
www.alno.co.uk
contemporary kitchens

Asselle
102 Alexandra Park Road
London N10 2AE
Tel: 020 8444 2422

14–18 Old Street
London EC1V 9BH
Tel: 020 7253 2806
www.asselle.co.uk
modular kitchens and wardrobes; lighting

Bulthaup
37 Wigmore Street
London W1U 1PP
Tel: 020 7495 3663
www.bulthaup.com
contemporary kitchens

Johnny Grey
Fyning Copse
Rogate
Petersfield
Hampshire GU13 5DH
Tel: 01730 821 424
www.johnnygrey.com
contemporary kitchens

Magnet
Allington Way
Darlington
County Durham DL1 4XT
Tel: 01535 661133 (head office)
for branches nationwide
www.magnet.co.uk
*kitchens and appliances; also bathrooms,
bedrooms and home offices*

Newcastle Furniture Company
Rutherford House
43 Bath Lane
Newcastle upon Tyne NE4 5SP
Tel: 0191 438 1342
www.newcastlefurniture.com
*kitchens and appliances; also bathrooms,
bedrooms and home offices*

Plain English Design
41a Hoxton Square
London N1 6PB
Tel: 020 7613 0022
www.plainenglishdesign.co.uk
Shaker kitchens

Poggenpohl
Ransome Road
Far Cotton
Northampton NN4 8AA
Tel: 01604 763482 (head office)
for suppliers nationwide
www.poggenpohl.co.uk
contemporary kitchens

Roundhouse
25 Chalk Farm Road
London NW1 8AG
Tel: 020 7428 9955
www.roundhousedesign.com
classic and contemporary kitchens

BATHROOMS

Alternative Plans
9 Hester Road
London SW11 4AN
Tel: 020 7228 6460
www.alternative-plans.co.uk
*bathroom fittings in stone, timber, glass
and stainless steel; kitchens*

Armitage Shanks
Rugeley
Staffordshire WS15 4BT
Tel: 01543 490253 (head office)
for suppliers nationwide
www.armitage-shanks.co.uk
bathroom fittings

Aston Matthews
141–147a Essex Road
Islington
London N1 2SN
Tel: 020 7226 7220
www.astonmatthews.co.uk
bathroom fittings

Avante Bathroom Products
Thistle House, Thistle Way
Gildersome Spur, Gildersome
Moreley
Leeds LS27 7JZ
Tel: 0113 2012240
for suppliers nationwide
ww.avantebathrooms.com
bathroom fittings including glass designs

Bathaus
92 Brompton Road
London SW3 1ER
Tel: 020 7225 7620
www.bathaus.co.uk
classic and contemporary bathrooms

Capital Marble Design
1 Pall Mall Deposit
124–128 Barlby Road
London W10 6BL
Tel: 020 8968 5340
www.capitalmarble.co.uk
marble bathroom fittings

CP Hart & Sons
Newnham Terrace
Hercules Road
London SE1 7DR
Tel: 020 7902 1000
and branches nationwide
classic and contemporary bathrooms

Ideal Standard
The Bathroom Works
National Avenue
Hull HU5 4HS
Tel: 01482 346461
for suppliers nationwide
www.ideal-standard.co.uk
classic and contemporary bathrooms

Lefroy Brooks
Ibroc House
Essex Road
Hoddesdon
Hertfordshire EN11 0QS
Tel: 01992 448300
for showrooms nationwide
www.lefroybrooks.com
classic and contemporary bathrooms

Majestic Shower Company Ltd
1 North Place
Edinburgh Way
Harlowe
Essex CM20 2SL
Tel: 01279 443644
for suppliers nationwide
www.majesticshowers.com
shower fittings

Vola UK
Unit 12, Ampthill Business Park
Station Road
Ampthill
Bedfordshire MK45 2QW
Tel: 01525 841155
www.vola.co.uk
contemporary taps

William Garvey
Leyhill, Upton
Payhembury
Honiton
Devon EX14 3JG
Tel: 01404 841 430
www.williamgarvey.co.uk
timber baths and basins

HEATING

Aestus
Unit 5, Strawberry Lane Industrial Estate
Willenhall
West Midlands WV13 3RS
Tel: 01902 632256
www.aestus-radiators.co.uk
glass radiators

Bisque
244 Belsize Road
London NW6 4BT
Tel: 020 7328 2225
www.bisque.co.uk
contemporary radiators

Eskimo
25R Horsell Road
London N5 1XL
Tel: 020 7609 9981
www.eskimodesign.co.uk
contemporary radiators

MHS Radiators
35 Nobel Square
Burnt Mills Industrial Estate
Basildon
Essex SS13 1LT
Tel: 01268 591010
www.mhsradiators.com
classic and contemporary radiators

Warmup
Unit 1, Roslin Road
London W3 8BH
Tel: 0845 345 2288
www.warmup.co.uk
electric stone radiators

FIREPLACES

B&D Design
Unit 2, Park Mews
213–215 Kilburn Lane
London W10 4BQ
Tel: 020 8964 5355
www.bd-designs.co.uk
bespoke contemporary fireplaces

CVO Fire
Unit 3, Mercury Road
Gallowfields
Richmond
North Yorkshire DL10 4TQ
Tel: 01748 821708
www.cvo.co.uk
contemporary fireplaces

Diligence
22 East Street
Ashburton
Devon TQ13 7AZ
Tel: 01364 654716
www.diligenceinternational.com
contemporary fireplaces

Elgin & Hall
Adelphi House
Hunton
Bedale
North Yorkshire DL8 1LY
Tel: 01677 450100
www.elgin.co.uk
traditional fireplaces

Lifestyle Fire and Flame
Garden Studios
Maynooth Road
Celbridge
Co. Kildare
Ireland
Tel: +353 1627 0099
www.lifestylefire.com
fire bowls and garden torches

The Platonic Fireplace Company
Phoenix Wharf
Eel Pie Island
Twickenham TW1 3DY
Tel: 020 8891 5904
www.platonicfireplaces.co.uk
contemporary gas fires

Real Flame
80 New Kings Road
London SW6 4LT
Tel: 020 7731 2704
www.realflame.co.uk
contemporary gas fires

Scan of Denmark
28 Diamonds Green
West Kirby
Wirral CH48 5DU
Tel: 0151 625 0504
www.warmfurniture.com
contemporary wood-burning stoves

Stovax
Falcon Road
Falcon Industrial Estate
Exeter EX2 7LS
Tel: 01392 474060 (stoves)
Tel: 01392 474055 (fireplaces)
Tel: 01392 474061 (gas, electric, oil)
www.stovax.com
traditional fireplaces and multi-fuel stoves

SALVAGE YARDS

Au Temps Perdu
30 Midland Road
St Phillips
Bristol BS2 0JY
Tel: 0117 929 9143
www.autempsperdu.com

Edinburgh Architectural Salvage Yard
Unit 6, Couper Street
Leith
Edinburgh EH6 6HH
Tel: 0131 554 7077
www.easy-arch-salv.co.uk

John Fyffe Architectural Salvage
4 Jennymount Street
Belfast BT15 3HW
Tel: 028 9035 1475

London Architectural Salvage and Supply Company (LASSCO)
St Michael's
Mark Street
London EC2A 4ER
Tel: 020 7749 9944

41 Maltby Street
London SE1 3PA
Tel: 020 7394 2101
www.lassco.co.uk

Nostalgia
Hollands Mill, 61 Shaw Heath
Stockport SK3 8BH
Tel: 0161 477 7706
www.nostalgia-uk.com

SALVO
www.salvoweb.com
directory of salvage dealers

Walcot Reclamation
108 Walcot Street
Bath BA1 5BT
Tel: 01225 444404
www.walcot.com

SPECIALIST SERVICES AND MATERIALS

Alma Home
12–14 Greatorex Street
London E1 5NF
Tel: 020 7377 0762
www.almahome.co.uk
leather furniture and accessories; floor and wall tiles

Arc Lighting
41a Upper St. James Street
Newport
Isle of Wight PO30 1LB
Tel: 01983 523399
www.arclighting.com
illuminated glass floors, walls and tiles

B&Q
Portswood
1 Hampshire Corporation Park
Chandlers Ford
Eastleigh
Hampshire SO53 3YX
Tel: 0870 0101 006
for branches nationwide
www.diy.com
DIY specialists

Bath & Glassworks
128-130 High Street
Hurstpierpoint
West Sussex BN6 9PX
Tel: 01273 831846
www.bathandglass.com
architectural glass, including radiators and bespoke bathrooms

Benchmark Woodworking
Kintbury
Hungerford
Berkshire RG17 9SA
Tel: 01488 658184
www.benchmarkwoodworking.com
design-led manufacturer of furniture and joinery; owned by Terence Conran

Bill Amberg Leather Design
10 Chepstow Road
London W2 5BD
Tel: 020 7727 3560
www.billamberg.com
bespoke leather furniture; floor and wall tiles

Bisca
Sawmill Lane
Helmsley
North Yorkshire YO62 5DQ
Tel: 01439 771702
www.bisca.co.uk
contemporary staircases in stainless steel, glass and timber

Bragman Flett
Unit 4
193 Garth Road
Morden
Surrey SM4 4LZ
Tel: 020 8337 1934
metal flooring, kitchens and stairs

Bulmer Brick and Tile
The Brickfields
Bulmer
Sudbury
Suffolk CO10 7EF
Tel: 01787 269232
handmade and bespoke bricks

Carlisle Brass
Kingstown Broadway
Carlisle CA3 0HA
Tel: 01228 511770
www.carlislebrass.co.uk
architectural brassware and fittings

Cast Advanced Concretes
Unit 4, Rempstone Barns
Corfe Castle
Wareham BH20 5JH
Tel: 01929 480757
www.castadvancedconcretes.com
concrete worktops and panelling

DuPont Corian
Maylands Avenue
Hemel Hempstead
Hertfordshire HP2 7DP
Tel: 0800 962 116 (head office)
and suppliers nationwide
www.corian.co.uk
*Corian surfaces for kitchens and
bathrooms*

Dura
4 Cambridge Terrace
St. James Road
Brackley
Northamptonshire NN13 7XY
Tel: 01280 706050
www.dura.eu.com
stainless-steel furniture and fittings

Fusion Glass Designs
365 Clapham Road
London SW9 9BT
Tel: 020 7738 5888
www.fusionglass.co.uk
*glass interior details, screens, stairs and
sculpture to commission*

Gooding Aluminium
1 British Wharf
Landmann Way
London SE14 5RS
Tel: 020 8692 2255
www.goodingalum.com
*aluminium sheet flooring, wall panelling
and casings*

Ibstock Brick
21 Dorset Square
London NW1 6QE
Tel: 0870 903 4013
www.ibstock.co.uk
*handmade and bespoke bricks; brick library
for smaller quantities*

Jim Lawrence Traditional Ironwork
Stoke by Nayland
Colchester
Essex CO6 4QG
Tel: 01206 265876
www.jim-lawrence.co.uk
wrought-iron fixtures and fittings

Pilkington Glass
Prescot Road
St. Helens
Merseyside WA10 3TT
Tel: 01744 629000
www.pilkington.com
*comprehensive range of glass products
including low-emissivity glass*

Sainsbury's Homebase
Beddington House
Railway Approach
Wallington
Surrey SM6 0HB
Tel: 0870 900 8098
for branches nationwide
www.homebase.co.uk
DIY specialists

Solar Century
91–94 Lower Marsh
Waterloo
London SE1 7AB
Tel: 0870 735 8100
www.solarcentury.co.uk
*solar technology, including photovoltaic
panels and solar slates*

Tin Tab
Units 5, 6 & 7
North Industrial Estate
New Road
Newhaven
Sussex BN9 0HE
Tel: 01273 515155
www.tintab.com
staircases, worksurfaces and flooring

Victorian Woodworks
54 River Road
Creekmouth
Barking
Essex IG11 0DW
Tel: 020 8534 1000
www.victorianwoodworks.co.uk
*reclaimed and new wood flooring,
panelling and beams*

Villavent
Avenue 2
Station Lane Industrial Estate
Witney
Oxon OX8 6YD
Tel: 01993 778481
www.villavent.co.uk
*heat-recovery ventilation and cooling
systems*

Zinc Counters
High Street
Markington
Harrogate
North Yorkshire HG3 3NR
Tel: 01765 677808
*zinc, pewter and copper cladding for
tables, counters and fascias*

ADVICE

British Interior Design Association
1–4 Chelsea Harbour Design Centre
Chelsea Harbour
London SW10 0XE
Tel: 020 7349 0800
www.bida.org.uk
publishes a list of members

The Building Centre Group
26 Store Street
London WC1E 7BT
Tel: 09065 161 136 (premium-rate guideline)
www.buildingcentre.co.uk
*information on everything to do with building
and building materials; advice service*

The Consumers Association
2 Marylebone Road
London NW1 4DF
Tel: 020 7770 7000
www.which.net
*testing and assessment of consumer goods
and services; publishers of Which? magazine*

**Council for Registered Gas Installers
(CORGI)**
1 Elmwood, Chineham Business Park
Crockford Lane
Basingstoke
Hampshire RG24 8WG
Tel: 01256 372200
www.corgi-gas.com
registers all gas-installation businesses

Crafts Council
44a Pentonville Road
London N1 9BY
Tel: 020 7278 7700
www.craftscouncil.org.uk
promotes contemporary crafts

Design Council
34 Bow Street
London WC2E 7DL
Tel: 020 7420 5200
www.designcouncil.org.uk
*can supply information on how to
commission designers*

Electrical Contractors' Association
Esca House, 34 Palace Court
London WC2 4HY
Tel: 020 7313 4800
www.eca.co.uk
technical information and referral to members

English Heritage
23 Savile Row
London W1X 1AB
Tel: 020 7973 3000
*preserves ancient monuments, historic
buildings and conservation areas*

Federation of Master Builders
Gordon Fisher House
14–15 Great James Street
London WC1N 3DP
Tel: 020 7242 7583
www.fmb.org.uk
publishes an index of members

Fire Protection Association
Bastille Court, 2 Paris Garden
London SE1 8ND
Tel: 020 7902 5300
www.thefpa.co.uk
information on fire prevention

Institute of Carpenters
35 Hayworth Road
Sandyacre
Nottingham NG10 5LL
Tel: 0115 949 0641
www.central-office.co.uk
information and referral to members

Institute of Plumbing
64 Station Lane
Hornchurch
Essex RM12 6NB
Tel: 01708 472791
www.plumbers.org.uk
publishes a list of members

Institution of Structural Engineers
11 Upper Belgrave Street
London SW1X 8BH
Tel: 020 7235 4535
www.istructe.org.uk
www.findanengineer.com
publishes a list of members

National House Building Council
Buildmark House
Chiltern Avenue
Amersham
Buckinghamshire HP6 5AP
Tel: 01494 735363
www.nhbc.co.uk
*publishes a list of members and registers
newly-built houses*

Public Health Inspectors
*Local councils will put you in touch with
public health inspectors: it is important
to contact them before undertaking any
alteration to drainage.*

Royal Institute of British Architects
66 Portland Place
London W1N 4AD
Tel: 020 7580 5533
www.riba.org
publishes a list of members

Royal Institute of Chartered Surveyors
RICS Contact Centre
Surveyor Court
Westwood Way
Coventry CV4 8SE
Tel: 0870 333 1600
www.rics.org.uk
publishes a list of members

ECOLOGICAL DESIGN

**Association for Environment Conscious
Building**
PO Box 32
Llandysul
Carmarthanshire SA44 5ZA
Tel: 01654 705 950
www.aecb.net
*publishes a range of titles covering aspects
of sustainable building and associated issues*

Building Research Establishment (BRE)
Garston Road
Watford WD25 9XX
Tel: 01923 664000
www.bre.co.uk
*information on reducing the environmental
impact of construction projects; includes
information on eco-homes and a materials
exchange for second-hand and unused
building materials*

Centre for Alternative Technology
Machynlleth
Powys SY20 9AZ
Tel: 01654 705 950
www.cat.org.uk
*information to inspire, inform and enable
society to move towards a sustainable future*

Construction Resources
16 Great Guildford Street
London SE1 0HS
Tel: 020 7450 2211
www.constructionresources.com
*ecological builders' merchant for sustainable
building materials and systems; detailed
technical information available*

Ecological Design Association
www.edaweb.org
*information on environmental issues relating
to the design and building professions;
promotes sustainable development*

Energy Saving Trust
21 Dartmouth Street
London SW1H 9BP
Tel: 020 7222 0101
www.est.org.uk
*information on creating energy efficient
homes*

Forestry Stewardship Council (FSC)
Unit D, Station Building
Llanidloes
Powys SY18 6EB
Tel: 01686 413916
www.fsc-uk.org
*international organization that sets
standards for timber management and
products worldwide; provides information
on suppliers of FSC-certified timber*

Friends of the Earth
26–28 Underwood Street
London N1 7UJ
Tel: 020 7490 1555
www.foe.co.uk
information on environmental issues

The National Energy Foundation
Davy Avenue
Knowlhill
Milton Keynes MK5 8NG
Tel: 01908 665555
www.greenenergy.org.uk
*information on sustainable and green
sources of energy*

Natural Building Technologies
The Hangar
Worminghall Road
Oakley
Buckinghamshire HP18 9UL
Tel: 01844 338338
and suppliers nationwide
www.natural-building.co.uk
*ecological designs and materials for walls,
floors and roofs*

**Scottish Ecological Design
Association (SEDA)**
12 Abbeymount
Edinburgh EH8 8EJ
Tel: 0131 6612500
www.inverarc.co.uk/seda
*promotes the design of materials,
products and systems that are benign
to the environment*

UNIVERSAL DESIGN

Care Design
Moorgate
Ormskirk
Lancashire, L39 4RX
Tel: 01695 579061
www.care-design.co.uk
*kitchen and bathroom specialists for
the elderly and disabled*

Centre for Accessible Environments
Nutmeg House
60 Gainsford Street
London SE1 2NY
Tel: 020 7357 8182
www.cae.org.uk
*information on how the built environment
can best be made or modified to
achieve inclusion by design*

The Disability Information Trust
Nuffield Orthopedic Center
Headington
Oxford OX3 7LD
Tel: 01865 227592
www.abilityonline.org.uk
*tests and assesses disability equipment;
publication of independent information*

Disabled Living Foundation
380–384 Harrow Road
London W9 2HU
Tel helpline: 0845 130 9177
www.dlf.org.uk
*information on disability equipment,
household gadgets and new technologies*

**Royal Association for Disability and
Rehabilitation (RADAR)**
12 City Forum
250 City Road
London EC1V 8AF
Tel: 020 7250 3222
www.radar.org.uk
*publishes a comprehensive range of
books and pamphlets*

INDEX

Page numbers in *italic* refer to illustrations and captions.

ACKNOWLEDGEMENTS

The following photographs have been specially commissioned by Conran Octopus:

Thomas Stewart (Stylist: Michelle Ogundehin): 20–21; 36–39 (Architect: Burd Haward Marston Architects); 40–43 (Designer: David Card of Mandolin Design, Contributions: Jo Ryan); 76–79 (Architect: Douglas Stephen Partnership); 97 (Architect: David Mikhail Architects); 108; 172 below and 173–175 (Architects: Buschow Henley Architects); 176; 185 (7) (Architect: David Mikhail Architects)

Hotze Eisma/Taverne Agency (Stylist: Reini Smit): 44

Dan Duchars: 151 (Architects: Phineas Manasseh Architects)

Peter Campbell Saunders: 182 (3–12); 183; 195 (3–11); 196 (3, 5, 7)

The publisher would like to thank the following photographers, agencies and architects for their kind permission to reproduce the following photographs:

Endpapers Ron Lowery/Corbis

2 Powerstock

6–7 Marco Tassinari/Paola Moretti Productions

9 above Helen Fickling (Design: Kamal Ifticen); centre above Peter Cook/View (Architect: Peter Feeny); centre below Catherine Gratwicke/Elle Decoration; below David George/Red Cover

10 above left Emmanuel Barbe/Marie Claire Maison; above right Ulkova/Studio Jaanis Kerkis/Courtesy of Siren Architects; below left José van Riele/Marie Claire Maison; right centre Ray Main/Mainstream

13 above Timothy Hursley (Architect: Rural Studio/Auburn University); below Edmund Sumner (Architects: Nicolas Grimshaw & Partners)

14 Brian Vanden Brink (Architect: Julie Snow)

15 Ignacio Martínez (Architect: Oskar Leo Kaufmann)

16 Peter Aaron/Esto (Architect: Adam Kalkin)

17 The Japan Architect (Architects: Takaharu Tezuka & Yui Tezuka/Masahiro Ikeda)

18-19 Louie Psihoyos/Katz Pictures

23 Guy Obijn (Architect: Karel Vandeneynden)

24 Mark Williams/Living Etc/IPC Syndication

26 Clive Frost (Architect: Genevieve Lilly)

27 above Amparo Garrido/Album; centre left Nicolas Tosi/Marie Claire Maison (Stylist: Catherine Ardouin); centre right Guy Obijn (Architect: Paul Alexander Linse); bottom left and right Eugeni Pons/Album

28 above left Tim Young/Homes & Gardens/IPC Syndication; above right Simon Whitmore/Living Etc/IPC Syndication; below left David Garcia/Living Etc/IPC Syndication; below right Per Gunnarsson (Stylist: Susanne Swegen)

29 above Nick Carter/Red Cover; below Graham Atkins-Hughes/Red Cover

30 above Polly Wreford/Narratives; below Paul Massey/Living Etc/IPC Syndication

31 above Alan Crow/View (Architect: 51% Studios); below left Guglielmo Galvin/Red Cover; below right Daniel Hertzell

32 above David Garcia/Living Etc/IPC Syndication; below Domininc Blackmore

33 left Minh & Wass (Owner: Robin Renzi); 33 right Christoph Kicherer (Designer: Torsten Neeland)

34 above left Stellan Herner (Owners: Sara Källgren & Jonny Vollner/Stylist: Lotta Noremark); above right Marianne Majerus (Designer: Paul Southern); below left Deidi von Schaewen; below right Verne Fotografie (Garden Designer: Andrew Ruth)

35 Polly Wreford/Narratives

46 Jake Fitzjones/Living Etc/IPC Syndication;

47 left Richard Davies; right Vercruysse and Dujardin (Architect: W. Depuydt)

48 above left Luc Wauman; above right Jan Baldwin/Narratives (Designer: Helen Somogyvari); below left Ray Main/Mainstream; below right Paul Massey

49 above and below Kristian Septimius Krogh/House of Pictures (Stylist: Lise Septimius Krogh)

50 Giulio Oriani/Vega MG

51 above left Uwe Spoering (Architect: Michael Croce Freier Architekt); below left Serge Anton/Inside/Red Cover; above and below right Grazia Ike Branco

52 above left Peter Tolkin (Architect: Tolkin & Associates); below left Jim Rounsevell (Architect: Neal Deputy); below right Courtesy of Tin Tab

53 above Frank Schott (Owner: Joe Sabel/Architect: AERO II Design); below Ray Main/Mainstream

54–57 Paul Ryan/International Interiors (Architect: Peter de Bretteville)

59 Jonathan Rose (Designers: Wayne & Gerardine Hemingway)

60 left Bieke Claessens (Architect: Peter Cornoedus/Interior Designer: Mieke Geraerts); centre Alexander van Berge; right Luke White/The Interior Archive (Designer: Caroline Gardener)

61 Winfried Heinze/Red Cover

62 above left Renée Frinking/Living/Sanoma Syndication; below left Verne Fotografie; right Ed Reeve/Red Cover

63 above William Howard/Dwell Magazine (Architect: David Hertz/Syndesis/Furniture Designer: Stacey Fong/Syndesis); below left Jeroma Darblay/Cote Ouest/Red Cover (Stylist: M. P. Faure); below right Verne Fotografie (Owner: Pierre Castelyn)

64 above left Paul Lepreux/Marie Claire Maison; below left Paul Massey/Living Etc/IPC Syndication; right Per Gunnarsson (Stylist: Ulrika Montan)

65 above left Kristine Larsen; above right William Howard/Dwell Magazine (Architect: David Hertz/Syndesis/Furniture Designer: Stacy Fong/Syndesis); below Allan Crow/View (Architect: Richard Hywell Evans)

66 Jean-Francois Jaussaud (Design: Lux-Productions)

67 above Stellan Herner (Stylist: Gill Rehnlund); below Per Gunnarsson

68 above left Courtesy of Rubner Blockhaus/Architects: Matteo Thun; above right Anneke de Leeuw/Ariadne/Sanoma Syndication; below left Ed Reeve/Red Cover; below right Bruno Boissonnet/Marie Claire Maison (Stylists: Catherine Ardouin/Maud Bury)

69 left Ray Main/Mainstream; right Peter Marlow/Magnum (Architect: Cartwright Pichard)

70 left Nathalie Krag (Architect: Christian Cold/Stylist: Gudrun Von Holck); above right Mel Yates (Owners: Alf and Nicola Lohr); below right Mirjam Bleeker/Taverne Agency (Stylist: Frank Visser)

71 left Hotze Eisma/VT Wonen/Sanoma Syndication; centre Alexander van Berge; right Renne Fickling/Ariadne/Sanoma Syndication

72 above Per Gunnarsson (Stylist: Ulrika Montan); below Jean Luc Laloux (Architect: Nico Steinmetz)

73 left Juliette Wade; right Jerry Harpur/Harpur Garden Library (Berry's Garden Co.)

74 Grazia Ike Branco

75 Hotze Eisma/VT Wonen/Sanoma Syndication

80–83 A. Ianniello/Studiopep (Stylist: Petra Barkhof/Patrizia Mezzanzanica)

84 Ingalill Snitt

86 Mirjam Bleeker/Taverne Agency (Stylist: Frank Visser)

87 above left Stellan Herner (Owner and Architect: Thomas Sandell/Stylist: Gill Rehnlund); above right Earl Carter/Taverne Agency (Stylist: Annemarie Kiely); centre La Casa de Marie Claire/Picture Press; below Ricardo Labougle (Owner and Designer: Hugo Ramasco)

88 above and below left Luc Wauman; centre Eric D'Herouville; right Paul Ryan/International Interiors (Architect: Olle Rex)

89 left Jean-Marc Palisse/Inside/Red Cover (Stylist: M. Duveau); right Julie Phipps/View (Architect: Tim Laurence)

90 left Misha Gravenor; centre Pere Planells/Inside/Red Cover; right Paul Ryan/International Interiors (Architect: Olle Rex)

91 above left Ryno/Visi/Camera Press (Interior Design: Block & Chisel); below left Verne Fotografie; right Mirjam Bleeker/Taverne Agency (Stylist: Frank Visser)

92–95 Christian Sarramon (Production: Ana Cardinale)

97 centre left Julian Cornish-Trestrail (Architect: David Mikhail)

98 left José Van Riele/Marie Claire Maison; right Marc Capilla/Album

99 above Ray Main/Mainstream (D-Squared design); below left Jerome Darblay/Inside/Red Cover (Stylist: M. P. Faure); below right Peter Cook/View (Architect: Mclean Quinlan Architects)

100–101 Eric Thorburn/Glasgow Picture Library

102 above and below left Imanol Sistiaga/Album; right Charlotte Wood/Arcblue (Architect: Burd Haward Marston)

103 Nicola Browne (Garden Design: Catherine Heatherington)

104 above Bill Timmerman (Architect: Rick Joy); below Jeff Goldberg/Esto (Architect: Rick Joy)

105–106 Jeff Goldberg/Esto (Architect: Rick Joy)

107 above right Jeff Goldberg/Esto (Architect: Rick Joy); below Bill Timmerman (Architect: Rick Joy)

117 Richard Glover/View (Architect: Reading & West Architects)

121 Alex Sarginson (Architect: Littman Goddard & Hogarth)

122 Mikkel Vange/Vogue Living

123 A. Ianniello/Studiopep (Stylist: Petra Barkhof/Patrizia Mezzanzanica)

124 above left Guy Obijn; above right Alex Sarginson (Architects: Littman Goddard & Hogarth); below Nigel Noyes (Architect: Clinton Murray/Painter: Bill Hollick)

125 Verne Fotografie (Architect: Peter Declercq)

126 Minh & Wass (Wall painted by Lulu Kwiatowski)

127 above left Undine Prohl (Architect: Alberto Kalach); above right Luc Wauman; centre right Courtesy of Designer Tracy Kendall; below left Ray Main/Mainstream; below right Nathalie Krag (Stylist: Tami Christiansen)

128 left Richard Glover/View (Architect: Tom Isaksson Architect); right Jan Verlinde (Designer: Agnes Emery)

129 *left* Ray Main/Mainstream; *right* Guy Obijn (Architect: Christel Peeters)

130 Nick Carter/Red Cover

131 *above left and right* Giorgio Possenti/Vega MG; *centre right* Annika Vannerus; *below left* Verne Fotografie (Architect: Axel Ghyssaert); *below right* Dan Duchars

132 *left* Guy Obijn (Architect: Will Arans); *right* Hotze Eisma/Taverne Agency (Stylist: Marielle Maessen)

133 Jefferson Smith/Arcblue (Architects: Tonkin Liu Architects)

134 Hans Petter Smeby/Design Interior

136 Grazia Ike Branco

137 *above left and right* Bieke Claessens (Architect: Toon Saldien); *below left* Guy Obijn; *below right* Ray Main/Mainstream

138 *left* Winfried Heinze/Homes & Gardens/IPC Syndication; *right* Antoine Bootz/*Marie Claire Maison* (Stylist: Daniel Rozenztroch)

139 *above* Guy Obijn (Architect: Carlo Seminck; *below* Richard Powers

140 *left* Verne Fotografie; *right* Guy Obijn (Architect: Piet Boon)

141 *above left* Vercruysse and Dujardin (Architect: Nathalie van Reeth); *above right* Guy Obijn; *below* Grazia Ike Branco

143 *above left* Geoff Lung (Architects: Robert McBride & Debbie-Lyn Ryan); *above right* David Sandison (Architect: Gabriel Poole); *below left* Adriaan Oosthuizen/Visi/Camera Press (Architect: Douglas Roberts/R&L Architects); *below right* David Matheson (Architect: Weir & Phillips Architects)

144 *above* Eugeni Pons/Album; *below left* Richard Powers; *below right* Hotze Eisma/Taverne Agency (Stylist: Reini Smit)

145 Tommaso Mangiola/*World of Interiors*/Condé Nast

146 *above left* Eduardo Munoz/The Interior Archive (Architect: Seth Stein); *above right* Cristina Rodés/Lovatt Smith Interiors; *below left* Ray Main/Mainstream (Property developers: Candy & Candy); *below right* Iben Ahlberg/Home Sweet Home Co.

147 Guy Obijn (Architect: Jo Crepain)

148 Ray Main/Mainstream (Architect: Littman Goddard Hogarth)

152 Ray Main/Mainstream

153 *above* Paul Massey; *below* Mirjam Bleeker/Taverne Agency (Stylist: Frank Visser)

154 Guy Obijn

155 *above and below left* Guy Obijn; *right* James Morris/Axiom Photographic Agency

157 *above* Guy Obijn (Architect: Nicolas Vanderhaegen); *below* Keith Collie (Architects: Azman Owens Architects)

158 *above* Jan Verlinde (Architect: A. Van de Walle); *centre* Jake Fitzjones/*Living Etc*/IPC Syndication; *below* Ray Main/Mainstream (John F Rolf Design and Build)

159 *left* Grazia Ike Branco; *right* Jake Curtis/*Living Etc*/IPC Syndication

160 *above and below left* Sue Barr/View (Architect: Found Associates); *below right* Jake Curtis/*Elle Decoration* (Owner: Derek Wylie)

162 *above* Chris Gascoigne/View (Architect: Eldridge Smerin); *below* Tham Nhu Tram/*Living Etc*/IPC Syndication

163 John Brandwood (Architect: Simon James Gonzalez)

164 Hotze Eisma/Taverne Agency (Stylist: Rianne Landstra)

165 *above* Clive Frost (Architects: Neil Choudhury Architects); *below* Jake Fitzjones/*Living Etc*/IPC Syndication

166 Paul Ryan/International Interiors (Designer: Schewen Design & Architecture)

168 Edmund Sumner (Architects: Thinking Space Architects)

169 *above* Mads Mogensen; *below* Mark Molloy (Architect: Sarah Featherstone/Featherstone Associates)

171 *above left* Patrick Reynolds (Architect: Architectus); *above right* Courtesy of Michael Gold Architects; *centre* Mads Mogensen; *below left* Michael Awad/Arch Photo (Architects: Shim Sutcliffe Architects); *below right* Jussi Tiainen (Architect: Aitoaho & Viljanen)

172 *above and centre* Nicholas Kane (Architect: Buschow Henley Architects)

179 Neil Marsh/*Elle Decoration*

180 (1) Jennifer Cawley; (2) Mikkel Vang/Taverne Agency (Stylist: Christine Rudolph); (3) Deborah Jaffe/*Elle Decoration*

181 (4) Jean Luc Laloux; (5) Pierre Even/*Marie Claire Maison*

182 (1) Helén Pe/House of Pictures (Stylist: Roth & Stone/Architect: Jonas Lindwall); (2) Jan Baldwin/Narratives (Architect: Jonathan Clark)

184 (1) Abode; (2) Doreen Dierckx; (3) Guy Obijn; (4) Hotze Eisma/Taverne Agency (Stylist: Rianne Landstra)

185 (5) Eugeni Pons/Album; (6) Alberto Piovano/Arcaid; (8) Minh & Wass (Architect: Patrick Naggar)

186 (1) Bernard Touillon/Inside/Red Cover; (2) Grazia Ike Branco; (3) Mel Yates (Architect: Block Architects); (4) Mads Mogensen

187 (5) Guy Obijn; (6) Michel Fernin; (7) Abode (Interior Architecture: Butterfield & Macpherson); (8) Verne Fotografie

188 (1) Paul Massey/*Living Etc*/IPC Syndication; (2) Giorgio Possenti/Vega MG; (3) Ray Main/Mainstream (Architect: Littman Goddard Hogarth)

189 (4) Bill Kingston/*Elle Decoration* (Design: Dominic Crimson); (5) Geoffrey Young/*Homes & Gardens*/IPC Syndication; (6) Dennis Gilbert/View (Architect: Penoyre & Prasad Architects); (7) Ray Main/Mainstream (Eltham Palace)

190 (1) Harvey Maria/Courtesy of Sinclair Till PR; (2) Alexander van Berge; (3) Karsten Damstedt (Architect: Kai Wartiainen/NCC Boende/Stylist: Hanna Holm); (4) Nick Allen/*Living Etc*/IPC Syndication

191 (5) Giorgio Possenti/Vega MG; (6) Alex Sarginson (Architect: Littman Goddard & Hogarth); (7) Eugeni Pons/Album

192 (1) Grazia Ike Branco; (2) Craig Knowles/*Living Etc*/IPC Syndication; (3) Clive Frost (Architect: Alfred Munkenbeck); (4) Sue Barr/View (Architects: Found Architects); (5) Andrew Wood/The Interior Archive (Property: Nobu: The Metropolitan); (6) Grazia Ike Branco

193 (7) Giles de Chabaneix/*Marie Claire Maison*; (8) Giulio Oriani/Vega MG; (9) Michael Moran (Designer: Moneo Brock Studio)

194 (1) Christophe Dugied/Inside/Red Cover (Stylist: J. Cole); (2) Paul Ryan/International Interiors (Architects: Tsao & McKown)

195 (13) Jake Fitzjones/Red Cover; (14) Verne Fotografie (Designer: Yves Goethals)

196 (1, 4, 6) Courtesy of Crucial Trading floor coverings; (2) Roger Oates Design

197 (8) Ray Main/Mainstream (Design: Filer & Cox); (9) Jonas Ingerstedt/House of Pictures (Stylist: Maja Elmer); (10) Mel Yates (Owner: Jo Warman); (11) Doreen Dierckx; (12) James Merrell/*Elle Decoration* (Owner: Henri Davies)

199 Peter Cook/View (Architect: Maygar Marsoni)

200 (1) Grazia Ike Branco; (2) Giorgio Possenti/Vega MG; (3) Alexander van Berge

201 (4) Peter Cook/View (Architect: Mclean Quinlan Architects); (5) Simon Upton/The Interior Archive (Architect: Michael Trentham); (6) Catherine Gratwicke/*Elle Decoration* (Owner: George Vinly); (7) Verne Fotografie (Architects: Bataille & Ibens); (8) Jan Baldwin/Narratives (Architect: Jonathan Clark); (9) Sue Barr/View (Architect: Beevor Mull Architects)

202 (1) Ken Hayden/*Country Homes & Interiors*/IPC Syndication; (2) Edmund Sumner (Architects: Thinking Space Architects); (3) David Sandison (Designer: Gail Hinkley); (4) Grazia Ike Branco; (5) Charlotte Wood/Arcblue (Architects: Burd Haward Marston)

203 (6) Peter Cook/View (Architect: Fiona McLean); (7) Julian Cornish-Trestrail (Architect: David Mikhail); (8) Ray Main/Mainstream (Designers: Mathmos)

204 (1) Jake Curtis/*Living Etc*/IPC Syndication; (2) Jan Baldwin/Narratives (Artist: Stephen Pearce); (3) Paul Ryan/International Interiors (Designer: Scott Bromley)

205 (4) Hans Zeegers/Taverne Agency; (5) Guy Obijn (Architect: Bart Lens); (6) Ken Hayden/Red Cover; (7) Andrew Twort/Red Cover

206 (1) Jake Fitzjones/Red Cover; (2) Winfried Heinze/Red Cover; (3) Jake Fitzjones/Red Cover

207 (4) Daniel Farmer/*Living Etc*/IPC Syndication; (5) Peter Cook/View (Architect: Fiona McLean); (6) Ray Main/Mainstream; (7) James Morris/Axiom Photographic Agency

208 (1) Alexander van Berge; (2) James Morris/Axiom Photographic Agency (Architect: Pip Horne); (3) Verne Fotografie; (4) Guy Obijn

209 (5) Chris Gascoigne/View (Architect: Alan Power Architects); (6) Henry Wilson/Red Cover; (7) Verne Fotografie (Architect: Bernard Declercq); (8) Chris Gascoigne/View (Architects: Alan Power Architects)

210 (1) Nick Hufton/View (Architects: Found Architects); (2) Paul Massey/*Living Etc*/IPC Syndication; (3) Ray Main/Mainstream; (4) James Mitchell/Red Cover; (5) Christian Brun; (6) Ray Main/Mainstream

211 (7) Jefferson Smith/Arcblue; (8) Luc Wauman; (9) Ray Main/Mainstream

213 Chris Tubbs/Red Cover

214 (1) Stellan Herner (Owner/Architect: Thomas Sandell/Stylist: Gill Rehnlund); (2) Luc Wauman; (3) Cristina Rodés/Lovatt Smith Interiors

215 (4) Huntley Hedworth/Red Cover; (5) Henry Bourne (Interior Design: Rupert Spira); (6) Deidi von Schaewen; (7) Graham Atkins-Hughes/Red Cover

216 (1) Tham Nhu Tram/*Elle Decoration* (Stylist: Emily Jewsbury); (2) Peter Cook/View (Architect: Mclean Quinlan Architects); (3) Hans Petter Smeby/Design Interior

217 (4) Grazia Ike Branco; (5) Liz Artindale/Narratives; (6) Andreas von Einsiedel (Designers: Nick & Gabriella Martin); (7) Ray Main/Mainstream (D-Squared design)

218 (1) Hans Zeegers/Taverne Agency (Stylist: Marianne Wermenbol); (2) Stellan Herner (Stylist: Synnove Mork); (3) Neil Marsh/*Elle Decoration* (Stylist: Amanda Smith)

219 (4) Kim Ahm/House of Pictures (Stylist: Vivian Boje); (5) Paul Ryan/International Interiors (Architects: Schewen Design & Architecture); (6) Per Gunnarsson (Stylist: Susanne Swegen); (7) Ray Main/Mainstream (Designers: Babylon design); (8) Tamsyn Hill/Narratives

220 (1–3) Paul Ratigan/Courtesy of Mary Thum Associates

221 (4) Bieke Claessens (Architect and Designer: Jeanine Van Den Bosch); (5) Per Gunnarsson; (6) Jake Fitzjones/Living Etc/IPC Syndication; (7) Richard Powers

222 (1) Lucy Pope/Living Etc/IPC Syndication; (2) Courtesy of Habitat; (3) Jonathan Pilkington/Living Etc/IPC Syndication; (4) Dennis Brandsma/VT Wonen/Sanoma Syndication; (5) Winfried Heinze/Red Cover; (6) Lizzie Orme/Living Etc/IPC Syndication

223 (7) Tim Evan-Cook/Elle Decoration; (8) Ed Reeve/Living Etc/IPC Syndication

224 (1) Solvi Dos Santos; (2) Paul Graham; (3) Daniel Hertzell; (4) Simon Whitmore/Homes & Ideas/IPC Syndication; (5) Giulio Oriani/Vega MG; (6) Courtesy of Molteni & C

225 (7) Harry Cory Wright/Homes & Gardens/IPC Syndication; (8) La Casa de Marie Claire/Picture Press; (9) Ray Main/Mainstream; (10) Kim Ahm/House of Pictures (Stylist: Vivian Boje)

226 (1) Ken Hayden/Red Cover; (2) Jan Baldwin/Narratives; (3) Jo Tyler (Interior designer: Ann-Katrin Berggren)

227 (4) Liam Quinonero/Album; (5) Verity Welsted/Red Cover (Architect: David Chipperfield); (6) Polly Wreford/Living Etc/IPC Syndication

228 (1) Polly Wreford/Narratives; (2) Jan Baldwin/Narratives; (3) Andreas von Einsiedel (Designer: Michael Reeves); (4) Polly Wreford/Narratives

229 (5) Tim Young/Living Etc/IPC Syndication; (6) Per Gunnarsson (Stylist: Susanne Swegen); (7) Helén Pe/House of Pictures (Stylist: Roth & Stone Productions/Designer: Michael Asplund); (8) Hotze Eisma/Taverne Agency (Stylist: Hanne Lise Poli); (9) Alexander van Berge

230 (1) Ricardo Labougle (Architect: Recondo); (2) Dennis Gilbert/View (Architect: Alison Brookes); (3) Luc Wauman

231 (4) Ed Reeve; (5) Christian Sarramon (Production: Ana Cardinale); (6) Jan Baldwin/Narratives (Architect: Melloco & Moore); (7) Guglielmo Galvin/Red Cover; (8) Richard Davies (Architects: 51% Studios)

233 Ray Main/Mainstream (Property developers: Candy & Candy)

234 (1) Jake Fitzjones/Red Cover; (2) Abode; (3) Courtesy of Santos

235 (4) Guy Obijn (Architect: Eyers); (5) Anders Schønnemann/Linnea Press (Stylist: Pernille Vest); (6) Jake Fitzjones/Red Cover; (7) Staffan Johansson; (8) Ray Main/Mainstream; (9) Eduardo Munoz/La Casa de Marie Claire/Picture Press (Architect: Seth Stein)

236 (1) Jan Baldwin/Narratives (Architect: Richard Rogers); (2) Hotze Eisma/Taverne Agency (Stylist: Rianne Landstra); (3) David Still/Homes & Gardens/IPC Syndication; (4) Guy Obijn (Architect: Bataille and Ibens); (5) Catherine Gratwicke/Living Etc/IPC Syndication; (6) Richard Powers

237 (7) Thomas Skovsende/Living Etc/IPC Syndication; (8) Paul Grootes/VT Wonen/Sanoma Syndication

238 (1) Hotze Eisma/Taverne Agency (Stylist: Hanne Lise Poli); (2) Luc Wauman

239 (3) Anders Schønnemann/Linnea Press (Stylist: Pernille Vest); (4) Sarah Maingot/Elle Decoration; (5) Jake Fitzjones/Red Cover; (6) Lepreux/Marie Claire Maison; (7) Mirjam Bleeker/Taverne Agency (Stylist: Frank Visser); (8) Luc Wauman

240 (1) James Mitchell/Red Cover; (2) Dan Duchars; (3) Ken Hayden/Red Cover

241 (4) Hotze Eisma/Taverne Agency (Stylist: Reini Smit); (5) Damian Russell/Living Etc/IPC Syndication; (6, 7) Giorgio Possenti/Vega MG; (8) Stephano Azario at Terrie Tanaka Management; (9) Luke White/Elle Decoration

243 Dan Tobian Smith/Marie Claire Maison (Designer: Matthew Williamson)

244 (1) Gianni Basso/Vega MG; (2) Dennis Gilbert/View (Architect: David Chipperfield Architects)

245 (3) Peter Cook/View (Architect: Fiona McLean); (4) Dennis Gilbert/View (Architect: Design Antenna); (5) Ray Main/Mainstream (Architect: Julie Richards)

246 (1) Ray Main/Mainstream (Architect: Julie Richards); (2) Guy Obijn; (3) Richard Glover/View

247 (4) Chris Gascoigne/View (Designer: Yakeley Associates); (5) Keith Hunter Photography; (6) Richard Bryant/Arcaid (Architect: Shideh Shaygan); (7) James Morris/Axiom Photographic Agency

248 (1) Ray Main/Mainstream; (2) Cora/Marie Claire Maison (Stylists: Marie Kalt and Gaël Reyre); (3) Kim Ahm/House of Pictures (Stylist: Pil Bredahl Ref. Verner Panton, Copenhagen); (4) Cora/Marie Claire Maison (Stylists: Marie Kalt and Gaël Reyre); (5) Courtesy of Habitat; (6) Bruno Helbling (Stylist: Mirko Beetschen); (7) Cora/Marie Claire Maison (Stylists: Marie Kalt and Gaël Reyre)

249 (8) Jonathan Pilkington/Living Etc/IPC Syndication; (9) Adrian Briscoe/Living Etc/IPC Syndication; (10) Andrea Jones (Owner: Trevyn McDowell/Designers: Paul Thompson & Ann-Marie Powell)

250 (1) Designer: Ross McBride for Max Ray Co./Courtesy of Normal. Photographer: Kozo Takayama; (2) Jean-Francois Jaussaud (Design: Luxproductions)

251 (3) Peter Marlow/Magnum (Architects: Knotts Architect); (4) Paul Massey/Living Etc/IPC Syndication; (5) Chris Craymer/Elle Decoration; (6) Luke White/Elle Decoration

252 (1) Helén Pe/House of Pictures (Stylist: Roth & Stone Production); (2) Guy Obijn (Design: Droog Design)

253 (3) Designed by Georg Baldele for Swarovski Producer: Lumen Mec Illuminazione SRL; (4) Adrian Briscoe/Elle Decoration; (5) Giorgio Possenti/Vega MG; (6, 7) Jefferson Smith/Arcblue (Architects: Tonkin Liu Architects)

Illustrations on the following pages are by Shonagh Rae: 23, 37, 41, 56, 76, 81, 93, 104, 110–115, 118–119, 173

Every effort has been made to trace the copyright holders and we apologise in advance for any unintentional omissions, and would be pleased to insert the appropriate acknowledgement in any subsequent publication.

The Publisher would like to thank Marissa Keating for her contribution to the picture research.

Architects and designers featured in the case studies and storyboards:

Pages 36–7
Burd Haward Marston Architects
Unit 9, 51 Derbyshire Street
London E2 6HQ UK
Tel: +44 207 729 7227 Fax: +44 207 729 3005
studio@bhm-architects.com

Pages 40–43
Mandolin Limited
133 Curtain Road, London EC2A 3BX UK
Tel: +44 207 739 2442 Fax: +44 207 739 3304
www.mandolinstudio.co.uk / info@mandolinstudio.co.uk

Pages 54–57
Peter de Bretteville Architects
315 Peck Street, Building 24, Unit 2G
New Haven CT 06513 USA
Tel: +1 203 785 0586 Fax: +1 203 785 0612
www.pdebarc.com / pdebarc@pdebarc.com

Pages 76–79
Douglas Stephen Partnership
140–142 St. Johns Street, London EC1 V4UB UK
Tel: +44 207 336 7884 Fax: +44 207 336 7841
www.dspl.co.uk / info@dsparchitecture.co.uk

Pages 96–97
David Mikhail Architects
Unit 29, 1–13 Adler Street, London E1 1EE UK
Tel: +44 207 377 8424 Fax: +44 207 377 5791
www.davidmikhail.com / info@davidmikhail.com

Pages 104–107
Rick Joy Architects
400 South Rubio Avenue, Tuscon, Arizona 85701 USA
Tel/Fax: +1 520 624 1442 / studio@rickjoy.com

Pages 148–149
Littman Goddard Hogarth Ltd
12 Chelsea Wharf, 15 Lots Road,
London SW10 0QJ UK
Tel: +44 207 351 7871 Fax: +44 207 351 4110
www.lgh-architects.co.uk / info@lgh-architects.co.uk

Pages 150–151
Phineas Manasseh Architects
37j Mildmay Grove North, London N1 4RH UK
Tel: +44 207 359 8886 Fax: +44 207 359 8886
phin@manasseh.plus.com

Pages 166–167
Schewen Design & Architecture
Guldgrand 1, S–118 20 Stockholm, Sweden
Tel: +46 8 643 6220 Fax: +46 8 642 4248
www.annavonschewen.com / anna.schewen@telia.com

Pages 172–175
Buschow Henley Architects
27 Wilkes Street, London E1 6QF UK
Tel: +44 207 377 5858 Fax +44 207 377 1212
www.buschowhenley.co.uk
studio@buschowhenley.co.uk